these sister nations, and finally, to adopt the position that the United States would "substitute political compromise for legal decisions" in controversies involving Latin-American governments and the property rights of United States citizens.

It was a policy which was influenced by the characters and ideals of the men who implemented it—men like Stimson, Hull, Sumner Welles, and Josephus Daniels, as well as by President Roosevelt, with whom it has come to be identified, and President Hoover, who supported it. This history has been documented with previously unpublished material from the archives of the State Department and the Franklin D. Roosevelt Library at Hyde Park, including numerous letters and records of conversations among these men and many others.

There is new information in these pages on the oil controversies with Bolivia, Mexico, and particularly Venezuela—a controversy in which the important role of the State Department is here made public for the first time. Businessmen, particularly those with Latin-American investments, will find the discussion of these crises in Part II of *The Making of the Good Neighbor Policy* informative. Any reader interested in present-day policies in Latin America and the Caribbean will gain a clearer understanding of why the United States has at times found itself in the position of giving tacit support to tyranny, and of the precedents and agreements which have been subscribed to in the interests of nonintervention and of being a Good Neighbor.

BRYCE WOOD has taught at Columbia University and Swarthmore College, and was Senior Administrative assistant in the Division of Special Political Affairs of the Department of State in 1942-43. At present he is a staff associate of the Social Science Research Council.

The Making of the Good Neighbor Policy

The Making of

the Good Neighbor Policy

Bryce Wood

Columbia University Press   *1961*

New York and London

In memory of my parents
Robina Evans Wood and
Richard Pike Wood

Acknowledgments

FOR ENCOURAGEMENT in the early stages of this study I wish to express my appreciation to Lindsay Rogers of Columbia University.

I am grateful to the American Philosophical Society and to the Rockefeller Foundation for grants that made research possible, and to the Social Science Research Council, which allowed me, as a member of its staff, to absent myself for two days a week for several years to examine documents in the archives of the Department of State. I wish to record my appreciation of their friendly interest in my research to Joseph H. Willits of the Foundation and to Pendleton Herring of the Council.

In the Department of State, John C. Dreier and Edward A. Jamison offered generous aid to a search for sources of the Good Neighbor policy, and G. Bernard Noble and E. Taylor Parks not only made me feel welcome in the researchers' room of the Historical Office, but also extended every appropriate assistance in obtaining documents and in speeding the review of the manuscript. Without their sympathetic concern, and that of members of their staff, Doris E. Austin, Margaret G. Martin, Marion Terrell, Dorothy A. Cross, and Anna Vukovich, this study would have been more limited in scope. To them and to Mary Ellen Milar and Clarence F. Holmes of the Records Service Center of the Department of State I wish to express my thanks for their assistance.

At the Franklin D. Roosevelt Library, Herman Kahn and the

members of his staff not only responded to requests for papers, but were more than helpful in seeking out additional materials to illuminate a line of inquiry.

To William T. R. Fox of Columbia University I am deeply indebted for reading the first draft of the manuscript and for frank and constructive criticisms. My colleague, Rowland L. Mitchell, Jr., read a part of the manuscript and has offered helpful comments; responsibility for the final text is, of course, mine alone.

Reviser, manuscript preparer, simplifier, isolator, foe of the unnecessary footnote, Virginia Staman Wood with this affectionate enrollment joins the wifely company of Corinthian editors who help keep authors and readers in communication.

BRYCE WOOD

Preface

THIS BOOK ATTEMPTS to delineate the rationale of the Good
Neighbor policy. It came to be written out of an interest in
the nature and limits of enduring, pacific, political relationships
between the United States, as a great power, and the Latin American
countries, as lesser powers, in the period from 1926 to 1943. The
chief problems with which it deals are those of the origins and
consequences of the formal and unreserved abandonment of the
use of force by the United States in its relations with Latin American countries. These relations did not develop haphazardly after
1926; they were guided at first by impulses and later by political
ideas that began to take the shape of principles with the sharpening
of appreciation of the nature of this interstate society from which
coercion was banned.

The focus of attention is on the development of ideas about
compromise, collaboration, and leadership in unfamiliar political
circumstances. This development is observable less in doctrinal
proclamations than in the significant residues from political controversies that were settled through processes of trial and error.
Outstanding among such controversies were those concerning the
interference of the United States in the domestic politics of
Latin American countries, and the efforts of Bolivia, Mexico, and
Venezuela to revise to their advantage the positions of United States
oil companies within their territories. Their courses are viewed

in relation to the growing desire of the United States for military and other assistance by Latin America in wartime. Attention is therefore given not only to intergovernmental affairs, but also to the issue of the role of private enterprise as affecting the foreign policy of a great power toward lesser powers.

From an examination of many policy decisions over a substantial period of time, certain patterns of policy actions emerge. An endeavor has been made to relate these patterns to the evolving objectives of the American governments as demonstrated in deed as well as in word, in order to frame tentative answers to questions about what the American states were trying to do in the era of the Good Neighbors, and what they accomplished.

The derivation of principles about political relationships from policy actions is a process that is, of course, subject to varied interpretations, and an effort has been made to provide a record sufficiently full and explicit so that other interpretations than those offered here may be tested. However, this study is not presented as a history of the Good Neighbor policy or its period, but as an essay about politics among sovereign states freed from the arbitrament of force but constrained by what they themselves called good neighborly aspirations.

B. W.

January, 1961

Contents

Introduction

Introduction

AT THE END of World War I, the United States found itself in an unprecedented position in its relations with the twenty
countries of Latin America. The power of the United States
throughout the Caribbean region was unchallenged by any European or Asiatic country. It was no longer necessary to assert, as
Secretary of State Richard Olney had done in 1895, that the United
States was "practically sovereign" in the Western Hemisphere.
Whatever Olney may have meant, there was no longer in Great
Britain or elsewhere, either the disposition or the capacity to raise
serious opposition to the "fiat" of the United States respecting any
of the approaches to the Panama Canal. As late as 1916, one of the
reasons for landing of United States Marines in Santo Domingo
was concern that a European state might take advantage of the
internal chaos there. By 1920, however, there existed little fear that
such a contingency might arise in the visible future.

Secure behind the oceans, its fleet, and its naval bases, the United
States was also incomparably stronger than any of the Latin American countries, alone or in concert. Having rejected membership in
the League of Nations, the United States was not only free from
the obligations of the Covenant but notoriously averse to the as-
sociative impulses arising in that organization.

Most of the states in the Caribbean area had experienced on their
own territory either extended occupation or brief incursions by

United States armed forces. In all of the Latin American countries there were strong feelings of distrust, suspicion, and fear of the alien nation of the north. What was to be the way of the strong with the weak, when strength was unrestrained save by inclination tempered by conscience?

Although the time was apparently ripe in 1920 for a reassessment of the position of the United States with respect to the Caribbean and to Latin America as a whole, the Department of State does not appear to have felt that it should strike out in a new direction, nor does any shift in policy seem to have been made in fact when the defense of the Panama Canal became a matter of routine.

There were two features of the policy of the United States that may account for the lack of a sharp break in the line taken immediately after World War I. In the first place, there existed no tendency on the part of any responsible statesman or party to extend permanent political control by the United States over the territory of any Latin American state. In the second place, the security argument for the use of force by the United States had usually been intertwined with other justifications, except in the case of Theodore Roosevelt's unabashed use of force to secure the independence of Panama as the means of acquiring the Canal Zone. These other justifications were the carrying out of obligations under a treaty as in Cuba, the protection of the lives and property of United States citizens, and the promotion of stable and democratic governments. High officials in the Department of State regarded these as sufficient reasons for the use of force in the Caribbean. The demotion of national defense as a necessary justification was not in itself important enough, therefore, either to make the employment of the Marine Corps inappropriate, or to make it essential immediately to reappraise policy toward Latin America.

After 1919, however, these rationalizations for the use of force, which had formerly been socially acceptable either as substitutes or reinforcements for the national security argument, lost much of their former persuasiveness among important sectors of public opinion in the United States, if not in the Department of State itself. Tutelary democracy began to be regarded as inconsistent with the principle of self-determination championed by Wilson at Versailles, and the use of Marines for the protection of business enterprise came to be opposed by influential leaders in both the major political parties.

On no less than twenty separate occasions between 1898 and 1920, United States Marines or soldiers entered the territory of states in the Caribbean area.[1] It should not be surprising that a certain sense of the normality, and even the propriety of calling on the Marines, should have persisted beyond 1920, independently of the nature of the formal justification for such action; it was an habitual, nearly automatic response to "disturbed conditions" or "utter chaos" in a Caribbean country.

Such intervention was regarded in the United States, Great Britain, and certain other countries as a legal right under international law, and on occasion coercion had been used to require Latin American states to accept arbitration for settlement of cases involving property rights of foreign nationals. This combination of methods for enforcement of an international standard of justice as interpreted by the great powers constituted the basic elements of a system of relationships between them and lesser countries that was not formally changed, at least for the United States, by the establishment of the League of Nations.

As late as 1924 Marines were landed in Honduras to protect the "American Minister and American colony" because "a condition of anarchy seems likely to develop."[2] This was one more, although almost the last, of the classic cases when the Marine Corps was called on for traditional reasons to go ashore in a Caribbean country.

This incident does not seem to have given rise to any need for a reappraisal of policy, but in 1927 a serious situation developed that marked a turning point. This was the intervention in Nicaragua that soon became a complicated and difficult undertaking, and was the principal experience that brought about durable and significant changes in policy before 1933. Its significance becomes apparent when it is remembered that with the Peace of Tipitapa in 1927 there commenced a period of about thirty years in which the United States refrained from the use of its armed forces to impose its will upon the nations of Latin America, whether for protection of its citizens or their property, for the promotion of democratic government, or for any other reason. The Nicaraguan affair, and the related "war scare" with Mexico, provided a basis in experience for a noninterventionist policy by the Coolidge and Hoover administrations. The Roosevelt administration also followed a noninterventionist policy, but only after separately founding it on experience in Cuba.

It was in the course of the Nicaraguan intervention that the men who managed policy in Washington realized that they were no longer adequately equipped to deal with the new situation in the Western Hemisphere brought about by the disappearance of any external menace and by the weakening of the persuasiveness of the other accepted rationalizations for intervention.

They needed new principles of action, since the Monroe Doctrine was a guide and justification only when there existed a threat from abroad, as was admitted when J. Reuben Clark wrote his *Memorandum on the Monroe Doctrine* in 1928. They also needed new techniques to carry out policy, since the Marine Corps was both too strong and too inflexible an instrument for use in situations where national defense could not seriously be claimed to be at stake.

With a simplicity perilously enhanced by distance, it is possible to look back at the two decades after 1918 and say that the problem of readjusting aims and methods was a fundamental one that confronted presidents and secretaries of state of the United States. They were struggling to find a new synthesis of purposes and techniques of policy toward Latin America in a new situation where they had no desire for conquest and no need for defense. The implications of the new situation were realized only piecemeal, with the occurrence of incidents, the building up of pressures, and the slow accumulation of knowledge. Questioning of the old policy arose from practical experience, and personal disenchantment seems to have been more important than intellectual analysis as a source of new policies.

Gradually, with some backsliding and some dissent, officials in Washington found themselves unable to escape the conviction that

their employment of force in the Caribbean was not only dispro-
portionately expensive in protecting citizens and property abroad
and ineffective in promoting democracy; it was also positively disadvantageous to their evolving conception of the national interest
of the United States. The maturing of this conviction forms the
first part of the story of the Good Neighbor policy and covers the
years from 1920 through 1933. This period may be described by
a phrase of Dean Acheson's: "the renunciation of domination."

It did not prove to be an easy and simple matter for the United
States, which possessed the power, and could spare the wealth, to
refrain from coercing its weaker neighbors, who were often quar-
relsome, wracked by civil strife, and disrespectful of what Washington regarded as the rights of foreigners. These attributes created
a standing temptation for intervention, for resort to force was easy
and free from retaliation in kind.

Nonintervention, however, was not enough; keeping the Marines
at home served policy objectives only negatively. The government of the United States continued to desire the protection of
the lives and property of its citizens and the advancement of
democracy in Latin America. Moreover it developed new objectives, since inter-American collaboration for the defense of the
hemisphere, and of the United States, became of vital importance
after 1938. How, in peaceful ways, could these old and new objectives most effectively be furthered?

The theoretical answer to this question was gradually crystallized in the idea of reciprocity. The policy answers, for they were
many, were found by trial and error. As the most satisfactory
policy answers were selected, they became accretions to the early,
unsophisticated notion of reciprocity, which was slowly refined
into working political principles if not into doctrine. Most simply,
the idea of reciprocity expressed the hope that, if the United States
did certain things desired by Latin American states, these states
would respond by doing other things desired by Washington. To
paraphrase a remark by Sumner Welles, the Good Neighbor policy
in this phase was the anticipation of reciprocity. For nonintervention and noninterference, would not Latin American governments
respond by "equitable" treatment for the property of United

States citizens and corporations? In general, the answer to this question was in the negative, and it therefore became necessary for the United States to adopt new policies with regard to the protection of its nationals in Latin America. These new policies were not only intergovernmental; they bore directly on relationships between the Department of State and private individuals and corporations. Companies in the United States whose investments abroad were adversely affected after 1933 by acts of certain Latin American governments and who turned for protection to the Department found not only that the traditional methods of protection were unavailable, but that the Department of State would bring effective influence to bear to induce them to change their policies and practices in order to further the national interest of the United States as interpreted by the Department. From this point of view, the decade following 1933 was one of transition in which the system of the international standard of justice was abandoned by the government of the United States in favor of a new set of understandings that were required when the national interest was found to be distinguishable from, and occasionally antagonistic to, the perpetuation of the old system of protection of United States nationals and their property abroad. On the whole, this set of understandings, in combination with policies in other fields, was reciprocally rewarded by Latin American approval of the measure of cooperation sought by the United States in World War II. It is the political process by which the understandings were reached that is here characterized as the evocation of reciprocity.

The policies here outlined represented conceptions of the national interest of the United States in inter-American affairs held by statesmen in the period between the two world wars. This period possessed its own peculiar and irreproducible attributes, and no attempt is made to suggest that the policies then found appropriate are applicable to the period following World War II. The names "Good Neighbor policy" and "Good Partner policy," however, have been officially employed to designate the postwar policies of the United States in inter-American affairs, so that it may not be entirely without political interest to examine the development and rationale of the original policy in the interwar period.

In a larger sense, however, these policies are of interest because they constituted an endeavor to discover how far, among sovereign states that differ greatly in culture and in power, it may be possible to engender certain neighborly attitudes, often found among individuals, that are as old as the hills and as young as tomorrow. The nature of these attitudes may be inferred from the words of William R. Castle, Under Secretary of State in the Hoover administration, who criticized Secretary Cordell Hull's Latin American policy for going too far in turning "the other cheek." [3] This criticism did not deter Hull, who was not unwilling that such an ancient and still respected precept should be part of the policy of reciprocity. And, although the focus of this study is on policies adopted by the government of the United States, it is probable that those policies alone would not have evoked reciprocity in Latin America unless Latin Americans had believed that the intent of the policies was, in truth, neighborly. Beyond words and even beyond deeds, there are engenderers of trust and confidence that formal intent can neither create nor mask. Diplomats are necessarily secretive, but their chiefs at home are public men, visible in a democracy alike to foreigners and to citizens. If the domestic policies of these public men are in harmony with their foreign policy, particularly when the foreign policy is one of limited diplomacy dependent upon good will and not on force, the effect will be greater on those whose friendship is sought. If neighborly virtues are discernible whether the newly aspirant neighbor is in slippered ease or cutaway, his reception will be both warmer and readier. When, for example, Mexicans may have wondered what manner of man not only sent Josephus Daniels to them as Ambassador, but kept him there, they could find out more by looking at the domestic policies of President Roosevelt than by reading the diplomatic correspondence. The spirit of the Good Neighbor, and the hopes aroused as much by its manner and style as by its words and deeds, figured in the response of its Latin American neighbors. That response was, finally, a welcome that constituted one measure of the policy of the United States, for it meant that the actions the United States desired Latin American governments to take in support of its own defense effort during World War II were, in general, undertaken as part of a mutual effort against a common enemy.

PART ONE

The Policies of Nonintervention and

Noninterference

CHAPTER I

The Nicaraguan Experience

WHEN AN OLD ORDER changes, particularly when the men identified with the old are also the custodians of the new, the justification of the past often receives no less solicitous attention than the planning of the future. The United States intervention in Nicaragua in 1926–27 was the occasion not only for one of the most elaborate official rationalizations ever made for the use of force in the Caribbean area,[1] but also for the then unrecognized beginning of the disintegration of the very policy so meticulously justified.

Eight years after the armistice ending hostilities in World War I, the slogan of normalcy had not lost its potency in the United States. There was no fear of aggression from abroad nor concern about possible involvement in disputes in distant lands. For the United States, minimizing its political activity abroad, it was no less true in 1926 than in 1933 that "among the foreign relations of the United States as they fall into categories, the Pan American policy takes first place in our diplomacy." [2]

Diplomacy in the Americas was still guided by the general intent of the Monroe Doctrine, by desires to mediate in keeping the peace among the Latin American states, to counsel the Central American and Caribbean countries about ways of avoiding revolutionary transfers of political power, and by temporary employment of force to protect the interests of United States citizens having trade with and investments in Latin America.[3] Beyond the maintenance of the security of the Panama Canal and of existing bases in Cuba and elsewhere, the United States had no territorial ambitions in the Americas.

In the shadows of this picture of bucolic calm in foreign affairs, however, there was hidden an imminent possibility of the outbreak of violence, namely, the decision by a major power that its citizens' lives or property were seriously endangered by the policy of, or the situation in, a minor power. Senator William E. Borah of Idaho was probably representative of prevailing official and unofficial attitudes of the time in the United States when he declared: "The great problem in international affairs at present grew out of the relationship between strong and weak nations." [4] The government of the United States was accustomed to employing armed force in the Caribbean and Central American states to preserve its interpretation of an international standard of justice for the protection of foreign nationals, and it entered upon an intervention in Nicaragua in 1926 without anticipating either a strongly adverse reaction at home or serious resistance in that small country.

Unlike the intervention in Honduras in 1924, the Nicaraguan intervention was complicated by policies of other powers; it involved support by Washington for one of the factions in civil strife, and it endured for six years.[5] It became, in other words, a political intervention, and not one carried out merely to protect the lives and property of nationals of the United States.

The political character of the intervention was due in part to the tenseness of Mexican–United States relations in the autumn of 1926 as a result of Mexican plans to expropriate lands owned by foreigners—plans which were opposed by the United States government as contrary to international law and equity. The dispute was exacerbated by strong feelings on the part of Catholics in the United States aroused by the campaign of President P. E. Calles to restrict certain practices of the Mexican clergy. In addition, the Mexican government engaged in activities in Central America which late in 1926 began to appear in Washington and in Central America as efforts to extend Mexican political influence over its smaller neighbors. For example, it was reported that the Costa

Rican government believed that "Mexico is attempting to develop a sphere of influence in Central America," and that "the Costa Rican mind does not approve of the radical political policies of Mexico." When Mexican diplomats in Costa Rica "subsidized a part of the local press," the government in San José was amusedly tolerant, but this attitude changed to one of alarm "when Mexico intervened in the Nicaraguan conflict. The presence of Mexican 'warriors' and of Mexican arms in Central America presented the possibility of Mexican hegemony in this region," and President Ricardo Jiménez was said to have "expressed grave concern over the possibility of the 'savages of Mexico' gaining a strong position in Central America through the Nicaraguan conflict." [6]

These and other reports caused serious concern in Washington. Whatever the intentions of the Mexican government and whatever the precise nature of its policy at the time, the view was held among high officials in the government of the United States that "the evidence before the Department [of State] shows an unmistakable attempt on the part of Mexico to extend Mexican influence over Central America with the unquestionable aim of ultimately achieving a Mexican primacy over the Central American countries," and of setting up governments in Central America "which will be not only friendly but subservient to Mexico and completely under Mexican domination." [7]

Decision to Intervene

However well founded Washington's fears of Mexican expansionism may have been, there seems little doubt that the Department of State's policy in Nicaragua after September, 1926, was based fundamentally on the assertion of the supremacy of the power of the United States in Central America. The immediate problem was that of preventing the Liberals, led by Juan Sacasa and General José Moncada, from gaining a victory in the Nicaraguan civil conflict, for that victory would have resounded throughout Latin America as a Mexican triumph over the United States. The longer range problem was to make it decisively clear to Mexico that the United States would not permit Mexican propaganda activities to blossom into political influence or control over any Central American country.

It may be said, without going into details, that pressure exerted by the United States in Nicaragua brought about (1) the resignation of Emiliano Chamorro as president, and (2) the election by a Nicaraguan congress of Adolfo Díaz as his successor; both men were Conservatives. On November 17, three days after Díaz's inauguration, he was recognized by the United States government, and shortly afterwards by other governments in Europe and Latin America; Sacasa was recognized as president by the government of Mexico. The constitutionality of the election of Díaz was challenged by Sacasa, and defended by the government of the United States, which undertook to interpret favorably article 106 of the Nicaraguan constitution.[8]

The election of Díaz restored to power an old and dependable friend of the United States, and, more importantly, the United States government now had in Nicaragua a recognized government, assertedly constitutional, which could be supported, if necessary, by the armed forces of the United States against a rebellion "financiered"[9] in Mexico.

Secretary of State Frank B. Kellogg apparently did not wish to intervene in Nicaragua, and he certainly had no intention of occupying the country or exerting direct control over the government. However, the weakness of the Díaz regime in the face of the able generalship of Moncada soon made it evident that the Mexican-supported Liberal cause would win the day unless United States troops were ashore in Nicaragua. The Department of State was warned that if the populace in western Nicaragua became convinced that support for Díaz were only "moral and indirect" and nothing were done to prevent additional aid from Mexico to the Liberal forces "a general uprising [would] take place resulting immediately in the speedy collapse of the government accompanied by conditions of anarchy."[10] This view was independently supported by requests for protection from men in the lumber business and other United States citizens in Nicaragua.

The combination of these factors provided the background for the landing of a force of United States Marines on December 23, 1926, at Puerto Cabezas on the east coast, where Sacasa had made his headquarters, and by January 8 the Marines were defending Managua and its railroad connections with the Pacific port of Corinto.

It would have been a serious blow to the prestige of the United States in the Caribbean area and in the world as a whole if its presidential choice for Nicaragua had been overthrown by Mexico's candidate. Although Kellogg may not have acted with this consideration in mind, other officials perhaps did. This motive was a strong one, sufficient to explain the later course of action of the United States, although it was not clearly, nor from the beginning, made the public basis for United States policy.

Intervention Creates Controversy in the United States

In contrast to the intervention of 1924 in Honduras, the Nicaraguan situation had, almost from its inception, become a matter of public concern. On the day after Díaz's recognition by Washington, the New York *Times* stated editorially that it did not think the Mexican government was aiding Sacasa, and issued a mild warning: "Intervention to protect American citizens is one thing. Intervention to pacify Nicaragua and assist in setting up a responsible government is quite another. It could not be entered upon lightly." [11] On the same day, an Associated Press despatch quoted Díaz as saying that Mexico was spreading Bolshevism in Latin America, and reported that the United States government was concerned that alleged Communistic tendencies in Mexico might be thrust into Latin American relations.[12] This despatch gave rise to a resolution introduced in the House of Representatives by Fiorello H. LaGuardia, asking for information on its origin.

Later, Senator George Norris introduced a resolution calling for an investigation of reports that Assistant Secretary of State Robert E. Olds had sent for the Washington managers of press associations and had made the charge that the Mexican government was "seeking to establish a Bolshevist authority in Nicaragua in order to drive a 'hostile wedge' between the United States and the Panama

Canal." Olds was claimed on this occasion (November 17, 1926) to have made the stipulation "that responsibility for any publication" about this charge should not be attributed to the Department of State. Secretary Kellogg denied that such a stipulation was made, but the press associations maintained their stand. The Norris resolution was defeated by an 8 to 5 vote in the Committee on Foreign Relations of the Senate. It was reported that one of the majority in this vote had said that the report "undoubtedly was true" but that an investigation would "embarrass the State Department"; to this the retort was made that "if we had a State Department of that sort, it deserved to be embarrassed." [13]

The clumsy attempt of Assistant Secretary Olds to influence the press and the public was a major blunder, for it only alienated both by arousing mistrust of subsequent explanations of its actions by the Coolidge administration.[14] This mistrust was heightened by the administration's irresolution and by the obvious inadequacy of its original official assertion of intent to account for the rapid enlargement of the role of the Marines in Nicaragua. Within the space of two weeks at the beginning of 1927, the administration offered to an increasingly skeptical and hostile public no less than nine distinct and chronologically separate justifications for its policy in Nicaragua.[15]

These several justifications were all attacked by a rising chorus of public opinion led by many powerful voices, including such redoubtable members of the President's own party as Senators William E. Borah and George W. Norris. Even the New York *Times*, which held that it was the President's duty to act if life and property of United States citizens were endangered, admitted that "the trouble arose only when we seemingly began to stretch or exceed our rights." It did not think Coolidge should have recognized Díaz as the legal president of Nicaragua, for "it is hardly becoming to outsiders to decide gravely constitutional points which the Nicaraguans themselves have long made almost a joke." [16]

The Mexican "War Scare"

The furor over Nicaraguan policy, however, cannot be laid only to the bungling of public relations by the Coolidge administration. Of greater importance was the deepening crisis with Mexico over the latter's expropriations of land owned by foreigners. When Olds's covert charges against Mexican participation in the Nicaraguan revolt became known, it was suspected by the administration's opponents that these charges were being made as part of a campaign to make war against Mexico acceptable to the people of the United States. Senator Borah publicly suggested that "oil interests" were encouraging an intervention in Nicaragua as part of an effort "to get this country into a shameless, cowardly little war with Mexico." [17]

A formal statement of the administration's Nicaraguan policy finally put an end to the day-by-day issuance of justifications by the Department of State, when on January 10, 1927, President Coolidge defended his action in a message to the Congress. He stated that conditions in Nicaragua "seriously threaten American lives and property, endanger the stability of all Central America, and put in jeopardy the rights granted by Nicaragua to the United States for the construction of a canal." Referring to Sacasa's "Mexican allies," the President quoted Díaz as saying that he could not protect foreigners in Nicaragua "solely because of the aid given by Mexico to the revolutionists," and stated that ships carrying arms from Mexico to Sacasa forces in Nicaragua had been fitted out in Mexican ports "with the full knowledge of and, in some cases, with the encouragement of Mexican officials and were in one instance, at least, commanded by a Mexican reserve officer." Concluding, Coolidge said:

The United States can not, therefore, fail to view with deep concern any serious threat to stability and constitutional government in Nicaragua tending toward anarchy and jeopardizing American interests, especially if such state of affairs is contributed to or brought about by outside influences or by any foreign power.[18]

This message for the first time made it officially clear that the Nicaraguan affair was a part of a crisis in relations with Mexico, since the Mexican government was specifically charged with responsibility for disorders in Nicaragua. The message also aroused a fear of conflict with Mexico, and initiated what may, without much exaggeration, be called a "war scare" which lasted for some two weeks.[19]

The administration's case was further explained by Secretary Kellogg in hearings before the Senate Committee on Foreign Relations on January 12. Kellogg presented a memorandum entitled "Bolshevist Aims and Policies in Mexico and Latin America," in which it was asserted that "the Bolshevist leaders" have "set up as one of their fundamental tasks the destruction of what they term American imperialism as a necessary prerequisite to the successful development of the international revolutionary movement in the New World." In support of these claims, quotations were offered from resolutions passed by various Communist organizations and from articles in Communist publications. This memorandum failed to persuade even the friends of the administration, and real fears of war with Mexico were aroused in active sectors of public opinion. The National Council for Prevention of War, a leading pacifist organization, mobilized its resources against the assumed intent of the administration, and in this instance found a readier response than in its campaigns for disarmament and other contemporary causes. It obtained the signatures of some five hundred prominent citizens to a statement published on January 19, favoring arbitration of the Mexican dispute. It got the support of experts in international law for a declaration that the dispute was suitable for arbitration. When Henry Parkes Cadman, head of the Federal Council of the Churches of Christ in America, declared on January 14 that he favored arbitration, the National Council for the Prevention of War sent copies of the statement to some seventy thousand clergymen, asking them to urge their congregations and their Congressmen to use their influence on behalf of peace. A torrent of letters and telegrams rushed to Congress, the White House, and the Department of State.[20]

For a week after the President's message there was in Washington a period of "excitement and rumors of war."[21] Then the administration, if it ever really had seriously contemplated the use of force against Mexico, suddenly changed its mind. First showing signs of internal indecision, it then asserted that its policy remained unchanged and adopted a new attitude toward Mexico that was as far from Coolidge's viewing "with deep concern" as day from night. As early as January 16, the press was able to note a new pacific temper in Washington, and on January 18, commenting on a resolution by Senator Joseph Robinson favoring arbitration of the land dispute with Mexico, Secretary Kellogg said he welcomed the resolution and added that for some time he had been giving "very careful consideration to the question of the definite application of the principle of arbitration to the existing controversy with Mexico." [22]

However, President Coolidge let it be known that he was opposed to arbitration of the Mexican controversy. It was reported that he saw no hope in arbitration; in his opinion "it is an inalienable right for people to own their property, and it should not be taken away by a Government unless paid for." [23] The discrepancy between the views of the President and his Secretary of State was not immediately clarified,[24] but the question of a pacific outcome of the dispute with Mexico was decisively answered on January 25 when the Senate by a vote of 79 to 0 adopted the Robinson resolution favoring arbitration of the issues with Mexico over oil rights and land legislation.[25] The resolution dealt only with the direct dispute relating to the position of the United States citizens in Mexico and did not refer to Nicaragua, but it had the effect of drawing the sting from charges against Mexico arising out of the Nicaraguan situation.

What had happened to dissolve the tension so quickly? The simple explanation seems to be the correct one: an outburst of popular opinion against the possibility of the use of force in Mexico caused the Coolidge administration to abandon its apparently threatening position. It is not necessary to assume that the administration actually contemplated the use of force, and no military moves appear to have been made; Coolidge had spoken of "deep concern," the press had spoken openly of the risk of war, and popular feeling and the Senate had expressed themselves swiftly and unmistakably for arbitration.

While the issue of the use of force against Mexico was thus decided, no such decision was made regarding Nicaragua where the government was already deeply committed. However, a "change of temper" was evident on the part of both the government and people of the United States. The people had not become pacifists, but, in contemporary judgment, they had "come into an entirely new idea of the alternatives to war. . . . The expressions from all parts of the country which have reached Washington, and been given to the public in the newspapers, show that this country is at present in the mood to insist upon reasonable compromise, methods of conciliation, submission to arbitration—all to be tried out honestly before there is any talk of the appeal to the ultimate reason of kings." In this view, although the United States had not joined the League of Nations, "it cannot isolate itself from League-of-Nations principles. They have been in evidence during the past ten days in Washington and will be so with, we must all hope, increasing power and success." [26] Further, President Coolidge got an expression of opinion from his countrymen that the difficulties in Latin America "were not worth fighting about. There came to be a swelling demand that some other way be found," and "a steady pressure from public sentiment" to make use of them, that amounted to "a kind of tacit consultation of the country by the President." [27]

The new temper may have been influenced by, or the weight given to it in Washington may have been increased by, expressions of opinion in Europe and Latin America. There appeared in the press as early as December 29, 1926, charges from Europe that the Nicaraguan intervention demonstrated that the United States had now become "frankly imperialistic." At that date, the New York *Times* was inclined to be defiant, for it stated that "all that we do has at least the motive of aiding and protecting the weaker republics on this continent, rather than of overriding or despoiling them. If this be Imperialism, make the most of it." However, the charges continued to come in, some of them denouncing Coolidge's speech of January 10 as a blunder, demonstrating "the hypocrisy of American moral philosophy in international politics," and others blandly welcoming the United States into the company of imperialist states.[28]

In Latin America, the Department of State was informed of a public meeting in Buenos Aires to protest the Nicaraguan policy of the United States, and of the fears of representatives of the Boston Bank and Standard Oil Company "that present situation will injure American interests." [29] The danger to United States commercial interests and to the country's general reputation in Latin America was a common theme of opponents of the administration's policy and the comment was made at the time that "one thing that must have swayed the Washington Administration was the evidence that its Nicaraguan and Mexican démarche had made an unhappy impression abroad. In South America and in Europe the critics of America used biting language." If, therefore, the change in Washington's policy were due to a triumph of public opinion, "it was world opinion that triumphed. Such is the gain, such the assurance, of knowing today that the considerate judgment of mankind is on the side of peace and positively against war." [30]

Intervention Becomes Occupation

The easing of the tension with Mexico was followed by new negotiations and by the sending of Dwight W. Morrow as Ambassador to Mexico in September, 1927, which opened a decade of friendlier relations between the two countries.[31] However, the Nicaraguan situation was not essentially changed by the passing of the Mexican crisis. The civil war continued, and the Liberal army under General Moncada slowly but steadily advanced on Managua.

It soon became clear that there were three alternative policy lines open to the United States: (1) to give up the attempt to maintain Díaz in office; (2) to order the Marines to destroy or disperse the Liberal army; (3) to arrange a negotiated settlement between the contending parties in Nicaragua. The first of these lines was out of the question, for in the eyes of the world it would have meant a Mexican victory on Washington's own admission and a humiliating loss of prestige for the Coolidge administration. The second policy line was almost equally distasteful, for President Coolidge, no less than Secretary Kellogg, wished to avoid responsibility for killing Nicaraguans who had no quarrel with the United States.

An attempt to make a negotiated settlement became urgent in

the early spring of 1927, not only because of the advance of Moncada, but also because of the pressure of public opinion against the intervention. President Coolidge appointed Henry L. Stimson on March 31, 1927, as his special representative to go to Nicaragua, to investigate and report on the situation, and, as Stimson later wrote, "if I should find a chance to straighten the matter out, he wished I would try to do so." [32] Stimson's instructions gave him wide latitude, and his mind was open; he had not previously come in contact with Nicaraguan problems, and, as he said: "So far as ignorance could free it from prejudices or commitments, my mind was a clean slate." [33]

Stimson soon reached two conclusions. The first was that the question of free elections was the "very heart of Nicaraguan problem as well as of general Central American problem." Since existing governments determined the outcome of elections, the only way for opposition parties to get into office was through revolution. However, leaders of revolutions would not be recognized as presidents by the United States or Central American governments because of the Washington Treaty of 1923. Hence existing party control of governments tended to be permanent, and the United States "becomes target of hatred of opposition." Stimson's solution for this problem was the "gradual political education of Nicaraguans in self-government through free elections," with the elections supervised by the government of the United States. As Stimson said, "naked intervention" by the United States with no attempt to improve Nicaraguan political habits, had existed in Nicaragua for thirteen years, from 1912 to 1925, and "peace lasted only twenty-five days after withdrawal of marines." [34]

Stimson concluded, secondly, that supervision would require the maintenance in Nicaragua of a force of United States Marines, and the establishment of a Nicaraguan constabulary that would "eventually greatly reduce number of marines necessary to guarantee stability." [35] Stimson's policy was approved in Washington, and he obtained its peaceful acceptance by the leaders of both sides in the Nicaraguan civil war, through the agreement of Tipitapa, May 4, 1927.[36]

Occupation: Anticipation and Theory

The Stimson policy was faithfully and conscientiously carried out by the United States through the following five years. The presidential elections of 1928 and 1932, and those for congress in 1930 were supervised, and their results accepted as fair by the Liberal and Conservative parties. A constabulary, known as the Guardia Nacional was trained by United States Marine officers, and Nicaraguan officers were trained in a military academy. All United States Marines were withdrawn from Nicaragua on January 2, 1933, following the election of Juan B. Sacasa of the Liberal party as President and the organization and staffing of the Guardia. General Anastasio Somoza, one of the leaders of the Liberals in their revolution of 1927, became commander of the Guardia.

This record appears, in these terms, to be a successful one. Why, then, did Stimson's own Under Secretary of State, Joseph P. Cotton, instruct the minister to the Dominican Republic in 1930: "You are not authorized to suggest any United States participation in or even supervision of the elections. The last thing we want is to get in a situation where that would result"? [37] Why then, also, did Admiral Clark H. Woodward, retiring chairman of the United States Electoral Mission to Nicaragua, recommend to Secretary of State Stimson that the United States should "seek, by every means possible, to avoid again becoming involved in a commitment of the nature of the three recent Supervisions of Elections in Nicaragua"? [38]

The answer to these questions is that by 1933, Stimson and his colleagues found supervision of elections in Nicaragua to be troublesome, embarrassing, and costly. In the six years, 1927 through 1932, more than five thousand separate documents are listed in Department of State archives dealing with Nicaragua. The vast majority of these are despatches and cables to and from Managua. A substantial amount of time was devoted to the study of Nicaraguan problems, which were more complicated and difficult than those arising with many other countries.[39]

The burdensome nature of the Nicaraguan intervention of 1927 was not apparent to Stimson at the outset. His analysis of the situation was logical enough, but it rested on two assumptions, both of which were unfounded. The first of these was that a demonstration of free elections would convince Nicaraguans that they constituted a superior way of selecting the men who would control Nicaraguan governments. The second assumption was that the presence of United States Marines would insure that the period of supervision would be a period of internal peace in Nicaragua. In addition, Stimson appears to have expected that electoral supervision and the maintenance of domestic peace would be a fairly simple and even an easy administrative operation. In all these expectations he was seriously disappointed. The life of Stimson's faith in the policy of supervision lasted only so long as it took his experience to triumph over his logic, a period of a little less than four years.

In anticipation, Stimson had reason to feel that electoral supervision could be simple. All that seemed to be necessary was to permit Nicaraguans to cast a secret ballot under conditions precluding fraud and intimidation, to see the votes were honestly counted, and to prevent revolutionary movements against the duly elected president and congress. From 1912 to 1925, peace in Nicaragua had been maintained easily by about one hundred United States Marines who, nominally serving as a legation guard, actually were effective in preventing governmental overturns by revolutions.

However, what actually happened was far from simple, and the United States found itself engaged in a wide range of unexpected activities, from studying tax revenues and the interest rate on paving bonds to the dropping of bombs on bandits who were called Nicaraguan patriots elsewhere than in Washington.

The type of intervention Stimson proposed was not quite like previous interventions, which had fallen into two general classes. In Cuba, Santo Domingo, and Haiti, the United States had undertaken military occupations, and actual control of governmental agencies had been exercised by military officers or civilians from the United States. In many other cases, United States Marines had been landed for shorter or longer periods to pursue brigands, to evacuate United States citizens or protect their property, to prevent revolutions, or for other similar purposes; in these cases, the Marines had not wielded governmental authority but had engaged in strictly limited operations.

In Nicaragua in 1927, however, a different kind of responsibility was accepted, and it resulted in a form of intervention intermediate between the other two, having the advantages of neither. Elections were to be supervised without the enjoyment of complete control of governmental machinery; and peace was to be maintained without the exercise of the full powers of a military occupation. Stimson here experimented with an unprecedented type of collaboration aimed simultaneously at the protection of the lives and property of United States citizens, their government's interests in the region of the Panama Canal, and the political education of Nicaraguans. As will be seen, the experiment was a failure on the first and third of these counts. It did, however, have two significant consequences, both unanticipated. By rendering electoral supervision highly distasteful, it was a prime source of political education for the Department of State, and by the efficient organization of the Guardia it was responsible, in significant measure, for the twenty years of political stability in Nicaragua provided after 1936 by the dictatorship of Anastasio Somoza.[40]

If Stimson, unfamiliar with Latin American affairs, was embarking on uncharted political waters, he was at least following, knowingly or not, the theory of an experienced and accomplished navigator. When Charles Evans Hughes was contemplating in 1924 the withdrawal of the Marines from Managua, he wrote that this action could be completed "with less danger of disorder in Nicaragua if the forthcoming elections are conducted in a manner which leaves no room for doubt that the successful condidate has the support of a real majority of the people . . . therefore . . . the Legation should exert every proper influence to bring about the holding of free and fair elections." [41] Here was the essence of the logic of Stimson's position of 1927, even though Hughes had not proposed electoral supervision. Similarly, in approving the organization of the Guardia, Stimson was in accord with the ideas of

Hughes, who had proposed the training of a constabulary in Nicaragua, so that the withdrawal of the Marines "should not be attended by any disorder or instability." [42]

A measure of sympathy is due to Stimson, and to Kellogg, for commencing an intervention that, if fundamentally motivated by military and economic interests of the United States, was also charged with high purposes of political melioration and at no time was intended to keep Nicaragua in permanent subjection to the United States. The Tipitapa agreement was generally accepted in the United States as perhaps the best way out of a difficult situation,[43] and Stimson justified the continued occupation and electoral supervision in Nicaragua in terms of an Isthmian policy that required the United States to be concerned about political stability in Central America in order to forestall possible European interventions. This justification amounted to a reaffirmation of the Roosevelt Corollary to the Monroe Doctrine, and Stimson approvingly quoted Roosevelt's well-known speech of 1905 in support of the Corollary.[44] Further, Stimson asserted that the United States action in 1927 was intended to promote Nicaragua's "independence and sovereignty in the most effective way. . . . Our promise thus to help Nicaragua has been made in the highest spirit of fellowship and cooperation." [45] It is of some ironic interest to note that Stimson's reincarnation of the Roosevelt Corollary was no more than a literary exercise; it came to life only in the pages of his book, *American Policy in Nicaragua*, for, when political instability came again to Central America in 1931, no attempt was made to apply the theory of the Corollary by the then Secretary of State, Henry L. Stimson.

Stimson's views were not greatly different from those President Coolidge voiced in his oft-quoted speech of April 25, 1927: "The person and property of a citizen are a part of the general domain of the Nation, even when abroad. . . . The fundamental laws of justice are universal in their application. These rights go with the citizen. Wherever he goes these duties of our government must follow him." This has been sometimes regarded as symbolic of Coolidge's whole policy toward the countries of the Caribbean area. If it was the high water mark in the declamatory assertion of the right to protect United States citizens abroad, it was, of course, the mark reached as the tide of policy turned.[46]

The perfection of expression of the nature of the old policy was attained just as a new policy made its appearance in the form of new actions—unlabeled, untested, strange alike to law, to theory, and to practice.

It is a curious feature of Stimson's position that the concluding pages of his book were devoted to a condemnation of public criticism in the United States of the Nicaraguan policy of the Coolidge administration. When the government of the United States was trying "to do an unselfish service to a weak and sorely beset Central American State," Stimson felt that it should not have been hampered by the disapproval of the public in the United States. His closing words were: "A policy of helpfulness, which was thus accepted by Nicaragua in the same spirit in which it was offered by our government, should not be poisoned and rendered of no effect by ignorant or partisan attacks in the United States." [47] The criticism of which Stimson complained was directed, not at Stimson's solution of what even defenders of Coolidge called the "Nicaraguan mess," but against the policy that had created the situation from which Stimson had rescued the President. Stimson had cause later on to rue the results of the Coolidge policy, but for the moment he chose to defend to the hilt that policy which, because of public criticism, it had become his responsibility to rectify.

Occupation: Experience Overturns Theory

Without attempting here a running account of Nicaraguan developments,[48] a review of some of the more important kinds of difficulties encountered before and during Stimson's Nicaraguan experience may provide an understanding of the growth, nature, and depth of his conviction as Secretary of State that intervention in Latin America was a policy that should not be indulged in by the United States. This conviction, nurtured and applied in Nicaragua, was rigidly expressed in his policy toward Cuba. The classification of problems given here is designed primarily to bring out what seem to have been the main reasons for the ultimate abandonment of the policy of electoral supervision, despite the fact that the supervision actually carried out did provide free and fair elections.

DIFFICULTIES OF ELECTORAL SUPERVISION

Washington found it impossible in several instances to bring about a reversal of actions which Nicaraguan authorities felt bold enough to take without previous consultation with the United States Minister in Managua.

The Tipitapa agreement provided that President Adolfo Díaz should remain in office until supervised elections were held in November, 1928. Díaz was a Conservative, and the Congress was controlled by his party. Following by-elections for Congress in November, the still Conservative Chamber and Senate seated a Conservative deputy and a senator on the basis of credentials described by Chargé Dana G. Munro as "fraudulent." Munro reported that this was the first time "in recent months where either party has openly disregarded a recommendation insistently made by the Legation." [49]

These members of Congress held their seats, and a serious situation developed in March, 1928, when the new electoral law, prepared by Harold W. Dodds of Princeton University, and approved by the Department of State, was rejected by a vote of the Chamber of Deputies. In January, Munro still hoped "to obtain a majority in the Chamber," but despite "unremitting pressure," a short vacation of Congress taken at the suggestion of Minister Charles C. Eberhardt, and warnings from Kellogg that supervision "must be executed" in any case by the United States, the Conservatives in the Chamber refused to adopt the law. Trying in every reasonable way to get the law passed, Eberhardt arranged for the rapid transit to Nicaragua of Carlos Cuadra Pasos, a leading Conservative politician, who was in Panama, after arranging for some modifications of the electoral law with General Frank R. McCoy, the head of the United States Electoral Mission. Eberhardt told Kellogg: "In view of the continued delay of Cuadra Pasos in Panama, the Admiral has invited him at our request to proceed at once on a warship. . . . He personally controls four votes and in case of a definite break with Chamorro he and the President could obtain the passage of the act." [50] This surely must be the most elaborate instance of that form of electioneering known as transportation that was ever undertaken by the United States Navy.

All was in vain, including Cuadra Pasos's expedited arrival, and, when Congress adjourned, there was no recourse but to get President Díaz to put the electoral law into effect by decree, despite Eberhardt's admission that "the legality of such a decree as a basis for holding an election may be questioned." [51]

On another occasion, President Moncada, leader of the Liberal party, who had been elected in the supervised election of November, 1928, imprisoned about fifteen members of the Conservative party, and Moncada told Eberhardt that, although the Conservatives had not been planning a revolution, they were "conspiring to promote intranquility and lack of confidence in his regime." [52] These and subsequent arrests caused concern in Washington. Chargé Matthew E. Hanna was instructed to tell Moncada that these measures "might very easily lead to greater evils than those which by this means he might seek to overcome," such as the loss by the Guardia of its nonpartisan character.[53] However, imprisonments continued, and eight Conservatives were deported to Mexico, for conspiring to create disorder. The Mexican government refused to admit the deportees, who proceeded to San Francisco where they were permitted to enter the United States.[54]

Moncada continued to employ the Guardia to suppress his political enemies, some of whom were charged with planning to assassinate him, and subsequent arrests and deportations were not ended until Stimson informed him that it was necessary for the United States "to assure itself that the Nicaraguan government should not, in the enjoyment of its immunity to serious attack from within, undertake measures against its political opponents which are open to the charge of being of a retaliatory or unjustifiably oppressive nature." [55]

A lesser effort by Moncada to strengthen the Liberal party was the removal of the municipal governments controlled by Conservatives in several towns and their replacement by councils composed of Liberals. Stimson instructed Hanna to inform Moncada that the

Department would "view with much regret the initiation of a policy which might be interpreted by his opponents as constituting unwarranted interference in the normal political and administrative activities of the Republic." [56]

On several occasions the Department of State found itself in the position of interpreting the constitution of Nicaragua in ways directly opposed to those of the president and other authorities of Nicaragua. In 1928, the Department approved the promulgation of the electoral law by presidential decree, although, as noted above, the procedure was of doubtful constitutionality.[57] In 1930, the Department protested against the desire of Moncada to make amendments to the electoral law by decree, because such action might "be exposed to challenge on Constitutional grounds." [58] Again, Moncada, toward the end of his four-year term, desired to convene a constitutional assembly to give him an additional two years in office and to make other changes in the constitution. The Department of State opposed this proposal as "contrary to the spirit of republican institutions," and because it did not think that an assembly could constitutionally be held in 1932. In that case, of course, Moncada's term could not be extended because presidential elections were due in November of that year. It is clear in the correspondence that officers of the Department of State had given careful attention to the legal questions, since they cited specific articles from the Nicaraguan constitution in support of their position. Although it was emphasized to a mission sent by Moncada to Washington that they "did not say that . . . this procedure 'must' be followed," the views of Departmental officers ultimately prevailed, and the 1932 elections took place as scheduled.

In these and in other ways, the Department had trouble in fulfilling its announced intention of helping the Nicaraguans to learn how to run their country on the premise that fair elections provided the best method for choosing governments. Moncada was frank in saying that he favored electoral supervision by the United States officials for many years; he felt that "neither Conservatives nor Liberals, by themselves, would give us free elections." [59] Stimson had by then decided to bring the Marines home, and he was unmoved by this proposal or by those made in 1932 by both Liberal and Conservative party candidates for the presidency, that the Marines should remain in Nicaragua.

When President Díaz had talked about retiring in 1927, Washington asserted such action "would strike at the very foundation of the transaction by which peace and order have been restored" and said his retirement could only be regarded "with the utmost disapprobation." [60] Díaz did not resign, but he later used his knowledge of his indispensability to put little pressure on Congress to pass the electoral law. Munro reported unhappily that Díaz "cannot be relied on. . . . If I press him too hard he threatens to resign." [61]

The Department also engaged in struggles to prevent the Conservative party from engaging in electoral maneuvers that might defeat the aim of supervised elections. In the 1928 election, the Conservative party at one stage planned to enter several candidates for the presidency in the hope of throwing the final selection into the Conservative Congress. This possibility alarmed Kellogg, who stated that a two-party election had been "clearly contemplated" by the Tipitapa agreement, and any effort to prevent the people from deciding in that manner would be viewed with "the gravest misgivings." [62] Whether or not this expression of concern was the cause, the Conservatives finally presented only one candidate.

Once again, in 1932, the Department of State was called on to remind the opposition party of its electoral duties. The Conservative candidate for president, General Emiliano Chamorro, said he was thinking of abstaining from the election because of "apathy" and "resistance to participation" within his party. Stimson asked Minister Hanna to tell Chamorro that, although "this question is of course an internal one" that the Conservative party must answer for itself, he was "unwilling to believe that the Conservative party sets so little store on the well being and enduring interests of Nicaragua that it would seriously contemplate abstaining from the presidential elections." Abstention would prejudice hopes for "peace and stability" and defeat the common purposes of strengthening and safeguarding "the principles of republican institutions," and the establishment of the Guardia "on a firm, nonpartisan basis for the future." [63] This appeal was successful, and Stimson must have been greatly relieved, in view of his earnest desire to give up his Nicaraguan responsibilities, and in view of the impossibility of coercing a reluctant candidate to take part in elections.

The Department of State took three principal positions on which it would admit of no compromises, and it was not hesitant in making demands on the Nicaraguan government to maintain these stands. First, it insisted on the complete execution of the terms of the Tipitapa agreement by all parties concerned, and it insisted on its own interpretation of those terms. It constantly returned to that agreement as the basis for its action and that of Nicaraguans. In the second place, it demanded, and obtained, all the powers that it deemed adequate to allow General McCoy to provide protection for voters and an honest count of the votes. Thirdly, it required that the government refrain from using the Guardia for political purposes, and, with the temporary exception already noted concerning political arrests, it was successful in imposing this requirement on the Nicaraguan authorities.

The negotiation and full execution of the laws and administrative measures necessary to make these demands effective in Nicaragua involved a nearly ceaseless vigil in Washington. That this watchfulness was becoming irksome as early as 1928 may be seen from the reply by Kellogg to a request from Eberhardt for a strong statement by the Department to dissuade the Conservative majority in Congress from rejecting electoral certificates given to four Liberal deputies by the National Board of Elections presided over by General McCoy. Kellogg did not make an official statement, but he authorized Eberhardt to say informally that "the United States Government, having at great trouble and expense to itself aided in the carrying out of a free and fair election at the request of both parties, and the elections having taken place in a manner generally accepted as completely acceptable, and all controversial questions relating to the election of individual candidates having been settled by the National Board of Elections in a thoroughly impartial manner and without respect to party considerations, the Department feels that there is a moral obligation for the Nicaraguan Congress to accept the certificates of the Board and thus to cooperate in making effective the will of the Nicaraguan electorate. For the

Congress to do otherwise would tend to nullify in part the results of these free and fair elections and the work of the National Board of Elections." [64] The Conservatives did not put this plaintive appeal to the test, and the deputies were seated.

On other occasions, the Department "insisted" that certain decisions be made,[65] and its wishes were respected, but it does not appear that it was necessary to make any direct threats of the use of force in order to bring compliance with the desires of the Department.

FAILURE TO ESTABLISH ORDER

When Stimson recommended the supervision of elections as elementary education in democratic politics for Nicaraguans, one of his assumptions was that supervision would take place in a peaceful country. The Tipitapa agreement provided for the surrender of rifles and other arms by both sides in the civil war, so that the Guardia and the Marines would enjoy a monopoly of weapons.[66]

However, one of Moncada's generals, César Augusto Sandino, rejected his chief's policy and retired with some four hundred armed men to the mountains of northwestern Nicaragua. For more than five years he directed sporadic raids, killing among others some fifteen United States citizens at mines, lumber camps, and plantations. Sandino claimed to be a Nicaraguan patriot, seeking to rid his country of North American invaders. This self-assigned role was widely accepted in Latin America, and also by some vocal individuals in the United States, who, in the view of the Department of State, should have known better.[67] In the Department's view, Sandino deliberately undertook

a program for the destruction of American and other foreign lives and property and the lives and property of Nicaraguans as well, not in open warfare but by the stealthy and ruthless tactics which characterized the savages who fell upon American settlers in our country 150 years ago. For these Americans who have been killed in Nicaragua during the past few days were first taken prisoner and then slaughtered.[68]

Because he eluded both the Guardia and the Marines, and because he continued boldly to make raids, Sandino became to many Latin Americans a symbol of triumphant defiance of the power of the United States. Long before the Marines were withdrawn in 1933 without having captured him, Sandino had become a continental hero.

Keeping order in Nicaragua was a four-fold task involving the prevention of violence at elections, the training of the Guardia, the protection of United States citizens, and the extirpation of Sandino's forces, described by the Department of State as "bandits." In the first two of these tasks, the Marines were entirely successful, but they failed in the latter two, principally because of nonmilitary features of the situation that were beyond their control.

At first, in 1927, the Marines, as well as the Department, were caught by surprise by the Sandino raids, which occurred during the rainy season when transportation was difficult in the northern mountains. In addition, it was asserted by the Legation in Managua that what it called "Conservative bandits" were also operating in that area. There were reports that Chamorro was aiding Sandino, to make it "more difficult to hold a free election in 1928," and Munro believed that Chamorro might be "working through some of the bandit leaders to foment disorders." [69]

A fundamental difficulty that plagued the Marines and the Department of State throughout this affair was that both Sandino's forces and the "Conservative bandits," when fearing capture by the Marines, were able to step over the northern border into Honduras. There they were not only safe from pursuit, but they were able to use Honduran territory for bases of operations. In Honduras they were able to sell property, such as coffee and gold, that they had seized in Nicaragua. They also were able to augment their numbers with Honduran recruits, and to purchase arms and other supplies.[70]

Kellogg wired Minister G. T. Summerlin to make "informal but emphatic representations" that the Honduran government should take measures for "more effective vigilance on the frontier" and for the prevention of the use of Honduran territory "as a base of operations by lawless elements in Nicaragua," but the bandits continued to enjoy immunity and replenishment in Honduras.[71]

Four and a half years later, Stimson complained of the existence of exactly the same conditions and asked Chargé Lawrence Higgins to discuss "very discreetly" with President Mejía Colindres of Honduras the proposition that he "raise no objection if detachments of the Nicaraguan National Guard should temporarily cross the frontier in hot pursuit of the bandits in an effort to abate this nuisance." Higgins replied that the President would probably not agree to such a request; further, he might well make it public, and "a very undesirable impression would be created if it became generally known that the United States government or its representative had suggested that he take a step in violation of his constitutional oath to defend the territorial integrity of Honduras." [72]

The Department, on receiving this advice, withdrew its proposal, but asked Higgins to take up with the President the question of improved controls along the Nicaraguan border. Higgins did so and found President Vicente Mejía Colindres cooperative; however, Higgins warned the Department that the result would be "entirely inconspicuous." Although Honduras had spent an estimated 500,000 pesos since 1927 in maintaining "a special expeditionary force" of from forty to one hundred and fifty men to prevent violations of the Honduran frontier, the results were "insignificant." In five years the force had captured one "bandit pack train" and found one arms cache. Twenty bandits had been captured and "reconcentrated" in the interior of Honduras, whence they had departed with no great difficulty. One Sandinista had actually been arrested and imprisoned, but had been "allowed to escape," and a few Nicaraguans had been refused entry into Honduras.[73]

The following month Minister Julius G. Lay reported that the Legation "has thoroughly reliable information" that arms stolen from Honduran government arsenals had been bought by Sandino's agents, and that "within the last few days mules were loaded with munitions, in daylight, in front of the Ritz Hotel in Tegucigalpa, destined for the frontier." The Department asked Lay to tell Honduran authorities that it "was surprised to learn of the theft and shipment of Honduran official war materials to Nicaraguan outlaws" and that it hoped the exportation of arms would in future be prevented in accordance with Honduran treaty obligations.[74]

In these circumstances, the failure to capture Sandino may be understood, even though the Marines were able from time to time to drive him and nearly all his followers out of Nicaragua. It was not surprising that "some officers of long experience [went] so far as to say that the task of exterminating the remaining bandit groups [was] not a military problem." Hanna took this view seriously and proposed a road building program for Nueva Segovia, that both would reduce banditry by giving regular employment to "reluctant bandits" and would provide highways for the rapid deployments of Marines and Guardia. The cost of this ingenious scheme would have been about $40,000 a month, but Stimson did not wish to recommend to Moncada "so large an expenditure," and he apparently had no thought of making a contribution for this purpose from the United States Treasury.[75]

The Marines also labored under an additional handicap in dealing with such Sandinistas as they were able to capture. Munro recommended that the Department of State should allow the Nicaraguan government to declare martial law in Nueva Segovia, since "the authorities are placed in a most embarrassing position when suspects or prisoners of war bring *habeas corpus* proceedings and the Marines and Guardia are being hampered in the actual conduct of operations against the bandits." Kellogg, however, replied that he would not agree to such action; martial law would have to be administered "practically by and under the direction of American officers," and he did "not desire to have Americans engaged in holding courts martial on Nicaraguans, even captured bandits." [76]

The Department tenaciously held to the position that banditry, even of the Sandinista type, was not a military offense, and that United States officers, whether commanding Marines or Guardia, could not try bandits in courts martial. The only alternative to courts martial was the trial of bandits by the civil courts, which, as Chargé Willard Beaulac declared, was "quite impracticable." [77]

The trouble with the civil courts was that if they were effective, they might be used for political purposes against the opposition Conservative party; this danger was avoided, however, because the Sandinistas were able to prevent the administration of justice both in Nueva Segovia and Jinotega. General D. C. McDougal reported that a *fiscal*, or special judicial officer, had been assigned to each of those provinces at the end of 1929; in the former, however, the *fiscal* "became very active in preparing different lists of Conservatives, whom he listed as bandit suspects, and also lists of Guardia [members] who had been formerly Conservatives and whom he wished to classify as ex-bandits. He took little interest in the bandit prisoners being held by Guardia and Marines for trial, beyond ascertaining which political party they belonged to." President Moncada had been asked to send commissions of civilians "to clear up these cases," presumably "under the military code or customs of the country of previous times," but the commissions never appeared, and the General understood that "no one could be found who was willing to serve, and thereby incur the enmity and the risk of retaliation which seems to be well founded." [78]

This situation left the Sandinistas nearly as safe in Nicaragua as they were in Honduras, so long as they avoided pitched battles with the Marines. General McDougal commented that the only effect of martial law, declared by Moncada, but unenforceable by Marine or Guardia tribunals, was "to prevent captured bandits from being released by the courts immediately after capture." He said that the Marines could locate many known bandits but it would only mean a loss of prestige for the Marines if they were captured and then released "for lack of machinery for handling the cases." Although he declared this situation "must be met in some way shortly if banditry is to be kept from increasing," the Department did not overcome its scruples, nor did the Nicaraguan courts become more efficient, and the General's prediction was borne out in 1931 by an especially revolting attack by Sandinistas on the northeast coast town of Cabo Gracias in which nine United States citizens were killed after being captured.[79]

These two principal sources of bafflement to the Marines and their pupils, the Guardia, were compounded by the fact that it was almost impossible for them to achieve surprise against the Sandinistas, except occasionally and with only temporary advantage, by the use of air bombardment.[80] Toward the end of 1931, Sandinistas became so bold as to loot a town on the railroad between Managua and Corinto, the principal port on the Pacific Coast. President

Moncada told Beaulac of his alarm over this development and said
"he would like to organize a volunteer force of Nicaraguans outside the Guardia to exterminate the bandits." Beaulac, however,
told Moncada, with Stimson's approval, that the organization of a
volunteer force would violate the agreement under which the
Guardia was to be the sole armed force in Nicaragua, and that the
President should maintain faith in the Guardia's handling of the
situation.[81] Beaulac thought that a volunteer force would be of
"very doubtful military value," but quoted Moncada as maintaining
that a force of 125 men recruited from provinces in the north
could "settle with the bandits," by "conducting real mountain warfare such as the bandits conduct." In the same published statement,
Moncada had recommended that the Marines should guard the
cities only; he had said he "felt sorrow" for eight Marines killed
in a recent ambush: "They fell in territory which they do not
know, assassinated rather than killed in real combat." [82] The Marine
officers, and the minister in Managua, however, opposed Moncada's
suggestion, and it was not carried out.

The only occasion when peculiarly Nicaraguan techniques of
antibandit operations were used was in Moncada's first year as
President. He engaged the services of a Mexican named Escamilla, as head of a force of "volunteers" that cooperated with the
Guardia against Sandino. Escamilla was described by Hanna as
"energetic and at times ruthless in his methods," and by the Conservative press as "a Mexican adventurer, a mercenary soldier, a
murderer and cut-throat." [83] One of Escamilla's chief exploits was
the capture and execution of a Sandinista leader named Jirón. The
execution was ordered by a court martial consisting of Escamilla
"and three or four of his colonels, all of whom being Mexican and
one Costa Rican," without reference to higher authority.[84] Three
other executions in the field were known to have been carried out
by the volunteers under Escamilla, but this technique of suppression, which might have become effective after a time, ceased to
be used in 1930 when Marine officers considered the Guardia well
enough organized so they could dispense with Escamilla's services.
Their decision was in accord with Stimson's desire that the volunteer forces should be disbanded; Stimson may well have felt un-

comfortable at delegating any of his responsibility for the pacification of Nicaragua to a Mexican commander of irregulars, however efficient.

The presidential election of 1928 was held without interference from Sandinistas, thanks to the presence of more than 5,500 Marines and Navy personnel and about 2,000 members of the Guardia. In May, 1929, General Dion Williams reported that the military situation was "excellent." Only two small bandit groups were in existence, and neither of these was allied with Sandino or was "in the field for Sandino patriotic motives." Sandino himself was out of Nicaragua, and Nicaragua "has never been in such a peaceful state," although it should be remembered that it would be "very difficult to stamp out all banditry," since it had always existed in Central American states.[85] Sandino was granted asylum in Mexico in July, 1929, and remained there for the better part of a year.

LIMITED PROTECTION OF UNITED STATES CITIZENS

Banditry, whether for loot only, or for loot and the independence of Nicaragua, did not cease with Sandino's departure. Nevertheless, the Marine forces, which had been reduced to about 2,600 men after the elections, were cut almost in half in August with the embarkation of 1,200 from Corinto. This reduction in force had been vainly opposed by Hanna, who asserted that order had not been restored, "extensive regions in the north [were] dominated by lawless elements," and the situation was not much better than it was in August, 1928.[86]

The attacks led by lieutenants of Sandino early in 1931 on the northern end of the east coast were apparently timed to take advantage of the chaos resulting from the earthquake that destroyed much of Managua at the end of March. Marines were landed to assist the Guardia to protect United States citizens, but Stimson was determined that they should not be sent into the interior, since "the problem of defense . . . [would have to] be worked out by the Guardia itself." [87]

In accordance with this decision, Stimson made the momentous declaration on April 18 that the United States could not undertake "general protection of Americans" in Nicaragua, because such action would "lead to difficulties and commitments which this Government [did] not propose to undertake." He therefore advised his co-nationals who did not feel sufficiently protected by the Guardia either to leave Nicaragua or go to coastal towns where they could be protected or evacuated by United States vessels.[88] This declaration gave rise to criticism in the press of the United States, and Stimson justified the policy in a long statement emphasizing that "it would be almost impossible for regular troops to operate effectively" against "outlaws" in the jungles of the east coast and pointing out that the Guardia, which had not existed in 1926, was now "highly efficient."[89] He felt that the United States, by helping to train the Guardia, was not only "furnishing the most practical and effective method of meeting the bandit problem," but was also recognizing that the bandit problem was one for the "sovereign goverenment of Nicaragua" to solve.[90]

To correspondents at his press conference Stimson remarked that it was "a matter of discretion with a government how far it will protect property of its citizens in another country"; if it determined that interposing to protect such property "may clash with broader international or governmental policies, it may perfectly well refuse to interpose. . . . This administration will hesitate long before becoming involved in any general campaign of protecting with our forces American property throughout Nicaragua."[91] So far, in just under four years, had the United States retreated from Coolidge's assertion that "the person and property of a citizen are a part of the general domain of the Nation, even when abroad," with the corollary that the government had a duty to prevent the pillage as well as the murder of its citizens in foreign countries. The Nicaraguan experience in those four years appears to have been the principal agent in creating this remarkable transformation of policy.

Stimson's statements were made less than three years after Hughes's well-known declaration at the Havana Conference of American States:

What are we going to do when government breaks down and American citizens are in danger of their lives? Are we to stand by and see them killed because a government in circumstances which it cannot control and for which it may not be responsible can no longer afford reasonable protection? . . . Now it is a principle of international law that in such a case a government is fully justified in taking action—I would call it interposition of a temporary character—for the purpose of protecting the lives and property of its nationals.

The vitality of the assertion of the right to "interpose" was so strong that it was not until ten years more had passed that the United States government accepted the proposition that no state had the right to intervene in another's domestic or external affairs. Within three years, however, Stimson was publicly saying that interposition to protect property might not be untertaken if it "clashed with broader international or governmental policies," [92] and he was privately writing in his diary that United States citizens on the east coast of Nicaragua "were a pampered lot of people" because they thought they had "a right to call for troops whenever any danger apprehends." [93] Probably without knowing it, Stimson was echoing the sentiments of Secretary of the Navy Josephus Daniels, some seventeen years earlier, who told a delegation of United States businessmen from Tampico that he would not provide protection for their property: "You went there to get rich quick; and now you want the whole country to raise an army of 500,000 men and send it to Mexico at this country's expense to protect you, and you won't pay a cent to support it there." [94]

The Department of State endeavored to explain that the Stimson declaration was not a new policy, and it pointed to previous cases at the outbreak of World War I, in China and in Mexico, where it had warned Americans "in disturbed foreign countries that it would be unable to protect them except at coastal points." [95] No comparable case, however, was cited in Central America and for this area the policy represented without question a new departure. Washington correspondents did not fail to comment that in his book Stimson had argued that the United States could not avoid responsibility for the protection of Europeans in Nicaragua. The administration's position, however, was that the new policy was simply a different way of offering protection: the situation in 1931 was not one of warfare in Nicaragua, but one of murder by guerrillas in the jungle; for this situation the most effective protection of United States citizens and foreigners alike required their moving to coastal areas while the Nicaraguan Guardia, now a strong force of 2,100 men, pursued the bandits.[96] Toward this dialectic even the normally friendly New York *Times* was unsympathetic; noting that Stimson "somewhat resentfully" said he was misunderstood, the paper remarked that "if so, he was misunderstood, by everyone." If the government was doing only what it could do in Nicaragua, rather than what it would like to do, there was no need "to have fired off a diplomatic gun about it. Moreover, it was a gun which seemed to be doing more execution at the breech than at the muzzle." [97]

Two months before this declaration, Stimson had publicly announced his determination to withdraw all Marines from Nicaragua "immediately after the election of 1932." [98]

Stimson's policy of relinquishment of responsibilities in Nicaragua was greeted with approval by influential members of the United States Congress and was supported by many people who had welcomed the change in policy toward Mexico in 1927. It was opposed principally by United States citizens having investments in Nicaragua, or living in Nicaragua, and by a substantial portion of the newspapers in the United States. Of especial interest, however, is the claim of one coffee planter who wrote to Stimson that he and his neighbors had never needed any protection before 1927. Until then, he said, they had enjoyed friendly relations with Nicaraguans, but "today we are hated and despised and in danger of massacre any time the Marines are withdrawn. This feeling has been created by employing the American Marines to hunt down and kill Nicaraguans in their own country. This was a fatal mistake. The intervention of the U.S. government in the internal affairs of Nicaragua has proved a calamity for the American coffee planters doing business in this Republic." [99] Under the existing circumstances, however, he appealed for the stationing of Marines at Matagalpa to prevent a possible massacre there by Sandinistas.[100] This letter may have helped to harden Stimson's determination to follow his policy.

Another, perhaps stronger, influence pushing him in the same direction was the cost of the antibandit campaign. From May 4,

1927, to April 16, 1928, twenty-one Marines had been killed, and the expense of maintaining the Marines in Nicaragua was estimated at $1,500,000 above the normal expenses for these forces.[101] In 1932, in the midst of the depression, it was found impossible in Washington to obtain permission either from Congress or President Hoover to spend the $750,000 thought necessary to send Marines to Nicaragua to insure adequate electoral supervision.[102] In Nicaragua, also, the financial situation was tight, and Stimson said that, if Moncada could not pay part of the electoral expenses, Washington should be informed immediately "in order that we can call the whole thing off at once and get the Marines out of Nicaragua." [103]

Moncada did find some funds, and so did Stimson, who, however, was not able to get them from Congress, which expressly stipulated that no part of the naval appropriation for 1932–33 should be used to send Marines to Nicaragua. The amount obtained by Stimson, presumably from other monies available to the executive branch, was only $200,000. This provided only for the arrangements offering the least protection against electoral intimidation among three contemplated plans, and made no allowance for the sending of additional Marines.[104]

Finally, after September 18, 1931, Stimson felt embarrassed in his resistance to Japanese policy in Manchuria by the continued presence of Marines in Nicaragua. To a question whether he would land forces "if they were needed to protect American interests in Chile and Colombia," he answered:

not on your life. . . . If we landed a single soldier among those South Americans now, it would undo all the labor of three years, and it would put me in absolutely wrong in China, where Japan has done all of this monstrous work under the guise of protecting her nationals with a landing force.[105]

Further evidence that the absence of Marines offered the best protection to United States citizens in Nicaragua was offered by the cessation of Sandinista banditry shortly after the Marines' departure. Sandino's methods were barbarous in the extreme, but he was in some respects different from many of his associates, such as Salgado, who was reported by Moncada to be "a dissipated, elderly bandit . . . who preferred to live by banditry." [106] Sandino immediately ceased his murderous raiding, and after 1933, political stability of a special kind characterized Nicaraguan internal politics. The commander of the Guardia, General Somoza, made use of the power given him in this position to secure his election in 1936, and dominated his country's administration for twenty years, either as President or as the controlling influence behind the presidency. The Guardia, originally intended as an impartial, nonpolitical constabulary that would keep order and insure fair elections in Nicaragua, was turned by Somoza into a force that, through coercion and intimidation, insured his victories in elections and prevented revolutions against his regimes. The probability of such a development was recognized in the Department of State as early as 1931, when Laurence Duggan wrote:

The fact is, however, a nonpartisan constabulary is impossible in Nicaragua. Not only is it contrary to Latin American political-historical development, but Nicaragua is handicapped by a special circumstance, namely, the vitriolic animosity of the two parties, which is as bitter today as it was two hundred years ago. Therefore it is difficult to understand why hope was ever entertained that a nonpolitical military force could be established.[107]

The hope was harbored by Stimson, since it provided one of the principal justifications for the evacuation of the Marines. On the day the last of the Marines left for home, the Department of State declared that the two obligations it undertook in the Tipitapa agreement—supervision of elections and organization of the Guardia—had been fulfilled. Concerning the Guardia, it was stated that it had "developed into a well-disciplined and efficient organization with a high *esprit de corps.* . . . Both political parties have agreed on their own initiative to a plan for insuring the nonpolitical character of that organization." [108]

The experience of the United States government from 1926 to 1933 in Mexico and Nicaragua provided ample reason for striking out in directions of policy different from those initiated by Theodore Roosevelt and Woodrow Wilson. Public and congressional opinion in the United States was increasingly unwilling that its government use force against Latin American countries either for the protection of the property of United States citizens or for the political education of Latin Americans. The Nicaraguan experience convinced Stimson that electoral supervision and bandit fighting were time-consuming and expensive, difficult and embarrassing. He extended his acquired distaste for intervention, interposition, or intermeddling to his policy in Cuba—a political arena Cordell Hull was soon to enter with an enthusiasm comparable to Stimson's in Nicaragua in 1927, and to leave with convictions, also based on experience, that were almost identical to those so deeply rooted in Stimson's mind by 1933. However, Stimson then was finishing his term as Secretary of State; the foreign policy ideas he had expressed in his book in 1927 had been relinquished if not repudiated. After 1931 he had been able only to retreat in Central America and the Caribbean. He had made a show of covering this retreat in Nicaragua by extolling the efficiency of the Guardia as the Marines were called home. When a revolution in El Salvador placed in power a dictator who stopped payments on the external debt, recognition was at first refused by Stimson, but was subsequently extended shortly before he left office. By the beginning of 1933, the Hoover administration had no desire to intervene in Central America, and it had ceased employing nonrecognition as a form of pressure on revolutionary governments. Nevertheless, it had gained little or no sympathy in Latin America as a result, for it had not found it possible to combine the doffing of former principles with the donning of new ones. Stimson, an active, free-swimming entrepreneur in the Caribbean in 1927, displayed markedly molluscan tendencies by 1933 as he withdrew hostages in Nicaragua, acquiesced in violent governmental overturns elsewhere in Central America, and cautioned his ambassador to refrain from any sort of intermeddling in the critical situation in Cuba.

CHAPTER II

The Cuban Experience I

THE ADMINISTRATION OF President Franklin D. Roosevelt had been in office only four months when it faced its first critical decision about applying the principles of a Good Neighbor. How should a Good Neighbor act toward Cuba, whose major city was just one hundred miles away, across the Gulf Stream, a country where over one billion dollars of United States capital was invested, a country which in 1933 was "economically prostrate, ruled by a tyrannical dictatorship to which 95 per cent of the people were fanatically opposed, a country . . . in which bombings, terrorism, and murder were daily occurrences?" [1]

Cuba presented a problem to the Roosevelt administration, oddly enough, because the two previous administrations had refrained from intervention in Cuban political affairs. In other countries of the Caribbean, revolutions had caused the overthrow of governments in power after the onset of the depression in 1929. In Cuba, however, President Gerardo Machado y Morales, who had been President since May, 1925, had built a strong political machine and had retained support of the army. In spite of economic distress caused by a decline in sugar prices, and in spite of revolutionary activity which became chronic in 1927, Machado's army and police remained masters of the country as a whole, and the economy continued to function amid a kind of guerrilla civil warfare carried on by anti-Machado groups in city streets and in the back country. To the Roosevelt administration this situation seemed to require ameliorative measures. Before exploring them, however, it may be well to look at the responsibility of the United States for the Cuban turmoil.

The Background of Policy

The United States, in its relations with Cuba, had obtained special rights of intervention through the provisions of the Platt Amendment to the Army Appropriation Act of 1901. These had been incorporated into the Cuban Constitution and also into the treaty of May 22, 1903, between the two countries. Article III of that treaty contained the political heart of the arrangement:

The Government of Cuba consents that the United States may exercise the right to intervene for the preservation of Cuban independence, the maintenance of a government adequate for the protection of life, property, and individual liberty, and for discharging the obligations with respect to Cuba imposed by the Treaty of Paris on the United States, to be assumed and undertaken by the Government of Cuba.[2]

The Platt Amendment, however, possessed three personalities, one quiescent and two active. The passive element was the text of the amendment itself, and the active components were two interpretations. How would the right be used? Secretary of War Elihu Root thought it should be used only in unusual circumstances, and he declared as early as April 3, 1901:

in the view of the President the intervention described in the third clause of the Platt Amendment is not synonymous with intermeddling or interference with the affairs of the Cuban Government, but the formal action of the Government of the United States, based upon just and substantial grounds, for the preservation of Cuban independence, and the maintenance of a government adequate for the protection of life, property, and individual liberty, and adequate for discharging the obligations with respect to Cuba imposed by the Treaty of Paris.[3]

This interpretation by Root was frequently mentioned and strongly relied upon by Department of State officials during the years from 1928 to 1933, in response to appeals for intervention both from citizens of the United States and of Cuba.

By "formal action" Root apparently meant the use of force, and whenever in this study the word "intervention" is employed it refers to the landing of troops of one state on the territory of another for other than ceremonial purposes. The words "interference" and "intermeddling" are used to refer to other actions, ranging from advice to economic pressures and the threat or show of force. This interpretation is more limited than that in general use, but only in this sense did the United States not intervene in Cuba in 1933, and this meaning most closely approximates the interpretation given by the United States government to the nonintervention pledge contained in inter-American agreements in 1933 and later.

There existed also another interpretation of the Platt Amendment, the "preventive policy" of Secretary of State Philander Knox, which permitted the landing of troops, as in 1912, as a measure only "of precaution and of ordinary protection of American life and property." [4] The preventive policy of Secretary Knox was intended to forestall the creation of situations "requiring" intervention as exercised in 1906–9, when the executive power was wielded by a United States official appointed by President Roosevelt and supported by United States military forces.

Subsequent administrations in the United States were as desirous as was Knox to avoid intervention in Cuba, and after his time, with the exception of the 1917 "war measure," the United States landed no armed forces in Cuba. The advisory half of the preventive policy was employed on occasion after 1912, although later secretaries of state did not generalize about it but applied it in specific instances, so that some of its significance, as well as its flamboyance, was dissipated.

The assertion of the right to follow a preventive policy did not define how it would be applied in a given case; that depended on what Washington decided was undesirable.

The Reelection of President Machado

In the spring of 1927 President Machado proposed amendments to the Cuban constitution that included the extension of the presidential term of office from four to six years. Ambassador Enoch H. Crowder commented that the action "cannot be interpreted

otherwise than as savoring of dictatorship" and added, propheti-
cally: "I greatly fear that the reaction upon the popular mind will
be such as to lend itself, should other conditions be ripe, to up-
setting the stability of the island." [5] In the Department of State,
it was recommended that, if it appeared that "an attempt is being
made to railroad the amendments through the Senate and a Constitutional Assembly, in spite of considerable popular opposition
which might lead to disorders, we would seriously object." [6] However, when Machado visited Washington shortly afterwards to
test whether his plans would be viewed as compatible with the
Platt Amendment, President Coolidge told him in words that found
frequent echo, that "the United States felt that this was a question for the Cuban people and their government to decide; that
the United States only desired that the people of Cuba should have
whatever government and constitution they themselves genuinely
wanted." [7]

To Machado this meant he could proceed without regard for
Crowder's admonitions. The amendments were voted in the spring
of 1928, and Machado was reelected for a six-year term beginning
on May 20, 1929.

The inner reasons for Coolidge's position are not known. His
statements may have been made without full appreciation of their
meaning and of their effect on Machado, or they may have been
uttered because Coolidge believed that Machado offered the best
prospect, among Cuban public men, of continuing a period of
relative stability in the island. Commenting on this policy several
years later, Laurence Duggan stated:

What emerges from this discussion . . . is that both the Department
and the Embassy put a premium on "order" in Cuba. Any qualms that
may have arisen over those factors of the Constitutional Amendment
Bill which made the Government less responsive, instead of more responsive, to the people were quashed, for President Machado had brought
internal peace to Cuba for the first time since 1917. Both Ambassador
Crowder and the Department indicated that their passivity to the constitutional amendments was due to their hope that under Machado peace,
order, and "political cooperation" would continue.[8]

In any case, two critical decisions had been made. Personally,
Machado had been approved by Washington; politically, his new

term and those of his supporters in Congress were not protested by Washington as contravening Article III of the Platt Amendment. Shortly afterwards, a third decision, no less important, but dependent on the others, was also reached. Despite charges by responsible sources in Cuba that the amendments were adopted unconstitutionally because changes were made in them after their passage by Congress, the Department of State decided not to raise the question with Machado at the time. Thus fortified, Machado must have felt that intervention by the United States against his rule in Cuba would be highly unlikely.

Secretary Stimson and Nonintervention in Cuba

The security of Machado's position was greatly enhanced by the commencement, about this time, of the antiinterventionist trend in United States policy that had developed in relations with Mexico and Nicaragua. The situation with regard to Cuba was different, because the Platt Amendment authorized intervention. However, the Root interpretation of the Amendment, proscribing intermeddling or interference, provided a ready refuge for a Department of State that was moving toward a general policy of nonintervention. When, after 1929, unrest in Cuba increased and protests from the United States public against Machado's rule grew in volume, Secretary Stimson found that the Platt Amendment itself was a positive embarrassment. He had a legal right to intervene in Cuba at his discretion. He was beset by clamorous groups in his own country who asserted, after 1929, that intervention would be justified. Opposition Cuban political leaders pleaded for intervention.[9]

To those who proposed that conditions in Cuba should be "righted," the Department of State replied that no action was needed: "Insofar as the Department is aware, no situation exists in Cuba which would make it incumbent upon the Government of the United States to consider the question whether it should avail itself of the rights implicit in this section [III] of the so-called Platt Amendment." [10]

To those who proposed that some effective action less drastic than that of intervention should be taken, the reply of the Department of State was that it was adhering faithfully to the principles of the Root interpretation of the Amendment.

These replies were formal ways of justifying inaction. They reflected, however, a genuine desire not to intervene and a growing conviction on Stimson's part that intervention in general was more costly and difficult than it was worth.[11] Another factor in the situation, which was appreciated only gradually, was that political developments in Cuba had outrun the Platt Amendment. The Amendment had been based in large part on the assumption that political stability and a favorable climate for foreign investment could only be assured by intervention or the threat of intervention. However, Machado had found ways to assure political stability and protection of foreigners in Cuba without positive help from the government of the United States. If the right of intervention were exercised against Machado, it must necessarily depose the only man who had achieved the conditions the Amendment had been designed to bring about.

The advisory, preventive policy of Knox had been intended primarily to protect the lives and property of non-Cubans, and so may not have been thought applicable to Machado's era, when, in the words of the Platt Amendment, there existed a government "adequate for the protection of life, property, and individual liberty," if it referred to the life, property, and liberty of foreigners, but not of anti-Machado Cubans. This point about the Platt Amendment had never been clarified by official interpretations. For the protection of whose life, property, and individual liberty did the United States have the right to intervene? The Platt Amendment left the question open. By its actions if not by its words, the government of the United States had made it clear that it was primarily, if not solely, concerned with the protection of United States citizens and other foreigners.[12]

Secure against his opponents in Cuba and safe from effective pressure by the United States, Machado was able to maintain his rule for more than eight years without granting either a share in governmental power to the opposition or social reforms to the Cuban people.

There developed concomitantly an underground resistance to

Machado's government that was different from normal Latin American political conspiracies and similar in significant ways to some of the drives behind the Mexican revolution. The objective of this movement, in which many different groups participated, was to bring about a social revolution in Cuba, if not on the Mexican model, at least with many of the same aims in mind. Its growth had serious implications for at least the property and individual liberty of foreigners in Cuba, but it does not seem to have been fully understood or appreciated in Washington, where experience, except with Mexico, had understandably created a stereotype of the army revolt as typical of Latin American countries.

The policy Stimson adopted was not easy to maintain; he was assailed in the United States for not helping the Cuban people to oust Machado, and his position was interpreted as having no other purpose than the defense of the interests of the United States banks and sugar companies with interests in Cuba.[13] Besides requests for aid from politicians like Carlos Mendieta, appeals were also made by private citizens of Cuba who took the position that the United States government owed them an obligation under the Platt Amendment.

In August, 1930, Abelardo Pacheco, editor of the weekly *La Voz del Pueblo,* was murdered. The paper had been critical of the Machado regime. Eight months earlier, Pacheco had called at the United States Embassy, and then had written a letter to the Ambassador, stating that he had learned of plans to assassinate him, and asking "that the Embassy provide for my life and my property the guarantee that the government of the United States undertook to give to all, according to article III of the Platt Amendment." [14] The Ambassador had, of course, been unable to give protection to the threatened editor.

Stimson was not insensible to these charges and appeals. He was also deeply disturbed by Machado's suspension of constitutional guarantees in February, 1931—an act authorized by Congress, but thought by Ambassador Harry F. Guggenheim to be of doubtful constitutionality since "many persons have been detained for more than ten days without their cases having been determined by the courts" and "courts have in many cases refused to grant writs of *habeas corpus,* throwing out applications therefor on technical grounds." [15]

This report disturbed two of Stimson's aides, who commented that "the report of the Embassy . . . strongly indicates that a government adequate for the protection of life and individual liberty is not now maintained in Cuba" and that "the denial of a writ of *habeas corpus* would seem to be in contravention of our Treaty provisions." [16] Stimson himself was not unmoved for he stressed to Cuban Ambassador Orestes Ferrara the importance attached in the United States, "with the background of a six hundred years' fight for constitutional liberties," to "the right of a man to be tried promptly." Ferrara explained that although Colonel Aurelio Hevia had been denied a writ of *habeas corpus* at least six times, he had not been held for more than three months, and he contrasted Cuba's tradition with that of the United States by saying that "the Cubans are not imbued with the sense of legality that prevails in this country [the United States] and there are two means of governing successfully there—one is through force, and the other through prestige. Being lenient with these people was damaging to Machado's prestige." Stimson concluded the interview by stating that "he appreciated fully what President Machado had been up against and what he had accomplished, and that of course the thing that he [Stimson] most wanted to avoid was a revolution with its concomitant, a possible intervention on our part." [17]

Henceforth, the Department's policy became one of drift, punctuated by spasmodic and gradually feebler attempts to persuade Machado to satisfy the press, the public, and the opposition by legislative reforms and by permitting a larger measure of civil liberties.

Stimson was, however, a prisoner of his policy of strict adherence to the Root interpretation, and he could not cry out against the denial of a fundamental right of the Cuban people, even though his own government was empowered by treaty to intervene to protect life, liberty, and property. To have done so would have been to express antipathy for Machado and, by so doing, to have intermeddled in Cuban internal affairs. Although the formal abrogation of the Platt Amendment was still two years and a United States election away, it is hard to deny or begrudge Stimson the credit for nullifying the Amendment in practice, since it may be assumed that he suffered a painful conflict between his better judgment and his bested feelings. A lawyer of Stimson's integrity could hardly have failed to be troubled by Machado's denial of *habeas corpus*. His lack of protestation may be presumed to have been due to his adherence to a principle he regarded as more important—that of avoiding intervention.

Stimson's bitter experience with intervention in Nicaragua may have convinced him that such action in Cuba would be no less troublesome, costly, unpopular, and, worst of all, ineffective, as is suggested in his response to a letter from a United States postal agent in Havana, which noted that many people in Cuba had been importuning the Department to intervene in Cuba for the past four years:

The attitude taken by these people in Cuba is similar to the attitude which is almost constantly taken by factions in other Latin American countries when the tension between them and their Government becomes acute. In many of these countries they seem to think that the United States exists in order to intervene in their behalf with the operation of the government in their own country of which they disapprove. If we complied with all of these requests, our hands would be full indeed and, however much these factions might like it, we should make ourselves extremely unpopular with every country in Latin America if we adopted such a course of action. . . .

It would be a very serious intervention for us to advise the President of Cuba to resign; an interference which I believe quite unwarranted either by international practice or by the Platt Amendment. Such an action would, of course, tend to break down all feeling of responsibility on the part of the people of Cuba to mend their own affairs and to conduct a responsible government.

So far as supervising an election in Cuba is concerned, that would be even more of an intervention on our part. We have done it in Nicaragua in order to bring to a termination a long period of civil war and anarchy and, in that case, we only did it upon the request of all parties and factions in Nicaragua. Even then, we found the expense and difficulty involved in such an operation, even in such a small country as Nicaragua, a very serious burden. Under present conditions, it would be quite out of the question in Cuba.[18]

A further explanation of the government's policy was offered by an official of the Department to a group of educators, who called to say that they felt "that this government should take some action to show its disapproval of Machado," because "conditions down there were dreadful." He replied to a suggestion that "a commission such as the Lytton Commission" might go to Cuba by saying that "the situation in Cuba is an internal political situation in a sovereign state, and it would be intermeddling imperialism of the most flagrant sort to intervene therein." To a comment that the Platt Amendment was at the root of the difficulty, the official pointed out "the benefits the Amendment has given to Cuba through the investment of capital to develop the country and the stability that has succeeded." [19]

One practical result of Stimson's policy was that, given a strong government in Cuba, there would be no intervention on the part of the United States, nor any preventive action whatever even if it were only an expression of sympathy for victims of oppression. In other words, the same treaty right demanded by the United States in 1901 to authorize its intervention, later became the principal reason for taking no action whatever. There emerged the paradox that, within the Stimson policy, the "dreadful conditions" in Cuba could be changed by the United States only if the United States freed itself from the Root interpretation of the Platt Amendment. Far from being any longer a burden upon the government of Cuba, the Platt Amendment had become Machado's principal strength, after his army and police. Far from being a cherished privilege of the United States, the Platt Amendment had become an inescapable doctrine of self-denial. The only time when the erstwhile privilege could be enjoyed would be when "chaos" came to Cuba, a condition Stimson dreaded. He could and did refuse to admit that it existed either in the revolution of 1931 or the continuing civil strife, simply by not using the word "chaos" to describe what was occurring. In the developing situation, however, the longer Machado clung to office, the greater became the probability that chaos would ensue when he left it. In these circumstances, the policy of the United States was gradually helping, by nonintervention in practice, to create a situation where intervention might well be unavoidable by treaty. There is a suggestion of a theme of classical tragedy in the self-destruction of the policy of the Platt Amendment through its application in the most austere, virtuous, and self-denying way. As will be seen, the drama did not end in a classic climax, because the policy was not carried out with classic stubbornness by Cordell Hull.

Secretary Stimson's policy was maintained until he left office on March 4, 1933. There was no improvement of conditions in Cuba. Although there was no organized revolution, terrorism increased and the government became more brutal in its measures of oppression. Students were murdered by the police after being arrested; [20] Vásquez Bello, president of the Senate, was assassinated. Guggenheim reported that:

February 24th being a national holiday, the customary precautions were observed from the 23rd to the 25th for the maintenance of order, and with the exception of eight bomb explosions on the night of the 23rd, the seizure of supplies of arms and ammunition in the building formerly occupied by the local Y.M.C.A. and numerous arrests of alleged conspirators, the day passed off quietly in Habana.[21]

There were, however, one or two moves made during this period which might be considered as at variance with a complete application of the policy of nonintermeddling.

When the Cuban Chargé, José Barón, called on Francis White in the Department of State to discuss the shooting of Cuban students, White went so far as to say that he had been "much shocked by the news that came from Cuba . . . [and that] this sort of thing was doing Cuba and President Machado's government a great deal of harm." White continued:

I said I realized the difficulty of dealing with some of the opponents of the Machado Administration but I thought it incumbent upon the government, as its first task, to try by some means to reestablish confidence in Cuba. I said that from this distance it was not possible to indicate the means by which this could be done; that that was something which the Cuban government would have to study over and find out for itself. I said I thought they should direct their attention primarily to this matter.

I said that of course Ambassador Guggenheim had taken an interest in this matter but he was only interpreting the general public sentiment in this country in counseling the Cuban government as I was doing, to do something to better conditions.[22]

This action exemplified the farthest point reached by the Stimson policy in the direction of counseling the Cuban government or protesting its actions.

Intermeddling and the Ousting of Machado (May 8–August 12, 1933)

When Cordell Hull took office as Secretary of State, "armed with the President's declaration of our Good Neighbor policy," [23] he followed only one of Stimson's policies toward Cuba: he intermeddled, but he did not intervene. He decided to take quite a different way of "interpreting the general public sentiment" in the United States than that of making half apologetic suggestions to Cuban diplomats in Washington. The principles that guided Roosevelt, Hull, and Sumner Welles are set forth in the instructions to Welles, who arrived in Havana on May 8, 1933, as the new ambassador.

Welles's instructions, though signed by Hull, were probably formulated in large part by Welles himself. They contained the text of the Platt Amendment and of the Root interpretation as well as a lengthy review of the course of the Machado regime. They stated that there was reasonable doubt of the legality of the constitutional reforms of 1928 and admitted that Machado had been given the "tacit approval" of the government of the United States for the prorogation of his term in 1927. The "campaign of violence" against Machado was noted, as well as the "repressive measures enacted by the Machado Administration," and special emphasis was given to the fact that the closing of the secondary schools and of the University of Havana for nearly three years had brought members of the student generation "to the conviction that changes in government in Cuba must be effected not by the orderly processes of constitutional government, but by the resort to measures of violence and revolution."

This situation gave "deep anxiety" to Washington, which was "forced" to the belief "that its friendly assistance and advice must be tendered to the Cuban people" in these "intolerable conditions," which might result in a rebellion in Cuba. Such advice—and here the policy of Philander C. Knox, the forgotten man of the history of the Platt Amendment, was adopted—would not constitute intervention but would be "intended to prevent the necessity of intervention." Terrorism and extreme repression alike must cease in Cuba, and Welles's "chief objective" would be to negotiate a truce between Machado and his opponents that would make new and fair elections possible.[24]

The meaning of this instruction in practice was worked out by Welles in the next several months. On at least one aspect of intent, the document was far from clear. Welles's "chief objective" was ambiguously stated, and it is highly improbable that he would have set off on his mission without having a more precise understanding of what it was he should do. Was the truce to continue until May 20, 1935, when Machado's term ended? If the opposition would not agree to a truce, what should Welles's attitude be? Could Welles suggest or demand Machado's resignation? It seems likely that questions of this order were discussed when the instructions were being drafted, although no record of them is available.

It is evident from Hull's *Memoirs* that he and President Roosevelt were no less anxious to avoid intervention in Cuba than Stimson had been. Hull's analysis of the situation was that Machado's government "was slipping its cinch after twelve years in the saddle, and revolution was plotting. . . . It was becoming evident that either Machado would resign or a revolution would force him out." On April 15 he stated publicly:

No consideration has been given to any movement in the nature of intervention. Nothing whatever is going on that would call for the slightest departure from the ordinary relationships and contacts between two separate and sovereign nations.[25]

Welles had previously written to Roosevelt:

The value of a policy of preventing the rise of conditions which lead to political disturbances, revolution, and civil war, in the Caribbean republics is, to my mind, far greater than the value of a policy which lets matters drift until civil war breaks out and then adopts measures of coercion.[26]

Similarly, Norman Davis, one of Roosevelt's most trusted advisers on foreign affairs, had attacked Stimson for abandoning "the policy of fostering the growth of democratic institutions and orderly government initiated by President Wilson and carried on by Secretary Hughes." [27]

Accompanying the adoption of a policy of prevention, there evidently existed also a desire to rehabilitate the reputation of Woodrow Wilson, a desire that pervaded the policy of Roosevelt and some of his associates, at least in the early days of the Good Neighbor policy.

There was more than this, however, in the origin of the new policy toward Cuba. The very real desire to aid Cuba in its economic distress by means of a larger quota on sugar imports into the United States could not be fulfilled without entrenching Machado in office, since he would obtain credit for any measure of prosperity. But this might not mean the end of the repressive measures of Machado or the violent opposition to his rule. Therefore, Washington followed the policy that "the prospect of increased economic advantages is a plum which will not be granted until the Cuban Government has taken positive and satisfactory steps to conclude the present unrest." [28] However, the impossibility of weakening Machado politically, while expecting to strengthen him economically at a later time, was quickly to be demonstrated.

Finally, neither Roosevelt nor Hull had taken part in Stimson's baffling experience in Nicaragua. They knew about it as outsiders, but they had not, intimately and recently, had to deal with a Sandino or even a Moncada, nor were they well acquainted with the Cuban situation. There were also other and more urgent things for them to do. The President was absorbed in the New Deal's domestic program; Hull was at the London Economic Conference throughout June, July, and the first week of August, 1933. Welles's position and prestige gave him, in these circumstances, an almost free hand to apply his ambiguous instructions as he saw fit in Havana.

Roosevelt himself seems to have given very little thought to the Cuban problem. On June 9 he told his press conference: "I have been so darned busy with other things that I have not read a single despatch from Welles," [29] and on the same day he wrote Welles that "in these last weeks of the Congress I have been altogether too busy to do more than keep in very sketchy touch with all you are doing, but it seems to me that things are going as well as you and I could possibly hope for." [30]

When Welles arrived in Havana, it was obvious to the opposition to Machado that they had everything to gain from his presence. Their major revolution, that of August, 1931, had been defeated, their principal leaders had been exiled, and the Cuban army remained loyal to Machado. The mediation was one of the forms of action by the United States for which they had pleaded unavailingly with Stimson and Guggenheim. Despite all Welles's verbal disclaimers of partiality in the Cuban situation, it was impossible that his actions would be regarded by Cubans as exhibiting impartiality. Most of the Cuban people wanted him to be partial, and the oppositon groups were avidly looking for evidence of partiality. Partiality was felt to exist when Machado restored constitutional guarantees in late July; when Machado protested against Welles's activities, Welles's partiality could be seen as proven. Finally, when the Department of State supported Welles, partiality was known to be authoritative. [31]

During June and July, 1933, Welles probed possibilities for a truce acceptable to both sides, but no agreement had been reached when on August 4 a general strike broke out in Havana. [32] Feeling he could wait no longer, Welles decided that "the only possible solution to prevent a state of utter chaos in the Republic in the near future" was to present to Machado a five-point plan that included the President's taking a leave of absence. Welles told Machado that, while the purpose of his own mission was to avoid the carrying out by the United States of its obligations under the Platt Amendment, he thought "disaster would arise" if Machado did not accept the plan. [33]

These words ended the mediation, in fact, although Welles continued to describe his role as that of a mediator. Welles had finally, if in a slightly veiled fashion, defined one occasion for intervention under the Platt Amendment: Machado's rejection of the five-point plan. This meant, to Machado, that Welles would recommend to Washington that armed forces of the United States be landed in Cuba to depose him, if the plan were rejected. This meant, to Welles, that he had become committed to one, and only one, way to emerge successfully from his mission: Machado must leave office immediately, but without intervention.

For the next few days the two men struggled desperately to save their positions and their prestige. In Cuba, Machado tried to regain his mastery of the political situation, and Welles sought to deprive him of his remaining support. In Washington, Machado tried to discredit Welles, and Welles repeatedly appealed for public and private endorsements by Hull and Roosevelt. At this stage of the mediation the spotlight turned to personalities rather than to issues. The issues had been stated; for the first time they had become clear and concrete. For the first time, also, important decisions had to be made in a few days rather than in an indefinite number of months.

Welles received support from the White House for the demands he had made on Machado, and, inferentially, for his warning to Machado of the possibility of intervention.[34]

For a brief time Machado refused to accept the proposals, and Welles was faced with a critical situation. He had to find a way, short of intervention, to force Machado out of office. His bluff was in grave danger of being called by Machado, who may have had some hope that Welles's hint of intervention was not a real threat, since it came from a man who had said that his purpose was to make intervention unnecessary. Welles undoubtedly was bluffing, since his intimation of intervention had not been specifically authorized by Roosevelt and since Roosevelt did not respond to a plea by Welles that Cuban Ambassador Oscar B. Cintas be told that "the United States will not evade its obligations" under the Platt Amendment.[35] Roosevelt saw Cintas on August 9, and, while he said Welles was acting with his "fullest authorization and approval," he added merely that "he had no desire to intervene but that it was our duty to do what we could so that there should be no starvation and chaos among the Cuban people." On the same day, Roosevelt told his press conference:

There is no government action on our part. It is simply saying to Welles, "Go ahead and help all you can" . . . . And, certainly, we cannot be in the position of saying to Machado, "You have to get out." That would be obvious interference with the internal affairs of another nation.[36]

In Havana, Welles was engaged in saying precisely what Roosevelt said "we" could not be in the position of saying; from being an interposer, he had assumed the role of a deposer.[37] Before hearing of Roosevelt's talk with Cintas, Welles recommended withdrawal of recognition of the Machado government; he believed this would mean that Machado would not then be able to remain in office "for more than an exceedingly brief period" and that the situation would not make necessary "even a brief armed intervention" by the United States. However, if this recommendation were adopted, Welles felt the prospects were ominous enough that "two American warships should be in Habana harbor with instructions not to land a man except in the gravest emergency the terms of which should be precisely defined beforehand." [38]

These recommendations were neither explicitly approved nor disapproved in any message sent to Havana. Hull, however, did say that he and Roosevelt appreciated Welles's "trying difficulties" in Cuba and had confidence in what Welles was "doing to be helpful"; while Hull said he placed no reliance on adverse comments that "the United States is attempting to coerce rather than to persuade," he hoped Welles would bear these comments in mind "and do what you can to correct them." [39]

There must have been qualms in the Department of State about Welles's conduct, for when Cintas suggested that Welles be asked to go to Washington for consultation so Machado could make concessions more freely, Under Secretary William Phillips told Roosevelt that

while I had been wobbling in my mind this morning as to whether or not there was something in Ambassador Cintas's suggestions, he had been pressing so hard and was so insistent upon getting Welles out of Habana that my suspicions were aroused and that I had come to the conclusion that this was not the time to ask Welles to come up here.[40]

Cintas's dampening of the amplitude of Phillips's wobbles may not alone have doomed Machado, but it did keep Welles in Havana, with long-range consequences for Cuba's political future. Roosevelt's message to Cintas was that Welles would not be asked to come to Washington; Roosevelt "was waiting for action by President Machado and . . . time was the essence of the whole problem." [41]

When Welles heard nothing definite from Washington in response to his recommendations, he decided to do his best with the local resources at his command. He reported on August 10 that he had had "a confidential talk with General Alberto Herrera," who had been for twelve years the chief of staff of the Cuban army, and was Machado's Secretary of War. Herrera gave Welles "his formal commitment" to accept his part in a new "solution" which Welles presented to him and said he would propose to Machado on the afternoon of August 11. The new plan was that Machado would offer as his counterproposal, which would be immediately accepted by Welles,

a request for leave of absence until a vice-president is inaugurated and the immediate resignation of all the members of his Cabinet with the exception of General Herrera, the latter then to become acting head of the government until a vice-president is inaugurated.[42]

Welles presented this plan to Secretary of State Orestes Ferrara on the afternoon of August 11, and in the early evening, Ferrara notified Welles that Machado accepted it and would ask Congress for leave of absence in a few days. This action by Machado, reported Welles, "was due to the fact that all of the ranking officers of the Army throughout the Republic had notified him that the Cuban Army would not support him further." [43]

Welles's plan was carried out except in one particular. Leading officers of the army decided that they could not support Herrera because they feared his close connections with Machado would cause "the great mass of the opposition" to refuse to accept him as provisional president. Herrera then told Welles that, since only a member of the cabinet could constitutionally succeed the president, he would, immediately after taking office, appoint as Secretary of State Dr. Carlos Manuel de Céspedes, who had formerly held that office, and then would resign the presidency in favor of Céspedes.[44]

Deserted by his army, Machado found it advisable not to defer his request for a leave of absence. He left Cuba by airplane on the night of August 12 and arrived safely in Nassau at daylight on the 13th. Nearly all the other leading members of the government also fled by air. Herrera, after hiding in the National Hotel, was personally escorted by Welles to the steamer "Santa Ana," which took the General and his family to New York.

Welles was regarded in Washington as having achieved a notable diplomatic triumph. Caffery cabled: "The President and Secretary have asked me to express their warm congratulations to you and their appreciation of what you have done." [45] A few hours before Machado's flight, Welles reported:

The determination of President Machado to act with this patriotism is due to the fact that he was finally and definitely informed last night that all of the ranking officers of the Army were unanimous in demanding that he leave the Presidency during the course of today. His action cannot therefore in any sense of the word be described either as the result of pressure by the United States nor as the result of a patriotic gesture on his part.[46]

Aside from Welles's sarcasm about Machado's "patriotism," this statement raises an important issue without disposing of it. Had there been no "pressure by the United States"? The fact that a mediation had been undertaken was a form of pressure, since it could end in no other way than in some form of demand upon Machado for a change in his policies or in his status and since it inevitably gave encouragement to the Cuban opposition. Welles's hint of the use of the Platt Amendment if Machado did not accept the compromise was another form of pressure. Welles's presentation of the five-point plan to Machado was a form of pressure, since that action put the full weight of the prestige of the United States government behind a proposal for Machado's relinquishment of office.[47]

Another statement in Welles's cable announcing Machado's impending departure also raises further questions:

Fortunately the solution which has now been elaborated and which I have every confidence will be acceptable to the enormous majority of the Cuban people has been worked out solely by the Cubans themselves and represents in my judgment the expression of the volition of very nearly the totality of the Cuban people.

The next few days will probably be difficult, but I now have confidence that the situation has been saved and that no further action on the part of the United States government will be necessary.[48]

Was this a Cuban solution to Cuba's problems? As early as June 2, Welles had told Machado that "the solution proposed by the Opposition which called for the immediate resignation of the President and his substitution by an impartial Secretary of State was not satisfactory to me."[49] Later, as indicated above, Welles said that he "had decided" on "the only possible solution to prevent a state of utter chaos in the Republic" and had presented his decision orally to Machado before having specific approval for it from Roosevelt or from the Cuban political groups. He had, however, submitted the general outlines of a solution to Roosevelt and Hull and had not received any reply from them, and he had acted only after long consultations with Cuban political leaders of both sides. How much agreement there was at the time he made his decision is not clear. He himself reported that "most of the factions of the opposition will agree to this compromise although certain of the more radical elements will probably demur."[50] The fact that the formula was accepted by all factions after it had been presented to Machado by Welles did not mean that this was the compromise which would have come out of the negotiations if they had not been ended by Welles's decision. However, when Machado later charged that Welles's acts and requests, "approved" by Roosevelt, had the aim of removing him from power, Roosevelt replied that Welles had not made a request but had simply transmitted a proposal adopted by the opposition groups.[51]

From the point of view of the opposition groups, the important thing about the proposal was that it provided for a quick departure from office of Machado. From the point of view of the government parties, the important thing about the proposal was that Welles had thrown his prestige behind it. This, to them, meant that it was likely that Machado was on the way out of office, and they had everything to gain, in that case, by allying themselves with the author of the proposal which was intended to shape the form of the coming regime. Hull had earlier spoken of a "Cuban plan" put forward by Welles on behalf of Cubans; this term was inspired partly by hope and partly by expediency, but it became a Cuban plan only after Machado and other Cuban politicians knew that in Welles's opinion the alternative to its acceptance was "utter chaos" with the probability of intervention under the Platt Amendment.

Did Welles have any influence on the action of the Cuban army? There does not appear to be enough evidence to answer this question with complete assurance, but it is a question that may well arise from objective considerations and not merely from unworthy suspicions. After Welles's "confidential talk" with General Herrera on August 10, did the Cuban army leaders tell Machado on the following day that they would support him no longer because they had received some word from Herrera, who was Secretary of War and the man to whom Welles had offered the interim presidency? The timing and unanimity of their decision suggests such a relationship. So, also, does the statement made at the time, that Welles "was able to report, before Machado himself knew it, that the army was about to desert the Cuban president." [52]

However, Welles's cables do not bear out this statement, and Welles does not appear to have admitted or claimed any connection with the army's decision. He did report that the "army is unanimously devoted to General Herrera," but he also repeated in the same cable the old Coolidge formula that the plan for Herrera's succession was "essentially a Cuban solution of the Cuban problem." [53]

On the other hand, Welles had cabled that Herrera was "exceedingly amenable to suggestions which represent the interest of the United States government." [54] A suggestion that the army could easily force Machado out, that otherwise intervention by the United States was likely, and that Herrera could become President of Cuba would have been entirely consistent with Welles's desires. It would have been politically astute since it was directed to the head of the army, the most powerful man in Cuba after Machado. It would have been logical since neither intervention nor withdrawal of recognition could be counted on from Washington; if Welles were to prevail against Machado he had to find potent allies in Cuba and not at home.

However, these considerations do not directly connect Welles with the army's action, for evidence is lacking to show precisely what Welles said to Herrera, and also to establish any immediately consequential link between Herrera and the leaders of the movement in the army. One of these, Horacio Ferrer, asserted that he and Colonel Manuel Sanguily had "fostered" the movement in the army to "save Cuba from American intervention." [55]

Even if this evidence were taken as showing that Welles had induced the army to turn against Machado, the principal result would be to prove that Welles merited the admiration bestowed on him for "needful guile" as well as for "consummate tact." [56] That he had been influential was obvious to all, and, since to cavil at Welles would have been to defend Machado, there were few indeed who, in August, 1933, failed to rejoice in Welles's diplomatic victory.

The Céspedes Interregnum

These questions, of interest to students of diplomatic techniques and to those seeking the origins of the Good Neighbor policy, were given little attention in 1933. The great fact was that Machado and his chief henchmen had fled from Cuba. Many of his lesser followers, whose status did not entitle them to escape by air, were hunted down and killed by jubilant Cubans bent on revenge. Satisfaction over Welles's achievement was voiced in the United States, and also in other parts of the world.[57]

Had Welles returned to the United States by the first of September, his mission might have been regarded as an unqualified success. Interestingly enough, Welles made precisely this proposal and recommended that the Department immediately announce that Jefferson Caffery would succeed him on September 1; Caffery "will obtain all of the needed influence immediately after his arrival, but it will be an influence exerted behind the scenes and not apparent to the public." [58] Once more Welles's recommendations were not approved in Washington. Roosevelt, without stating his reasons, replied that "it would be preferable" for Welles to remain in Cuba until September 15; announcement of Welles's return would be made "shortly." [59]

However, Welles was not a good political forecaster of Cuban political affairs, for the "solution" that had brought Céspedes to power lasted less than a month.[60] The new government immediately declared martial law, but there was some rioting and looting throughout the country. Two United States destroyers, the "Taylor" and "Claxton," arrived in Havana harbor on the morning of August 14. Welles stated:

I feel very confident that the visit of these ships was essential for its moral effect alone. If the strike is broken today as I anticipate conditions may become normal rapidly and in that event the two ships might well leave after forty-eight hours.[61]

Céspedes, on Welles's advice, announced that the government would take steps to deal in an orderly way with officials of the Machado regime, but the situation continued to deteriorate. The economic situation was serious. Welles reported that poverty and destitution "exist throughout the Republic. Under such conditions no government can stand, and particularly not a government which has come into power under existing conditions, when almost every Cuban will expect it to perform miracles without a moment's delay." He recommended an immediate loan by the United States and the conclusion of a commercial treaty to increase the amount of Cuban sugar permitted to enter the United States.[62]

A few days later Welles gave up hope that the Céspedes government could govern as a constitutional government, and he developed a new plan for holding elections in three months, combined with an immediate increase in the Cuban sugar quota under the United States tariff. However, the decree calling for new elections was ineffective and no action in the economic field was taken by Washington. In any case, the center of powerful unrest in Cuba was neither on the political nor on the economic stage but in the military. In the early morning of September 5, the rank and file of the army deposed their officers in a mutiny throughout the island and installed a revolutionary junta of five civilians as the new Cuban government.

This sudden end of the Céspedes regime was a surprise, and must have been a great shock to Welles, for in a real sense the Céspedes government was his government, and the mutiny was a blow to his newly-gained prestige no less than an attack on the position of the traditional ruling groups in Cuba.

The Grau San Martín Regime and the Verge of Intervention

The proclamation of the new regime was signed by the leader of the soldiers, Sergeant Fulgencio Batista, and, Welles reported, "by a group of the most extreme radicals of the student organization and three university professors whose theories are frankly communistic." Reiterating his desire to avoid intervention by the United States, Welles told Washington that such a step might have to be taken, since

It appears hardly likely that a so-called revolutionary government composed of enlisted men of the Army and radical students who have occupied themselves almost exclusively during the last ten days with assassination of members of the Machado government can form a government "adequate for the protection of life, property, and individual liberty." [63]

In an interview with opposition leaders not directly connected with the new junta, Welles said he suggested "that through consultation among themselves they determine whether they can devise any plan to prevent the utter break-down of government which in my judgment is inevitable under the present regime." [64] This statement could not have been taken by these leaders as other than an invitation to organize a new opposition, again with support from Welles. They were not slow to accept the invitation.

Welles's initial hostility to the new regime did not waver, and during the next three months he followed three lines of policy in a continuous effort to restore Céspedes to power. First, he tried to oust the new government by intervention; second, he hoped that nonrecognition by the United States would be sufficient to cause its downfall; third, he tried to induce Cuban groups to re-place it.

On three occasions he asked fruitlessly that United States troops be landed in Cuba. The first of these was in the midst of the shock of the Batista mutiny, when Welles said in a telephone talk with Hull and Caffery that it was "absolutely indispensable that men be brought from the ship [the destroyer "McFarland"] to the Em-bassy and to the [National] hotel." Caffery tried to reassure him by saying that "the 'Mississippi' is on the way. She is 32,000 tons," but Welles said he thought he would have some men come ashore from the "McFarland" immediately.[65] This remark disturbed Hull, who spoke with Roosevelt and called Welles within an hour to suggest that unless Welles were "in physical danger" he should not request men from the "McFarland." Welles did not insist.[66]

The next day Hull called again to emphasize that he did not wish to intervene unless "we are absolutely compelled to do so. . . . Because if we have to go in there again, we will never be able to come out and we will have on our hands the trouble of thirty years ago." [67] At a cabinet meeting on September 8, "it seemed clear that the decision of everyone, from the President down, was against intervention unless it was actually forced upon us." [68]

Welles's second proposal for a landing of United States troops was made shortly afterwards, not on the basis of imminent danger to himself and others, but as a calculated move to restore the Céspedes government. He took the extraordinary step of proposing a "limited intervention" by the United States that would support a counter-revolution led by Horacio Ferrer, Secretary of War in the Céspedes cabinet. Such action would require "the landing of a considerable force at Havana and lesser forces in certain of the more important ports of the Republic," since a great portion of the Cuban army had mutinied, and the new government would require aid until a new army could be organized.

The justification for such a limited intervention was made by Welles in his customary imposing and persuasive style; he even managed to bring the "lending of a police force" within the as yet unstaked boundaries of the Good Neighbor policy:

The disadvantages of this policy, as I see them, lie solely in the fact that we will incur the violent animosity of the extreme radical and communist groups in Cuba, who will be vociferous in stating that we have supported the Céspedes Government because that Government was prepared to give protection to American interests in Cuba and that our policy is solely due to mercenary motives. It is worth emphasizing, however, that we always have had and always will have the animosity of this group and that the adoption of the measures above-indicated will merely offer them an excellent opportunity for attack. Consequently, since I sincerely believe that the necessity of full intervention on our part is to be avoided at all hazards, the limited and restricted form of intervention above outlined would be infinitely preferable. When the recognized and legitimate government of a neighboring republic, with which republic we have special contractual obligations, is confronted by mutiny in the army and can only maintain order and carry through its program of holding elections for a permanent constitutional government through the assistance of an armed force lent by the United States as the policing power, it would seem to me to be in our best interests to lend such assistance, and it would further seem to me that since the full facts of the situation here have been fully explained to the representatives of the Latin American countries, the landing [*sic*] of such assistance would most decidedly be construed as well within the limits of the policy of the "Good Neighbor" which we have done our utmost to demonstrate in our relations with the Cuban people during the past five months.[69]

Welles's argument may have been hard for Secretary Hull to swallow; but he recounts that "the moment I finished digesting the telegram I took it myself to the President at the White House and had him read it." He added:

I then strongly expressed to him my opinion that we could not and should not think of intervening in Cuba even to a limited extent. It seemed to me that Welles was overinfluenced by local conditions in Cuba and misjudged the disastrous reaction that would follow throughout Latin America if we agreed to his request. From my previous conversations with the President I knew that he was as resolved as myself to stay out of Cuba. Mr. Roosevelt readily agreed with my viewpoint. He said he would merely send a cruiser to Cuban waters, where we already had some light units. The naval vessels were strictly forbidden to send forces ashore unless it were necessary to evacuate American citizens caught between the contending Cuban factions.[70]

Hull drafted a reply himself, obtained Roosevelt's approval, and sent it to Welles the same evening:

We fully appreciate the various viewpoints set forth in your telegram. However, after mature consideration, the President has decided to send you the following message:

"We feel very strongly that any promise, implied or otherwise, relating to what the United States will do under any circumstances is impossible; that it would be regarded as a breach of neutrality, as favoring one faction out of many, as attempting to set up a government which would be regarded by the whole world, and especially throughout Latin America, as a creation and creature of the American government. . . ."

All of us appreciate the heavy load you are carrying and hope you may bear up well in order to get the best possible results in these trying circumstances.[71]

Shortly before receiving this message, which, however vague, meant that Welles's scheme for a limited intervention was rejected, Welles had cabled his impression that the junta was breaking up, and that "the sergeants and ringleaders of the mutiny are in a state of panic." He concluded, apparently confident that his recommendations would be approved in Washington:

I am beginning to have the hope that the situation may turn out so that we may be able to avoid any act of intervention other than that of the landing of a moderate force, at the request of President Céspedes, to assist his government, if it is reconstituted, in maintaining order.[72]

Welles's hopes were dashed. Ferrer's plans were not carried out, and reports that the junta would itself restore control of the government to Céspedes were unfulfilled.

Finally, Welles made a third, albeit anachronistic, effort to bring about intervention. He reported on September 8 that there was "cumulative evidence from every province that complete anarchy exists." Welles here used words that had been avoided by Stimson, who would have felt that, had he admitted that there was anarchy in Cuba, the United States would have had the obligation to intervene. Welles probably intentionally pulled the trigger of the Platt Amendment by this usage, but the old blunderbuss did not go off, for Hull had changed the magic words from "complete anarchy" to "actual physical danger" to the persons of United States citizens. In this same telegram, Welles favored "affording police service" in Cuba in the form of "the moral assistance a small number of Marines would create," and he distinguished between such action and "a military intervention." [73]

To this final interventionist effort by Welles, no formal reply was forthcoming, but Roosevelt apparently decided Welles had to be brought up short. He telephoned Havana at 11 o'clock on the night of September 8. Apparently as the direct result of this unrecorded conversation, Welles's position underwent such a marked transformation that he reported to Hull: "I am more than ever confident that in view of the very difficult situation which has now been presented the only path for the United States to take is that which the President indicated to me on the telephone the other night, namely one of watchful expectancy." [74] Welles talked no more of intervention or the restoration of Céspedes; he even spoke for the moment of the possibility of recognition, under certain conditions and in consultation with Latin American states. Roosevelt must have spoken plainly and strongly to have wrought such a change in Welles's attitude.

For five days after the mutiny frantic negotiations continued among the junta, Batista, Welles, Céspedes, and various party leaders, aimed at a government of national concentration, but these failed. Finally, a professor of biology at the University of Havana, Ramón Grau San Martín, was named by the junta as provisional President of Cuba. The crucial point in the negotiations seems to have been Céspedes's refusal to promise, if returned to the presidency, that he would confirm Batista as Colonel and Chief of Staff of the Army, titles which had been conferred on him by the junta. The two thousand men in the army then gave their support to Grau. Since they were the principal element of power in Cuba, their action was decisive.[75]

With the proclamation of Grau as provisional President, there also was passed a crisis in the development of the policy of the United States. Limited intervention by a United States police force for the purpose of restoring a constitutional government to power was not to be a principle of the Good Neighbor policy, nor was it to be contemplated even as an aberration. Hull made it clear in talking with correspondents at his press conference that he would feel compelled to intervene only if such action were absolutely necessary to save the lives of citizens of the United States. When asked to clarify whether naval forces would be used to guard property as well as lives of United States citizens, Hull replied that "we had not taken up the question of emergency aid except in the possibility of danger to the persons of Americans." [76] Welles informed the managers of several sugar plantations that in case of danger they and their families should "go to the nearest port where an American warship was stationed to seek protection and in no sense to expect American landing parties to be sent from these American warships inland. I made it very clear that under present conditions we had no intention of landing forces to protect property." [77]

The concern of Hull with protecting lives and not property was indicated in his remark to Welles that

I am telling people who have property there to let it be injured a little, while the Cubans are establishing a government themselves, because should the Cubans themselves establish a government, the outbreaks will gradually cease, business will return to normalcy, and the owners will recover their losses.[78]

Hull, of course, was preoccupied with plans for the Montevideo Conference, and, since he was away from Washington from November 11, 1933 to January 22, 1934, his influence on policy in the last half of Grau's tenure of office was negligible. Had he remained in Washington, able to give his attention to Cuba, particularly after Batista quelled an attempted coup on November 8, the course of policy might have been different, in view of his primary concern for protection of persons. The only United States citizen killed during the period between Machado's fall and the end of the Grau regime was one Lotspicht, who was struck, apparently by "a stray bullet," when he ventured on a balcony to watch the siege of the army officers in the Hotel Nacional early in October.[79]

Warships Are Sent to Cuba

Although Welles's pleas for intervention were rejected, warships of several classes were sent racing to Cuba, and in a few days about thirty of them, ranging in type from battleships to Coast Guard vessels, had appeared at Havana and at a number of other Cuban ports. There was newspaper talk that Cuba was surrounded by vessels of war,[80] but Roosevelt and Hull rejected this allegation. Hull regularly referred to the ships as "little vessels," and Roosevelt played word games with his friendly enemies, the White House correspondents. He told them that "this talk about its being a large armada and a great display of strength is sort of silly." He liked neither "fleet" nor "flotilla," saying that "where you have twelve or twenty ships all scattered along twelve hundred to fourteen hundred miles of coast, I don't think there is any particular word for it." He likewise did not accept "cordon" because "there is no connection between the different outlying boats." He refused to apply any one term to the operation.[81] He did emphasize that except for the "Mississippi" and the "Richmond," all the ships were "little bits of things."

The purposes the ships were intended to serve, and the ways they were used, are of some interest. The 32,000 tons of the "Mississippi" were presumably mentioned by Caffery in order to bolster Welles's own morale. Although she stayed out of sight of Havana during most of her stay, the "Wyoming," which replaced her, "spent most of the day close to shore, having a calming influence on resident Americans." [82]

When Hull spoke of the "moral effect" of the presence of the ships,[83] he seems to have meant that their appearance in a harbor would disincline Cuban revolutionists to injure or kill United States citizens. Thus the ships would help prevent the sole occasion that Washington admitted would bring about intervention in the form of the landing of troops. Hull also had domestic political considerations in mind, for he said that if vessels of war were "somewhere within reach . . . we would not be accused of neglect." [84] The ships were not specifically despatched for the purpose of evacuating United States citizens, although such action might have been taken had the danger to life become sufficiently great. When asked by a correspondent if "naval forces" might be used to guard property of United States citizens, Hull replied that he "had not taken up the question of emergency aid except in the possibility of danger to the persons of Americans. Of course, if a state of lawlessness should become sufficiently aggravated to call for such action it might or might not affect the other phases."

It is clear that Roosevelt and Hull wished to avoid intervention if at all possible. The President's passionate attachment to the Navy did not embrace the desire to see it in action against Cubans. His reluctance to intervene was so sincerely manifested that there seem to have been no charges by Latin American statesmen or by responsible newspapers that he was looking for an opportunity to put Marines ashore.[85] His first orders to the cruiser "Richmond" were merely that it should "proceed from Canal Zone *towards* Cuba." [86]

The guns of the ships were quiet throughout the period of some five months when the presence of the ships as silent witnesses was deemed necessary. There seem to have been only two occasions when men from the ships were said to have gone ashore, and these occasions were without importance. In one, it was reported that some United States sailors were putting up a signaling light on the Embassy in Havana for purposes of communicating with the ships in the harbor. In the other, it was said that a squad of Marines had been landed at Puerto Cabeza at the urgent request of a frightened United States citizen; the Marines returned to their ship the next morning, having found they were not needed. In general, Hull told his press conference, the ships were under instructions "merely to appear and stand off, having as their mission nothing except the exclusive function of protecting American life in case it is in imminent danger. They are not expected to take the place of the rural guards or other officials of the country." [87] For example, he announced at this conference that "at Antilla American lives were somewhat threatened and a coast-guard vessel will probably drop in there."

When Secretary of the Navy Claude Swanson, who had previously planned a visit to the Pacific aboard the cruiser "Indianapolis," stopped in Havana, Roosevelt instructed him to stay aboard, where he would be visited by Welles, and then to proceed as originally intended.[88]

In Havana harbor a cruiser and several destroyers kept constant vigil. Elsewhere along the coast, at smaller places, destroyers and smaller ships appeared and disappeared as local conditions seemed to require. When the "Mississippi" was withdrawn at the end of the September crisis, her replacement was stationed not far from Cuba. When fighting broke out at the beginning of October, Welles requested the battleship to approach near to Havana but to remain out of sight from the harbor. Welles felt, and Hull agreed, that "if she is brought within sight now, it would be regarded by the people in the government as an effort on our part to lend moral support to the officers and people opposed to the government." [89]

At one time in September, Welles asked Hull to speak to Roosevelt about the suggestion that it might be useful if a destroyer cruised up and down along the Havana waterfront directly in front of the Hotel Nacional.[90] It does not appear that Hull mentioned this proposal to Roosevelt or that Welles requested such a demonstration on his own authority; it may or may not have been consistent with Hull's interpretation of his own view that the ships should do no more than "stand off" at various points.

In addition to protecting the lives of the 5,500 United States citizens in Cuba, the presence of the ships may have been desired to restrain Cubans from undefined revolutionary excesses, such as the burning of sugar mills, which might possibly bring about intervention, although Hull would probably have tolerated a considerable amount of property damage before ordering an intervention. In fact, little serious damage was done; a number of sugar mills were seized and occupied by groups of Cubans, but actual destruction of buildings and machinery was on a remarkably small scale. Whether this resulted from the presence of the ships or from the Cubans' recognition that it would not be sensible to destroy a prime source of potential income, or from some other cause, is difficult to say.

It is evident that Welles thought that the ships had some effect on restraining revolutionary activities against the Grau regime. In October he recommended the withdrawal of destroyers from four ports where there was relative quiet, which had been "due to the continued presence of American destroyers." If the ships were not removed, he thought the United States might be "rightfully suspected of maintaining ships for purposes other than those officially announced by us."

However, if the presence of ships had a salutary effect in safeguarding life, Welles felt that the absence of ships might also have an effect of a different kind. He added: "I see no advantage to be gained by us in retaining the destroyers in Cuban ports and thereby strengthen the position of the present government by assisting in preventing disturbances of public order." [91] This statement should not be interpreted as evidence of unconcern on the part of Welles about the lives of United States citizens. He undoubtedly felt that, if revolutionary disturbances should break out against the existing government, they would be initiated by groups which would be desirous of restoring sugar mills to their former owners and in protecting United States nationals. This statement is, however, entirely consistent with Welles's opposition to the Grau regime.

The ships were gradually withdrawn from various points along the Cuban coast, but this action appears to have been taken by Washington solely because the danger to United States citizens had disappeared, and not because Hull agreed with Welles's policy of withdrawal in order to help revolutionists against Grau.

CHAPTER III

The Cuban Experience II

Nonrecognition of the Grau San Martín Government

THE UNITED STATES withheld diplomatic recognition through-out the duration of the Grau government, which continued in power for slightly over four months, until January 15, 1934, when it was succeeded by a coalition headed by Carlos Mendieta.

On the day following the Batista mutiny, Welles told Hull that "for the time being we ought not even to consider recognizing any government of this character," and Hull replied: "Until it has shown its ability to preserve law and order." [1] In this conversation, Welles did not protest this single criterion for recognition offered by Hull, but he did succeed in adding another that in a few days became embodied in the formal position taken by the government in Washington as to the requirements that the Grau regime would have to meet. On the same day he reported that the Cuban govern-ment "is an undisciplined group of individuals of divergent tend-encies representing the most irresponsible elements in the city of Havana with practically no support whatsoever outside the cap-ital," [2] and on September 11 he recommended a public statement by Hull that the United States would not accord recognition un-less "conclusive evidence is presented" that the Cuban government "effectively represents the will of a majority of the people of the Republic." [3]

Hull did not go so far as Welles recommended, but in effect his response was satisfying to his representative in Havana. Explaining its position to its missions in Latin America and elsewhere, the Department of State declared that it did not intend to intervene and that it hoped the Cubans themselves would form a government capable of maintaining order. "We have not, and shall not, attempt to influence the Cubans in any way as to choice of individuals in the government." [4] Publicly, in a statement quite different from that desired by Welles, who wanted an announcement that Washington would not even consider recognition of "the revolutionary group at present in power," [5] the press was told on September 12 that the United States government "has no interest in behalf of or prejudice against any political groups or independent organization which is today active in the political life of Cuba . . . [it] is prepared to welcome any government representing the will of the people of the Republic and capable of maintaining law and order throughout the island. Such a government would be competent to carry out the functions and obligations incumbent upon any stable government." [6]

The formal conditions for recognition were, therefore, that the Cuban government represent the will of its people and demonstrate its capacity to maintain law and order. The Cuban government made every effort to fulfill these conditions in the course of the following four months, but it was not able to convince Washington that it had done so, or could ever do so.

Although Welles had asserted that "no government here can survive for a protracted period without recognition by the United States," [7] this was a truth that Roosevelt and Hull either did not understand or did not demonstrate that they understood. They appeared hopefully to regard the delay in recognition as permitting the Cubans to establish a government "themselves," without realizing that the simple continuance of nonrecognition prevented the Cubans "themselves" from establishing a government, and would ultimately doom the Grau regime. Roosevelt and Hull seemed to be willing to consider recognizing Grau, if he should succeed in satisfying them that he could keep order and obtain popular support, but they showed no signs of understanding that the policy of nonrecognition made Grau's success impossible, and they depended largely on Welles for advice and information on these points. Welles, however, was fully aware that this was the case, and his unvarying recommendation for the continuance of nonrecognition, regularly approved in Washington and supported by his successor in Havana, played an important part in limiting Grau's span of power. Although Roosevelt and Hull did not share Welles's determination that Grau should not remain in office, they appeared satisfied with a policy that they could justify as consonant with democratic principles and the doctrine of nonintervention. Welles was largely satisfied with the same policy, since it meant that the Grau regime could not survive, even though Céspedes could not be reinstalled.

On the question of representation of the Cuban people, who were the Cubans "themselves"? Were they the political leaders who, with Welles, had agreed that Céspedes should head the government that followed Machado? Were they the rank and file of the army, and the students and workers who had turned Céspedes out of office? Were they other Cubans who might later turn Grau out of office? So long as recognition were deferred, opponents of Grau would be encouraged to organize revolutions against him. So long as recognition were deferred, Grau would be unable to give Cubans the hope of economic recovery by a treaty reducing the United States tariff or increasing the Cuban quota on sugar. So long as recognition were deferred, the Cubans "themselves" both within and without the Grau government would base their actions on the controlling assumption that the Grau regime was unacceptable to the United States.

Welles more than once referred to the leaders of the "large political parties" opposed to Grau, but there was some doubt about both their size and cohesiveness. The only legal parties between 1928 and 1933 were three that supported Machado, of which the Liberal was the largest. No recent election had been held to measure the importance of these parties, and it is unknown whether, in September, 1933, any or all of them would, in a free election, have been able to muster more votes than the groups supporting Grau.

The opposition to the Grau regime came from three main sources. The strongest of these was the officer corps, and its two attempts at rebellion were crushed in October and November. The second group was composed of a small number of communists, a few labor unions influenced by them, and a splinter group of students that joined with the communists, in opposing Grau. This element was not powerful, and Welles did not base his policy on danger from this source. The third group consisted of the political leaders of the established parties that had entered the Céspedes cabinet, the majority of Cuban businessmen, and probably certain other elements. The main activities of this group were the issuance of formal statements denouncing the Grau regime and refusing to give it cooperation.

Support for Grau, or at least acceptance of his regime, appears to have been given by the main body of the Cuban people. At this point, however, it should be noted that the accuracy of this statement was disputed by Welles at the time and afterward. In the absence of polls, plebiscites, or elections during the Grau regime, there was no objective test of popular opinion, and the fact that Grau did not, in four months, attempt to hold elections for a legislature or for a constituent assembly, casts doubt on the solidity of the assurance he professed that his regime had majority support among Cubans.

There is sufficient evidence to suggest, however, that the main body of the Cuban people at least did not reject the Grau government. One line of evidence is furnished by Russell Porter, who reported that "official American circles view with alarm the failure of the students to differentiate between the passive acquiescence with which the public has accepted their governmental experiment and the positive support that is regarded as essential to its success and to its recognition." [8] Noisy enthusiasm, as distinct from quiet acceptance, was then, and happily remains, a rarely used criterion for recognition of a foreign government.

A second kind of evidence is provided by Jefferson Caffery, who replaced Welles in Havana in December. Caffery reported that he agreed with Welles "as to the inefficiency, ineptitude, and unpopularity with all the better classes in the country of the *de facto* government. It is supported only by the army and ignorant masses who have been misled by utopian promises." [9] Thus Caffery, the political theorist, minimizing the quality of the support given by "ignorant masses" to a government he hoped would fall. When the new Mendieta government was having trouble with rioters two months later, Caffery reported: "The fact must not be lost sight of that, in numbers, the ignorant masses of Cuba reach a very high figure." [10] Thus Caffery, the political observer, maximizing the quantity of "ignorant masses" opposing a government he hoped would endure.

Caffery's judgments may be compared with the consistent claims of Welles, who, in a major speech in justification of his Cuban policy, asserted:

The most searching and reliable reports sent to me by Cubans and by Americans from every section of the country showed that the opposition to the [Grau] regime was participated in by the peasant in the country, by the small farmer, by the merchant in the provincial village, by the average Cuban in whatever station of life or of whatever origin he might be. Organized labor as such likewise proclaimed its opposition. [11]

He also said in this speech that Grau's regime "was violently opposed by every one of the groups that had opposed Machado . . . with the exception of a small percentage of the University students." Welles's view of the position of the political groups was supported by Adolf A. Berle, Jr., a temporary member of his staff, who said that "practically every organized element except the army had declared itself in opposition" to Grau. [12]

Concerning the second criterion for recognition, what constituted the maintenance of order? Hull thought "that we ought to keep our minds primarily and paramountly on American lives and that if the Cubans set up a government stable enough to protect lives, the property of Americans is very apt to fare pretty well." [13]

Shortly after Grau became provisional president, Hull posed the question of recognition to Welles in a telephone conversation:

Secretary: If they [Grau and the opposition] should reach a stage where they would get together in a broad way, would we want to take up then, as rapidly as we could, the question of dealing with them further?

Ambassador: Yes. I think under those conditions, it is the only possible solution.

Secretary: That would cause the more unintelligent people everywhere, who do not know our real attitude, to see that we were doing our best to go along with the Cubans.

Ambassador: Exactly. Under those conditions I think we could safely waive the maintenance of order question, because no government here will be able to maintain absolute order for some time to come.[14]

These few remarks are suggestive with regard to the bases of United States policy. Hull apparently desired to recognize as soon as possible; he was looking ahead to the Montevideo Conference of American states, scheduled for December. Welles's remark that the question of the maintenance of order might be waived indicates that he did not at the moment consider this point essential. Hull did not make any comments on Welles's statement, and it may be reasonably inferred, therefore, that the United States was withholding recognition from Grau for a reason other than his incomplete maintenance of order.

Welles's evaluation of the Grau regime seems to have been accepted uncritically and without serious consideration by Roosevelt, who told his press conference:

The situation is that Mr. San Martín is sitting there in the Presidential Palace, and he has his local army with him, which consists of about fifteen hundred men and a bunch of students. Apparently they are not collecting any taxes anywhere on the island, and, of course, their government cannot go on there forever without taxes.[15]

Nevertheless, the Grau regime managed to maintain itself. Batista's troops put down two movements led by former army officers in Camaguey and Oriente provinces in the third week of September, economic disaster was staved off, and the demands of the opposition for Grau's resignation and the creation of a nonpartisan government were successfully resisted. In a battle on October 2, the ex-officers of the army, who had on September 8 occupied the Hotel Nacional where Welles was staying, were captured; fourteen of them were killed, and eighty soldiers and civilians lost their lives. Welles had moved out of the hotel a few days previously, and other United States nationals had left on the morning of October 2. In a telephone talk with Hull, Welles said: "I do not see that there is anything we can possibly construe about it as deliberate endangering of lives of American citizens." He did not think any help from Washington was needed, except that the battleship "New Mexico" might be ordered to move close to Havana but to keep out of sight of land.[16]

These actions appeared to indicate at least that the forces under Batista were both loyal to Grau and capable of crushing insurrections. Was this evidence of the capacity of the Grau regime to maintain "law and order throughout the island," as required by the declaration of September 12? If, as Welles had said in the Céspedes interregnum, no government could maintain complete order under post-Machado conditions, how was Grau's record to be evaluated?

As Stimson never admitted the existence of "chaos" in Cuba under Machado, Welles never admitted the existence of "order" under Grau. At most, Welles conceded only that "where quiet prevails, it is the quiet of panic." [17] Berle's comparably critical view of Cuban tranquility was that the situation was one of "passive anarchy"; he did not think there was serious danger to the lives of United States citizens, "but the danger to property is real." [18]

Two days after the battle of the Hotel Nacional, Welles and Batista had a long talk. Welles told Batista that he was "the only individual in Cuba today who represented authority." His troops had defeated the officers and were taking effective action against communists and radical elements elsewhere. This action had "rallied" the support of commercial and financial interests, and he had won the support of the press by refusing to let Grau give control of the papers to the students. In addition, said Welles, the opposition leaders, except Menocal, "were in accord that his control of the army as Chief of Staff should be continued as the only possible solution." This admission of Batista's power, however, was significantly distinguished by Welles from the status of the Grau regime, which, he said, "did not fill any of the conditions which the United States Government had announced as making possible recognition." In Welles's view, the Cuban government had not adopted a single constructive measure; it possessed far less popular confidence than when it came into existence; it lacked "support of the commercial and financial interests in Cuba." Without recognition by "foreign governments," Welles stated, the financial situation would soon make it impossible for government to function in Cuba; and, "should the present government go down in disaster, that disaster would necessarily inextricably involve not only [Batista] himself but the safety of the Republic, which he had publicly pledged himself to maintain."

Welles added that the only obstacle to a political truce "was the unpatriotic and futile obstinacy of a small group of young men, who should be studying in the university instead of playing politics, and of a few individuals who had joined with them from selfish motives." He urged Batista to "act as intermediary between the groups now at variance and, through the force of authority which he represented in his person, to insist that an immediate fair and reasonable solution be found so that Cuba might once more possess a government which had the confidence of all and which would have a fair opportunity to tide over the critical situation which now lay ahead." Emphasizing that Batista's influence "must necessarily be regarded as preponderant," in view of the important position he now held, Welles urged him to seek a solution that "represented effectively the desire of the Cuban people and which at the same time would make it possible for confidence in government to be restored in the Republic."

In sending the report of this talk to Washington, Welles admitted:

The situation as regards my relations with Batista is, of course, anomalous. I feel it necessary to make plain, however, that there does not exist at the present time in Cuba any authority whatever except himself and that, in the event of further disturbances which may endanger the lives and properties of Americans or foreigners in the Republic, it seems to be essential that this relationship be maintained.[19]

This talk marked the first time that Welles reported giving a perfectly clear indication that he had told any Cuban that the United States would not recognize the Grau regime. Taken in combination with the rest of the cable, this intimation strongly suggests that Welles was appealing to Batista to dissociate himself from Grau and the students and to bring into power a new government composed of the opposition parties. This attempt to bring about the downfall of the existing, if unrecognized, government, was far more "anomalous" than the fact that talks between the two men were being held at all. The intensity of Welles's antipathy for the Grau government may be estimated from the boldness with which he proposed that Batista's pledge to maintain the "safety of the Republic" authorized Batista to intrigue against his government, since its only end could be "disaster" because of the nonrecognition policy to which Welles himself was committed. Welles appeared to have no great concern about involving the Cuban army, a mutinous army at that, in Cuban politics; he was here dealing with a Cuban reality as he saw it and not with a theory about civil-military relations in a democratic polity. Welles here made use again of the tactics he had employed in consulting General Herrera when Machado seemed unlikely to be brought down by other means.

Hull discussed this important telegram with Roosevelt, and he informed Welles in a brief reply that the President thought that

public opinion . . . here seems to regard the capture of the officers as indicating a consolidation of the position of the present government. . . . Cuba now is going through a period of storm and stress, and . . . given all the circumstances, there must be some latitude, on the part of ourselves and of other states, in the application of the customary principles of international practice (e.g., as regards recognition) in view of these conditions.[20]

This telegram must have seemed to Welles to threaten the whole policy he had pursued during the previous month, for "consolidation" was close to "order." He immediately cabled Washington that "the capture of the officers does not indicate consolidation of the position of the government but solely a decidedly increased prestige for the army as distinguished from the government." The army "mutiny," he said, had occurred not to bring Grau to power, but solely to oust the officers, and "was not, as appears to be believed in the United States, in any sense responsible to a social movement. . . . The divergence between the army and the civilian elements in the government is fast becoming daily more marked. As Batista becomes more influential the power of the students and Grau San Martín diminishes." Welles repeated his view that the regime was opposed by business and political groups and "by a very great majority of the people as well." In addition, while recognition "would undoubtedly help to keep the present government in power for a while," there would be "popular reaction against it," and the government would either be overthrown or "plunged into utter anarchy."

Finally, he said, "I consequently most earnestly recommend that in the true sense of the term we give the Cuban people a further opportunity to settle their own problem without hindering that end through premature action on our part." This recommendation apparently overcame Roosevelt's inclination to recognize Grau, and, on October 10, the Under Secretary of State publicly affirmed the continuation of the nonrecognition policy by reiterating the essential points of the declaration of September 12.[21]

This action satisfied Welles for the moment, but he may have feared this evidence of uncertainty in Washington. Within a week he proposed "a permanent policy towards Cuba which [would] further the ultimate interests of the United States, both political and commercial, not only in Cuba but on the continent as well." Setting forth his appraisal of the Cuban situation, he contended that nonrecognition of Grau was a policy based on justice to the Cuban people," and further it was:

one which will hasten rather than retard the creation of a constitutional government in Cuba and one which will expedite eventual stability. Our own commercial and export interests in Cuba cannot be revived under this government. Only confidence can accomplish that, and there is no confidence either in the policies nor stability of this regime, whether it be recognized or not.[22]

No reply was made to this cable. However, no action was taken either, and this fact meant that the nonrecognition policy was continued, a policy that Grau called "a new type of intervention—intervention by inertia," that "intensifies the very ills it claims to pacify, maintaining a condition of intranquillity in our social and economic structure."[23]

The rationale for nonrecognition was now complete. If a political calm prevailed for a time in Cuba, it was characterized by Welles as a "quiet of panic" and by Berle as "passive anarchy." If the calm were broken by violence and the rebels were quelled by Cuban government forces, the demonstration of such ability was not admitted by Welles to be maintenance of "law and order," and he went so far as to praise nonrecognition as a policy based on "justice to the Cuban people." However, this position was not in itself strong enough, since observers outside the United States Embassy in Cuba could make independent judgments about "order" that might carry weight in Washington. For example, Russell Porter commented in the New York *Times* on October 15, 1933, that, "although the Grau government has not yet attained sufficient popular support to insure recognition, its army . . . has shown surprising restoration of discipline and ability so far to restore authority and maintain law and order."

Therefore, as has been indicated, Welles and Berle placed emphasis on the lack of support for Grau by leaders of political parties and by other organized groups as demonstrating that the "will of the Cuban people" was not represented by Grau; and Caffery held that Grau was supported only by the army and by "ignorant masses." If the masses were as numerous as Caffery later admitted, and if Grau represented them, such a relationship would not necessarily have been relevant to recognition policy because Caffery had placed the issue of representation beyond empirically verifiable judgment. Even if the "ignorant masses" that supported Grau were admitted to outnumber the "organized groups" that opposed his government, the issue of representation would not have been settled. The declaration of September 12 referred not to the Cuban people as a statistical entity from which Grau's capacity for representation might have been derived by a majority vote or even by estimates of majority support, but to the "will" of the Cuban people, and Caffery's description of the masses as "misled by utopian promises" indicates that he did not shy away from making an external, normative judgment about the quality of the will of the Cuban people. Such a judgment would of course provide an unassailable position for the defense of a steadfast policy of nonrecognition.

In the meantime the political crisis continued. In the interior of Cuba several sugar mills were occupied by groups of laborers who declared themselves to be the new owners and set up what Welles called "soviet government" for the operation of the properties.[24]

The Cuban politicians were in a deplorable state of indecision.

Welles's cables reported the daily ups and downs in the influence of Grau and Batista and of various opposition leaders. Batista was carrying on negotiations with the opposition independently of Grau, and he also had difficulties with some of his own colleagues in the army. The main body of the splinter group known as the "ABC Radicals" left the government and denounced Grau's regime as "a worse dictatorship than that of Machado." [25]

Within the government there were frequent resignations of cabinet ministers. Welles said that the Secretary of the Treasury resigned after being visited by a group of armed men and boys who demanded that a treasury employee be ousted.[26] The "Student Directorate," which represented some fifteen hundred former students and other youths of university age, was deeply divided as to policy and tactics. The Directorate was not an official body, but it was a significant political force because most of the students were armed, and many of them had become accustomed to violent methods of politics when the University had been closed and they had fought Machado's police. The Directorate needed Grau as a leader, and Batista needed him also as the only candidate for the presidency who would recognize and validate the army revolt.

If, as Welles had said in mid-September, "a social revolution" was in progress,[27] it was not directed by professional revolutionaries, although there apparently were a few communist agents who enjoyed some local successes.

If the Grau regime exhibited at this time few of the characteristics of a stable government, it must also be said that the opposition groups showed little capacity to maintain a solid front or to define a policy which would gain them Batista's support. At one point during the almost continuous negotiations between the opposition and government representatives, Mendieta appeared to have the support of Batista and at least two opposition parties for the formation of a new government. However, Mendieta suddenly refused, at the end of October, to accept the provisional presidency, ostensibly because he feared both that Batista could not control the army and also that he "would merely be Batista's prisoner." [28]

Welles considered affairs in Cuba in early November "more precarious than they have been at any moment during the last two

months." In these circumstances, he thought it best, after a telephone conversation with Phillips, that he should remain in Havana,
rather than return to Washington. However, in the next few days,
Welles apparently got word of a possible modification of Washington's recognition policy, for he cabled for and obtained permission
to go to Washington for a few days for discussions with Hull and
Roosevelt. In this cable Welles stated: "Should the policy we have
followed until now be changed, it would be preferable for Caffery
to substitute me as special representative as it might be preferable
in any event." [29]

Why was there talk of a change in policy? The materials are
lacking to permit a clear answer to this question. It may be suggested, however, that there were several possible reasons for change.
An important consideration was probably the fact that the Grau
regime had maintained itself for over two months and had put
down several movements against it. A second consideration may
have been that Washington was not happy about the continuation
by Welles of his "anomalous" relationships with Batista and the
kind of intermeddling that they unavoidably entrained. A third factor may have been public opinion in the United States, which was
showing some signs of feeling that the Grau regime had proved
its capacity to govern. A fourth factor may have been Washington's sensitivity to reports from Latin America indicating that there
was growing sympathy for Cuba and less support than at first for
United States policy. In the first half of November, Ambassador
Daniels in Mexico transmitted several editorials from the Mexican
newspapers *Excelsior* (Conservative) and *El Nacional* (Government) expressing criticism of United States policy. Finally, not
only did Grau hang on to his position, but the possibility that the
United States might have to intervene to protect United States citizens remained a real one. In the revolt of November 8–10, there
was artillery fire in Havana, and Welles once more said: "I anticipate a condition of complete anarchy after nightfall." [30] Some
stray shots hit a United States destroyer in the harbor. Since Welles
had been sent to Cuba in order to ward off a situation leading to
intervention; since, after three months, Cuba was still girdled by
United States warships, and Welles reported anew that anarchy was

imminent, it was not surprising if Washington should begin to think of changing both its policy and its ambassador in Havana.[31]

This is all speculation since there are not available any records of the talks which Welles had with Roosevelt at Warm Springs on November 19 and later in the Department. At any rate, Welles again quelled Washington's doubts about the policy he advocated, and, although his mission was terminated on December 13 after a brief return to Havana, he apparently induced Roosevelt to issue a statement on November 24 in which the President said that because of special treaty relations "recognition by the United States of a government in Cuba affords in more than ordinary measure both material and moral support to that government." Therefore,

> We have not believed that it would be a policy of friendship and of justice to the Cuban people as a whole to accord recognition to any provisional government in Cuba unless such government clearly possessed the support and the approval of the people of that Republic. We feel that no official action of the United States should at any time operate as an obstacle to the free and untrammeled determination by the Cuban people of their own destinies.
>
> We have been keenly desirous during all this period of showing by deed our intention of playing the part of a good neighbor to the Cuban people. We have wished to commence negotiations for a revision of the commercial convention between the two countries and for a modification of the permanent treaty between the United States and Cuba. . . . No progress along these lines can be made until there exists in Cuba a provisional government which through the popular support which it obtains and which through the general cooperation which it enjoys shows evidence of genuine stability.
>
> As has already been officially stated, the Government of the United States has neither partiality for nor prejudice against any faction or individual in Cuba. It will welcome any provisional government in Cuba in which the Cuban people demonstrate their confidence. We earnestly hope that in the near future through a spirit of compromise on all sides, the Cuban people themselves will reach some peaceful agreement which may result in general support of a government and thus avoid continued civil disturbance with its attendant tragic loss of life and grave prejudice to the economic interests of the Republic.[32]

This statement also announced the termination of Welles's mission "in the near future," his resumption of the position of Assistant Secretary of State, and his replacement in Havana by Jefferson

Caffery. In order to avoid legal problems concerning recognition, Caffery, a career officer with extensive experience in Latin America, was sent to Cuba as personal representative of the President and not as ambassador.[33]

Roosevelt's statement was, in effect, and probably in intent, both a death blow to the Grau regime and an invitation to the Cuban opposition groups to continue to refuse to accept the existing government of Cuba. It was also a victory for Welles even though he was not to be present for the *coup de grâce*. If the United States were eager to engage in commercial negotiations and in the changing of the permanent treaty, and if the obstacle to these desirable ends was the lack of a government that "clearly possessed the support and approval of the people," the implications for Cubans were as clear as they were when Welles began mediating between Machado and his opposition. The Cuban government must be changed if the Cuban sugar market in the United States were to be expanded, if the Platt Amendment were to be repealed, and if Cuba were to emerge from economic distress so serious that it had brought many people to the verge of starvation.

Roosevelt effectively adopted Welles's estimate of the situation in saying to the press:

We are not taking sides in any way. It is up to the Cuban people to decide and so far it appears at the present time that we haven't yet got a provisional government that clearly has the support of the majority of the Cuban people. What can we do? We can't do anything. The matter rests.[34]

News reports that Welles would return to Havana "with the full confidence and support of the President" met with a reaction in Havana "very favorable in all quarters excepting, of course, those identified with the Grau regime." [35]

In response to a cable sent by Hull on his way to Montevideo asking for "the controlling facts and conditions to date against recognition" of Grau, Acting-Secretary Phillips cabled the following summary of the United States position:

We have maintained that the criteria of Cuban recognition are: (1) popular support, and (2) ability to maintain law and order and carry on the functions incumbent upon any stable government.

The Embassy at Habana insists that these criteria have not been met. With regard to No. 1, Mr. Welles emphatically expressed to me his judgment that Grau does not have the confidence of the mass of the Cuban people, but is supported by a minority bent upon remaining in power despite all costs. With regard to No. 2, Mr. Welles believes that the Grau regime can maintain order only by the most extreme and dictatorial methods (although it appears to have strengthened itself by the suppression of the November 8th revolt which has tended to discourage counter-revolutionary movements).[36]

It may be of importance to observe that, in this cable, Phillips did not say he shared in the judgments of Welles and that he remarked that the Grau regime might be stronger since November 8. Since Roosevelt's declaration had made it clear that there was to be no change in attitude toward Grau, the general policy line recommended by Welles was to be continued. However, this cable suggests that there may have been the feeling in Washington that Welles's personal involvement in Cuban affairs had become so constraining that it was desirable to replace him with a man who, being uncommitted, might be able to judge more impartially, and to observe with greater calmness and, perhaps, with greater clarity.

On his return to Havana, Welles vainly resumed his conferences with representatives of Grau, Grau himself, and leaders of the opposition. He ended his mission on December 13.

For lack of evidence beyond the diplomatic correspondence, it is difficult to go very far in understanding Welles's motivations for his inflexible opposition to the recognition of the Grau regime. The most puzzling aspect of his policy was the advocacy of a limited intervention to restore the Céspedes administration, for this proposal was inconsistent with his own previously expressed views and, as he well knew, with those of Hull and Roosevelt. A strong impulse must have been behind this action; it does not seem to have been fear, either for himself or for other non-Cubans, nor is it probable that he was primarily concerned about the security of the property of United States firms in Cuba, although these may have played a part. The stronger motive may have been the desire to regain the prestige he had won with the flight of Machado and lost with the deposition of Céspedes. Welles was at the height of his early career for the brief month's life of the Céspedes government, and its fall, while he was still in Cuba, may be assumed to have been a bitter blow to his pride. If he was no longer the impartial envoy, it is possible that he confounded the interests of his government with his own and confused "those classes in Cuba which in reality constitute the dominant portion of public opinion" [37] with the "will of the Cuban people themselves." In so doing, he could have failed or refused to see, as Caffery did, that very great numbers of the Cuban people supported the regime of Grau San Martín. Whether this element of his motivation retained its force throughout the whole of his subsequent policy toward the Grau administration is a matter for speculation, for he appears to have become genuinely concerned that Grau and his colleagues could not under any circumstances secure the support of the professional and financial groups that possessed the expertise to operate the Cuban governmental machinery in its established patterns. However, even when the restoration of Céspedes became manifestly impossible, Welles's efforts to oust Grau did not diminish, and he laid down the line, both in rationale and techniques, that Caffery carried out to what Welles must have regarded as a successful conclusion.

Welles had asserted, as we have seen, that a "social revolution" was taking place in Cuba under Grau, and it is possible that he may have regarded its suppression as his principal objective in the last months of 1933, although he does not emphasize this point in his communications to the Department of State. If this were the case, he accepted a mission that had sombre portents for the future. This possibility was recognized by two Mexican commentators whose remarks are worthy of recall.

Foreign Minister José M. Puig Casauranc said at the Montevideo Conference that the Cuban situation under Grau was not the result of a "barracks revolution," but that "Cuba is trying to complete her independence" and, "by an accelerated process of a social order, to secure the adaptation of her masses to the realities of the moment." Without referring directly to the United States, he strongly criticized its policy by implication:

When, in these conditions, the 'recognition' of the strong, of the country definitely involved in the political life of another people, is not forthcoming, then there arises—whether the strong country desires it or not

—the incentive to evil . . . Then an indirect invitation, consciously or otherwise, is given to our people to continue an 'abnormal status'. . . . Out of such periods of confusion and delayed results, the ultimate moral responsibility belongs to those who deny the swift and definite cementing of the popular forces which at a given moment are attempting to direct situations.[38]

A similar view, expressed in quite different terms was voiced by Roberto Córdoba, Mexican agent on the General Claims Commission, who said that, while no military intervention took place when the United States government surrounded Cuba "with a threatening line of battleships," he considered that "the kind of intervention practiced on that occasion was one of the most effective and skillful interventions ever carried out by the American government." [39]

Caffery Replaces Welles and Grau Resigns

The day after Welles's departure, and before Caffery's arrival on December 18, Batista and several students called on Chargé H. Freeman Matthews. They said that the Grau regime was comparable to the New Deal in the United States and denied that the regime had any sympathy for communism or that it was anti-American or anti-foreign. They noted that communists were opposing the government, and they blamed them for "the continuing nightly bomb explosions." Both Batista and the students minimized the strength of the opposition and claimed that it would lose its influence if Grau were only recognized by the United States. They asserted that the Grau regime had proved its stability by remaining in power for nearly four months and emphasized as proof the opening of schools and the planned opening of the University in January.[40] This, in outline, was the case of the Grau government for recognition by the United States.

The situation in Havana in December was one of disorder and disunity. Nightly bombings continued, although casualties were low and, with few exceptions, "these bombs have been exploded in a manner calculated to cause little material damage." The opposition to Grau apparently wished to create an impression of disorder, while prudently avoiding the destruction of real property.

The Embassy reported that "the population [was] in a condition of nervous tension and terror," the streets were patrolled by soldiers "assisted by irresponsible armed civilians of the type of the *'porrista'* of the late Machado régime," and several students had recently been killed by soldiers. The National Confederation of Labor had denounced Grau's labor legislation as "fascist" and "the extension of Batista's activities beyond military affairs . . . as a threat of a swing to a military dictatorship." In this view, the "Cuban better classes" had finally begun to abandon hope for the solution of its problems through American intervention, but they still hoped that recognition of Grau would be withheld.[41]

The change from Welles to Caffery did not mean that the policy of nonrecognition had changed; its permanence was merely made more explicit. Within three days of his arrival, Caffery spoke frankly to Carlos Hevia, Grau's Secretary of Agriculture, reporting the conversation thus:

"As the situation appears today (I repeated some of the well-known deficiencies of the regime) we cannot recognize your government; you say that you are only a provisional governor with no political affiliations and no political interests and that your only object is to hold honest elections and then get out; but I do not feel that you offer adequate assurances for guaranteeing free elections for the proposed constitutional assembly."
I said also that we had been disturbed at seemingly communistic tendencies in the present regime and at the apparent lack of preparation with which important decrees affecting some of our interests had been issued; some of these decrees, such as that affecting the electric light rates, appeared confiscatory and others, such as the Workmen's Compensation Law, appeared entirely unworkable.[42]

It was not long after this that the British Minister stated that

in his view the authority of the Grau [San] Martín Regime extends further than American reports indicate and that unsatisfactory as the regime may be it is better to look towards some action stabilizing it rather than let the situation drift into increasing disorder and resultant damage to foreign property.[43]

Caffery told the British Minister in Havana that it would be a mistake to recognize Grau at the moment. From Washington, Phillips informed Caffery that the British government took the view that it wished to cooperate with the United States in this situation, but that, "had a similar situation existed in some other Latin American country, Great Britain would be on the brink of recognizing a regime similar to the Grau San Martín government." Phillips said he had advised the British Ambassador that "the sentiment of the Latin American governments in the great majority was against such recognition." [44]

If the policy remained unchanged, why was Welles recalled? In addition to considerations already mentioned, Roosevelt may have felt that Welles had become so personally involved in Cuban politics that any change in the Cuban government would inevitably be attributed to his "mediation" and, therefore, to interference by the government of the United States. In this case, if a new man were sent to Havana, one who was not personally known to the Cuban people or their leaders, two purposes could be served at the same time: the new man, Caffery, would be uncommitted, in so far as his personal prestige was concerned, by the turbulent events of Cuba's immediate past; and, in the second place, the policy he would express would be unquestionably that of President Roosevelt. From this point of view, it seems probable that one, and perhaps the most important reason for changing ambassadors was to demonstrate beyond question that the Grau regime could never obtain recognition from the United States. Another explanation was, however, given by Hull at the Montevideo Conference. In a talk on December 17 with Herminio Portell Vilá, one of the Cuban delegates, Hull was reported to have answered Portell Vilá's protests against "intervention" against the Grau regime by saying that Caffery was going to Cuba "to study the situation and inform the Department of State about it." [45]

Caffery does not appear to have received written instructions, as did Welles in April. In any case, Hull was not in close touch with the Cuban situation, as he had sailed for Montevideo on November 11, two weeks before Welles's meeting with Roosevelt at Warm Springs. Further, Caffery's first telegram from Havana contained the information that he had told Hevia that the Grau regime could not be recognized; this was hardly the action of one whose instructions were to study and report.

Until mid-December, Grau might persuade himself and Batista that the reason for Washington's refusal to recognize him was a combination of Welles's influence in Washington and Roosevelt's unwillingness to embarrass Welles by repudiating his policy. After Caffery told Hevia that the United States could not recognize the regime, Grau must have realized that he could not stay in office even long enough to hold the elections for a constitutional assembly which he had called for April 22. Batista, for his part, must have made similar calculations, and he quickly came to the conclusion that the best and perhaps the only chance for his continued leadership of the new Cuban army depended on coming to terms with the most likely successor to Grau. Batista's army revolt had not only dispossessed the whole group of previous officers of the army but had also outraged the majority of the wealthy class of Cubans, with whom a large number of the officers were connected by social and family ties. Batista was determined that he and his fellow noncommissioned officers were going to maintain their new, hard-won status in Cuba, even though other groups, such as some of the students and labor leaders, were to be disappointed in their revolutionary aims.

Assuming that Grau would be forced from office if recognition were withheld, Batista presumably envisaged three possibilities. One was intervention by the United States; this would mean the defeat and dissolution of his army. A second was a successful revolution against the Grau regime; this would have the same result. Preferable to either a third, which lay within his power to achieve, was to bring into office, through his support, a new government that would legalize his army and his position as its commander.

Batista bluntly asked Caffery on January 10 what the United States "wanted done for recognition." Caffery replied: " 'I will lay down no specific terms; the matter of your government is a Cuban matter and it is for you to decide what you will do about it,' (Having in mind our reiterated declarations as to our position on recognition.)" [46] A statement of this kind to the man possessing effective but illegal military power in Cuba could hardly be looked at otherwise than as an invitation to him to arrange a settlement most effectively serving his own interests. Batista knew that Grau would not be recognized; with this exception, Caffery did not apparently place any conditions on Batista's action. Therefore, within a week, Grau resigned because Batista had come to terms with Mendieta, the opposition leader who Batista knew was most likely to gain recognition from Washington.[47]

Caffery's estimate of the situation on January 10, only a week before Grau resigned, illuminates both United States policy and the situation in Cuba. After referring to Grau's support by the army and by "ignorant masses," as previously quoted, he cabled:

> However, unless Dr. Grau decides voluntarily to give up power, it is my opinion that he can be forced to do so only by the armed intervention of the United States unless there is a break in the army, which is now standing strongly behind the government. The military have plenty of arms and ammunition and, realizing that they will be sheep exterminated in a successful revolution, they will be fighting for their lives. The opposition declare that they are organizing a revolution, but it will be very difficult for them to overcome the organized military forces. I find in the opposition little tendency to compromise and an insistence that the only way to clear up this situation is for us to intervene. They refuse to believe our insistent declarations against intervention.
>
> On the other hand matters cannot with impunity be allowed to drift interminably in the direction they are now drifting: the *de facto* authorities in view of the fact that they have no support from the better elements of the country are relying more and more on radical and communistic elements and we may soon be faced with the [a?] [*sic*] very grave situation in connection with the protection of our manifold interests on the island.[48]

Caffery need not have been concerned, for he had already given Batista his cue. On January 11 Batista talked with Mendieta, and on the 13th he told Caffery that he would support Mendieta as president. At the same time, Mendieta told Caffery that he was "willing to assume the Presidency (provisionally, of course) at once but only if he [knew] in advance that the United States [would] recognize him." Assurance to Mendieta of advance recognition was recommended to Washington by Caffery, on the ground that "if this is not done, Batista will probably turn definitely to the left with definite disaster for all our interests here (or declare himself military dictator.)"[49]

This recommendation involved problems of such importance that the matter was taken to President Roosevelt, who decided that

It is of course impossible to pledge recognition of any individual or group before certain conditions are an accomplished fact. The position of the President has been made abundantly clear in previous statements. This government will recognize a Cuban provisional government which is substantially supported by the Cuban people and is able to maintain law, order, and the normal functions of government. A reiteration of this to any or all leaders or parties is entirely in order, but we cannot be in a position of promising recognition to any individual or group in advance of the fulfillment of the conditions we have consistently set forth.[50]

Grau, apparently informed by Batista and what Caffery called a "junta of officers" that they would no longer support his government, said on January 14 that he would resign. On January 15 he relinquished his office to Carlos Hevia, his Secretary of Agriculture, who held the presidency for three days until the accession of Mendieta.

Grau's account of this occasion was as follows: He had been advised that Mendieta, Batista, and Caffery had requested an interview with him. He had replied that he would talk with Caffery only if some international problem were involved. He had therefore talked only with Mendieta and Batista and had agreed to resign, because, as he put it:

On the one hand there was Col. Batista, head of the army, representing all the military forces in the country, and on the other was Col. Carlos Mendieta who was said to be the only man capable of reuniting all Cubans.[51]

This story was energetically denied in several particulars by Batista in an interview in *El Avance* (Havana), November 8, 1934. Concerning the final interview with Grau, he said that it had not been requested by himself, Mendieta, or Caffery, and that Caffery's name had not been mentioned at all during the course of the talk. Concerning his own talks with Caffery, which he readily admitted, he said: "As chief of the army, and in those days, even more as chief of the revolution, I had the duty to receive any foreign diplomat who requested an interview with me." Caffery does not appear to have made any public statement in response to Grau's charges.

The debate among Cubans about United States policy from Machado's fall to Mendieta's accession has been intense and prolonged and can only briefly be mentioned here. Approval of Welles's mediation in bringing about Machado's resignation had been nearly unanimous.[52] On the other hand, there was much less openly expressed support for the nonrecognition of the Grau regime. The Cubans who welcomed Mendieta probably formed a minority of the population and were understandably less than eager to credit the United States with bringing them to power, but the adherents of Grau felt little restraint in asserting that his downfall was caused by the policy of the United States.

Hevia, having received the provisional presidency, was unable to obtain the support of the whole of the Nationalist party, headed by Mendieta, and he was faced with a move by Grau's former Minister of Interior, Antonio Guiteras, to call a general strike throughout the island. Caffery reported on the second day after Grau's resignation, that

Batista has just sent me word that, in view of the very precarious strike situation (seriously endangering enormous American properties) provoked by Guiteras and also in view of Hevia's inability to secure the full support of Mendieta group, he has decided to declare Mendieta President this afternoon. He may meet with armed resistance from the Cuban navy.[53]

Batista overcame the navy's objections to Mendieta on the evening of January 17, and the way then was clear for him to make Mendieta president. Hevia resigned, and the Secretary of State, Márquez Sterling, was entrusted with the presidential powers for a few hours before Mendieta took the oath of office as provisional President on January 18, before the Supreme Court.[54]

Caffery thought that the Mendieta government would have "large public support . . . the government is dealing firmly with the situation and it is my opinion that it will be capable of maintaining law and order. There is a very evident feeling of relief and enthusiasm throughout the city." [55]

Recognition and Maturation of the Mendieta Government

The alliance between Mendieta and Batista finally achieved the combination Welles had failed to bring about since September: control of the presidency by the most popular of the political leaders who had opposed Machado, and support of the new President by the new Cuban army which wielded physical power in the island. Although Mendieta and his supporters represented what Caffery had called the "better classes in the country," Batista's army, which was now led only by former noncommissioned officers, had for months been denounced by the "better classes"; some ex-officers who were also political leaders, such as M. G. Menocal, had refused to deal with Batista. However, Batista's success in defeating the ex-officers, and then in easily suppressing the November rebellion, had made it clear that no power in Cuba could dispossess him and, no less importantly, that the United States would not help his enemies, at least in any positive fashion. In the course of the Batista–Mendieta talks, it presumably became mutually evident that Batista's need for legitimacy by way of formal sanction of the position he had gained in leading the mutiny and Mendieta's need for the army's backing in keeping order under the new government were sufficiently vital to the two men that their essential interests would impel them to collaborate for a substantial period of time. In addition, while they did not have advance assurance of recognition by the United States, the course of United States policy over the preceding four months was such that their hope for recognition must have been so strong as to verge on expectation. In this they were not to be disappointed.

A few hours before Mendieta was sworn in, Acting Secretary Phillips told a press conference that the situation in Cuba looked more hopeful and might work out satisfactorily; he thought that it was a "good sign" that the army and navy were working together.[56] Caffery told Hull, who was on the way home from the Montevideo Conference, that Mendieta had "strong public support" and would probably be recognized soon by Latin American countries.[57]

After talking with Hull at Key West, Caffery cabled the Department that the Mendieta government was maintaining order and carrying out the "normal functions of government"; it was supported by "all the political groups, except those of the extreme left and except possibly the adherents of Machado."[58]

Roosevelt made up his mind swiftly. On the afternoon of January 22, he told a meeting attended by the representatives of seventeen other American states that the United States would recognize the Mendieta regime, and on the 23rd, five days after Mendieta took office, formal recognition was accorded.[59]

Hull's statement on the occasion called the recognition "a sort of culmination" of the Montevideo Conference: "The almost universal support by the people of Cuba points strongly to the maintenance of a stable government and the continuance of law and order in that country." [60] On the 22d, having just arrived in Washington, Hull had told a press conference that "when the army and the navy and other political elements on the island are behind the government," the correspondents could draw their own conclusions about the probability of recognition by the United States.[61]

Grau had sailed for Mexico on January 20. On his arrival he gave an interview in which he expressed pride that he had not been recognized since others who were "bandits and criminals" had been recognized by the United States. He also made some sarcastic remarks about the "arts of divination" which permitted Washington to decide in a few days that Mendieta's government would be stable, while the stability of the Grau regime had not been admitted even though it had lasted for four months.[62]

The Mendieta regime was stable in that Mendieta peacefully relinquished the presidency shortly before elections in January, 1936, following a revision of the constitution, and Miguel Mariano Gómez, the electoral victor over Colonel Menocal, peacefully became President. There are, however, two features of the Mendieta government which indicate the special character of its stability. The first of these was that the government had to contend with a considerable amount of popular unrest in the form of strikes, riots, and attempted revolutions for a period of about two years. The second special characteristic of the regime's stability was that Mendieta's government was given strong support by the United States, a support which had been refused to the government of Grau San Martín.[63]

In a gesture of confidence in Mendieta, Washington withdrew one destroyer from Havana and one from Nueva Gerona, on the day Mendieta was recognized.[64] However, Caffery cabled that it would be a "decided mistake" to move the battleship "Wyoming" from Havana unless its force of Marines were transferred to another ship which would remain.[65] A few days later, Caffery reported that the railway, bus, and tobacco workers were on strike, that a general strike had been declared in Santiago, that two bombs had exploded in Havana, and that the government had prohibited any popular manifestations.[66] Mendieta, in a message to the Cuban people, said he was obliged "to confront and resolve most grave problems of public order and a social disturbance." [67]

In June, 1934, Roosevelt proclaimed that "there exist in Cuba such conditions of domestic violence," that they might be promoted by exports of arms from the United States. He thereby brought into effect the provisions of the joint Congressional resolution of January 31, 1922, prohibiting the export of arms to American countries in such circumstances.[68]

The social disturbance continued for more than a year and grew in seriousness. In December, 1934, Mendieta roused memories of Machado by suspending the writ of *habeas corpus;* on January 15, 1935 all constitutional guarantees were suspended for a period of three months, and penalties of death or life imprisonment were established for persons convicted of such acts as burning fields of sugar cane.[69]

It was not until after March, 1935, when a general strike directed at the government itself was suppressed by the army, that the slowly improving economic position combined with political developments to bring about a gradual subsidence of political unrest.

These disorders were the aftermath of what Welles had belatedly recognized as a "social revolution" in Cuba. The revolutionary movement had been nurtured by desperate economic conditions in Cuba and by Machado's years of repression. It had been encouraged by the freedom it enjoyed during Grau's brief presidency, and it was not extinguished until some time after Batista and Mendieta joined forces. Caffery reported that "the Mendieta government has been fighting for its life against the communistic elements, and, although it has thus far strengthened its position in the country by its recent firm attitude, the communists have by no means given up hope and will continue to be a menace for some time to come." [70]

The identity of the "communistic elements" was not clarified by Caffery,[71] but, as late as October, he reported that Batista had been "endeavoring to have President Mendieta understand the importance of his having a Cabinet that meets with some support among the public—a condition which his present Cabinet, of course, does not meet." [72] Either the communists had suddenly become much stronger than Welles had claimed that they were, or Caffery was employing a more elastic definition than Welles had permitted himself to use in referring to the main body of the Cuban people.

Mendieta was a provisional President, pledged to make arrangements for elections in which he would not be a candidate. The plans for the elections gave rise to an intense conflict among political groups, and Caffery found himself acting in a mediatory capacity comparable in some ways to that of Welles in July, 1933. In March, 1935, at the time of a serious and widespread strike, Caffery reported that he had talked with Batista about arrangements for the holding of a constituent assembly and that he would "pass on" the views of Batista to the political parties.[73] Some of the party leaders told Caffery that they would accept Batista's proposals on condition that Batista persuade Mendieta to resign, but the Ambassador informed Washington that he had told them he "could not advise Batista to accept their proposal (if Batista weakened on this, the army might break down with consequent immediate chaos)." [74]

There were some protests against Caffery's activities in the press of the United States. Hull answered one of them by stating that "the cornerstone" of the Good Neighbor policy was "noninterference in the internal affairs of any other country. That this policy has been adhered to in our relations with Cuba will be apparent, I believe, upon impartial study of the facts." He noted the abrogation of the Platt Amendment and the completion of the trade treaty, and added:

These are only the more outstanding examples; our assistance has been requested and given in connection with many other minor matters, but that such assistance could be termed interference in Cuban internal affairs is baseless. I have no doubt but that our policy has been misinterpreted in certain quarters, but this does not alter the true facts of the matter.[75]

Caffery had to tread a narrow way amid the pressures brought to bear upon him. He recorded, for example, that a mine manager had asked him for assistance in breaking up a labor union that was alleged to be violating the law. Caffery told the manager that he could not lend support "to any attempt to break up the union. [He] explained that that would be counter to well-known policies in the United States; that the Embassy could not possibly be identified with endeavors to smash labor organizations." [76]

One of the types of assistance provided by the United States to Cuba was that of technical advice in preparing for the presidential elections. Professor Harold W. Dodds of Princeton University went to Cuba in December, 1935, at the invitation of Mendieta, and, with the approval of nearly all the Cuban political parties, developed procedures for the holding of elections which were then enacted into law by the provisional government. [77]

Mendieta resigned on December 11, 1935, because of opposition to his being in office at the time of the election. He was succeeded by his Secretary of State, José A. Barnet, who held the elections on January 10, 1936, that brought President Miguel Mariano Gómez to office.

Following the failure of the general strike in March, 1935, and even more clearly after the presidential election, it may be said that attempts to bring about a social revolution in Cuba came to an end. A gradually improving economic situation and a growing desire for internal peace, together with the return of traditional political parties to power, restored a political, social, and economic situation basically similar to that existing during the early years of Machado's administration in the late 1920s. This does not mean, of course, that there were no important changes. But two significant features of the Cuban system emerged, still recognizable after five years of unrest: the pre-1930 social and economic class structure was retained, and the important place in the Cuban economy held by foreign-owned enterprises was not fundamentally disturbed.

Labor had created for itself a position of such strength that greater recognition was in future given to its demands for improved wages and working conditions, and improvements were shortly made in educational opportunities for the general public.

These changes, however, were made gradually and peacefully, and not as the result of a revolutionary reorganization of Cuban society.

There was, however, one new and notable development of the revolutionary period which was to leave a lasting effect in Cuba. This was the active entry of the Cuban army into politics and the emergence of Batista as the dominant figure in Cuban public affairs.

Batista had come to national prominence by organizing a successful mutiny against all, or nearly all, the commissioned officers of the Cuban army. For at least two months thereafter his position had been insecure, because the army officers had remained organized and armed for the first month and because he did not fully gain personal ascendancy over all the armed forces until he had put down the insurrection of November 8, 1933. He and his fellow mutineers must have been anxious, even frightened men in those tumultuous days. However, in those months, and before the fall of the Grau regime, he learned the full implications of the vital fact that he and his army were indispensable to the formation of any Cuban government capable both of securing recognition by the United States and of attaining constitutional possession of power in Cuba. He owed his political education not only to his being courted by Cuban politicians, but also to his being told by both Welles and Caffery that he had it within his power to bring into power another Cuban government in place of that headed by Grau. Neither Welles nor Caffery could promise him that such a government would be recognized by the United States, but, after he threw his support to Mendieta and Mendieta was recognized within five days of taking office, he needed no further evidence of the extent of his actual political power nor, it may be assumed, of his political potentialities.

It is not intended to suggest that Batista would not have come to exert great political influence in Cuba if the United States had quickly recognized the Grau regime. Batista might well have developed into a political as well as a military leader, given the weaknesses of the Grau government. This, however, is speculation. As the course of events actually unfolded, the combination of the

Cuban political situation and the policy followed by the United States provided not merely an opportunity but positive encouragement for the assertion by Batista of decisive political influence at a critical point in Cuban history.

The limitations of this statement should be clearly stated. It is not meant to suggest that the United States was wholly responsible for Cuban political developments after 1933, nor is it intended to suggest that the United States government wished either to enlarge the political role of the Cuban army or to promote Batista's rise to the presidency of Cuba. It is clear, however, that, given the determination of Washington not to intervene by landing troops and at the same time to refuse recognition to Grau, the powerful influence of Welles and Caffery was exercised in such a way that Batista, as head of the army, became the most powerful individual in Cuba.

There seems to be every reason to believe that Washington hoped that normal, democratic, constitutional government in Cuba would be reestablished after the fall of the Grau administration. There do not appear to have been formulated any political balance sheets evaluating the possible risks of encouraging Batista to bring in Mendieta as President, as compared to those of giving recognition to Grau. The immediate decision was the most important one to the United States. It seemed vital to find an immediate way to end a situation which might develop so that the dreaded intervention would become unavoidable. Cuban internal developments were of course important, but their character was secondary so long as they did not involve the possibility of intervention.

Consequently, strong support was given to Mendieta shortly after his assumption of office. This support was not only directly political, such as the prohibition of arms exports without license, but was of other types. The Platt Amendment was abrogated by treaty on May 29, 1934, to the accompaniment of secret sighs of relief in Washington and the public exchange of congratulatory messages. All rights of intervention in Cuban affairs were renounced by the United States, although Cuba continued to permit the United States to maintain the naval base at Guantánamo. Although the signing of the treaty was in one way a victory for the Mendieta administration, it seems to have had little immediate effect on calming political strife in Cuba. In any case, nonrecognition, which had been effective in ousting Grau, was a policy operative quite independently of the Platt Amendment, and the actions of both Stimson and Hull had demonstrated the extreme unwillingness of Washington to use the Platt Amendment as a justification for intervention or interference of any kind in Cuban affairs. It may be said that by 1933 the Platt Amendment, far from providing a desired right of intervention, had become for the United States a burdensome responsibility involving duties to maintain order which appeared not only incompatible with the Good Neighbor policy but also expensive and troublesome. At the same time, the abrogation of the Amendment had long been desired by Cubans, and the event was justly hailed in both countries as the enlightened termination of an unequal relationship and the beginning of a new era of collaboration. The Platt Amendment had been a symbol of inequality, and its abandonment was an act, as distinct from a mere expression of intention, that quickened the appreciation of the Good Neighbor in other countries. In Peru, for example, "enthusiastic commendation" was heard, and Ambassador Dearing reported that the moral standing of the United States was high in Lima and that "even most distrustful of our illwishers are beginning to believe the Good Neighbor is a reality." [78]

The new era was also marked by the completion on August 24, 1934, of the first of the trade agreements completed under Secretary Hull's program of bilateral treaties for the enlargement of the foreign trade of the United States. The treaty reduced the tariff on Cuban sugar to slightly less than half of the tariff on sugar from countries paying the full duty. In conjunction with the application of the provisions of the Jones–Costigan Act, which permitted an increase in the total amount of Cuban sugar imported into the United States, the effect of the treaty, coincident with a general improvement in economic conditions, was to bring about a substantial increase in Cuban exports to the United States, and a consequent increase in Cuban imports.[79]

Although the exertion of United States influence in Cuba did not later reach the 1933–34 peak, the old habits and relationships continued for some time. Toward the end of 1936 a dispute arose over legislation, supported by Batista and opposed by President Gómez, to impose a tax of nine cents a bag on sugar to raise funds for building rural schools. Caffery reported that the Secretary of Agriculture had asked him to make "a public declaration that the United States government would support President Gómez in vetoing the rural schools bill." Caffery replied that since such a declaration "might involve the probability of our having to land troops back here . . . under no circumstances would my government authorize me to make such a declaration." [80]

Gómez's determined opposition to the bill, which by December 19 passed the Senate unanimously and the House by a large majority, stirred up a serious political controversy. There was some sentiment among officers in the army for violent action to oust Gómez.

After 1933 the officers in the army had become increasingly active with respect to domestic political issues. This was true not only of those at the very top, but of the commissioned officers in lower ranks as well, and Batista, perhaps with an early eye to a political career, had expressed support for the development of rural schools. Such political activity on the part of the army had been nearly unknown before 1933, partly because many of the pre-Batista officers had been trained in military schools in the United States and had been influenced to some degree by the tradition of civil-military relations that prevailed there.

The school issue quickly became converted into a fundamental one of the dominance of the civil or the military authorities in Cuba. The situation was clearly understood in the Department of State. Duggan wrote, in a memorandum sent to the White House, that, since 1933,

the military has not confined its interest and jurisdiction to purely military affairs. It has assumed civil functions to such an extent that with regard to those matters in which it is interested its word is final. Congress, aware of the seat of power, has followed the desires of the army. Gómez, elected at reasonably fair elections, took office apparently firmly resolved to restore the prestige of the civil arm of the government. In this he has not succeeded.[81]

In Cuba, the solution to the crisis came quickly. Gómez's announced intention to veto the bill spurred a movement to impeach him. Desperate but still determined, Gómez instructed his ambassador in Washington to see President Roosevelt and deliver a memorandum described by the Acting Secretary of State as of a "purely informative character." The memorandum, delivered on the morning of December 19, in substance declared that Batista had informed congressional leaders in Havana of his desire to have Gómez impeached, "and that, if this takes place, a military dictatorship will be established with consequent impairment of democratic and constitutional government." [82]

The next day, a less covert appeal was made by the Secretary of Treasury, who called on Caffery "and intimated that the only solution of the present crisis was to be found in a 'moral' intervention by our government." Caffery told him that in his opinion Washington "could not intervene in this crisis." [83]

This appeal for "moral intervention" was laid before President Roosevelt, who stated that "he had no intention of intervening, either morally or otherwise, in the Cuban crisis." However, he thought that Caffery might point out to the proper persons, presumably Batista among others,

that what President Gómez had done in calling in legislative leaders to lay before them his attitude with regard to the sugar tax bill was exactly what he [Roosevelt] and other presidents in democracies had frequently done and that this action was not considered in other countries to give grounds for the charge of infringement of legislative prerogatives.

Caffery was given this message by Acting Secretary R. Walton Moore, and the Ambassador replied "that he had taken the liberty of pointing this out on a number of occasions, but that the opposition to President Gómez had given little heed to his observations." [84]

On December 21 Gómez vetoed the schools bill, and Caffery reported that he had been "endeavoring personally and informally of course to have the two houses of Congress confine their activities this afternoon to a consideration of the President's veto," rather than proceeding to an impeachment. [85] However, the army was determined to get rid of Gómez, and it brought pressure to this end that amounted to what Caffery called "intimidation" in certain cases. On December 22, the Cuban lower house voted by 111 to 45 that impeachment proceedings be instituted, and on the 24th the President was impeached by the Senate by a vote of 22 to 12. The Vice-President, Laredo Bru, was sworn in as President on the same day, and the crisis was over.

The military had succeeded without violence, but not without threats, in constitutionally forcing the President from office. The observance of legal forms may have been due in large part to the urgings of Caffery. The substantive victory was carried, however, against the implications of Roosevelt's cautiously phrased suggestion that Gómez had acted like presidents of other democracies. Such influence as Roosevelt and Caffery felt able to exert was given to the upholding of the civil power in the Cuban state. However, Batista, the man who first learned the full measure of the political implications of his military strength when he was encouraged to make Mendieta president in 1934, was not the man to give more than ceremonial satisfaction to admonitions from Washington in 1936 when a challenge was made to the very heart of his hard-won position.[86]

Ex-President Gómez issued a public statement, justifying his course of action and expounding his efforts to maintain a proper separation between the civil and military authorities. The crisis was really closed, however, when Batista informed Caffery that he did not know about any plans for further changes in the Cuban presidency.[87] Some rumors persisted in Cuba, fanned by unhappy but hopeful partisans of Gómez, that the United States government might exert economic pressure on Cuba in retaliation for the impeachment proceedings. However, these rumors died out after it became apparent that Washington had no such intentions. It was a still longer time, however, before Cubans who were opposed to their own government could bring themselves fully to accept the fact that they could no longer look to Washington for assistance in bringing about a change in a Cuban regime. Nearly two years later, a Cuban politician tried to get an expression of opinion from the United States Embassy toward a possible movement against the existing government. Chargé Beaulac reported that he had made it "abundantly clear" that his inquirer "could expect no opinion, support, advice, or sympathy from us toward any illegal change of government in Cuba" nor would it do any good to go to Washington to try to get help from officials there.[88]

The United States government in 1938 would do no more than recall, as did Duggan to the Cuban Ambassador when he told him that President Bru might resign, that

when Dr. Gómez was removed from office . . . he [Duggan] clearly remembered the concern felt both by the President and the Secretary, and their disappointment that an administration so auspiciously begun should so soon have terminated, and in circumstances so disquieting.[89]

With the refusal of Roosevelt to undertake "moral intervention" in Cuba in the civil-military crisis of 1936, the results of the experience of 1933–34, and of the abrogation of the Platt Amendment, were finally crystallized in action as well as in understanding and implications. The last, lingering hopes of the political opponents of Batista that the United States might help them and try to foster what with some justification they might claim as the cause of democracy were extinguished in November, 1938, when Batista made an official visit to Washington at the invitation of the Chief of Staff, General Malin Craig. The invitation was formally issued by the War Department, and Batista accepted as Chief of Staff of the Cuban army, but the occasion was also profoundly political in importance. When the invitation was made known, Ambassador J. Butler Wright reported that this fact had "enormously strengthened" Batista's position in Cuba. He reported:

It appears to be the general opinion that, if Colonel Batista can be convinced that it is to his advantage to follow constructive policies from now on, much good will come. If Colonel Batista's prestige merely increases and he fails to take steps to improve conditions within the government and the army, it is generally believed that the trip will not only fail to do good but will result in prolonging the present unsatisfactory political situation in Cuba.[90]

Batista was met at Union Station by General Craig and Sumner Welles, and he talked with President Roosevelt and Secretary Hull, as well as with military officers. Although the nature of the talks is not fully known, they dealt with hemisphere defense, and

Batista heard something about the commercial policy of the United States and some guarded suggestions concerning Washington's hopes for the progressive development of democratic institutions in Cuba.

On his return to Havana, Batista claimed that his visit would result in "economic, social, political, and even military and strategic benefits to Cuba." He stated that President Roosevelt had expressed fear that Cuba might become "a victim of totalitarian influences," but that he, Batista, had assured the President that Cuba would "cling to democratic principles." [91] Batista also announced that an oral agreement reached in Washington would bring about a reduction in the United States tariff for Cuban sugar, together with lower Cuban duties on rice and other exports of the United States.[92] It seems safe to assume that the prestige acquired from this visit was of help to Batista in his first successful campaign for the presidency of Cuba in 1940.

CHAPTER IV

Origins of the Good Neighbor Policy

LATIN AMERICAN FEARS of intervention by the United States were not allayed by the friendly speeches of Presidents Hoover and Roosevelt. For some time after Hoover's good-will tour in 1928, Latin American statesmen and publicists demanded deeds in addition to words as evidence of the good faith of the United States. However, even such deeds as the evacuation of Marines from Nicaragua and the strictly shipboard role of the Marines in the Cuban affair were not enough to convince Latin Americans that intervention would be abandoned. They insisted that the policy of nonintervention be elevated to the level of a legally binding pledge of nonintervention. This Latin American demand had been successfully resisted by Charles Evans Hughes at the Havana Conference in 1928, but Cordell Hull recognized the political desirability of translating his own intention into a public promise not to intervene.

At the Montevideo Conference in 1933, therefore, Hull signed the Convention on Rights and Duties of States, article 8 of which declared: "No state has the right to intervene in the internal or external affairs of another." Further, Hull told the conference that "the United States government is as much opposed as any other government to interference with the freedom, the sovereignty, or other internal affairs or processes of the governments of other nations," and that "no government need fear any intervention on the part of the United States under the Roosevelt administration." [1] This pledge was based on assumptions that were only half formulated at the time, as is demonstrated by the United States reservation to article 8, which stated that the policy of the United States would follow the ideas embodied in speeches by Roosevelt and Hull, "and in the law of nations as generally recognized and accepted." This statement reflected, if not some uncertainty on Hull's part, a divergence of opinion among his advisers, some of whom opposed a sweeping renunciation of the right of intervention, particularly because of its possible weakening of the international standard of protection of nationals. What Hull's reservations really meant, therefore, was that the United States renounced the use of force in regard to domestic political affairs in Latin America but was not yet ready in a legally binding way to renounce the use of force for the protection of the lives or property of United States citizens in Latin America.

Hull's openness and sincerity of manner at Montevideo, combined with his signature of the Convention, met with a generally favorable response in Latin America, but the United States reservation gave rise to a new Latin American campaign for a complete renunciation of the right to intervene. This campaign culminated at the Buenos Aires Conference of 1936, but it would be a mistake to assume that the action of the United States at that conference was due simply to repeated demands from the Latin American governments. Between the two conferences, the Department of State underwent a second test of policy in Nicaragua from which it emerged with a new policy of noninterference. In part as a consequence of this experience, the United States government was fully prepared to accept without reservations an even stronger nonintervention obligation at Buenos Aires. The action at the conference, however, may be regarded primarily as a ratification of policy, rather than as the formation of policy; in Chapter V, the latter will be traced through several significant decisions affecting Central America from 1934 to 1936.

The suggestion that the Buenos Aires conference saw the ratification of policy, rather than its formation, should not be taken to mean that ratification was unimportant. It was regarded in Latin

America as of vital importance to secure a binding pledge of nonintervention by the United States. To Latin America such a pledge meant either the "burying" [2] of the Monroe Doctrine or the elevation of the Monroe Doctrine to the status of a principle accepted equally by all American states with respect to their extrahemispheric relationships and freed from the possibility that it might be interpreted unilaterally by the United States in order to justify interventions.[3] In this way, the Monroe Doctrine would lose its character as a "mystical social dogma" in the United States, and as a "taboo or hobgoblin" [4] in Latin America, and would regain the high regard in which it was held, as a theory of defense against European or other aggression, before the days of the Roosevelt Corollary.

In a broader sense, an unqualified pledge of nonintervention would affirm the respect of the United States for the principle of the legal equality of states, thus permitting all the Latin American countries to say with pride: "Now there are no little nations." [5]

In still a third way, a nonintervention pledge would remove from Latin American governments the fear, remaining after the Montevideo Conference, that the United States might employ its armed forces to protect its nationals or their property if endangered by disorder or by governmental action.

The form approved by the United States for the ratification of its policy of nonintervention is found in article 1 of the "Additional Protocol Relative to Non-Intervention": "The High Contracting Parties declare inadmissible the intervention of any one of them, directly or indirectly, and for whatever reason, in the internal or external affairs of any other of the Parties." [6] This formulation was regarded in Latin America as stronger than that approved at Montevideo, despite the use of the nontechnical expression "inadmissible" instead of the phrase "No State has the right . . ." Latin American commentators emphasized that this protocol was approved by the United States without reservations and that it was broader in scope than its predecessor because of the addition of the words "directly or indirectly."

One of the interesting features of the eagerness of the Latin

American countries to secure a pledge of nonintervention was the implied compliment to the integrity of the United States. A second feature was that Bolivia and Mexico undoubtedly counted upon the protocol for protection against intervention at the time of their successful actions in 1937 and in 1938 to gain control of the properties of oil companies within their jurisdictions. Action of this type had been feared by some members of the United States delegation to the Montevideo Conference, but by 1936 the Department of State had become so committed to the policy of nonintervention that it was willing to accept without protest or reservation the public ratification of that policy. The Bolivian and Mexican actions do not appear to have been anticipated in Washington, so it could hardly be said that such drastic measures were accepted as calculated risks. When the actions occurred, however, it does not appear that the Department contemplated for a moment the use of force, and, as will be seen, it gradually worked out pacific political solutions in both cases.

Whether, on the part of either the Bolivians or the Mexicans, plans had been laid for confiscation or expropriation before the Buenos Aires Conference met in 1936 is a question that cannot be fully answered on the basis of available information. Such foresight seems improbable although its possibility cannot be excluded. There is no question, however, that the Mexican delegation took the lead at Buenos Aires in pressing for the adoption of a new convention, and that there was considerable elation in Mexico City when that enterprise was successful. The head of the Mexican delegation at Buenos Aires, Francisco Castillo Nájera, stated that the protocol was "the principal objective of Mexico." [7] Later, when Castillo Nájera was asked whether Mexico had not feared intervention as a result of the oil expropriations, he said that Mexico had confidently relied upon the Buenos Aires protocol and on the good faith of President Roosevelt. [8]

It is also interesting to note that there was some difference of opinion in America, or at least some difference of emphasis as to the allocation of credit for the adoption of the protocol. The Mexican press understandably stressed the Mexican initiative [9] and quoted diplomats of other countries who had admitted Mexican authorship of the protocol. On the other hand, Dr. Manuel Castro Ramírez, the Salvadoran chief delegate, was quoted in *La Prensa* (San Salvador), January 21, 1937, as saying:

I who was always a determined opponent of imperialism, declare without reserve that the American policy has completely changed its direction, and that, as a result of the work of Roosevelt and Cordell Hull, it signifies the most absolute respect for all the peoples of America, condemning every kind of intervention.

A third view, expressed with that impersonal sense of social responsibility characteristic of *La Prensa* (Buenos Aires), one of the greatest newspapers of America, was that the protocol was the work of the conference as a collective body which "unanimously and without the slightest reservation condemned all acts of intervention in the life of a state." [10]

In the United States the tendency was to regard the terms of the protocol as a concession by the United States government. The prevailing attitude seemed to be that this concession was in the national interest since it was one of the several ways of promoting closer and more friendly political and commercial ties with other American countries. A minority view, maintained with considerable feeling, was that the United States had gone too far in abjuring intervention for the protection of United States farm owners, ranchers, and businessmen in Latin America.

The protocol was a form of words indicative of little more than inclination and intent, but policy was already being shaped by the growth of an understanding of the implications of this form of words and by the performance of acts in response to situations arising in Latin American countries. It is with this emergence of policy that Part Two of this study is concerned.

The Institution of Consultation

Another understanding reached at Buenos Aires that had significant consequences included the agreement that the American states "shall consult together for the purposes of finding and adopting methods of peaceful cooperation," if the peace of the

American republics were menaced.[11] This understanding was repeated in the Declaration of Lima, in 1938, with procedural addi-
tions to make it easier to convene a meeting.[12]

This was only an understanding, for there was no obligation to
consult, and it seemed insignificant to some of Hull's ready critics,
including the eminent Mexican statesman, José Vasconcelos, who
wrote that

> instead of the alliance, instead of the dream of a League of American
> Nations, he [Hull] has again, as at the Montevideo Conference, had to
> content himself with a vague declaration of principles regarding the de-
> fense of democracy and the cooperation of the nations of the New
> World in case of manifest European aggression, and nothing more.[13]

However, the bond of sympathy between the American governments in 1939 was sufficiently strong so that it did not require
binding institutional ties. Hull needed nothing more than a vague
declaration about consultation in 1939, for his country was gaining
the good will that disregarded legal gaps and invented ways of
collaboration when the time of crisis arrived. The results of the
Panama (1939), Havana (1940), and Rio de Janeiro (1942) meetings of ministers of foreign affairs gave ample evidence that,
Argentina apart, policy coordination in the pursuit of mutual aims
was possible for the American states without the previous definition of obligations in treaty terminology.

The Origins of the Good Neighbor Policy

During World War II the Good Neighbor policy came to be
regarded with general satisfaction in the United States. Some
fairly good-natured controversy, however, has arisen over the
assignment of credit for the origination of that policy.

Herbert Hoover, after reviewing Latin American relationships
during his administration, declared:

> As a result of these policies, carried on throughout my administration,
> the interventions which had been the source of so much bitterness and
> fear in Latin America were ended. We established a good will in Latin
> America not hitherto known for many years, under the specific term
> "Good Neighbor." [14]

Hoover renewed this assertion in supporting the Good Neighbor policy against the attack upon it made in 1943 by Senator Hugh Butler. On this same occasion, however, prominent members of the Republican party cited Elihu Root and Charles Evans Hughes as originators of the Good Neighbor policy,[15] and they were correct in recalling that the phrase "Good Neighbor" had been used by these statesmen. If the employment of a phrase were equivalent to the founding of a policy, credit might have been given to the Mexican Commissioners who negotiated the Treaty of Guadaloupe Hidalgo, establishing peace between Mexico and the United States in 1848, and who were apparently responsible for the inclusion, in the preamble, of the statement that the treaty should "assure the concord, harmony, and mutual confidence wherein the two peoples should live, as good neighbors." [16]

The fundatory declarations of Hoover have been supported by an agreement of scholars, a group hazardous to engage, especially when surrounded by multifloral verbiage and cloaked in a rising myth. The myth is that the Good Neighbor policy, commonly associated with the administrations of Roosevelt, was actually Hoover's creation.

The agreement offers several varying but congruent judgments that may be arranged in order of the strength of their support for Hooverian claims. One view refers to "Hoover's Good Neighbor policy" and declares that, in its essentials, "the Good Neighbor policy had its roots in the Hoover administration; Roosevelt only adopted and expanded it." [17] Others are: "Taken with other features of the Hoover-Stimson Latin American policy, it [the Clark Memorandum] warrants the assertion that those two statesmen laid the basis of the 'Good Neighbor policy' of the 1930's." [18] "In fact, the Good Neighbor policy was born under Hoover, though it was baptised and came to maturity under Roosevelt." [19] "Herbert Hoover completed the foundations for Franklin D. Roosevelt's Good Neighbor policy." [20]

An appraisal of the degree to which these claims may be valid requires a review of some features of Hoover's policy and of the early approach of Roosevelt to Latin America.[21]

After the Havana Conference of 1928, the government of the United States began, in a neighborly spirit, to take certain initiatives toward Latin America. The first move was ceremonial. In that year, between his election and his inauguration, Hoover visited ten countries in Central and South America, "for the purpose of paying friendly calls upon our neighbors to the south." [22] Hoover encountered some evidence of hostility in the form of demonstrations in certain countries, but he was courteously received by the officials of the ten countries he visited from Honduras to Chile, Argentina, and Brazil. The press was less hospitable in some countries than in others. Before Hoover left the United States on November 19, 1928, an editorial in *El Mercurio* (Santiago, Chile) of November 12 warned him that "in South America the Republican [party] is considered more frankly imperialistic than the Democratic party"; the paper hoped that the tour might make Hoover realize that "imperialism is damaging to the United States: it enrages the countries that suffer from it directly and creates jealousy, lack of confidence, mistrust, and animosity in all the others." However, in Guayaquil *El Telégrafo* on December 4 said that Hoover's visit had been welcomed "because of the important and spontaneous declarations he made for the welfare of Ecuador and Latin America, and in support of international morality, as well as for his favorable statements concerning aid by United States capitalists in the development of Ecuadoran industries." Personally, Hoover made a good impression on those who saw and talked with him, and a sympathetic response was enhanced by the presence of Mrs. Hoover.[23]

One incident occurred during the trip that had an immediate bearing on policy and was the cause of some embarrassment to Hoover. He was quoted by *La Epoca* (Buenos Aires), on December 18 as saying in an interview with President Hipólito Irigoyen of Argentina that "in future the United States government would never intervene in the internal affairs of other countries, but would respect their sovereignty." The paper suggested that Hoover had implied that he was not in accord with the policy followed by Coolidge. Secretary of State Kellogg inquired of Ambassador Robert Woods Bliss in Argentina about the editorial and asked whether Hoover intended to issue a statement on the subject.[24] Bliss replied that Hoover had not stated that he disagreed with Coolidge's policy; he had said that both he and Coolidge were opposed to intervention. The Ambassador had been authorized by Hoover to make a statement to the Argentine press, but he had thought it best not to call attention to the matter by starting a controversy.[25] Bliss added that he had talked with Irigoyen, who had agreed that Hoover had not made the statements attributed to him by *La Epoca;* the incident seems to have been no more than an effort by an enterprising journalist to create a stir.[26]

On the question of intervention, Hoover said publicly (New York *Times*, December 17, 1928) that "the fear of some persons concerning supposed intervention ideas of the United States are unfounded. The facts are gradually demonstrating more clearly and more fully that in my country there prevails no policy of intervention, despite any appearances of such an intention." This statement was greeted with satisfaction in Latin America; it found a mixed reception in the United States where the president-elect was thought by some to have prematurely commented on a question of foreign policy.

An interesting feature of the many speeches made by Hoover on his trip was his frequent reference to "Good Neighbors." He said, for example: "We have a desire to maintain not only the cordial relations of governments with each other but the relations of *good neighbors.*" [27]

In the area of active policy, it is a matter of record that the Hoover administration did not intervene in Cuba, and, although it was unable to escape criticism for keeping Marines in Nicaragua for four years, it withdrew them when it considered that obligations undertaken following the Coolidge intervention were discharged. Further, Hoover and Stimson adopted a policy that did not attempt to make use of nonrecognition as a method of unseating Latin American governments.

In the declaratory sphere of policy, Hoover stated publicly that "it ought not to be the policy of the United States to intervene *by force* to secure or maintain contracts between our citizens and foreign states or their citizens. Confidence in that attitude is the only basis upon which the economic cooperation of our citizens can be welcomed abroad. It is the only basis that prevents cupidity encroaching upon the weakness of nations—but, far more than this, it is the true expression of the moral rectitude of the United States." [28] He also, although apparently with some reluctance, permitted the publication of the well-known *Memorandum on the Monroe Doctrine*, by J. Reuben Clark.

Hoover's above-quoted remark, "We established a good will in Latin America not hitherto known for many years," is probably correct, at least if it were meant to point to a contrast between 1928 and 1933. It is, however, a comparative statement that does not necessarily claim that there was a substantial amount of good will existing in 1933, and it gives a different impression from that of Hull's equally partisan declaration that, in 1933, "our inheritance of ill will was grim." [29] It is also of interest to note that there were some expressions of regret in the Latin American press when Hoover was defeated in the election of 1932,[30] and during Hoover's administration there was evidence of a favorable response to the notable differences between his policies and those of Coolidge.[31]

On the other hand, Hoover labored under several serious disabilities in trying to develop good will in Latin America. In the first place, he was the leader of the Republican party, and "in Latin America the idea has been rather widespread that imperialist tendencies have had their most effective interpreters among the Republicans, while it has been understood that the Democrats have been generally opposed to imperialism." [32] It is an interesting phenomenon that, despite Wilson's interventions in Haiti, Mexico, and Santo Domingo, the Democratic party was generally regarded with greater good will than the Republican party. This attitude may be due to the linking of the latter with intervention or at least "interposition" to protect United States investors abroad, and by the difference in the public statements of the leaders of the two parties. The Republicans were identified with such catch phrases as "the big stick," "dollar diplomacy," and "I took Panama." The Democrats, despite Wilson's interventions, had avoided being labeled with easily remembered phrases resented by Latin Americans.[33]

The Republican party's unpopularity in Latin America might have been greatly reduced by Hoover had he been able to carry his policy through a second term, but four years was too short a time to overcome this handicap, particularly when it was aggravated by the continuation of the Nicaraguan intervention. Moreover, Hoover's term of office fell just between the Havana and Montevideo conferences of American states, so that he did not have an opportunity, such as Hull seized at Montevideo, to sign a pledge of nonintervention—an action that was in accord with Hoover's principles and practice.

Finally, the passage in 1930 of the Smoot-Hawley tariff, with Hoover's approval, aroused great antagonism in Latin America. *El Mundo* (Havana), February 18, 1936, declared that "insistent and ferocious protectionism had built a Chinese Wall between the United States and the republics of Central and South America." [34]

A review of the development of Roosevelt's thinking about Latin America may begin with an article he was asked to write as a campaign document for *Foreign Affairs* in 1928. Roosevelt gave serious attention to the article, and he received assistance in its composition from Norman H. Davis and Sumner Welles. His frame of mind in approaching it may be glimpsed from a letter to Senator Carter Glass: "Is it not time, in view of the Nicaraguan slaughter, to revive the Wilson Mobile speech and his invitation to other American republics to join with us in solving local difficulties?" [35]

In the article, Roosevelt stated:

The outside world views us with less good will today than at any previous period. This is serious unless we take the deliberate position that the people of the United States owe nothing to the rest of mankind and care nothing for the opinion of others so long as our seacoasts are impregnable and our pocketbooks are well filled.

Associating "dollar diplomacy" with the Republican party, he claimed that it had placed "money leadership ahead of moral leadership." Wilson, however, had restored "high moral purpose" to our international relationships.

Although praising Hughes's achievements at the Washington naval disarmament conference, he attacked the Republicans on other questions, and then turned to the subject of the Americas, "in many ways, most important of all." He admitted that the interventions in Haiti and the Dominican Republic, in the first of which he had played an important part, were "not another forward step," because little attention had been paid "to making the people there more capable of running their own governments." In Mexico, he reluctantly conceded that "we were better off" than in 1927, but he gave the credit to Dwight Morrow and Charles Lindbergh. Elsewhere throughout the Americas, however, recent policy "has allowed a dislike and mistrust of long standing to grow into something like positive hate and fear."

Concerning intervention, Roosevelt felt that, if a Latin American country should in future need "a helping hand to bring back order and stability," it was neither the right nor the duty of the United States to extend its hand alone, but only in association with other American republics, and "in the name of the Americas." "Single-handed intervention by us in the internal affairs of other nations must end; with the cooperation of others we shall have more order in this hemisphere and less dislike."

Referring to the "nine gray years" since 1919, Roosevelt claimed there had been bungling in Nicaragua and a failure in the Tacna-Arica dispute, and the only success that he saw was in Hughes's staving off a hostile majority on the nonintervention resolution at the Havana conference in 1928. Linking good will in Latin America to increased trade, he called for the opening of a new chapter in relations with that area. If the spirit behind United States leadership were great, the United States could "regain the world's trust and friendship," move once more toward a reduction of armaments, and "for all time renounce the practice of arbitrary intervention in the home affairs of our neighbors. It is the spirit, sir, which matters." [36]

Although this article was written as a campaign document, it is significant because it stated five themes that were dominant in the Latin American policy of his administration: (1) a deep concern for securing good will in Latin America; (2) the idea that good will would increase trade; (3) a favorable attitude toward working in association with Latin American states; (4) hostility to "arbitrary intervention" in the domestic affairs of Latin American countries; and (5) emphasis on "the spirit" of United States policy.

The remote and immediate origins of the Good Neighbor policy
in the thinking of Roosevelt were described by the President himself in 1942. He was asked by his Secretary, Stephen Early, to
dictate about five hundred words on the origin of the Good
Neighbor policy for use by Vice-President Henry A. Wallace in a
speech accepting for Roosevelt an award from *The Churchman*.
The President dictated the following statement, which is quoted
here in full since it has received little attention:

The origin of the Good Neighbor Policy dates back to a day in the
President's life when, as Assistant Secretary of the Navy at the beginning
of the first Wilson Administration, the United States realized that Mexico
had become critical. President Wilson decided that the insult to the
American Flag at Tampico was more than this country could tolerate,
in view of the unfriendly and undemocratic Administration then in power
in Mexico. The Fleet was ordered to take Vera Cruz, which United
States forces occupied for several months. History may show that this
whole episode was realistically necessary but the fact remains that many
were killed on both sides and the bad feeling throughout Latin America
created by this action lasted for a generation. The President has always
believed that the germ of the Good Neighbor Policy originated in his
mind at that time.

In 1915 the atrocious conditions in the Republic of Haiti, ending with
the brutal murder and cutting up of the President of Haiti, was causing
unrest in other parts of the Caribbean, including Cuba, Santo Domingo
and Jamaica. The United States, under a policy which had lasted for
many years, restored order both in Haiti and in Santo Domingo by sending
Marines there and by occupying both Republics for a long period.

In all of these operations, President Roosevelt was impressed with the
great emphasis placed on trade and finance in lieu of an approach from the
standpoint of the right of self-determination and the use of a quarantine
system for the restoration of order rather than the use of force in occupations. After he left Washington at that time, the President saw a rebirth
of dollar diplomacy and the occupation of Nicaragua.

Soon after he became Governor of New York the terrible depression,
starting in this country, spread all over the world, including Central and
South America, and during the next four years most of our discussions
with Latin America were still largely based on dollar diplomacy. This was
accentuated by the fact that during the period from 1925 to 1930 New
York banks, aided by the trips of Professor Kemmerer to various Republics, forced on most of these Republics unnecessary loans at exorbitant
interest rates and huge commission fees.

The President, therefore, began to visualize a wholly new attitude toward other American Republics based on an honest and sincere desire, first, to remove from their minds all fear of American aggression—territorial or financial—and, second, to take them into a kind of hemispheric partnership in which no Republic would obtain undue advantage.

After the President's election in the autumn of 1932, he discussed this subject with Senator Hull, Senator Robinson, and with a number of others.

In February, 1933, he began to formulate his Inaugural Address. In a discussion of the Address with Professor Moley he drew the analogy between the relations of the American Republics and the relations between a citizen in a small community with his own neighbors and said, "What we need in a small community is the man who is a good neighbor to the people he associates with every day." This use of the words "Good Neighbor" was seized by Professor Moley as just the right term, and the President put it into his first draft of the First Inaugural.[37]

This significant document shows signs of being hastily dictated and may not have been read by Roosevelt afterward. Among its interesting features are the linking of the origins of his conception of the Good Neighbor policy to the Vera Cruz incident and the definition of the two aims of the new policy—to banish the fear of territorial or financial aggression by the United States, and to form "a kind of hemisphere partnership." It is also of interest that, in 1942, when asked by Early to write about the Good Neighbor policy, Roosevelt not only accepted the invitation and himself applied the phrase only to Latin America, but stated that its immediate origin in the first inaugural address was to be found in a discussion about the American republics. In that address, the policy of the Good Neighbor was related to the whole "field of foreign policy," and, at first, Roosevelt hoped that his declaration might find a response throughout the world. However, in Europe there was no affirmative response from Germany or Italy, and in Asia Japan remained unmoved. It was with Latin America that the policy quickly became identified, and it is therefore understandable that Roosevelt in 1942 should emphasize the Latin American origins of the policy ideas as well as of the phrase itself.

The source of the diversity both of statesmen's claims and historians' interpretations resides in a confusion between objectives and policy. Hoover and Roosevelt earnestly desired to establish and maintain friendly relations with the Latin American states, and the use of the term "Good Neighborly" to describe the attitudes of both would probably receive general approbation. The actions of the two administrations, however, differed so significantly that the claim that the term "the Good Neighbor policy" applies to both, or the assertion that Hoover's policy was "only adopted and expanded" by Roosevelt, refuses to grant the word "policy" its customary meaning. Such contentions require the demonstration of continuity in policy, and such demonstration is difficult.

If the Roosevelt administration had admitted or declared that it was maintaining the policy of its predecessor, the question would be easy, but it did not do so. Instead, it appeared to feel that new and different policies must be found to overcome the political antagonism and economic resentment that Cordell Hull said he found in Latin America when he came to office. He declared that long before March 4, 1933, he had "resolved that one of our principles in dealing with Latin America would be religious adherence to the principle of nonintervention," and that he and Roosevelt had "for some years . . . already been thinking on the same line." [38]

The question of continuity does not arise with regard to the highest policy objective since both Hoover and Roosevelt gave primacy to nonintervention. Hoover's declarations were clouded by the presence of Marines in Nicaragua until two months before the end of his administration, but his Cuban policy demonstrated the tenacity of his attachment to nonintervention.

It is, rather, with regard to lesser objectives and the policies initiated to attain them that the question of continuity may be raised. Hoover and Stimson refused to regard any mitigation of the tyranny of Machado in Cuba as a policy objective of the government of the United States, and apparently on the basis of their experience in Nicaragua they had shunned intermeddling in Cuba. Roosevelt and Hull, on the other hand, regarded the Cuban situation in 1933 as intolerable, and Welles was sent to Havana to try to bring about a "truce" between the contending political factions. By such intermeddling and, later, by refusing to recognize the Grau San Martín regime, Roosevelt reversed two policies followed by Hoover. By pursuing the objectives of political reform in Cuba through the adoption of these policies, Roosevelt was brought to the verge of intervention when Welles requested the landing of Marines. He decided not to intervene, but it was not until then that he appreciated the extraordinary difficulty of combining a policy of interference in Cuban politics with a policy of nonintervention.

The Cuban experience, then, demonstrated that the Roosevelt administration did not adopt, build upon, or follow the policies of its predecessor. Subsequent analysis of this experience persuaded Hull and Welles that avoidance of intervention required noninterference, but, again, this was a lesson self-learned and not borrowed from Hoover or Stimson.

As for other features of the policy of the Roosevelt administration, notably the reduction of duties under the Trade Agreements Act of 1934, there seems little reason to maintain that these were "expansions" of policies of the Hoover administration. Stimson and Hoover were able to engage in policy retreats, but, committed to a high tariff policy, they had none of the freedom of movement in the direction of positive policies of cooperation that was enjoyed by their successors.

Despite these policy differences, one common motivation toward the formation of Good Neighborly attitudes may have originated, oddly enough, in the administration of Calvin Coolidge. The intent of the articulate public that force should not be used by the United States in dealings with Latin American countries had been clearly expressed in the Mexican dispute and the Nicaraguan intervention in 1927. Although Coolidge and Stimson had protested against public criticism and alleged misunderstanding of their policies, they had finally moulded their policies in accord with the popular will. The 1927 outburst, although it is rarely mentioned in official correspondence, was memorable enough to have left lasting impressions, and it seems reasonable to assume that it created an atmosphere or policy climate favorable to the growth of friendly and pacific relationships as the alternatives to intervention and other forms of coercion. Thus Hughes at the Havana Conference in 1928, retreated from intervention to "interposition"; thus Hoover visited Latin America at the end of the same year to talk with his "Good Neighbors." As an alternative to force, if investments were to thrive and commerce increase, some stable and mutually acceptable set of new relationships had to be established. Given the situation when he came to office, the time at his disposal, and his political orientation, President Hoover made certain moves toward such relationships.

Starting with different policies, President Roosevelt discovered they brought him to the verge of a pre-1927 intervention, and these policies were consequently changed. In other ways the policies of the two administrations were different, but with respect to nonintervention they became similar, because their inspiration was derived from the two common sources of popular antipathy to the use of force in Latin America and from separate, but similarly unhappy, experiences with policies of interference.

Among Latin Americans the impression was widespread that the Roosevelt administration, and consequently the Democratic party, was solely responsible for the changes in policy that became associated with the idea of the Good Neighbor. Despite the occasional appreciations of Hoover's policies that appeared in the Latin American press, and despite the occasional comments of informed observers such as Bauer Aviles and J. M. Yepes,[39] the prevailing view credited the Roosevelt administration with the new orientation of policy that won general approval in Latin America. *El Plata* (Montevideo), May 21, 1936, expressed the fear that the Republican party, which under "Coolidge and Hoover had opened such a deep abyss between the United States and the other nations of America," might return to power. This was a common theme of newspaper comment during the 1930s. When, in 1945, Ambassador Spruille Braden said in a speech at the Universidad del Litoral at Santa Fé, Argentina, that the Good Neighbor policy had begun as early as 1928, a Central American diplomat stated that "most Latin Americans had been unaware that it originated prior to 1933." [40] On February 28, 1936, the prestige of *La Prensa* (Buenos Aires) was lent to the view that President Roosevelt "initiated the 'Good Neighbor' policy," which had given happy results in the Americas, and other papers expressed similar opinions.[41]

It is possible that, given a longer period as president, Herbert Hoover would have followed policies toward Latin America that would have been generally recognized as being indeed Good

Neighborly. The temper of the American people manifested during the Nicaraguan intervention as well as the course of world affairs then and afterward were conducive to the development of a different policy in the Americas. The Hoover administration had shown itself responsive to the new situation, notably in Stimson's decision to protect United States citizens only along the Nicaraguan coast, but it did not find it possible to make positive moves toward collaboration with Latin American nations, particularly in the field of economic relationships. If Hoover's claim and that of his supporters were not that he had founded or initiated the Good Neighbor policy but that he had followed certain lines of action which were consonant with the requirements of a Good Neighborly attitude, there would be few who would disagree. Roosevelt ultimately came to similar conclusions, but he, with Hull and Welles, gave up intervention as a legal right, developed new policy ideas, and over a span of twelve years created confidence among Latin Americans that pre-1928 policies would not be revived. His lines of action were approved by Hoover and nearly all other leaders of the Republican party, so that the policy known as that of the Good Neighbor received strong bipartisan support by the end of 1941.

In this sense, three administrations each played a part in transforming the peaceful desires of the people of the United States into policies in which all have reason to claim some, if different, shares. There is satisfaction here for members of both political parties, and little reason for political argument, whether to salvage or maintain the reputation of individuals.

CHAPTER V

The Policy of Noninterference

BY THE POLICY of nonintervention and by its pledge at the Buenos Aires Conference, the government of the United States meant that it would not employ its armed forces in support of its objectives in Latin American, particularly Caribbean, countries. Adoption of this policy did not mean, of course, that the United States also gave up all means of influencing Latin American governments in all spheres of policy. In one sense, indeed, influence was undivestible. It was a radiation, for the prestige and the economic power of the United States were so great that governments around the Caribbean would have based some policies on their anticipation of Washington's reactions even had the Department of State declined to express its attitudes.

In its exercise of influence after 1933, the Department distinguished between the foreign and the domestic affairs of the Latin American states. By foreign affairs, it meant those relationships in which the United States government had a special interest, such as economic policy, the treatment of the persons and investments of United States citizens, and, in the later 1930s, issues of hemisphere defense. To attain its objectives in this sphere, a new policy of reciprocity was developed as a form of influence; this will be described in Part Three. In relations among the Latin American states themselves, the United States largely limited itself to impartial participation in conciliation in the Chaco, Leticia, and Marañon conflicts and in several Central American boundary controversies. The role played by the United States in these disputes was entirely consistent with the policy of noninterference.

By domestic affairs of the Latin American states the Department of State meant internal politics, including all matters relating to party struggles and revolutions. In this sphere, a new policy was also developed between 1927 and 1936, one that may be called the policy of noninterference. The policy of nonintervention renounced one technique, the use of armed force, for the pursuit of any and all policy objectives.[1] The policy of noninterference renounced any and all techniques of influence for the pursuit of certain former policy objectives. These latter objectives were the spread of democratic institutions in Latin America and the avoidance of situations usually described as instability, chaos, or anarchy. Democracy and stability in Latin America continued to be desired in Washington, but they ceased to be objectives of policy since no direct measures were taken to achieve them. It was possible, of course, that the example provided by the political institutions of the United States might inspire imitation or that increased commerce resulting from the reciprocal trade agreements might enhance political stability, but these were indirect influences indeed.

As with nonintervention, noninterference also found its origin in practice and improvisation, rather than in principle. In principle, if not in practice, the right of intervention was upheld throughout the Hoover administration. Interference, in the form of advice, warnings, and other types of tutelage, lay in the sphere of political relationships rather than in that of law, and, except in Cuba, it was indulged in when judged opportune. When the Roosevelt administration came to office, it showed no disinclination to interfere, and it reversed Stimson's policy of detachment in Cuba. However, its involvement there did not encourage it to make further experiments at intermeddling by ambassadors unsupported by the Marine Corps. In Washington the Cuban experience gave rise to the realization that interference was capable of creating situations where intervention might become unavoidable. One intervention, or even the repetition of the admonitory naval display off Cuba might wither blossoms of good will cultivated in other ways. Therefore, if the policy of nonintervention and the pledge of Montevideo were to be maintained inviolate, it was essential that interference, which created responsibility for political developments, should cease.

Not again would anything like the "moralization" program of General Enoch H. Crowder be attempted in Cuba or anywhere else. No more would special United States envoys swoop down on Central America and hold conferences of warring politicians on the decks of United States naval vessels. Not only were such obvious assumptions of superiority and predominance forsworn, but the Department of State by 1936 entered upon a policy of nearly complete neutrality in the domestic political affairs of its neighbors. The nature and scope of this policy of noninterference is of long range political significance, and it has given rise to a good deal of criticism not only by Latin American political exiles and opposition parties, but also by some sectors of public opinion in the United States.

The policy of noninterference was not, of course, applied immediately nor with the same rigor in all countries. The Department of State felt responsible for the Mendieta administration in Cuba and advice and counsel were given to it by Ambassador Caffery. In Nicaragua where intermeddling had become almost habitual, the United States Minister continued for at least two years after 1933 in an active tutelary role. Here, as in Cuba, the experience ultimately, although not immediately, fortified a determination to refrain from interference.

In the Nicaraguan election of 1932, supervised by United States Marines, Juan B. Sacasa, the revolutionary of 1926, was elected president. The Guardia, trained by the Marines in order to maintain internal peace and assure free elections in Nicaragua, was placed in command of General Anastasio Somoza. It was generally believed in Nicaragua, and in the circumstances it seems highly probable, that Somoza was chosen either by, or in consultation with, the United States Minister, Matthew E. Hanna. Somoza was an able officer who spoke English and had received a part of his education in the United States, and these considerations may have made him appear more likely than other candidates to promise to give strictly military, as distinct from political, leadership to the Guardia.

When the Marines were withdrawn on January 2, 1933, the Department of State announced that the "special relationship" between the United States and Nicaragua had terminated and that command of the Guardia had been given over to Nicaraguans. The two presidential candidates in the 1932 elections had made an agreement to insure the nonpolitical character of the Guardia, which had "developed into a well-disciplined and efficient organization with a high *esprit de corps.*" [2]

Secretary Hull was asked at the Montevideo Conference by the Nicaraguan Foreign Minister, Leonardo Argüello, whether the Department of State would consent to the desire of the Nicaraguan government to "reorganize the National Guard." This request was a warning signal, for it probably meant in essence that President Sacasa was having trouble controlling General Somoza and was seeking a way to remove him from command of the Guardia. If "consent" were given by Washington, Sacasa's hand would be strengthened. The opinion of the Department, transmitted to Hull by Sumner Welles, was that it could not make an official comment on the reorganization of the Guardia any more than on comparable action by any other sovereign state.

This incident illustrates the first step in the development of the policy of noninterference, namely, the avoidance by the Department of State of official, written expressions of opinion or advice on internal political affairs of Caribbean countries. This step toward irresponsibility or impartiality was an easy one.

However, when a copy of this message was sent by Welles to Minister Arthur Bliss Lane in Managua, Welles added:

It is the Department's opinion, nevertheless, that the continued maintenance of a Guardia Nacional organized substantially as at present is important to the future peace and welfare of Nicaragua, and it believes that the maintenance of the nonpartisan principle, in particular, constitutes one of Nicaragua's strongest guarantees of peace.[3]

It was more difficult for officials in the Department of State to refrain from authorizing informal, conversational remarks of "concern" or "distress" or "encouragement" by the chiefs of mission in the Caribbean area. Further, it was for a time quite impossible for those chiefs of mission, besieged by local politicians for some sign of favor of the United States government, to keep from listening, advising, and warning. Ministers such as Hanna and Lane had matured in the foreign service in an era when it was regarded as the duty of the United States Minister to tell an ambitious Central American president that he should not pack a legislature to change a constitution to give himself a second term, or to confer with a frustrated member of the opposition who was known to be planning a revolution and urge on him the desirability of avoiding the use of violence.

A striking example of the enduring quality of established diplomatic practices in Nicaragua, as well as of the animosity they could create against the United States, was offered by the activities of Minister Arthur Bliss Lane only two months after the Montevideo Conference. In February, 1934, General Sandino came to Managua to talk with President Sacasa about the termination of an agreement of February 2, 1933, which had allowed Sandino to maintain an armed force—"a state within a state," as Sacasa called it. Friction had developed between Sandino and General Somoza, and Sandino refused to turn over his arms to the Guardia, which, he declared with some reason, was an "unconstitutional" force since it had been established and maintained under the authority of an executive decree rather than by legislative enactment. Given the revolutionary traditions of political life in Nicaragua and the characters and positions of Sandino and Somoza, civil strife before the elections of 1936 seemed highly probable.

Somoza, however, had other plans. On the night of February 21, 1934, in Managua, Sandino was murdered by members of the Guardia acting under orders from Somoza.[4] During that day, Lane had talked with Somoza at the legation, and at Somoza's home. In the evening, after the murder, at Sacasa's request, Lane not only agreed to try to persuade Somoza to go to the President's residence, but he took Somoza there in his own car and remained with the two men during their interview. Three days before the murder, Lane had attended a baseball game with Somoza.

Lane, of course, had nothing to do with the murder of Sandino. He had, however, known that something might happen to Sandino, and his talks with Somoza were in the nature of urgent efforts to prevent harm to Sandino. He reported in sincere if not entirely fortunate phraseology that Somoza had given him "his word of honor on four separate occasions—the last at 6 P.M. on February 21—that he would take no action against Sandino without my consent." A year later Lane reported:

When I recall that twice on February 21, 1934, Somoza gave me his "word of honor" (he used that expression in English) that he would take no violent action against Sandino—at a moment when he was actually perfecting the plans for Sandino's murder—I cannot place great confidence in his promises.[5]

Curiously enough, however, the tone of Lane's reports suggests that he had not expected that the mere fact of his having associated with Somoza would give rise to what he called the "apparently growing and strong feeling that I conspired with Moncada and Somoza to have Sandino killed." [6] This feeling arose in other Caribbean countries as well, where the assumption was made that the United States government was supporting the Guardia and therefore Somoza, "as contrasted with the government," in a tense, but peaceful, struggle for political control of the country.[7]

The following year Lane was confronted with a proposal from his Mexican colleague in Managua that Mexico and the United States should cooperate to improve relations between Sacasa and Somoza, principally by telling Somoza that "he cannot be President." The Mexican Chargé, Octavio Reyes Spindola, supported his proposal with an embarrassing argument: "It would be most unfortunate for the prestige of the United States in Latin America if Somoza, known to have been responsible for the death of Sandino—a hero in Latin America, yet a mortal enemy of the United States—was to become President. It would be said that the United States had put him in power as a reward for having killed Sandino." Lane replied that he would have nothing to do with this proposal, and as dean of the diplomatic corps he refused to convoke it for any mediatory purpose. He added that "if anything untoward" should happen after action by the diplomatic corps, its members and the United States government in particular would be blamed. To Reyes Spindola he said: "The criticism of what I had tried to do to help in the Sandino situation was still too fresh in my mind to be caught again. 'Once bitten twice shy.' " [8]

Lane's caution in this instance appears to have been due primarily to his determination to avoid any public, official action that could be construed as interference in Nicaraguan politics,[9] for he continued privately and informally to consult with and to offer advice to Nicaraguan politicians about the coming presidential elections. In so doing he appeared to be acting in accordance with the previously mentioned course suggested by Welles in connection with the reorganization of the Guardia.[10] However, the distinction between these two types of interference was apparently not entirely clear, and it was difficult to maintain in practice. On two occasions, Lane attempted to draw the distinction in general terms and to place specific instances in the framework of general policy.

The first of these occasions arose when, in the spring of 1934, the Nicaraguan Foreign Minister told Lane that Secretary Hull had said at Montevideo that the Department of State had no objection to the reorganization of the Guardia. In reply to Lane's report, Hull said that Argüello had "evidently misunderstood" him, and he repeated that the Department would express no opinion on this matter.[11] Lane approved this position, but, probably with his continuing advisory activities in mind, he endeavored to relate these to the Good Neighbor policy:

I consider, however, that it is not inconsistent with the Department's policy and on the other hand that it is in harmony with the President's policy of the "Good Neighbor" for me to do all I can through personal conversations to calm those persons whose ambitions and passions may lead them to commit acts which might have a disastrous effect on the well being of the country.[12]

A little later, elevating both lines of action to the plane of general policies, Lane wrote:

There has been at times some question in my mind as to how the "Hands Off" and "Good Neighbor" policies should or may be reconciled. I feel . . . that we should not interfere in Nicaraguan internal affairs; should we feel, however, that a word from us might serve to maintain the peace of the country and consequently avoid bloodshed and disorder, we should not refrain from assuming the responsibility of the "Good Neighbor" by expressing our views, preferably as the personal views of our diplomatic representative.

This interpretation of policy was formally approved by Sumner Welles on behalf of the Secretary of State.[13]

In the following year, Lane's cautionary influence appears to have been decisive in preventing the execution of a would-be assassin of Somoza, an action which, if carried out, might have brought about civil war.[14] Again, Lane's action was approved by Welles, who said that Lane's "wise and friendly counsel aided materially in preventing the development of a situation of great danger to Nicaragua, which might likewise prejudice American interests in that country." [15]

It thus seemed that, with the sanction of the Department of State, or at least that of Sumner Welles, the Good Neighbor policy was to consist of two elements: an official, formal policy of noninterference and an unofficial, informal policy of "responsibility" through which the chiefs of mission in the Caribbean countries would make known the desires of the Department for peace and order and, perhaps, would also impart some suggestions as to how these goals could best be achieved.

However, there appeared to be some doubt among highly placed officials in Washington as to the validity of the distinction between these two types of interference, and these differences subsequently resulted in a significant policy shift. A sharp contrast between the activities of Lane in Managua, as approved by Welles in mid-1935, and the line followed by officials in the Department itself was demonstrated in the autumn of that year by the remarks of Willard L. Beaulac, assistant chief of the Division of Latin American Affairs, to a delegation sent by President Sacasa in an attempt to gain the support of the Department in his growing struggle with General Somoza. Beaulac wrote that for two hours Federico Sacasa, the head of the delegation, "endeavored to induce me to give him some 'advice' with reference to the situation in Nicaragua," contending that the United States had some responsibility for what the Guardia did, since "we created it." Beaulac rejected this argument along with one that "advice" would not constitute "intervention." Beaulac would say no more than that he hoped peace would be preserved in Nicaragua, and that "the only durable peace would be one arrived at through the efforts of the Nicaraguans themselves." In closing his account of the talk, Beaulac wrote: "Our conversation was of the friendliest nature, and as we parted Dr. Sacasa said that he regretted that I hesitated to give him advice. I said that there was no hesitation at all on my part; that I was determined not to give him advice." [16]

Lack of success with Beaulac did not deter Federico Sacasa from carrying his appeal to higher authority; he called on Sumner Welles and received essentially the same response. He said that what he desired from the Department was neither intervention nor interference, but only its "friendly moral assistance" such as "some expression of the friendly interest of the United States in seeing Nicaragua work out her problems satisfactorily." Welles replied that if the Department made any such declaration "this would be regarded as intervention or interference in Nicaraguan affairs." [17]

These views were expressed within a few days of Lane's having reported that, although "intervention is a thing of the past," unless he were instructed to the contrary, he would "endeavor personally to prevent any ill-advised action tending to disturb the peace of the country." [18] There appeared to be less than a full meeting of minds between Washington and Managua as to the nature of non-interference.

The uncertainty about the Good Neighbor policy that had bothered Lane in 1934 was also a source of worry on the part of the Minister in El Salvador, Frank P. Corrigan, and his request for enlightenment resulted in the working out of a theory and declaration of noninterference that remained for many years the accepted policy of the United States government. Corrigan asked the Department in January, 1936, "for an instruction which might begin to develop or clarify to this and other missions similarly situated the positive aspects of the Good Neighbor policy." [19] Corrigan said he was concerned because "powerful dictatorially inclined leaders" were taking a cynical attitude toward constitutional government since they felt that the "nonintervention feature of the Good

Neighbor policy [gave] them a free hand in the reestablishment of the old order of rule by force." Corrigan felt that the Department might desire to take "possible preventive steps" in view of undesirable political developments in El Salvador, and his statement of the policy problem is important enough to deserve quotation:

The powerful influence of our missions is an established fact which leads political elements in these countries, and the public as well, to expect either opposition or cooperation. A completely negative position is unlikely of acceptance and subject to misinterpretation. Failure of a mission to use its influence constructively may become a sin of omission with consequences fully as grievous as the former sins of commission. . . . Liberal elements, some of which have been formerly active critics of the United States and bitter opponents of intervention have indicated to me that the cooperation (by diplomatic means) of the United States is more than welcome when it seeks to retain progress, and prevent bloodshed and the establishment of autocratic regimes and actual setting up of dictatorships such as the Machado regime in Cuba and the Gómez dictatorship in Venezuela. They feel that a liberal government, like that of the United States with its immense power and moral influence, should lend its aid and cooperation in every peaceful way to retain progress and ideals and to aid the evolution of these countries toward real democratic republican government such as at present exists in Costa Rica.

Corrigan's despatch gave rise to differences of opinion within the Department of State that concerned the fundamental nature of the Good Neighbor policy. The questions it raised were probably given point by riots in Nicaragua in February, 1936, and by renewed intermeddling on the part of Minister Lane, who told President Sacasa: "I must insist, as Dean of the Diplomatic Corps and American Minister, that order be maintained for the protection of the lives and property of American and other foreigners." Sacasa complained to Lane that General Somoza was refusing to obey orders, and Lane agreed to talk with Somoza "and ascertain whether appropriate measures had been taken to guarantee order." [20] Shortly afterward, Lane was replaced as Minister by Boaz Long, who was instructed to refrain from interfering in Nicaraguan politics "even though such interference is requested or suggested by Nicaraguans." Hull stated further: "I am firmly convinced that it is essential not only to decline comment or advice, but scrupulously to avoid giving ground for belief that this government is taking any part in Nicaragua's domestic affairs." [21]

However, despite the Nicaraguan situation, when Assistant Secretary Welles came to comment on Corrigan's despatch, he wrote that he had for some time been "unhappy" because of his realization of the existence of the facts reported by Corrigan, and he considered that "the personal influence of the American Minister, if exerted tactfully, quietly, and without publicity, and with regard to matters that affect the general relations between the Central American republics, and, inferentially, their individual or joint relations with the United States, should be of the utmost value." He added that "noninterference should not be considered as a negation of helpful and friendly advice on matters in which the Central American republics and ourselves, as well as, in a broad sense, all of the American republics, have a legitimate interest." [22]

This view of Welles's was opposed by Laurence Duggan, chief of the Division of Latin American Affairs. Duggan, who thought it would be desirable to prepare "a clarification of the basis upon which our relations with the Central American republics are to rest," did not consider that United States diplomatic representatives should be permitted to "use their discretion" along the lines Welles had suggested. Duggan argued that in many delicate situations "no action will be better than action the precise consequences of which cannot be foreseen," and that it might not be possible for United States diplomats "to maintain an impartial attitude" when in the midst of a local situation. In the second place, the opinion of a minister, even when expressed in his personal capacity, "is usually taken to mean the considered judgment of this government and is given great if not conclusive weight." Thirdly, Duggan maintained that it would be unwise to give discretion in a general instruction as suggested by Welles, because the "abilities and standing" of United States ministers varied greatly. "On more than one occasion inept handling of situations by our own representatives has not only served to make these situations worse but has resulted in embarrassment for and intense criticism of the United States." [23]

A subsequent talk between the two men resulted in a fundamental change in Welles's position. He requested Duggan to prepare an instruction stating that, "in their official relations with the governments to which they are accredited," United States ministers in Central America "should conduct themselves exactly as if they were dealing with one of the great republics of the south or with any non-American power; that is to say, that they should religiously abstain from offering advice as regards any domestic question and that, if they are requested to give such advice, they should refuse to take any action except upon specific instruction from the Department of State."

Welles continued to maintain that "the personal confidence which our ministers may inspire in the officials of the republic where they are stationed should be a power for good if properly exercised," but he agreed with Duggan that "in the last analysis activities of this kind should only be undertaken when specific authorization is given by the Department in special cases. The only way to handle this, of course, is through personal conferences and not through official instructions." Welles did not think Minister Long should become "embroiled" in the existing Nicaraguan political controversy, nor should any minister use his "personal good offices" in any other Central American country. "We will, therefore, make no exceptions to the general prohibitions until and unless we think the situation demands it and the man on the spot capable of keeping within the required limit of tact and discretion."

Welles considered the proposed instruction to be "a very important one, since to all intents and purposes it constitutes a new precedent." He did not wish it to be worded so as to give an impression that the United States was "assuming a sterile policy of aloofness, but rather that it wishes to carry out in all sincerity a policy of constructive and effective friendship solely provided that neither this government nor its representative are drawn into any domestic concerns of any one of the Central American republics." [24]

The resultant instruction of April 30, 1936, sent to the ministers in Costa Rica, El Salvador, Guatemala, Honduras, and Nicaragua, embodied the Department's decision that the policy of the United

States would no longer be "guided" by article II of the General Treaty of Peace and Amity in extending or denying recognition to Central American governments.[25] The instruction also declared the "considered policy" of the Department on the attitude to be taken by United States representatives abroad when "they are requested, or there appears to be an opportunity, to use their influence or good offices" in connection with internal political situations or with relations between Central American states. The view had been expressed, it stated, that "the friendly advice or good offices of our representatives might be helpful in overcoming situations apparently prejudicial to the country or countries concerned, and that such action on the part of our representatives would constitute real assistance within the meaning of the Good Neighbor policy."

Concerning informal advice relating to "purely internal affairs" in these countries, the Department expected its representatives "to abstain from offering advice on any domestic question, and, if requested to give such advice, they should decline to do so." It was noted that governments or important elements in the Central American countries had in the past shown a tendency to "seek our advice," and that in many cases

we have yielded to the requests of those Governments or groups. *It has usually developed, however, that such advice rapidly came to be considered as intervention and, in fact, sometimes terminated in actual intervention. The result in a majority of cases was that, at the best, doubtful assistance was rendered to the governments, and the relations of the United States with those governments, and with other Latin American governments, were actually prejudiced.*

This instruction, signed by Secretary Hull, closed by stating that the Department of State was in this manner

in the fullest sense, applying the Good Neighbor policy to Central America. This government is desirous of carrying on with the Central American republics a policy of constructive and effective friendship, based upon mutual respect for each other's rights and interests. It would obviously be incompatible with this policy to become involved in the domestic concerns of any of the Central American republics. It has been adequately demonstrated that there is great danger that such involvement in matters which are not directly of concern to us will prejudice not only the interests of the United States in Central America, but the interests of the countries of Central America as well.[26]

This policy of abstention from interference, normally followed in the countries of South America, was extended also to the other Latin American states, including Mexico, Cuba, the Dominican Republic, Haiti, and Panama. The adoption of this policy clearly indicated that the Department had become wary of the ease of taking a downward path from interference to intervention, and it also reflected a feeling that previous interventions had both failed to promote democracy and had been harmful to friendly relations among the American states.

The new policy was applied immediately. Within two weeks of the date of the instruction, an official of the Salvadoran foreign office expressed concern to Corrigan about the Nicaraguan situation; Corrigan told him that the United States attitude would be one of "complete and friendly detachment." Corrigan commented that the official appeared to be "nonplussed and did not want to believe it—so strong is tradition! I emphasized the sincerity of our 'hands off' policy and apparently convinced him. But the suspicion lingered in my mind that he was a man convinced against his will but of the same opinion still." [27]

Disbelief in Central America about the noninterference policy could hardly have survived for long after 1936, for in that year, despite earnest entreaties from Nicaragua and elsewhere, the United States refused to exercise any influence in the revolution and subsequent election that brought General Somoza to power.

As early as May, 1935, it was learned that General Somoza was determined to become president in 1936, and the Department of State had to withstand an avalanche of requests for interference. In May, 1936, Hull was asked by the Nicaraguan Chargé to say "anything possible" to avoid a revolutionary outbreak. Hull said:

there was not a single word I could say about the domestic affairs of Nicaragua, either pro or con; that the attitude of the twenty-one nations towards each other, I felt sure, was a hope and a prayer for the good welfare of each and for the fullest measure of success for the people in each country . . . . all of our twenty-one nations had been steadily preaching the doctrine of noninterference with the domestic affairs of each other and naught could be said or done that would lend color to the opposing view.[28]

This policy of "a hope and a prayer" was maintained by the Department of State with nearly complete rigidity. Minister Boaz Long was instructed not to make "any statement, however informal, with reference to the internal political situation, or in any other manner endeavor to influence events in Nicaragua." [29] The days of the "responsible Good Neighbor" as interpreted by Lane in Nicaragua had definitely come to an end.

Thinking ahead, the Department determined that, if the situation in Nicaragua should become so critical

as to threaten life and property, and, if requested by all contending factions, this government would consider the possibility of rendering some assistance, but that this government would not act alone, but only in company with a group of nations, and that even under these circumstances this government would not take the initiative.[30]

Civil war broke out in Nicaragua on May 31, and General Somoza was in complete control of the country by June 8. Although President Sacasa had repeatedly asked the United States for help, none was given, and, of course, General Somoza made no request for good offices. Indeed, the above conditions made it utterly impossible for the United States to "render some assistance," for, once convinced that the United States would not interfere except at the request of all factions, that faction which had most hope of winning would never request assistance.

Although the officials in Washington do not appear to have relaxed the austerity of their view of the policy of noninterference, they had to withstand one more appeal by Corrigan, who wished to try to prevent President Maximiliano Martínez of El Salvador from getting himself reelected by changing the constitution to permit a second term. Returning to the charge, Corrigan said: "There arises in this instance the old question of reconciliation of the completely cold 'hands off' interpretation as against the warmer implications which seem to me to be inherent in the 'Good Neighbor policy.' " Although "forcible intervention" was a thing of the past, still "the moral influence of this and other missions in the American republics continues to be a potent factor which can be utilized for good ends. I am sure no American would wish these missions to lose prestige so long as that prestige is based on good will and fair dealing." However, "a negative attitude" in this case could have "a positive result" by Martínez's continuance in office, and Corrigan suggested that there was "a moral responsibility implicit in the interpretation of the 'Good Neighbor' policy. The simile of a fire in the neighbor's barn is here in point." Corrigan appealed to past practice by recalling Welles's approval of Lane's interference in Nicaragua in May, 1934,[31] and he asked for the Department's instructions "with relation to the deeper and more positive implications of our established continental policy of the 'Good Neighbor.' "[32] The Department, however, dashed cold water on Corrigan's burning desire to do good in El Salvador; Welles instructed him to be guided by the instruction of April 30, 1936:

If this government is not to become involved in the internal political situation in El Salvador, it is obvious that we must avoid expressing opinions or giving suggestions with reference to internal politics in that country. It is believed that you can consistently decline to comment on the developing situation without in any way impairing the prestige of your mission.[33]

This occasion appears to have been the last time before the outbreak of World War II that the policy of noninterference, as laid down in the instruction of April 30, 1936, was questioned by an officer of the Foreign Service. Here and elsewhere that policy was maintained, whether or not it was a "sterile policy of aloofness," as Welles had suggested it should not be. Aloof it was, and aloof it remained.

The policy of noninterference was known and appreciated outside diplomatic circles. *La Prensa* (Buenos Aires) of July 9, 1936, praised President Roosevelt for having "proven" the Good Neighbor policy not only by withdrawing troops from Latin American states, but also for having refused to comply with "requests and suggestions made by Latin American politicians seeking at least the friendly influence of his government." Such requests and suggestions continued to be made occasionally after 1936,[34] but they were uniformly rejected.

The governments in Latin America were of course unanimously in favor of nonintervention, and with only occasional lapses or doubts they approved the policy of noninterference. That policy, however, was strongly criticized by certain elements of public opinion in the United States and elsewhere, principally because the influence of the United States was thereby prevented from having any adverse effect upon Latin American governments that were disliked by the critics. Why should the United States not take steps to remove from power individuals who headed governments that were, as *La Prensa* said, "vulgar tyrannies"? One answer to such a question was the Nicaraguan experience. Another answer was a counter-question: Would the new government be less tyrannical? A third answer was that the United States was, after 1936, under the obligation not to intervene, and that it had learned that it might not be able to avoid intervention if it indulged in interference. These answers did not solve the problem or still the appeals by political exiles or by newspapers that disapproved of dictators in other countries than their own. The Department meanwhile refused to interfere, rejected the argument that because the United States was capable of overthrowing tyrants it had a responsibility to do so, and justified its course on the ground that Central Americans would have to learn how to govern themselves, however bitter the process.

A more sophisticated and difficult question was sometimes asked. Rául Victor Haya de la Torre in *El Mundo* (Havana), on February 20, 1938, observed that, when President Roosevelt went to Buenos Aires, he had said pleasant words about the "dictators" of Argentina and Brazil; on the other hand, he frequently attacked "dictators" in Europe. Haya de la Torre asked why Roosevelt, in the name of democracy, did not seek to promote civic education in Latin America by accusing Latin American "dictators" of despotism. Then, he added, the common man in Latin America would not cynically call Roosevelt "the Good Neighbor of tyrants."

This question could hardly be answered convincingly in terms of the ethical or educational principles in which it was posed. An indirect answer to questions of this type was given by Roosevelt when he said: "The maintenance of constitutional governments in other nations is not a sacred obligation devolving upon the United States alone"; it was the affair of the nation concerned unless conditions in that nation affected other states, and in that event it might become "the joint concern of the whole continent in which we are neighbors." [35] The real if unexpressed answer, it may be suggested, was a political one. If the United States hoped to secure economic or political cooperation from Latin American governments, it could hardly denounce the heads of those governments for violating democratic principles, especially when the list of those denounced might well be a long one. Roosevelt and Hull certainly did not approve the practices of dictatorships in Latin America, nor did they have two moral standards in their personal judgments of dictators in the Americas and in Europe. It was, however, politically desirable to express their antipathy to the latter, but not the former. It was, of course, possible for Latin Americans to make their own comparisons and conclude that their own Mussolinis were equally disliked by North Americans who preferred not to name Latin American names.

There is one more question on this subject that was occasionally raised by those who were willing to admit the political wisdom of the stand of the Department of State on the two previous questions. Was there no way whatever of discriminating among Latin American countries so as to demonstrate in negative, if not denunciatory, fashion a disapproval of dictators and so to weaken their political grip?

The principal objection to "discrimination" was that it either created ill will or was ineffective, or both. Measures like the refusal to negotiate a trade agreement, or a return to the policy of nonrecognition, would certainly have been resented by Latin Americans as disguised forms of intervention if, as in Cuba, they were effective in dislodging a regime. Even if they were effective, it was simply unrealistic to assume that the alternative to a dictatorship was necessarily a democratic administration, rather than another dictatorship.

These considerations, which formed the basis for the policy of noninterference, left very few areas of policy in which discrimination might be practiced by Washington. Shortly before Pearl Harbor, Sumner Welles even took the position that the United States should not unilaterally intervene in any Latin American country on the ground that its government was acting under the influence of one of the Axis powers; such intervention, he felt, would endanger "the whole structure of inter-American cooperation" and the issue, if it arose, should be handled by joint measures agreed upon with all the other American states.[36] It does not appear that Roosevelt responded directly to this letter, but it may be doubted that the President would, in a specific case, have gone so far. In a press conference in 1938, Roosevelt had asked newsmen to assume that certain European governments might try to do in Mexico what they had done in Spain—organizing a fascist revolution, taking over the government, and building up the Mexican army and air force. He asked: "Do you think that the United States could stand idly by and have this European menace right on our own borders? Of course not. You could not stand for it." [37]

There remained, however, one area of policy where the policy of noninterference was occasionally applied with slightly less than full rigor. This was the ceremonial aspect of the Good Neighbor policy. The White House and the Department of State had it within their power to express the whole range of intensity of their approval or disapproval of Latin American regimes that lay between the coolness and warmth of official relationships. Correct they must be, not only in terms of diplomatic protocol, but also in the application of all other aspects of the policy of noninterference, but they did not have to be cordial toward dictators and democrats alike.

President Roosevelt was rather proud of "getting on to a social footing with our Latin American neighbors," which was what he called a new and unofficial relationship with Latin American officials.[38] Thus there was a series of visits of presidents, foreign ministers, and generals, beginning with the arrival in Washington on October 9, 1933, of President Harmodio Arias of Panama. This manifestation of Good Neighborliness, however, was apparently not intended to be a mark of favor for democratic, as distinct from dictatorial, rulers in Latin America, for in 1939, President Anastasio Somoza of Nicaragua was invited to visit Washington. President Roosevelt established a precedent by going to the railroad station to meet Somoza, and an impressive military parade was held in the visitor's honor.[39] Somoza stayed overnight in the White House and thus became the only guest so hospitably entertained after having been officially reported by a United States Minister as having planned and been responsible for a murder.[40] Such a welcome for a dictator of infamous reputation gave rise to expressions of incredulous indignation in Latin America.

A year later, Latin Americans were no less indignant, although perhaps less incredulous, when General Rafael Leonidas Trujillo, then Chief of Staff of the Army of the Dominican Republic, but with the presidency safely within his reach, visited Washington and was entertained at a tea at the White House by President and Mrs. Roosevelt.[41] This ceremony took place after dictatorial control by Trujillo had been firmly established in the Dominican Republic and only a year and a half after Welles had drawn Roosevelt's attention to a despatch from Minister R. Henry Norweb containing an account of the killing by the Dominican national police and army of at least one thousand Haitian civilians in peculiarly horrible circumstances, following a series of border incidents. The account, given to Norweb by the Auditor of the Receivership General of Dominican Customs, stated that the Haitians were "murdered" by Dominican troops "apparently with the approval of President Trujillo." [42]

On at least one occasion, however, use was apparently made of a ceremonial occasion for purposes of influencing the course of internal politics in Mexico. In 1940 there were rumors that a revolution would be attempted to prevent President-elect Avila Camacho from taking office, and the attitude of the government of the United States was made abundantly clear by the announcement that Vice-President Henry A. Wallace would attend the inauguration of Avila Camacho as President Roosevelt's official representative. Whether or not this admonitory gesture was effective, it stands almost alone in the decade after 1933 as an attempt at interference in the domestic politics of a Latin American state.

PART TWO

The Policy of Pacific Protection

CHAPTER VI

The Evolution of a New Policy

THE POLICY OF nonintervention was the refusal to employ armed force in order to secure any policy objectives of the United States in its relations with the countries of Latin America. The policy of noninterference was the refusal to influence in any way the course of domestic political affairs in Latin American countries. The adoption of these two policies, however, did not mean that the United States gave up all methods of influencing all aspects of the foreign relations of its neighbors, as the United States defined those relations. The United States government divested itself neither of its concern with Latin American commercial and military policies nor with policies affecting the lives and properties of its citizens living or having investments south of the Rio Grande. Further, the United States continued to employ the customary methods of diplomacy to influence the policies of Latin American governments in these fields of concern. These methods, in general terms, combined the propagation of the idea of reciprocity with financial inducements, protests, discriminatory practices of an economic or ceremonial character, as well as various measures designed to create positive collaboration among the American states.

From the early days of the Good Neighbor policy, the idea of reciprocity, that is, of a neighborly response to neighborliness, had been an essential assumption of the new spirit. As expressed by Roosevelt in his first inaugural address: "I would dedicate this nation to the policy of the Good Neighbor—the neighbor who respects his obligations and respects the sanctity of his agreements in and with a world of neighbors." All Good Neighbors were presumed to have obligations and to be willing to respect them.[1] The idea of reciprocity was obliquely referred to by diplomats in calling the Good Neighbor policy "a two-way street," and they persisted in the hope that somewhere near its middle the Latin American countries would come to meet the United States.

The spirit of the Good Neighbor and the idea of reciprocity did not, of course, constitute a policy. Where did the United States expect to meet its neighbors? How neighborly would it have to become? What could it do to persuade the Latin American states to be more neighborly, if they appeared to be staying at their own end of the street, knowing that the United States Navy would not sail south? These questions could not be answered in abstract terms; the answers were found in specific decisions made in specific cases of difference of opinion among neighbors. The idea of reciprocity could not serve as a basis for decision within the policy of noninterference, because the United States made no conditions for noninterference. The Department of State did not say that it would refrain from interfering only if Central American politics were orderly and democratic; it asserted in effect that it would not interfere even if they were chaotic or tyrannical. In other words, a Latin American state could be looked upon as a Good Neighbor regardless of its form of government or the civic liberties its citizens possessed. The tie between noninterference in domestic politics and the idea of reciprocity was that the Department of State expected that, in response to its nonintervention and noninterference, the Latin American governments would reciprocate by neighborly policies in other types of relationships. These other types of relationships were, principally and immediately, the treatment of United States nationals and their property and, later, cooperation for the defense of the hemisphere. It is with the application of the idea of reciprocity to the first of these relationships that Part Two of this study is concerned.

When the United States intervened in Nicaragua and interfered in Cuba, it did so both to change the political situation in the two countries and to protect the lives and property of its citizens. Although renouncing the use of force to attain either of these aims, both in practice and in form, the United States government relinquished a policy concern only about the first of them. If only for considerations of its own political support in the United States, it was not to be expected that the United States government could be as indifferent to the fate of its citizens and their property as it was, officially, to the type of government enjoyed or suffered by Central American peoples. To revert to the elementary terms of the Good Neighbor policy, a neighbor could not be a Good Neighbor, whatever his form of government, if he did not treat United States citizens and their property in ways acceptable to the government of the United States.

In Washington, noninterference in domestic politics and the assurance of nonintervention in either domestic politics or "external affairs" was regarded as creating on the part of Latin American governments a reciprocal obligation of equitable treatment of United States citizens as "equitable" was defined in Washington. It was, however, precisely this assumption of reciprocity that was not accepted by Mexico and certain other countries, who refused either to allow the United States unilaterally to define the content of "equitable" treatment or to subject their own policies in this area to the test of any tribunal that would base its decision on the rules of international law.[2]

From the point of view of the United States, adoption of nonintervention and noninterference policies transformed it into a Good Neighbor, a position solidified and strengthened by the negotiation of reciprocal trade agreements. As Hull stated, for "background" information for United States missions in the Latin American countries shortly after the Mexican oil expropriation decree:

The policy of this government during the last five years has been the policy of the Good Neighbor. During these years the American Government has repeatedly evidenced its fulfillment of that pledge. Moreover, because of the universal applicability of the basic principles on which that policy is premised, they have had the support of other governments of this hemisphere. This policy of equity and of reasonable and just treatment must have a reciprocal character if the peoples of the New

World are to progress steadily toward a higher level of international relationships.[3]

From the point of view of certain Latin American countries, however, the nonintervention and noninterference policies constituted merely the password to a Good Neighborhood, and the addition of the trade agreements program was insufficient to make of the United States a Good Neighbor. They could not consider the United States as a Good Neighbor until it accepted the elimination of what they regarded as an equally offensive interference in their internal affairs, namely, that measure of support from Washington that would enable certain types of North American business enterprise to maintain the power and status they had secured before 1933.[4] If Nicaraguans and other Latin Americans could not feel independent until after the last United States Marines had left their countries, Mexicans did not regard themselves as citizens of a fully sovereign state until they had broken the old form of the alliance between the United States government and North American oil companies. Only then did they consider themselves as emerging from what they called "economic vassalage," and only then did they accept the United States as a Good Neighbor, a status ardently desired by Roosevelt and Hull as World War II drew closer to the Americas.

This difference in point of view might have been clarified earlier had there been a meeting of minds over the protocol on nonintervention of the Buenos Aires Conference, which declared intervention inadmissible "directly or indirectly, and for whatever reason, in the internal or external affairs of any other of the Parties." To the United States delegation, "intervention" meant the use of armed force; "internal" affairs meant only domestic politics; and "directly or indirectly" meant the landing of troops or the threat of such action. This interpretation by the United States delegates is strongly supported by the failure of a committee of the Conference to agree on a convention concerning pecuniary claims which would have bound the signatories to refrain both from force and from "diplomatic intervention" for the collection of public or contractual debts. Futher, the Conference did not even give serious consideration to the subject of diplomatic protection of nationals. The United States delegation would almost certainly not have accepted the nonintervention protocol if it had considered that instrument to have prevented or inhibited it from protecting its nationals in Latin American states by traditional, pacific methods of diplomatic protestation.[5]

However, to some Latin American delegations, especially that of Mexico, it appears that these terms had a meaning that placed greater limitations on the admissible action of the United States. An important explanation of the Mexican point of view was given in a public address by Roberto Córdoba, Mexican agent on the General Claims Commission. After a review of United States interventionist policy, Córdoba said that the Buenos Aires text had fundamentally modified that of Montevideo because of the change

in the connotation of the principle of nonintervention with the words "directly or indirectly," in such a way as to include therein not only the armed intervention of one country in another, but that other intervention, at present of much greater interest to us, *consisting of intervention which we might call peaceable but which has the same effect as . . . political, preventive, or repressive interventions.*

Córdoba added:

As far as I know, the scope of the words "indirect intervention" was not the subject of special explanation, but, in view of the antecedents of our international policy, I am convinced that in the mind of the Mexican delegation which proposed the wording of the Protocol, those words refer clearly to that class of unarmed intervention.[6]

Córdoba clarified his point and his interpretation of United States policy by a consideration of the action taken in Cuba in 1933. He said that, owing to the "prudent attitude" of the White House, no "military intervention" took place in Cuba. However, he continued, "this did not signify a refraining from intervention in the internal affairs of the Cuban people, and I believe that I can safely affirm that the kind of intervention practiced on that occasion was one of the most effective and skillful interventions ever carried out by the American government." By withholding recognition from the Grau San Martín government and permitting his opposition to obtain arms in the United States, added Córdoba, the United States "little by little attained the realization of its wishes, namely, the stabilization of a government more in harmony with the interests of American capital in Cuba and more in harmony with the American government itself."

To the Mexicans, therefore, there were several kinds of "intervention," all of which were made "inadmissible" by the Buenos Aires protocol, but to the United States government only the use of force was justifiably called intervention and it was only the use of force it had agreed was inadmissible. To Mexicans, the test of "intervention" was not the means employed, but the effectiveness of the use of any means whatever by the United States to cause a Latin American state to change its policy against its will, in what that state regarded as "internal affairs," notably its policy toward United States corporations. To the United States, the test of intervention was simply whether armed force was employed.[7]

This difference in interpretation, which was not harmonized at Buenos Aires, was of crucial significance to the subsequent development of the Good Neighbor policy. It may be exemplified, curiously enough, by an exchange of correspondence between Ambassador Josephus Daniels, who well represented the Mexican point of view on this occasion, and Secretary Hull. Daniels inquired how the Department of State by "taking sides" with the oil companies in Mexico could reconcile its action with the nonintervention articles signed at Montevideo and Buenos Aires and with the Good Neighbor policy. In reply, the Department pointed out that, if a foreign government took a position adversely affecting the interests of aliens, "it is proper for the aliens' government to inquire into the controversy for the purpose of determining whether its nationals are being accorded treatment consonant with principles of international law." If the treatment given them were "unfair or unreasonable," then "remonstrance in their behalf would not constitute intervention in the internal affairs of the foreign state. It would be simply a matter of protection. It is not always easy to draw a sharp line between matters purely of an internal or domestic character and those of an international character." Elucidating the Good Neighbor policy, Hull then added:

The Good Neighbor policy, in which you and I are firm believers, is inherently a two-sided policy. If American nationals in Mexico are treated in such a manner as to make it possible for them to prove that they have suffered injustice through the imposition of unreasonable demands or the expropriation of their property without adequate compensation, public opinion in the United States, and notably in the Congress, will undoubtedly protest against the continuation of a policy by the United States toward Mexico which is in its results one-sided and which implies a continuing to give without receiving.[8]

This exchange indicates certain essential points of the Department's position on the question of reciprocity. The United States had made concessions; in return it expected fair treatment of its nationals; if such treatment were not afforded, the Department would "remonstrate"; the test of fairness was to be found in principles of international law; if fair treatment were not forthcoming, the Department would probably find itself obliged by public opinion at home to change a policy that would be looked upon as one of unrequited giving.

A comparable situation arose in 1939, when Daniels was instructed to register a protest against a proposed amendment to the Mexican constitution affecting foreign investors. Daniels wrote to Welles that such a protest

seems to contravene our commitments at Montevideo, Buenos Aires, and Lima. . . . The Good Neighbor policy calls for patience, toleration, justice, mutual helpfulness. Like Democracy, it can be purchased only at a heavy price, but no other policy can be upheld by a nation which respects the sovereignty of small countries and believes in self-determination.

Daniels did not consider that we could justify making the protest in view of the obligation of the United States "not to intervene 'directly or indirectly.' " Welles accepted Daniels's position in this matter, and the protest was not presented in Mexico. Welles wrote:

The position of this government is based on the accepted principles of international law. That position will presumably remain the same whether or not the proposed amendment to the Mexican Constitution is adopted. I think consequently it would be inexpedient, as well as contrary to the position this government has taken with regard to noninterference in the domestic affairs of other countries in this hemisphere, for the government of the United States to make any such official approach as that proposed to the Mexican government.[9]

When the prop of armed force was withdrawn from the international standard of protection of nationals, the states against whom it had formerly been enforced refused to accept the jurisdiction of arbitral tribunals that would have applied it. The stand-ard did not collapse, but it assumed a new form, and political, rather than legal, methods were sought as buttresses. The Depart-ment of State, which was described by an eminent international lawyer as being, in the 1920s "just a big international law office," was converted in the late 1930s into a center of diplomatic negotia-tion for the protection of nationals in Latin America. The language of discourse was changed from charges of denial of justice to pleas for equitable treatment, and the techniques of settlement from courts to foreign offices and commissions.

The transition from juridical to political modes of settlement of disputes involving the status of North American business enter-prise in Latin America was a major development of the period between 1936 and 1943. The Hoover administration had largely freed the Department of State from the political burdens formerly assumed in helping holders of Latin American government bonds in the United States to secure full payment for their loans. The Roosevelt administration successfully asserted the claim of the De-partment of State to make independent judgments concerning the degree to which the protection of direct investments by North Americans in Latin America was consonant with the general for-eign policy of the United States. In brief, the Department of State ceased to be a collection agency for bondholders or bankers,[10] and it sharply curtailed without completely shutting off its legal services for business firms having contract or concession difficulties with Latin American governments.

When it gave up being the policeman of the Caribbean, the United States could hale no offenders before an arbitral tribunal or court of justice. Although the Department of State continued for a time to talk of arbitration, it got no one to arbitrate. Casting about for a substitute for legal obligations, it hit upon the neigh-borly "obligation" of reciprocity for good deeds. However, the Latin American states did not respond satisfactorily to mere ex-hortations of reciprocity; they confiscated or expropriated the properties of United States citizens.

The United States, having denied itself the luxury of the use of armed force, could stiffen exhortation only by remonstrances, discriminations, and inducements. It could also add to nonintervention and noninterference one more renunciation; it could cease insisting on international juridical settlements of disputes between United States citizens and corporations and Latin American countries. This the United States did by reaction rather than by planning. The specific measures adopted over a period of some six years form an ultimately consistent whole that is here called the policy of pacific protection.

For how long a time and at what level of insistence would the United States remonstrate? Would remonstrance be accompanied by any positive measures to encourage fair treatment? Were there any policy alternatives to remonstrance? These were hard and real questions, and the Department of State had not formulated the answers to them at the time of the Buenos Aires Conference. It worked out answers over a period of several years in dealing with issues raised by the attitudes of Bolivia, Mexico, and Venezuela toward North American oil companies. In so doing, it did not surrender its claim to exert influence in order to assist the companies, nor were its efforts on their behalf entirely unrewarded. It found neighborly methods for dealing with these issues that substituted political compromise for legal decisions, and, in substance, it established as a fundamental principle of the Good Neighbor policy that there was a national interest of the United States in its relations with Latin America, different from and superior to the private interests of any sector of business enterprise or of business enterprise as a whole. That interest, it became clear in 1939, was nothing less than the security of the United States, and there is good reason for the assertion that it was well served by the policy of pacific protection. This policy was worked out through a process of political bargaining on a grand scale that is described in the following chapters.

CHAPTER VII

The Principle of Discrimination: Bolivia

SUDDENLY AND without warning, the government of Bolivia, on March 13, 1937, annulled the petroleum concession of the Standard Oil Company of Bolivia and confiscated its properties. The decree of March 13 alleged that the Company had defrauded the Bolivian government by avoiding payment of taxes and by the illegal exportation of oil to Argentina in 1925–26 via a pipeline under the Bermejo River.[1]

The Company, a subsidiary of Standard Oil of New Jersey, had been prospecting for oil and operating wells in southeastern Bolivia, following the grant of a concession on July 27, 1922, which was a continuation of an earlier concession of 1920 to Richmond Levering and Company. An investment of about $17,000,000 had been made, largely in the Villa Montes–Tarija area. However, the Company had ceased drilling new wells about 1932, and the impression had arisen in Bolivia that the Company had little interest in the development of the oil fields. This impression was strengthened by the opening in 1936 of negotiations for the sale of the Company's assets to the Bolivian government.

The action of the Bolivian government was not an expropriation, for which compensation might have been offered. Instead, relying on its claim of fraud, the government took the position that it could cancel the concession and take title to the properties without making any compensation whatever.

Foreign Minister Enrique Finot told United States Minister R. Henry Norweb that, aside from the legal grounds for the action, "there is a moral justification arising from the company's noncooperative attitude during the Chaco war," and that "it was 'a natural aspiration of a country to control its petroleum resources.' "[2] During the Chaco War, 1932–35, the Company had refused to make a loan of several million dollars, which had been requested by the government, and in other ways it had not provided the full measure of assistance that La Paz had desired. The very fact of the confiscation, even without Finot's charge that the Company had not cooperated during the war, may have given a wry pleasure to officials of the Company, who remembered the almost constant attacks by the press in Paraguay and other countries that it had been inciting Bolivia to attack Paraguay and had been financing Bolivian purchases of military equipment.

There may have been some desire in Bolivia to take revenge on the Company, and perhaps even to assuage disappointment over the loss of the war with Paraguay, by gaining a victory over a weaker if no less well known opponent. However, Finot justified the action on different grounds. He told Norweb that Bolivia had to "dispel the impression current throughout the world that the weak and impoverished Bolivia had been merely an instrument of the all-powerful, imperialistic world monster, the Standard Oil Company—that the Chaco War had been fought merely to protect the Standard Oil properties."[3]

The Company held that the confiscation was unjustified, since its contract included a provision authorizing it to produce and sell oil either in Bolivia or abroad, and that the exportation of 704 tons of oil in 1925–26 had taken place with the knowledge of Bolivian customs officials and without their having made any objections, although the Company had not made a formal request for permission to build the Bermejo pipeline. With regard to alleged tax frauds, the Company admitted that it owed some back taxes, but pointed out that a suit to determine the amount was still pending in the Bolivian courts.

Beyond and behind the legal, moral, and "natural" origins of the decree of March 13 lay political and economic motives. Although there had been no fighting with Paraguay for nearly two years, the boundary had not yet been determined in the Chaco, and it was known that Paraguay yet hoped to gain control of the oil fields, which were in sight of its troops on the cease-fire lines. Despite the feeling in Bolivia, which was shared elsewhere, that Argentina had materially aided Paraguay in the war, Finot had "put aside his personal dislike and distrust of the Argentine and Dr. Saavedra Lamas" and had made a visit to Buenos Aires at the end of 1936. Norweb concluded that Finot had decided that, since Bolivia could not expect assistance from any country other than Argentina in the Chaco settlement, he must try to come to terms with Saavedra Lamas. The most plausible way of reaching an agreement "would be for Bolivia to accede to the Argentine's eagerness" for access to Bolivian oil. Finot found that Argentina demanded, in return for supporting Bolivia at the Chaco Peace Conference, no less than "full possession of the Bolivian oil resources." If Bolivia refused to give Argentina an oil concession,

Argentina has intimated that it will not be favorably disposed, and Paraguay may eventually be allowed to obtain control of the fields. . . . In other words, in making the Standard Oil concessions available to Argentina, such action would guarantee Bolivia a powerful neighbor, who would never again let Paraguay menace its territory.

The talks were supposed to have become so specific that Argentina offered Bolivia 14 percent of the returns from an oil concession, as compared with the 11 percent received from the Standard Oil Company.[4]

The immediate, public result of Finot's talks in Buenos Aires was the signing of a convention in which Argentina undertook to extend a railway northward from Yacuiba toward Santa Cruz de la Sierra in return for joint exploitation arrangements in Bolivian oilfields. In December, 1936, the Yacimientos Petrolíferos Fiscales Bolivianos (YPFB) had been created by the Bolivian government with the ostensible purpose of developing oil production in new fields and in those where the Standard Oil Company had already allowed its concessionary rights to lapse.[5]

It seems safe to assume that the private result of Finot's talks was the Bolivian determination to gain control of the properties of Standard Oil. It seems highly probable that Saavedra Lamas was aware of this determination. He certainly knew that Bolivia had no proven oil resources beyond those operated by the Company. As a final political element in this affair, it may be taken for granted that Finot hoped that his own political prestige would be enhanced if, after the ouster of the Company, he could negotiate a still more advantageous agreement with Argentina.

All of these potential material advantages to Bolivia apparently were more important in La Paz than concern that the United States might take any action to help the Company that would seriously harm the interests of Bolivia. Finot was little worried about diplomatic pressure from Washington "for he [had] repeatedly asserted to friends that the policy of the United States is to let American investments abroad take care of themselves." [6]

Good Neighborly Measures of Protection

The first diplomatic move of the Department of State was to instruct Norweb to make an oral statement to Finot that it "regrets to see difficulties arise" out of interpretations of contracts between United States companies and foreign governments. It did not express any opinion about the issue created by the March 13 decree but limited itself to the "hope that the present difficulties . . . [would] be resolved in a manner equitable to all concerned through friendly discussions carried on in an atmosphere conducive to a satisfactory settlement." [7] A few days later, Finot told Norweb that "we had to drive the Standard Oil Company out of Bolivia for political reasons. It will never be allowed to return." [8] At this interview, Finot also said that he had not been surprised that he had not been given a copy of the Department's oral message, and added: "As I always contended, the American Government will never lift a finger in defense of the Standard Oil Company; the informal presentation of the views of your Government proves this, so informal, in fact, that I have forgotten what you said nor do I recall what I answered." [9]

Until it learned of these intemperate remarks of Finot, the attitude of the Department of State had been a cautious and moderate one. The Department was experimenting with the good neighborly gesture of trying to protect United States business concerns in Latin America and elsewhere through friendly representations, rather than through formal protests based on the traditional legal claims for such protection. However, the Department quickly adopted a slightly stronger, if still amicable, position in the face of Finot's contemptuous attitude. Hull told Norweb that he was "increasingly disturbed" about the situation, especially since the Bolivian government appeared to have "no present intention of reaching a fair adjudication of the equities involved in this case, whatever these equities may in fact be." He therefore instructed Norweb to deliver in writing a "personal message" to Finot. The message referred to Hull's "friendly association" with the foreign minister, and expressed his "personal concern" at a situation "which may prejudice the steady growth of . . . confidence on the part of all of the peoples of the American republics one towards the other." Hull continued, explaining for the first time his understanding of the Good Neighbor policy as applied to a case of this type:

> During these recent years the "Good Neighbor" policy, as an inter-American policy has made tremendous strides. It has no more able and consistent advocate that Dr. Finot. It contemplates, of course, a general friendliness, complete faith of governments and peoples in each other, and a wholehearted disposition to cooperate each with the other for the promotion of their mutual interests and mutual welfare. One of its foundations must, of course, at all times be the recognition and the practice of fair dealing and fair play on the part of governments and peoples towards each other. This policy of equity and reasonable and just treatment cannot by its very nature be a one-sided policy. It must in its very essence have a reciprocal character, if the peoples of the New World are to progress steadily towards a higher level of international relationships. . . .
>
> The government of the United States, in accordance with its consistent efforts to practice the policy of the Good Neighbor to the fullest extent, does not at any time or in any instance contemplate support for one of its nationals who seeks to exploit the government of another country or the nationals of such government, or who pursues methods or practices inherently unfair or unwarranted.

Further, said Hull, Bolivia had not shown any evidence that it intended to compensate the Company for its "seizure" of the

Company's properties or that it intended to "arbitrate or otherwise adjudicate any rights or equities which may be involved." The Secretary said he would not deal with questions of fact or law, but hoped that in the interests of avoiding prejudice to "mutual confidence," Bolivia would take steps "at an early opportunity" to offer compensation or arbitration or adjudication as a means of settlement.[10]

Finot's immediate response to this appeal was to become more "guarded and temperate" in his comments, but he gave to Norweb the impression that he was more interested in justifying the seizure than in accepting Hull's request for compensation or arbitration.[11] On May 12 he sent a long reply to Hull, upholding the legality of the decree of March 13. He stated that Hull could be assured that he would not regard Hull's message as "the instrument of a diplomatic move in defense of private interests," since neither the United States policy of nonintervention, the principles of Bolivian policy, nor the legal background of the case could justify such action. Finot concurred with Hull that the "policy of the good neighbor should rest on the foundation of 'fair play'" between governments and the nationals of other governments. However, he argued that since the Company did not own "properties" in Bolivia, but merely had a concession, the Bolivian government did not take confiscatory action and was under no obligation to make compensation; it had merely applied a penal clause in the concession contract because the Company had committed frauds in its dealings with Bolivia. He would try to demonstrate that Bolivia "guarantees and protects foreign capital," and to this end, he concluded with courteous effrontery, he counted on Hull's cooperation.[12]

There was no sequel to this inconclusive exchange, and the relations between the two governments became for some time less important than those between Bolivia and the Standard Oil Company. These relations opened with efforts to reach a settlement by direct negotiations. The Company met its first defeat with the refusal of the Bolivian government to cancel the decree of March 13. Although the Company wished to sell its holdings and did not intend to resume operations in Bolivia, it was determined to uphold the legality of its claims. The Company's representative in

Bolivia, F. C. Pannill, told Norweb that this case "might be made a good precedent to all Latin American countries, particularly the Argentine and Peru, that the Standard Oil Company prefers to accept financial losses than to allow these countries to get the impression that it can be forcibly expulsed [sic]." [13] Norweb shared this view, and felt that the Company would do well to wait until the political "set-up" in Bolivia, which he thought was "wobbly," had changed, and then try to get the decree canceled. Otherwise, the Company would merely encourage other Latin American governments to follow Bolivia's example.

Mr. Pannill left Bolivia early in June, and the Bolivian government astonished Chargé John J. Muccio by regarding the expulsion of the Company as "a closed incident." Muccio thought "something should be done to keep the issue alive" in these circumstances, but his best suggestion was that a statement might be made at a press conference that the Department hoped that "a friendly adjustment" might be found before long. He thought that "strong official representations" to President David Toro or Minister Finot would do no good. He stated further,

Should the United States unduly press such representations, forcing a successful conclusion, the political repercussions would likely be such as to precipitate the downfall of the present military Junta. This, in turn, would provide political capital to opponents of the United States and give rise to possible criticism of undue interference in internal matters of a friendly country. Furthermore, it would adversely affect the influence of the United States in the Chaco Peace Conference, possibly endangering the success of those negotiations.[14]

Domestic developments brought about a change in the Bolivian political situation when, on July 14, Colonel Germán Busch led a revolt that ousted President Toro. However, the new government, of which Enrique Baldivieso was Foreign Minister, was no more willing than its predecessor to consider either revocation of the March 13 decree or other proposals made by the Company. Instead, it issued a second decree, on October 22, which had the effect of requiring the Company to file suit against the government within ninety days. The legislation amended by this decree had allowed a period of thirty years during which a suit might be filed in a comparable case.[15] Following the expression to La Paz of the opinion of the Department of State that this brief period might justifiably be extended to give the Company sufficient time to prepare its case, an additional two months was granted.[16]

In the meantime, Baldivieso resigned and was replaced by Eduardo Diez de Medina, and President Busch gave a press interview in which he expressed his belief that the Standard Oil Company had been guilty of illegal acts. This statement gave rise to the following comment by Minister Robert G. Caldwell, who had succeeded Norweb:

On an issue so sharply and publicly drawn, it seems to me almost impossible for either this Government or any other which is likely to succeed it to give a decision favorable to the Company. . . . This difficulty applies not only to the executive branch but also to the judiciary which is—as I believe reliably reported—to be completely subject to the control of the executive.[17]

Shortly afterward, on November 27, the Bolivian government further darkened the prospects of the Company for a fair hearing in the Bolivian courts by deporting to Argentina Dr. Carlos Calvo, a Bolivian citizen who was the Company's attorney in La Paz. The official reason for the deportation was that Calvo had engaged in "subversive political activities," but Caldwell said there was little doubt that "a leading reason was his connection with the Standard Oil Company, which was regarded by military leaders as unpatriotic." [18] The Department of State did not make any protest against the deportation of Dr. Calvo.[19] The Company was informed later that the reason for Calvo's deportation was that he had publicly questioned the legal validity of the decree of March 13, but the loss of Calvo's services did not have any effect on the filing of the Company's formal appeal to the Court.

Throughout this period of several months, the Department took no overt action other than to propose the extension of time for filing of the Company's suit and to permit Caldwell to read to Baldivieso the statement read by Norweb to Finot on April 26. The Department was aware that the Argentine government opposed any strong pressure on Bolivia from Washington, and it circulated to its missions in Buenos Aires, La Paz, and Rio de

Janeiro a statement by Argentine Foreign Minister Carlos Saavedra Lamas that "President Roosevelt would not countenance an official protest to the Bolivian Government over its confiscation of the Standard Oil properties, since to do so would destroy all the good effects obtained by the Good Neighbor policy to date." [20]

The new Bolivian government asked Caldwell to obtain for it a copy of Hull's personal message to Finot of May 7 and of Finot's reply, because Finot had left no copies of these messages behind when he left office with Toro, even though his departure was presumably rather hurried. However, the Department, with a sudden access of diplomatic delicacy, informed Caldwell that since Hull's note to Finot was "a personal and confidential message," it could not allow the Bolivian Foreign Office to have a copy of it unless Finot gave his consent. As for Finot's reply, the Department suggested that Baldivieso get a copy from Finot himself.[21] The Department's records do not reveal whether or not Finot's consent was obtained; if not, the government headed by Busch was deprived of the benefit of Hull's stand that Bolivia should provide either compensation or an offer of arbitration of its dispute with the Company.

The Department's position at about this time seemed to be rather weaker than that taken in Hull's message to Finot. In an instruction to Caldwell, Welles said the Department held "that the Company should exhaust all of its remedies in Bolivia, and that every effort should be made to continue conversations between the Bolivian government and the Company, looking toward a possible solution of the present difficulties." [22]

The conversations took place, but they did not produce a settlement. The Bolivian government was willing to make a payment in cash to the Company, but a member of the Cabinet told the Company's negotiator that

no compromise of any kind could be reached on the fundamental question of principle . . . the good faith of the Bolivian Government had been committed as to the complete legal validity of the decree of March 13, 1937, through international agreements . . . with the Argentine Republic on November 19th, and with Brazil on November 25th.[23]

For reasons mentioned above, the Company did not wish to accept a settlement of this kind.

The agreement with Argentina provided in part for Argentine participation in the development of Bolivian oilfields. During the negotiation of the agreement, Ambassador Alexander W. Weddell had reported that Foreign Minister Saavedra Lamas was understood to have told the Argentine negotiators that "Bolivia should disregard the Standard Oil in any negotiations with that company." [24] Article 7 of the agreement provided that references to Bolivian oil were understood to refer to "petroleum and by-products belonging to the Bolivian State and originating from fields of its exclusive property." This article was regarded in Washington as being based on Bolivia's retention of the confiscated oil lands. Welles was sufficiently concerned to call in Felipe A. Espil, the Argentine ambassador, and point out to him that "the Bolivian Government had not developed any oil fields of its own nor did it possess any 'of its exclusive property.'" He suggested that Argentina would not wish to be understood in the United States as "entering into contractual relations with Bolivia covering oil properties to which the title was definitely not clear and which had been properties owned by United States interests for which no equitable compensation had been offered by the Bolivian authorities." Espil said he agreed with Welles, but that it would be unwise to take the matter up now in Buenos Aires, since Saavedra Lamas had negotiated the agreement and since it could not in any case be ratified until after the inauguration of President Ortiz in February. He felt that the new administration would not complete the agreement until Bolivia and the Standard Oil Company had come to terms.[25]

Talks between Bolivian officials and the Company's representative, H. A. Metzger, dragged on for months. These were punctuated from time to time by Welles's inquiries of Minister Luis Fernando Guachalla as to whether progress was being made and gentle urgings to Bolivia to reach an equitable settlement. By February, 1938, Welles had concluded that an international arbitration was the only way out that would both satisfy Bolivian dignity and afford hopes of justice for the Company. He told Guachalla of his decision and added, in a softly admonitory tone, that "the only way in which public opinion in this country was going to support the 'Good Neighbor' policy as a permanent part of our foreign policy would be for the policy to be recognized throughout the continent as a completely reciprocal policy and not one of a purely unilateral character." [26] Guachalla apparently reported his talks with Welles to La Paz and personally recommended resort to arbitration, but without avail.

As March 22 drew near, the last date on which the Company could file suit in the Bolivian courts, a solution by way of an international arbitration was again urged on Guachalla, this time by Duggan. However, La Paz maintained a stony silence, and Washington did not insist on arbitration. Caldwell wrote from La Paz that the controversy was important because of its "effect on American prestige and especially on those just and friendly relations with a South American republic which, if violated with impunity, may very readily weaken the foundations of the 'Good Neighbor' policy, not only here but in other countries where similar policies might be adopted." He thought it was "perfectly clear that the Bolivian Government would never have dreamed of applying a similar policy of confiscation to the property of any one of its neighbors, as, for example, Chile, which has a large amount of capital invested in Bolivia." Since the appeal to the Bolivian courts would "merely give apparent justification to the policy of confiscation," arbitration seemed to him the only available solution.[27]

On March 21 the Company filed its suit, under protest, "in order that it may not be alleged that the Company has not exhausted all local remedies." [28] This decision was taken after consultation with officials of the Department of State who thought that, while the responsibility for the decision must be taken by the Company, the existence of the Calvo Clause in the Company's contract "did raise a difficulty," even though it did not prevent the United States from "intervening" by formally requesting an arbitration. It was also thought that such intervention, based on a claim of a denial of justice after the judicial process in the Bolivian Court, would be less difficult "than to assume in advance that the Supreme Court of Bolivia is of such a character that it could not be expected to do justice, even though we may believe this to be the case." [29] Company officials were assured by the Department that "in the event of an adverse decision by the Bolivian Supreme Court which, in the opinion of the Department, is a manifest denial of justice, the Department would support a claim for arbitration." [30]

A definition by the Department of its own role at the end of 1938 was made in response to a request from the Standard Oil Company for permission to include the following paragraph in a report to stockholders:

The Department of State has taken an active interest in this case and has protested to the Bolivian government against the confiscation. When the Bolivian government arbitrarily cut down the statute of limitations to ninety days and expelled the Company's chief counsel, the Department requested an extension of the time for filing suit. While realizing the denial of justice involved in the whole proceeding and informally requesting international arbitration of the entire issue, the Department considered it desirable for the Company to exhaust local remedies before presenting the issue formally for settlement by diplomacy or arbitration.

This picture of its activity apparently painted the Department in a style too close to that of Delacroix for Welles's taste. His reply, stating that "there would be no objection" to the following statement, seems more like a sober, brown self-portrait from a calm, good neighborly pupil of Rembrandt:

The Department of State has taken an active interest in this case and has exercised its good offices informally in an effort to assist the Company and the Bolivian government to reach a mutually satisfactory settlement. When the Bolivian government cut down the statute of limitations to ninety days, the Department requested an extension of the time for filing suit. The Department of State, without expressing an opinion concerning the merits of the case and without making any commitment with respect to its possible future attitude or action, considered it desirable for the Company to exhaust its local remedies in Bolivia as a first step in the attempt to effect a settlement of the case.[31]

The Supreme Court took a year to hand down its decision. A delay in the proceedings resulted from the promulgation by President Busch of a new constitution and the consequent appointment of a new Supreme Court, some of whose members had not participated in previous deliberations. The period of waiting for the decision was enlivened by renewed efforts to arrive at a settlement outside of court, and also by a series of incidents which brought into grave question the independence and impartiality of the

Supreme Court itself. The new negotiations came to naught and need not be detailed here. It may be of interest, however, to observe some of the pressures exerted on the legal process in Bolivia. The nature of these pressures gives some picturesque meaning to the legal phrase "exhaustion of local remedies" and illumines the situation to which United States policy was quietly accommodated at the time.

One form of pressure on the Court was exemplified by the passing of a resolution by an organization called the Workers Federation of Sucre, affirming the justice of the decree of March 13, and asking the Bolivian Bar Association "to disqualify those lawyers who defend the interests of the Standard Oil Company, to whom the exercise of their profession would then remain impossible." [32]

Pressure was also brought by the initiation of what was regarded in the Department of State as a strenuous press, radio, and labor campaign against the Standard Oil of Bolivia. The campaign was apparently inspired by the YPFB and aimed to awe the Supreme Court into a decision favorable to the government.

Welles voiced to Guachalla his "expectation" that there would be a fair trial, and said that he and Hull "would be very glad if the Minister pointed out to his government the unfavorable atmosphere which the press and radio campaign was causing and the difficulty which might be created for the Supreme Court in rendering a fair decision under such circumstances." [33]

In the press campaign, the Standard Oil Company was accused of being "the worst enemy of Bolivia in the Chaco War" and with having furnished maps of the Chaco to Paraguay, as well as refusing to produce gasoline for Bolivian airplanes.[34] The Company was charged with carrying on propaganda, subornation, conspiracy, burning of oil wells, and even "the victimization of persons standing in its way, in order to safeguard its dark domain." [35] The lawyers of the Company, who were Bolivian citizens, were assailed as unpatriotic, as part of this slanderous campaign.[36]

In the spring of 1939, shortly before the decision was expected, threats were made in the press against the members of the Supreme Court. Portions of a radio speech made by the Director General of Police were reproduced in *El Debate* (La Paz), February 19, 1939:

It is just at this moment that we should make the members of the Supreme Court understand our decision to tear out their entrails and burn their blood, in case they should decide against the sacred interests of the country, and in favor of Standard Oil. How long are they going to delay their decision? Are they afraid, perhaps that we, the Bolivian people, veterans of the war, will destroy them with our own hands?

Evidence that members of the Supreme Court felt themselves under strong extralegal pressures was afforded by the resignation of Justice Placido Molina M. a few days before the decision was handed down. In a letter printed in *La Fronda* (Sucre), March 5, 1939, Justice Molina stated that he was resigning on account of his health, but he noted at the same time that "enraged threateners" had gone so far as to "menace the members of the Court with violent popular reactions and even with capital punishment." Justice Molina thought that "it is necessary that both within the country and abroad, it should be known that Bolivian courts possess independence in deciding cases, and that their decisions are the result of probity and study by the judges. What would be thought of a decision which, it might be said, had been obtained through intimidation?"

The remaining members of the Court decided unanimously on March 8 that the Standard Oil Company did not possess a legal status in Bolivia which entitled it to enter a suit against the State. This decision meant that the Company had unsuccessfully exhausted all legal remedies in Bolivia. The Company turned to the Department of State, and the Department inquired within itself about its next step.

One view in the Department was that it should inform the Bolivian government that it considered the decision of the Bolivian Supreme Court "neither just or reasonable" and that it request that the dispute be submitted to an arbitral tribunal. However, Secretary Hull, in talking with Guachalla, initially adopted a less rigid position. He said that "in this dangerous, chaotic world situation there was never such a ripe plum dangled before a hungry person

than Latin America appears to be to . . . lawless nations, hungry
as wolves for vast territory with rich undeveloped natural resources such as South America possesses; that it is all-important
for the American nations to pursue a lawful, friendly and reasonable course with each other; and that the dollars and cents involved
in the oil seizure were small compared to the great injury that
would result to Bolivia, as well as to my own and other countries,
if that sort of an act should go uncorrected and the friendship between the two countries should be seriously impaired." [37]

Guachalla expressed agreement with Hull, and said he would
"take the matter up in all earnestness looking towards some method
of adjustment."

Officials of the Department also talked with representatives of
the Standard Oil Company, following the decision of the Bolivian
Supreme Court. In a memorandum written as background for this
talk, these considerations, among others, were noted as significant:

1. An important factor in inter-American relations is involved, namely,
the maintenance of the principle of immediate and just compensation in
case of expropriation.

2. The Department's study of facts and information available to it
indicate that the company has a strong legal case with respect to denial
of justice in the decision of the Bolivian Supreme Court on the company's
appeal from the decree of March 13, 1937. . . .

The first principle might be served if compensation were paid
the Company by Bolivia, and the fact of payment would amount
to a "tacit admission of a reversal of its policy" as set forth in the
decree of March 13. On the second point, the Department might
urge both parties to make a direct settlement, or failing this,
propose that Bolivia agree to arbitrate the dispute. Concerning
another point, it was stated that the Bolivian government claimed
to have documentary evidence that the Company had violated its
contract, while the Company disputed the validity of the charges.
However, in view of the political importance of the case in Bolivia,
the government "must be given an opportunity to save face in
order to avoid its own downfall," which might unfavorably affect
the Company's interests.[38]

These views were given to officers of the Company in an interview on April 28, at which one of the officers indicated that the Company was much more concerned about the withdrawal of the charge of fraud against the Company than about compensation for its Bolivian investment. It was agreed that the Company would draft a proposal safeguarding the Company's interests in other countries against charges of fraud like those made by Bolivia, and would also allow the Bolivian government to maintain the legality of the decree of March 13. The proposal would also provide for compensation to the Company based on an appraisal of the value of its properties by impartial experts.[39]

The Company's draft of a proposal was not found satisfactory by the Department, and a new draft was prepared with the expectation that it might be transmitted, through the good offices of the Department to the Bolivian government, as a proposal from the Company. However, Guachalla told Duggan that he was authorized to send to La Paz only suggestions from the Department itself, since the Bolivian government "takes the attitude that it has nothing further to discuss with the Company." He also informed Duggan that his government "could not accept international arbitration." However, he would send to La Paz a proposal by the Company if it were accompanied by "at least the Department's analysis of and comment upon" it, since La Paz felt that it must deal with the Department and not with the Company at the outset of negotiations. From this talk, Duggan concluded that a third draft should be made of the proposal, which then could be sent to La Paz with a statement that it had the approval of the Department "as a basis for a possible satisfactory settlement of the case." [40]

This procedure was followed, and Welles handed to Guachalla, on June 15, a proposed agreement between Bolivia and the Company as a basis for negotiations approved by the Department. Welles said, however, that this action was taken "not officially as on behalf of this government but unofficially as an evidence of the friendly interest which this government had in paving the way for a solution." Guachalla agreed to this and said he thought the moment was "propitious" for settlement, both because the new Foreign Minister, Alberto Ostria Gutiérrez, shared his own point of view, and "since there was no Congress now in existence in Bolivia, the Bolivian Executive would determine a question of this kind without having to obtain the consent of the leaders of the various parties, which consent for political reasons might not be forthcoming." [41]

Guachalla's acceptance of the proposal was only a personal action; he did not forward it to his government, nor did he even tell La Paz that he had talked with Welles and Duggan. He gave Duggan a memorandum with some comments on the proposal, and said that he thought his government "would never agree to any formula . . . that the government owed the Company an amount for compensation for the Company's properties. The Supreme Court decision of March 15 now made it impossible for the government to admit that it possessed any legal obligation to pay compensation to the Company." He thought the only possible formula was one which would allow "a board" to determine amounts due the government by the Company, as well as amounts due to the Company. [42]

On the basis of this talk, the Department went back to the Company, and a new proposal was prepared, calling for payments both by Bolivia and by the Company, based on the determination by a three-man tribunal of the dollar value of the Company's property in Bolivia in 1937 and the amount of taxes still due to Bolivia from the Company. [43] This proposal amounted to an international determination of these two questions; it did, however, leave entirely untouched the question of the legality or justice of the decree of March 13, 1937. [44]

Desultory talks between Guachalla and officials of the Department, and between the latter and Company officers, continued until February, 1940, when the text of the arbitral proposal was actually sent to La Paz by Guachalla. However, hope of a solution along this line had to be abandoned, following the publication of a United Press despatch in *La Razón* (La Paz) on March 20, 1940, stating that United States government officials had declared that an agreement for an arbitral tribunal would probably be signed. Guachalla immediately made a public statement that Bolivia would never accept arbitration and that he did not have knowledge of any alleged conversations about arbitration of the dispute. Guachalla's untruthful if diplomatic denial was circulated widely in Bolivia. It effectively repudiated the negotiations that had been going on for months, and it served to strengthen what Minister Jenkins called "the prevalent Bolivian public opinion that the Standard Oil case is settled and that the Standard Oil Company was dealt with according to its deserts by the Bolivian Supreme Court." [45] This incident ended all attempts to arrange a settlement via arbitration, but the case was by no means closed.[46]

By this time the Bolivian government had discovered that it was not within the power of its own Supreme Court to "settle" the controversy with the Standard Oil Company, principally because the Department of State, contrary to Finot's expectations in 1937, had not completely abandoned the Company. The Department did not question the legality of the decree of March 13, 1937, nor did it challenge the decision of the Supreme Court. The Department did not assert that the Company was in the right and Bolivia in the wrong, nor did it claim that a denial of justice had occurred. Finally, it did not insist that Bolivia accept arbitration or any other specific procedure for finding a solution. The Department did, however, take the position that the Company was entitled to some form of compensation for the value of the refineries and other installations which had been confiscated. This position was essentially the same as that adopted in the Mexican oil expropriation, even though the Bolivian action was of a different kind.[47]

The Policy of Discrimination

The Department of State did not attempt to bring any affirmative pressure to bear on the Bolivian government in the form of economic measures, and its positive diplomatic representations were of the restrained character already described. However, the Department was not altogether without resources of a negative kind, and it used these in such a way as slowly to influence the policy of successive Bolivian governments. The Department's actions in this case provide an illustration of the thinking of its officials about the principles of the Good Neighbor policy in the period of crisis just before the outbreak of World War II, and in the two years preceding the entry of the United States into the war.

The Department of State followed two principal methods of bringing influence to bear on La Paz: it tried to prevent Bolivia from obtaining help from its immediate neighbors in exploiting and exporting oil, and it refused to recommend the extension of governmental loans or technical assistance from the United States until the Bolivian government had come to terms with the Standard Oil Company.

In dealing with Bolivia's neighbors, Argentina and Paraguay, the Department was only partly successful. A tentative agreement with Paraguayan officials was reached by the YPFB on April 21, 1939, for preferential importation of Bolivian oil in the Paraguayan market.[48] This agreement was regarded as objectionable in the Department, and the question was taken up with the President-elect of Paraguay, General José Félix Estigarribia, who stated that it had been made without his consent. He told Department officials that he had no intention of proceeding to honor the agreement. Shortly after President Estigarribia's inauguration, Duggan informed the Paraguayan Chargé, who was to become the new Minister of Economic Affairs of Paraguay, that the retiring Minister had told Ambassador Norman Armour that the Paraguayan government "feeling under obligation to the United States for the consideration it had shown in connection with the Export-Import Bank credits, would not wish to do anything that could be interpreted as unfriendly to the United States," and that therefore it hesitated to approve the tentative agreement with Bolivia without knowing whether the United States "would have any objections." Duggan told the Chargé that Welles had suggested to Estigarribia that "countries with undeveloped resources could hardly expect to attract the capital necessary to develop them unless they gave security to that capital." The Chargé agreed with this suggestion and said that, besides this consideration, Estigarribia had decided not to ask the Congress to ratify the agreement because it appeared that Bolivia would obtain the major benefit from the agreement. In his new position, added the Chargé, he would do all he could to prevent the ratification of the agreement, although he thought the issue had already been settled.[49]

The agreement was not ratified by Paraguay, but, in view of the low production of the Bolivian wells and the difficulties encountered by the YPFB after the ousting of the Standard Oil Company, it is doubtful in any case that any substantial quantity of oil would have been available to Paraguay from this source.

The previously mentioned arrangements with Argentina, from which so much had been anticipated by Finot in 1937, had produced no tangible results, and on April 2, 1940, a new arrangement was signed concerning the proposed railroad from Yacuiba to Santa Cruz, for joint exploitation of the oil fields and for deliveries of Bolivian oil to Argentina in partial return for its assistance. This development stirred the Department to express its views directly to the Argentine government—an action it had not previously taken—despite several requests from the Standard Oil Company. Ambassador Norman Armour presented an *aide mémoire* to the Argentine foreign office on May 7, pointing out that some of the oil received by Argentina under the agreement would come from fields where United States nationals had "been given the exclusive rights to extract and sell petroleum." The United States government believed that the Argentine government "would wish to bear this in mind" with regard to making any commitments about oil to which United States interests "have definite claims." If any agreement adversely affected the rights of such interests, "the government of the United States would feel constrained to reserve its rights under international law."

The Argentine reaction did not give Washington much satisfaction. Foreign Minister José María Cantilo told Armour that he did not understand the reference to "international law," and Armour was instructed to explain that the *aide mémoire* "merely constituted a broad statement of this government's point of view and a reservation of its citizens' rights in the event that they might be adversely affected by any arrangements entered into. It was felt that a failure to clarify the position of this government might give rise to a subsequent misunderstanding, and that a friendly statement of our government's position would be of interest to the Argentine government as well as to other governments concerned." [50]

The formal Argentine reply, dated May 16, asserted that "it is not incumbent upon the Argentine government to decide, or even to enquire, whether the decision [of the Bolivian Supreme Court] is fair or not, whether it constitutes or not a denial of justice," and stated that it "would be unable to discuss the lawfulness of the rights claimed by the Bolivian state over the petroleum produced within its territory." [51]

Although Armour had regarded his communication to the Argentine foreign office as confidential, Cantilo immediately informed La Paz of what had taken place, and Ostria Gutiérrez expressed disapproval of Armour's action. The statement of the Department's position did not disrupt the Argentine-Bolivian plans, and the first shipment of Bolivian oil to Argentina was made in September, 1940, when a small amount was delivered for testing. [52] Shortly afterward, public announcement was made that the YPFB and the Argentine State Railways had entered into a contract for the sale by the former of 15,000 tons of fuel oil in return for the opening of a credit of 120,000 Argentine pesos. [53] This was a small transaction that did not go far toward fulfilling Finot's 1937 anticipation for rapid development of the oil fields.

This agreement gave rise to a request by the Standard Oil Company that the Department of State follow up its earlier interposition by "protesting" against the execution of this contract. The Department, however, replied that it did not think it would be "to the best interests of the Company" to make a protest, because it would "jeopardize" efforts to reach a settlement of the general question of the differences with Bolivia. [54]

Thus, the attempt of the Department to induce other countries to refrain from aiding a confiscatory government was no more successful than a comparable effort against Mexico. [55] Greater success, however, was obtained by the Department through the refusal of loans and technical assistance to Bolivia.

The Bolivian government was told as early as August, 1939, that a loan to Bolivia by an agency of the United States government would not be made before settlement of the oil dispute. [56] This position was reluctantly maintained by Welles in talks with Bolivian officials at the Panama Conference, and on various other occasions this policy position was repeated, notably by Warren L. Pierson, president of the Export-Import Bank, during a visit to La Paz in October, 1940.[57]

Changes in the Bolivian government at this time did not result in any immediate modification of its policy although they undoubtedly affected the course of the dispute in the long run. On August 23, 1939, President Busch had committed suicide. He was succeeded by General Carlos Quintanilla, under whose direction elections were held in the spring of 1940, and the new president, General Enrique Peñaranda, was inaugurated on April 15, 1940. The Peñaranda regime, like those of Busch and Quintanilla, continued both to desire financial aid from the United States and to provide no compensation to the Standard Oil Company. Jenkins reported that on one occasion Foreign Minister Ostria Gutiérrez "actually expressed annoyance at the fact that the Department was disposed to let the case stand in the way of a loan to Bolivia." [58] However, Bolivian officials finally came to recognize that the Department was determined to use its refusal of loans to pry a settlement of the dispute out of La Paz. Bolivian government officials wished to clamber on the long end of Washington's financial lever, because of their knowledge that nearly all the other Latin American countries were obtaining loans from the Export-Import Bank, particularly after the Panama Conference. However, they found it impossible for a long time to make a settlement because of their fear that the opposition might overthrow the Peñaranda regime with an alleged "surrender" to the Standard Oil Company as the issue.

The Bolivian Minister presented a memorandum to the Department on December 26, 1939, formally requesting various kinds of aid. In response, the Department gave to Guachalla a "Record" of its position as explained orally to him earlier. The memorandum stated that the Department would consider several possibilities, such as the furnishing of a committee of experts to report on the economic possibilities of Bolivia and an expert to give technical advice to the Ministry of Mines and Petroleum; the facilitation of credits by the United States to carry out projects approved by the committee of experts; and encouragement to private interests in the United States to assist in executing the experts' recommendations. However, the Standard Oil Company dispute still blocked the way to this vale of promise:

In view of the fact that satisfactory achievement of this economic co-operation in all respects must depend upon assurance that the under-takings will rest on a secure basis, and in order to secure the necessary support and cooperation of American private interests, it is believed to be essential before American financial assistance is given that a settlement will have been reached of the unfortunate controversy that has arisen in regard to the cancellation of concessions of American oil properties in Bolivia. If the plans for economic cooperation are to be fruitful, it is believed that this difficulty must be gotten out of the path, and it is hoped that the Bolivian government will proceed promptly with the necessary measures.

In addition, the program of assistance would depend on the understanding "that there exists a desire on the part of the Bolivian government also to adjust in an equitable manner the present default on its outstanding dollar bonds and in the hope that the improvement in Bolivian economic affairs will make this easier to achieve." [59]

The position of the United States government, so far as loans were concerned, was made public by Jesse Jones, president of the Reconstruction Finance Corporation, and Warren L. Pierson, head of the Export-Import Bank, when they told a committee of the Senate that they would not make loans to "a country that is confiscating our property." [60]

The broad policy problem posed by the Standard Oil issue was stated in mid-1940 by Laurence Duggan. Noting that the failure to settle this issue was the only reason why a loan had not been made to Bolivia, he considered that it was not possible to "buy" a settlement with specific credits or concessions, principally because the Bolivian government might then come under irresistible pressure from the opposition, which would allege a "sell-out" by the government to the United States interests. Noting that two members of Bolivian opposition parties were in the United States at the time, he suggested holding informal conversations with them about a possible long-term program of economic development for Bolivia in which the United States could be of financial and technical assistance. It might be anticipated that as part of the arrangements for such a program, a settlement of the Standard Oil problem could be reached, although he did not favor making settlement as a condition of the negotiation of the development program. The settlement of the oil issue would become

a matter of good faith and mutual confidence based squarely upon other advantages which both parties desire and are willing to work for. . . . In this crisis, are we to make our relations with Bolivia—with all that implies in the political, economic, military, and cultural fields—contingent upon a settlement of the Standard Oil question? [61]

The answer to this question became more pressing as war neared the Americas.

In its essentials, the situation remained unchanged until shortly before the Rio de Janeiro Conference that followed Pearl Harbor. The United States refused to make loans or provide technical assistance, and the Bolivian government, while desiring to reach a settlement of the oil question in order to obtain financial and other aid, could not find any way to do it that would not create serious popular opposition, with consequent risk of a revolution. In the early part of 1940 La Paz apparently did not fully believe that the position of the United States was a firm one, but in June Bolivian officials recognized Washington's determination and began to try to find a way out.[62]

Seeking an escape from the impasse, Bolivian officials proposed to their Congress in the autumn of 1940 that they be given authority to negotiate an agreement with the Standard Oil Company. They declared that they would under no circumstances agree to a solution that would submit the case to arbitration, call into question the legality of the decision of the Supreme Court, or provide for a return of the Company to operation or ownership of oil properties in Bolivia. One of their principal arguments, in lengthy debates, was that the United States would make no loans nor provide technical assistance to Bolivia until a settlement were made with the

Company. The authority they requested was granted by the Senate but ultimately refused by the Chamber of Deputies, which adjourned on April 30, 1941, without taking action on the request.

However, even if the Bolivian government had been authorized to make an agreement at this time, the attitude of the Standard Oil Company would probably have prevented a successful outcome of negotiations. During the course of the legislative debates in Bolivia, Guachalla suggested to Duggan that informal talks with Company officials might be reopened. The Company at first refused even to permit its officers to talk with Guachalla, although it later consented to do so after a personal appeal from Welles to President W. S. Farish.

The stand taken by the Company was that it wished to continue to press for a solution by arbitration along the lines of the proposal sent to La Paz in February, 1940, because "it did not wish to take from its international plane an arbitrary act of confiscation of the property of aliens and because it wished to avoid the imputation that it was selling its property to Bolivia under such circumstances." In addition, the Company would be willing to receive proposals from Bolivia through the Department of State, although it did not favor "private conversations with the Bolivian Minister," because "they would have an unfortunate effect on our interests generally, for it might indicate that confiscations by a foreign government are merely private matters between the government and its victim, although such confiscations materially impair the interests of all American citizens in the confiscating country and in others." [63]

In his reply, addressed to W. S. Farish, Welles said he was "disappointed in the position which the company has taken"; he believed Guachalla's suggestion for talks "offers a promising method of approach and that, in view of all the considerations, it would be advisable for the company to reconsider its position on this matter." [64]

After some delay a meeting between Guachalla and Company officials was arranged, but it was found impossible for the Bolivian government and the Company to come to terms directly. If an arbitral solution were out of the question, the Company preferred that the Department of State participate in negotiating a settlement, but this the Department did not wish to do. The Company keenly desired to prevent the dispute from being demoted from the status of an international, intergovernmental negotiation, to that of a private matter between itself and La Paz, and, if the role of the Department of State were to be no more than that of a provider of good offices, as distinct from that of an active supporter and negotiator with or on behalf of the Company, such demotion would take place. The Company's reluctance to engage in direct negotiations with Guachalla was thus the procedural corollary of its substantive position that the Bolivian government had violated international law through its act of confiscation.

The Company wished to see the Department both assert that a denial of justice had occurred and insist on redress by way of arbitration. The Department, however, at no time declared that a denial of justice had occurred, nor did it say there had been no such denial. The Department avoided the discussion of the dispute on legal grounds entirely; it recognized the existence of a dispute between Bolivia and the Company and tried to bring about a settlement as between them, but it carefully refrained from getting into a position where it might be regarded as a party to the dispute. It would not arrange for loans to Bolivia so long as the dispute was unsettled, but it would not charge Bolivia with a breach of international law.

The Department's position was influenced by its concern to maintain the most intimate cooperation with other American states in view of the European war. Further, as will be seen in the following chapter, a firm stand for arbitration in the Bolivian affair would have been inconsistent with the Department's decision in 1940 to seek a settlement with Mexico by means other than arbitration. If in 1941 it were to demand that Bolivia accept an arbitral decision, an impression would probably have been created abroad that a return to the practices of earlier administrations with respect to the protection of nationals was being made by Washington. Such an impression was not one that Hull or Welles desired to create at this moment in world politics or at this stage in the cultivation of the spirit of the Good Neighbor.

The action of the Department of State in the controversy between the Bolivian government and the Standard Oil Company consolidated into policy the decision taken toward the Mexican oil expropriations. The new policy, which does not appear to have been stated explicitly by the Department of State, may, it is suggested, be regarded as being based on the principle that the interests of United States business enterprises in Latin America were not identical with the interests of the government of the United States but were of substantially less importance. The interests of business enterprises would be protected so far as protection did not interfere with what the Department regarded as the essential requirements for the maintenance of good political relations with Latin American countries, but protection would not be offered if it did interfere with such relations. After 1931, when Stimson refused to provide Marines to defend the property or lives of United States citizens in the interior of Nicaragua, the armed forces could not be successfully called on by United States companies to protect their holdings in Latin America. Following 1939, the Department of State could no longer be regarded as an international law office automatically responding to requests for the presentation to international tribunals of cases affecting United States companies. This change in policy, no less important than Stimson's, did not mean that no protection whatever would be given to United States enterprises, but it did mean that the protection would be of a different kind and that it might provide remedies which were both less prompt and less adequate in the view of the enterprises affected.

However, a new stimulus to a different kind of solution of the problem came from an entirely different direction. The question was raised with the Department of State whether it was wise to continue to refuse economic aid to Bolivia. Officials of the Bureau of Mines suggested to Assistant Secretary Breckinridge Long that the Standard Oil Company dispute prevented any exploitation of Bolivia's oil resources with United States capital, and that there was a danger that "German agents . . . will get the concessions for German account and will open up credits in blocked marks as the payment for furnishing the mining materials necessary to do the drilling and production." Long consequently suggested to Welles that "it looks as if some effort should be made by this Department" to dispose of the Standard Oil Company case.[65]

No immediate action followed this idea nor one by Minister Douglas Jenkins that "it does not seem wise on our part to allow a troublesome question like the Standard Oil case to remain open like a festering sore, if any means can be found to dispose of it or ease it in some way," [66] but these comments may have helped prepare the minds of Department officials for a change in policy. The change was further prepared by the adjournment of the Bolivian Chamber of Deputies on April 30, with no action on the government's request for authority to negotiate a settlement of the oil dispute.[67]

The Department's awareness of Bolivian attempts to develop economic collaboration with Germany and Japan had given rise to the recommendation in Washington that

it might be advisable for the United States government to undertake reasonable measures of economic and financial cooperation with the Bolivian government, in the hope that there might be engendered a cooperative attitude on the part of the Bolivians which would produce a favorable atmosphere for further consideration of the Standard Oil case and also for consideration of settlement of the defaulted dollar debt of the Bolivian government.[68]

These slow currents were gradually changing the attitude of the Department of State, which had taken no affirmative action since February, 1940, when it had given its approval to the fruitless proposal for arbitration. A sudden change in policy in the direction of these currents resulted from the discovery in July, 1941, of a plot to overthrow the Peñaranda government, in which the Bolivian Military Attaché at Berlin, Major Elías Belmonte, and the German Minister to Bolivia, Ernst Wendler, were thought to be implicated. Washington immediately offered Bolivia assistance in resisting Nazi activities, and an agreement for the sending of a military mission to Bolivia was signed on September 4, 1941. In addition, on August 1, the United States presented to Bolivia a plan for economic collaboration, including the possible extension of credits from the Export-Import Bank for highway and other developments. This plan, intended to go into effect following a report from an expert mission, was accepted by the Bolivian government, and the mission, headed by Merwin L. Bohan, arrived in La Paz on December 17, 1941.

Although the Standard Oil Company expressed the hope that no credits would be given to Bolivia "without some understanding concerning further consideration of the Standard Oil case," the Department of State took the position that it was nevertheless

prepared to cooperate in giving effect to recommendations arising out of thorough technical and economic surveys of Bolivian communications needs and agricultural and mineral potentialities. . . . This cooperation is not contingent upon the solution of any specific problem, such as the Standard Oil case, but it has been made known to important political circles in Bolivia . . . . that this government expects the cooperation to be unqualifiedly bilateral.[69]

Considerations relating to the war, to continental solidarity, and to the national interest of the United States in speeding the economic development of Bolivia were now viewed in Washington as of greater importance than receiving prior assurance from Bolivia that the claims of the Standard Oil Company would be satisfied. However, reliance was placed on the desires of Bolivian officials for a settlement of the case, as expressed by them in the legislative debates, and also on the good will which it was hoped would be engendered by the removal of the settlement of the case from its key position as a condition of economic aid.

As it turned out, this reliance on reciprocity was not misplaced. The Japanese attack on the United States put a new face on the whole affair, and, at the Rio de Janeiro Conference, in a few days agreement was reached over a controversy which had by then lasted almost five years. The Bolivian Foreign Minister, Eduardo Anze Matienzo, arrived at the Conference with authority from President Peñaranda to secure an agreement on the Standard Oil Company case. He gave Welles a draft text, providing an "indemnity" to the Company for the rights it claimed to hold in Bolivia. Matienzo suggested that Bolivia would be willing to pay $1,000,000 to the Company. Welles suggested a procedure like that arranged with Mexico, but Matienzo preferred a quick solution, arranged at the

Conference, in order to help his president to obtain political support for the agreement.[70]

Duggan informed Welles that Standard Oil officers wished to avoid the term indemnity, "in order to safeguard their overall international position," and wished to make the agreement in the form of a sale of the Company's rights and property. However, the officers evinced a spirit of compromise and stated that, in view of the importance Welles attached to an immediate settlement, and since they did not wish to "handicap any other matters which may be considered of more far-reaching importance at this stage," they would place themselves "in his hands with respect to the final wording of the agreement." They added that they had hoped to obtain $3,000,000 from the sale of their Bolivian properties, but they left the amount, and the rate of interest, to the discretion of Welles. Duggan said that he and other officials favored the simple agreement of sale as suggested by the Company.[71]

Welles quickly completed negotiations with Anze Matienzo, and, on January 27, an agreement was signed by the latter for Bolivia and by H. A. Metzger for the Standard Oil Companies of Bolivia and New Jersey. The agreement provided for the payment by Bolivia to the Company (New Jersey) of $1,500,000, within ninety days, "for the sale of all of its rights, interests, and properties in Bolivia," with interest at 3 percent from March 13, 1937. The agreement, "freely entered into," also provided that on the completion of this payment, there would remain no issue between the parties.[72]

The settlement provided some measure of satisfaction to all parties concerned. To Bolivia, the way was fully opened for economic collaboration, and an agreement providing for a $25,000,000 economic development program financed by the United States government was announced at Rio de Janeiro on January 28. Bolivia also had the satisfaction of making a positive move toward reciprocity and continental solidarity by coming to terms with the Standard Oil Company. To the Company, the agreement could be defended on the ground that it was a business transaction, and neither a forced sale nor an indemnity, which, in view of an investment of about $17,000,000, would have seemed grossly inade-

quate and would have established a precedent which other countries
might have regarded as an invitation to expropriation or confiscation. The amount received was small. However, it may have been
some comfort that the principles for which the Company had been
contending had not been expressly violated, although for all practical purposes Farish and his colleagues must have realized that
henceforth they were on their own. They could no longer push
the Department of State ahead of them as a parental shield in their
disputes with Latin American governments.

From the point of view of the United States government, the
agreement gave grounds for satisfaction. Since it had already determined to aid Bolivia ultimately, despite the oil controversy, and
since the initiative had come from La Paz, there was little ground
for charges that the settlement had resulted from "pressure" by
Washington. Bolivian officials were pleased with the arrangement,
and the suddenly cooperative attitude of the Company, in marked
contrast to its previously inflexible stand, was gratifying to the
Department of State.[73]

The signing of the agreement did not mean that the struggle was
ended. Duggan recognized the need for quickly following up the
Rio de Janeiro accord, lest opposition in Bolivia be given a chance
to arise, and he cabled Chargé Allen Dawson in La Paz, to use the
influence of the Legation "in every appropriate and tactful way
to press for the immediate issuance of the supreme decree that will
terminate the Standard Oil of Bolivia problem." [74]

The reaction of the Bolivian press and public to the news of
the signing of the agreement was reported as "favorable" by Dawson, and on February 24, the supreme decree which constituted
governmental approval of the agreement was issued. The decree
summarized the agreement, noted that all claims between Bolivia
and the Standard Oil Company were terminated, observed that "the
Export-Import Bank has offered to the Bolivian government an
initial credit of $5,500,000 for the development of the oil industry,"
declared that the agreement "is in accord with the national interest,"
and announced the formal approval of the Cabinet.[75]

The Bolivian Congress was not in session at this time and would
not meet until August. This consideration appears to have been

of major importance at Rio de Janeiro in the fixing of the time limit of ninety days for the making of the payment to the Company, for then the Congress would not be able to meet until after completion of all the terms of the agreement. Although the government had not received express congressional authorization to negotiate with the Company at the end of the long debates in 1940 and 1941, neither had Congress voted that the government could not negotiate. The government thereupon boldly decided to present the Congress with the accomplished fact, not only of a signed agreement, but of the irrevocable action of a cash settlement. However, the publication of the supreme decree did not complete the transaction, and the political opponents of Peñaranda made every effort to prevent it.

The leader of the Genuine Republican party, Demetrio Canelas, who was also the chairman of the Foreign Affairs Committee of the Chamber of Deputies, declared in a letter to the press on February 27 that the fulfillment of the agreement would be unconstitutional without the consent of the Bolivian legislature. This letter caused what Dawson described as "consternation" in government circles. Dawson told the Department that he would continue his efforts "to put some backbone into the responsible Bolivian officials," and he said to Foreign Minister Anze Matienzo that he would "be glad to tell any of his colleagues or the President himself that I considered the Standard Oil settlement a cornerstone of the economic cooperation program and to express my earnest hope that it would be put into effect as agreed upon in Rio de Janeiro." [76]

Following Canelas's letter, there was a renewed debate within the Cabinet, and the decision to make the payment to the Company was apparently made only by a narrow majority. Dawson reported that, while his own efforts and those of Bohan had been of some influence, the major credit for the final decision should go to Anze Matienzo.[77] After further delays caused mainly by financial complications among Bolivian agencies, a check for $1,729,375 was delivered to the Standard Oil Company on April 22, eighty-five days after the signature of the agreement at Rio de Janeiro. Dawson cabled, for himself and Bohan, that "it has been pulling hen's teeth to accomplish what we have." The Company and the Department graciously overlooked the minor irregularities that the check was delivered through the Chemical National Bank of New York, instead of through Guachalla, and that interest was paid through April 18, instead of through April 22, and the Company delivered to Bolivia its maps and geological studies of the oil regions.

In Bolivia the case was not closed until, in November, 1942, a motion of censure failed of passage by a single vote in the Chamber of Deputies. A speech by President Peñaranda fittingly closes the story of the dispute, since it both expounded the position of the government and associated his administration with the Good Neighbor policy. The President emphasized that, while the agreement was signed with the Company, the negotiations at Rio de Janeiro were carried on with Under Secretary of State Welles, "thus giving the matter its correct significance as a political problem related to the cooperation between two countries clothed in the necessary respectability." The agreement had been followed by promises of economic aid by the United States, including assistance in the development of the petroleum industry. The President declared that the agreement was constitutional, and pointed to its financial desirability, by commenting not only that the sum paid by Bolivia was only 10 percent of the $17,000,000 invested in Bolivia by the Company, but also that the maps and surveys furnished by the Company "are so important that technicians value them at four times the price agreed to at Rio de Janeiro."

In defending his own actions, the President both criticized and defended the policy of the Department of State:

Capital from the United States of America could not be attracted on the basis of a decree [that of March 13, 1937] which, in spite of all explanations made in good faith, was considered to be confiscatory. Unfortunately, the Department of State, which is always consulted in such emergencies, did not seem to disagree with this reasoning. Thus, future investments in Bolivia were hindered since by tradition the investments and activities of American companies in foreign countries are supervised to a certain extent by the Department of State.

I wish to establish definitely and with complete satisfaction that the Department of State always acted in this matter—and it could not have done otherwise—with great respect for the highest Bolivian interests; it never sought to modify the terms of the decree.

President Peñaranda significantly proclaimed a new orientation
of Bolivian foreign policy toward the United States and away from
Europe, and so provided for Washington a source of genuine satisfaction with its own course in the dispute:

My government, departing from the ominous policy of isolation,
adopted the more cordial and more advantageous policy of narrowing
each day, more and more closely, its relations with European countries.

As a result, it was my duty to eliminate the obstacles which prevented
complete cooperation with the government in Washington—to clear the
road so that the confidence of that government could be gained and it
would be possible to work in an atmosphere of fruitful cooperation.

Finally, the President made a contribution toward the growth
of an understanding of the Good Neighbor policy on the part
of Bolivians and other Americans, by expressing his views about
the idea of reciprocity with an amplitude unusual among heads of
state of the countries of Latin America:

The putting into effect of the American "Good Neighbor" policy was
accompanied by a sense of reciprocity, that is, the point was made clear
that this doctrine implies mutual respect between countries and reciprocal
safeguarding of the interests of nationals. Making this concept even
clearer, the Department of State declared that it did not object nor could
it object to acts of expropriation which might be decreed if they were
in keeping with the interests of the governments, as long as adequate
and acceptable indemnity was provided. Thus, the "Good Neighbor"
policy is based upon two premises: Reciprocity and just and adequate
indemnity for all property expropriated.

That is the position adopted by the United States in its economic relations with Latin American countries. It is up to these countries to
decide freely to accept or to refuse that policy based on equitable reciprocity. . . .

The agreement at Rio de Janeiro put into effect the doctrine of the
"Good Neighbor" policy between Bolivia and the United States. On the
basis of reciprocity, it assured the economic and technical cooperation
of that great country without limitations of time or capital, which will
grow in proportion to our economic solvency and the human possibilities
of labor.[78]

This speech happily closed an episode in the relations between
Bolivia and the United States that had opened unpromisingly with
Finot's hostile attitude. The work of the Commission of Experts
proceeded, and a second commission to examine problems of tin
production was despatched early in 1943. The course of collabora-

tion so favorably inaugurated was not a smooth one, for the Peñaranda government was overthrown in December, 1943, by an army group headed by Major Gualberto Villaroel, which was refused recognition for seven months by the United States and all other American countries, except Argentina. The Standard Oil case was not, however, reopened, and, after a hiatus, technical assistance from the United States was resumed.

CHAPTER VIII

The Principle of Accommodation: Mexico I

WHEN PRESIDENT Lázaro Cárdenas expropriated the properties of Dutch, British, and United States oil companies in Mexico
on March 18, 1938, he initiated a struggle over high stakes. The
value of the oil lands under concession to all the companies was
nearly $500,000,000; United States companies' estimates of the
worth of the lands to which they held title was about $200,000,-
000, and their investments in drilling and other equipment came
to about $60,000,000 on the basis of their own appraisals.

The continuity of the Cárdenas administration and of the direction it had given to the Mexican revolution were higher stakes
that were also in play, for Cárdenas could not be sure of the outcome of the contest. The oil companies were influential and un-
compromising, and they might be able to secure effective support
from their governments. If Cárdenas should thereby suffer a severe
loss of prestige, there were influential Mexicans who opposed the
pace and course of Cárdenas's policies and who might try to oust
him by force.

The expropriation decree was Cárdenas's response to the refusal
by the oil companies to accept the full terms of a decision by the
Mexican labor board in a labor dispute that had begun in 1936.
Cárdenas told Ambassador Josephus Daniels that the decree would
not have been issued if the companies even at the last moment
had been willing to abide by the decision.[1] In a speech ten years

afterward, Castillo Nájera, Mexican ambassador in Washington in 1938, recalled that as late as September, 1937, Cárdenas had spoken to him only of "control" of the companies, and the Ambassador interpreted the final decision as follows:

The obstinacy of the companies in disobeying the law, and the threat implied in their declaration "that they would not be responsible for the consequences" of the dispute, which amounted to their considering themselves as powerful as the government, was decisive in bringing about the action taken on the night of March 18, 1938.[2]

Cárdenas was of course aware that the United States had signed pledges of nonintervention at Inter-American conferences in 1933 and 1936, but, although the expropriation was consistent with his administration's vigorous prosecution of social reforms, the timing of the decree seems to have been due more to anger and exasperation at the oil companies' policies than to the climax of a calculated course of action.

On the other hand, some oil company representatives believed that the Cárdenas administration intended from the beginning to expropriate the oil properties, but as late as January, 1938, Daniels did not think this was Cárdenas's policy. Daniels thought the controversy was primarily a wage dispute, and that it was "a mistake to suppose, as some of the oil men here do, that the strike originates in a desire to use it as an excuse for governmental expropriation of all oil fields."[3]

The Department of State was surprised by the expropriation. It had not been asked for assistance by the oil companies before March 18, and until then Under Secretary of State Sumner Welles was ready to let constitutional procedures in Mexico take their course. He told the British Ambassador, Sir Ronald Lindsay, in February, that the United States did not propose to take any action in the dispute, which then had taken the form of an appeal of the labor board's decision by the oil companies to the Mexican Supreme Court. Welles calmly said that since the Mexican government appeared to be operating in accordance with Mexican legislation, "if the Court upheld the previous award of the Labor Board, there would seem to be no more reason for this government to interpose in the matter than there would be for the Mexican government to interpose if the decision had been rendered by the Supreme Court of the United States." [4]

In the fall of 1937, Ambassador Daniels had urged both Cárdenas and company officials to try to avoid an impasse in the negotiations. When, in March, 1938, the Supreme Court approved the labor board's decision, Daniels advised the company representatives that "no settlement was possible unless they agreed to pay the full amount upheld by the Supreme Court, in view of the fact that President Cárdenas had pledged that the twenty-six million peso award would be the maximum sum they would be called upon to pay. They said they could not pay that sum." [5]

However, on March 16, all the oil companies agreed to pay the amount of the award but stated that they could not accept certain other requirements established by the labor board. Encouraged by this concession, Daniels talked with Under Secretary for Foreign Affairs Ramón Beteta and urged him "to secure conferences between the oil men and the labor leaders." Further talks did not bring full compliance from the companies, however, and the expropriation decree was then issued. There is some evidence that the British companies would, at the end, have accepted fully the decision of the labor board, but that the United States companies got them to hold out on the expectation of "strong backing from Washington." [6]

This chapter is presented, not as a full account of the course of the expropriation controversy, but rather as a study of policies followed by officials of the United States government that expressed their differing and developing conceptions of the range and style of action of a good neighbor, as affected by Mexican ideas on this same subject. [7]

Chronologically the controversy may be separated into four phases. The first phase ended on April 2, 1938, with the public understanding that the United States would accept the legality of the expropriation and that Mexico would accept the obligation to compensate the oil companies. A second phase of about two years of negotiations and experimentation with different policies was terminated in April, 1940, with a formal proposal by the United States for arbitration of all aspects of the question of compensation due the companies. This proposal was rejected by Mexico, and a third phase, lasting until November 19, 1941, was marked by Washington's acceptance of the Mexican counterproposal of a two-man commission for settlement of issues of compensation, and the vain efforts of Hull and Welles to gain acceptance of this procedure by the oil companies. The fourth and final phase was completed in the spring of 1942 by the decision of the commission, and the subsequent acceptance by the companies of the terms of the award.

Analytically, the policy of the United States appears in these several phases as a series of probing operations that demonstrated that there were certain techniques of influence and methods of settlement that officials either would not employ or would employ only in limited fashion in the light of their individual conceptions of Good Neighborly behavior, and others that were gradually found to be both consistent with those conceptions and acceptable to Mexico. No code of conduct had been formulated, and policy was the resultant of such factors as the prestige, location, independence, and access to President Roosevelt enjoyed by different individuals, in addition to judgments about the national interest of the United States with respect to Mexico and the oil companies.

Before a mutually satisfactory way of settlement was found, there were four fields of action that, with respect to Mexico, were placed outside the pale of neighborly behavior. One was the use of force (this was not contemplated within the Department of State but was proposed from without). The other three were discovered to be unneighborly only after they were tried out by the Department itself. These were: (1) the delivery and publication of an "ultimatum" (the word is Daniels's); (2) economic measures having coercive effects on Mexico; and (3) insistence on arbitration for settlement of any issue in the controversy. It may be said that these were "discovered" to be unneighborly since the expropriation was an unanticipated test of a Good Neighbor, and Washington had no strategy to deal with such an eventuality. The Bolivian experience offered little aid, since the stakes there were far smaller and the dispute could be treated as an incident, while in the Mexican case the expropriation was regarded in Washington as part of a well-established Mexican policy already being carried out with respect to farm lands owned both by Mexicans and foreigners.

An Ultimatum Is Not the Way of a Good Neighbor

The expropriation "surprised and shocked" Cordell Hull, and Sumner Welles told Ambassador Castillo Nájera that the Mexican policy was "suicidal" and might make friendly and satisfactory negotiations impossible. Welles went so far as to suggest that Cárdenas should rescind the expropriation decree, but the Ambassador doubted that this was possible in view of the popular excitement in Mexico.[8]

Castillo Nájera was right on this point, for the climate of opinion in Mexico was stormy. *El Nacional,* the government newspaper, published an editorial on March 19 declaring that this was no time for retractions; even if "the belts of Mexicans may have to be pulled ten holes tighter," the thread of history would be renewed: "first, political independence, then internal emancipation, today the inexorable rupture of this umbilical cord which ties us to imperialism . . . The country writes its history with its own blood." Daniels saw a "wave of delirious enthusiasm" sweeping the country,[9] and Cárdenas had been so angered by the manner and duration of the resistance of the oil companies that he was in no mood to reconsider.

Looking back, Cordell Hull saw his policy as "firm" but "friendly," in keeping with "the spirit of the Good Neighbor." [10] In the unbounded but fairly narrow area between these neighborly precepts Hull's policy moved slowly and tentatively. From the beginning, however, there were two solid positions about which United States officials were unanimous. On the one hand, Mexico's right to expropriate was admitted, but, on the other, the companies would be supported in their claims for compensation. The type and intensity of support remained to be explored between firmness and friendliness.

The view of the Department of State was expressed privately as early as March 21 by Laurence Duggan, chief of the Division of

American Republics, in saying that even while awaiting the oil companies' "brief" he had thought "of the possibility of our delivering a note in the near future, not only for the record but for the effect it might have on the Mexican officials. It would have to be worded carefully, but should make it pretty clear that we expect real compensation." [11] Even Daniels "saw no course open but to seek to aid the companies in securing compensation." [12]

Beyond these elementary points there appears to have been no agreement, because there had been no serious consideration of alternative lines of policy. The Department of State "learned the angles" of the good neighborly game as its shots caromed off the Mexican foreign office and the Standard Oil Company of New Jersey. For a long time the Department made only misses, which may have been fortunate in view of the final score.

The danger in the situation immediately after expropriation was that the reaction of the United States government would be so peremptory as to close the door to negotiations by causing a defiant Cárdenas to break diplomatic relations. Indeed, the first note from the Department of State to Mexico almost certainly would have had that effect, had not Ambassador Daniels, by a remarkable combination of insubordination and suppression of information, prevented the note from ever gaining formally recorded status.

Ambassador Daniels made on March 18 the first public statement by a representative of the United States government. Asked whether he had engagements to see Mexican officials or intended to file a protest, he said that he had kept the Department of State informed and had sent it copies of the decree and of President Cárdenas's accompanying speech. He also stated that he had told Foreign Secretary Eduardo Hay and Under Secretary Ramón Beteta before March 18 that it would be "a serious calamity to all concerned" if an agreement were not reached.[13]

This interview was remarkable for what it omitted, rather than for what Daniels said. He did not express any personal or official protest against the expropriation, and so made it possible for Mexicans and others to interpret his attitude, and that of Washington, as one of acceptance if not of approval. Daniels's silence and inaction, particularly when contrasted with the presentation by March 21, of a note of protest by the British minister, was regarded in Mexico as "meaning that we are backing the Government up." [14] Daniels's reticence reflected his lack of instructions in the event of expropriation; it also reflected his desire to avoid making a crisis of the situation, for his sympathies throughout were with the Mexican government and not with the oil companies.[15]

In Daniels's first, postexpropriation interview with Cárdenas, the President said that he had "the sincere intention of proceeding immediately to begin offering compensation" and that the companies could take legal action in the Mexican courts against the expropriation decree.[16] Although both Cárdenas and Daniels considered these verbal assurances as having crucial significance, they were not regarded in Washington as adequate bases for negotiation. Consequently, on March 26, a note was sent to Daniels for delivery on March 27 to Foreign Minister Eduardo Hay. When it was delivered, Daniels was to go to Washington for consultation and the note was to be published in Washington, together with a separate statement that the Treasury Department would "defer continuation of the monthly silver purchase arrangement with Mexico until further notice."

The note of March 26 commenced with President Roosevelt's dedication of his country to the "policy of the Good Neighbor," made in his first inaugural address. The principles of this policy, stated the note,

include a real friendship between nations, complete confidence of the respective governments and peoples in each other, the adjustment of difficulties by processes of negotiation and agreement, fair play and fair dealing, and the wholehearted disposition to cooperate each with the other for the promotion of their mutual interests and mutual welfare. [This policy] must of its very essence have a reciprocal character if the peoples of the New World are to progress steadily toward a higher level of international relationships.

The note then stated that the United States government had "been mindful of the high social objectives" of the Mexican government. To this end, the development of natural resources in Mexico had been stated by President Cárdenas to be necessary.

"For such development, capital has been required," and in the past a large amount of American capital had been invested in Mexico, and it had been welcomed there.

However, the United States had "noticed with anxiety the increasing number of instances of disregard of legitimate and uncontroverted private property interests of its nationals," in the cases both of agricultural and oil properties. The United States government had previously represented to Mexico that,

while it has not been disposed to question the right of the Mexican government to take over and distribute large holdings of real property, such action should not amount—as it has in effect—to the confiscation of such property, but that under every rule of generally recognized law as well as equity, the rightful owners are entitled to the payment of just compensation, having a present effective value to the owners from whom their properties are taken.

The United States reserved the rights of itself and its nationals in these matters, and it had "taken attentive note" of a statement by Cárdenas that Mexico would not refuse to pay for what had been expropriated.

In view of these considerations, and Cárdenas's statement, Hull concluded:

My government directs me to inquire in the event that the Mexican government persists in this expropriation, without my government undertaking to speak for the American interests involved, but solely for its preliminary information, what specific action with respect to payment for the properties in question is contemplated by the Mexican government, what assurances will be given that payment will be made, and when such payment may be expected. Inasmuch as the American citizens involved have already been deprived of their properties, and in view of the rule of law stated, my government considers itself entitled to ask for a prompt reply to this inquiry.[17]

The emphasis given in the note to the reciprocal character of the Good Neighbor policy was an expression of deeply felt hurt in Washington. Hull was aggrieved. He felt he had been a good neighbor, and could point to many friendly gestures as proof. He had been angered by the raising of the Mexican tariff at the beginning of 1938, and he felt that the oil expropriation, added to five years of Mexican dilatoriness on compensation for agrarian expropriations, was poor recompense for his sincere efforts to create an atmosphere of good will. He was also, of course, under pressure from oil and other interests to protest the expropriation. Here, and in other cases, Hull learned that it was fruitless for him to charge a Latin American government with not being a Good Neighbor; this charge was more effective when made by Latin Americans against the United States, for was it not President Roosevelt alone who had dedicated his nation to that policy?

It was here that Daniels changed the course of policy. He did not like the tone of the note, saying later that he felt, "My dear friend, Cordell Hull, let his Tennessee temper lead him into undue sharpness in a message to Mexico." [18] He, therefore, cabled Hull immediately, desiring to fly to Washington before "anything in the nature of an ultimatum" was delivered, since "every possible step should be taken to prevent the threatened break in the relations between the two countries." [19]

Daniels's remonstrances caused Hull to change his tactics in one important way: publication of the note would be withheld "for the time being, and definitely if a satisfactory solution is found." [20] However, the note was to be delivered to Hay in accordance with the original plan, without any verbal changes, except the elimination of the word "very" in the phrase requesting "a very prompt reply to this inquiry." Word of the ending of the silver purchase agreement had already been given to the Mexican Ambassador on March 25, and the termination was publicly announced in Washington on March 27.

After gaining his point against publicity, Daniels made no further protests. Saying in his memoirs that "as a good messenger [he] obeyed orders," [21] he reported to Hull that he saw Hay on Sunday, March 27, "and delivered note to him as you sent it." Hay read the note and said that "Mexico was resolved to pay." He added that he would make an early response, and that he would not publish the note since Daniels told him that the note would not be published in Washington "in view of his [Hay's] promise to . . . make a prompt reply." [22] Daniels recalls in his memoirs that Hay was surprised that Hull had made an "arraignment" and an "indictment" of Mexican policy, and quoted Hay as saying: "This note seems to have been written without the knowledge of the oral assurance made to you by President Cárdenas."

Daniels engaged in a bit of independent, personal policy in this meeting with Hay that later gave rise to misunderstandings. He records in his memoirs:

> While I was in full accord with Secretary Hull's insistence upon payment for properties expropriated, I could not feel that a resort to note-writing would achieve the results sought, particularly since both the Foreign Minister and President Cárdenas had plighted their word orally to do what Hull asked in his note.
>
> Seeing that we might be in for long and inconclusive note writing, I said to the Foreign Minister: "Since the President has promised payment for property expropriated, it may be as well to consider the note as 'not received' and I will convey again to my government the promise to pay." [23]

Daniels did not, however, inform the Department of State at the time that he told Hay that the note could be regarded as "not received."

Two days later, Hay told Daniels that Cárdenas wished to request that the note of March 26 "be withdrawn and altered," because it made no reference to Cárdenas's assurances of compensation made orally to Daniels on March 22. Daniels recommended to Hull that the "last page of the note be altered in conformity with request." [24] This recommendation was not adopted in Washington.

A few hours after sending this cable, Daniels talked with Hull by telephone. Daniels had a sore throat, and part of the talk was carried on through Counselor Pierre Boal. Boal said that he himself had informed the Mexican foreign office that it was a "large order" to ask that the note be revised; the response had been that the note might be held up for a few days so that Mexico could state in writing what Cárdenas had told Daniels on March 22 about compensation.

Hull felt that it was difficult "to withdraw a note in effect or put it in cold storage," not knowing yet that Daniels had been the iceman. However, since the Mexican government might consider it necessary to argue the question raised by the note as to whether it was following a policy of reciprocity within the spirit of the Good Neighbor, Hull adhered to his decision that it would be best not to publish the note, for a short time at least.

Daniels came on the phone, and Hull said that the note had been sent so that the Department of State would be able to respond to inquiries in Washington by saying that it had developed plans and had taken action to secure compensation for the oil companies. Hull noted that his policy toward Mexico had been friendly, and he hoped for evidence of reciprocity on the part of the Cárdenas administration. To Daniels's inquiry whether he might tell the press that no ultimatum had been issued, Hull replied that Daniels could say that the note was simply one of inquiry.[25]

The matter of the note was left in this confused status. Daniels had told Hay it could be regarded as "not received" but had not reported this to Hull. Hull thought the note might be held for a few days without being made public, but he expected that the Mexican government would make a reply to it.

That a meeting of the minds of Hull and Daniels had not occurred did not appear until a second, if less serious, crisis three months later, but in the meantime the situation was greatly eased by suave diplomacy on the part of both governments. While awaiting a reply to the note of March 26, Hull felt he had to make some public statement to amplify his March 21 announcement of "concern." To satisfy clamor at home,[26] he made on March 30 a further statement on the Department's position substantially in accord with the essential terms of the note of March 26, but without referring to the note or saying that a note had been delivered. This was a brief and moderate declaration that did not refer to "anxiety" or mention the Good Neighbor policy; Hull even remarked that the oil expropriation was "but one incident in a long series of incidents of this character and accordingly raises no new question." [27]

The conciliatory note struck by Hull found an immediate echo in Mexico, where Cárdenas on March 31 read to Daniels a formal note addressed to him as Ambassador, stating that the President and people of the United States had "won the esteem of the people of Mexico" by the "proof of friendship" shown in the attitude of the United States government. During the "last few days" the Mexican nation had known "moments of trial" when it "did not know whether it would have to give rein to its patriotic feelings or to applaud an act of justice" on the part of the United States. Mexico, said Cárdenas, "will know how to honor its obligations of today and its obligations of yesterday."²⁸ This statement and an appreciative reply by Hull were published on April 2. On April 1, Roosevelt had told a press conference that Cárdenas's message was "very satisfactory."²⁹

This exchange completed the first phase of the oil controversy. Cárdenas seized on Hull's March 30 statement with relief and pleasure as something he could accept with dignity and friendly warmth, and his reply to that statement was in effect his reply to the note of March 26, which otherwise never was answered. The published approval given the reply in Washington meant that negotiations could be opened, although it did not mean that they would be short, simple, or harmonious. Daniels was probably right as well as picturesque in saying: "There are plenty of hurdles ahead, but we have safely vaulted over the highest. . . . It is to our interest as well as our good neighbor duty to facilitate and aid where we can in the fulfillment of the intention expressed by President Cárdenas. Freedom from strife here and stabilization of the peso will facilitate the payments."³⁰

This highest hurdle, however, had to be vaulted once more by Daniels when in July, 1938, Cárdenas told newsmen in Mexico that "the United States Department [of State] had made no demands upon Mexico in regard to the expropriation and had sent no formal note." Hull immediately asked Daniels for confirmation of this report, saying that "the Department . . . of course assumes that the Government of Mexico has always regarded" the note of March 26 "as having been delivered. . . ."³¹

Daniels reported that Hay had given him a statement, and that Cárdenas's remarks did "not justify the impression that Secretary Hull had not, from the first, insisted through the Embassy in behalf of American oil companies that they be paid for the oil properties expropriated."³²

This statement was far from satisfactory to Hull, since it made no reference to the note of March 26. Hull was to hold a press conference on July 21, and Duggan telephoned to Daniels in the morning to review the situation. It was only at this time that the Department learned what had really happened when Daniels "delivered" the note to Hay. Duggan said that "we did not contemplate either the permanent sidetracking or the suspension of the note; that the idea was that the note would remain with the Foreign Office, but that their observations, whatever they were, could be made without any reference to our note, just as though it had not been delivered, although it was actually in their possession." The conversation continued:

Mr. Daniels: That is all right. After we had talked about it I went to see General Hay and as I understand it he said if the President [Cárdenas] is going to pay or promise to pay for it, I [Hay] will regard the note as not received.

Mr. Duggan: Do they have the note? Does the Mexican government have physical possession of the note?

Mr. Daniels: Yes. Hay said, "I will keep the note, but I will treat it as if not received," and I assented to that.

Mr. Duggan: Of course the Secretary meant that if the Mexicans wanted to get to us the observations that President Cárdenas earlier had made to you, they could do so as on their own initiative and without direct reference to our note.

Mr. Daniels: But the Mexicans had already said that they were going to pay so that the note was no longer necessary.[33]

This talk took place in the morning, while Hull and Welles were drafting a statement for release at Hull's press conference in the afternoon. At 1:35 P.M., Daniels telephoned Duggan to ask if the press had been told that a note had been sent on March 26. Duggan read him the press release approved at 1:30, which stated that Daniels had "handed to the Mexican Minister for Foreign Affairs at the Foreign Office a note from this Government which General Hay read." It further stated:

The note in substance reserved all American rights as to property of every kind expropriated, or in the act of expropriation by the Mexican government. This government acknowledged the sovereign right of another government thus to expropriate, but coupled with the transaction the condition that adequate, prompt, and effective compensation should be made in accord with the universally recognized principle of international law and equity.[34]

On hearing the text of the approved release, Daniels told Duggan: "I feel bound to say that General Hay will consider that statement bad faith." Duggan then put Hull on the wire. The Secretary told Daniels that he had understood that Cárdenas had wanted to send the essence of his talk with Daniels to Washington, but not in the form of a reply to the March 26 note, and that Cárdenas had not wanted publicity on either message. Hull added that he had been "entirely agreeable to accommodate and oblige them," but he "never remotely thought about canceling our note."

Daniels said that Hay had not thought the note was canceled. He continued:

General Hay told President Cárdenas that he had said to me that he would act as if the note hadn't been received. That made it perfectly reasonable to Cárdenas that the note had never been officially received. . . . I think this, that Cárdenas thought he was being accurate when he said that he hadn't received any note. He, of course, has the note in his possession. He read the note. He knows everything in it. I have been continuously pointing out our position to the Mexican government.

Daniels again urged that no public reference to the note of March 26 be made, even though some oil men knew of its existence. Hull said: "We have to answer the questions that the press is asking in some way." The two men then agreed there had been a "misunderstanding":

Secretary: In the first place, the Mexicans construed this beyond any idea that we dreamed of as a permanent thing and in the second place, there was some misunderstanding by Boal and you in regard to what I said.
Ambassador Daniels: There was a misunderstanding. I told Hay to write his note as though our note had not been received. Maybe I ought not to have done that. Cárdenas's attitude, therefore, has been that he hadn't received our note. In your press statement I would say that I [Hull] had sent notes and that the Ambassador has made oral representations. If you could leave out reference to that one note to save them embarrassment, everything will be all right.
Secretary: The Mexicans will keep hanging on to that point.
Ambassador Daniels: I talked with Beteta this morning and he now appreciates that no further denials can be made that no note has been received on the oil matter. . . .
Secretary: I will have a talk with my associates and go into all phases of the matter. Today we are sending the Mexican government a note on the small landholders. We are sending you the text by cable.[35]

Daniels's appeals were heeded, and at the press conference, postponed until the next day, Hull parried a question about Cárdenas's statement by saying that he "had not gone into details of the despatches from Mexico City." He added that he did know that the note to the Mexican government on agrarian claims, sent on July 20 and now published, "spoke for itself," and he did not propose to discuss it. He added that the Department had been carrying on "conversations and exchanges of views" with Mexico "both orally and otherwise" during the past months, and that he did not intend to go into "minor phases of the mechanics of the matter." [36]

The incident was closed by Hull's instruction to Daniels to inform Hay that the Department "had not contemplated that the note would be suspended or withdrawn, inasmuch as it was delivered and received in the regular procedure in such matters," and therefore, the Department regarded the note "as regularly delivered and valid in every respect." In view of the misunderstanding that had arisen, however, the Department would try not to mention the note of March 26.[37]

If Daniels was right in attributing the note of March 26 to Hull's "Tennessee temper," the air around Hull was probably blue in July when he learned the full details about Daniels's envoyship. Even before this incident, Henry Morgenthau's diary recorded that Hull had said to Morgenthau: "Well, we are having lots of trouble in Mexico, and you know the President and Daniels have given the Mexicans the impression that they can go right ahead and flaunt everything in our face. . . . Daniels is down there taking sides with the Mexican government, and I have to deal with these communists down there and have to carry out international law." [38] If these words expressed Hull's private feelings at the time, the temperateness of his public and other formal statements is a remarkable tribute to the influence exerted by his commitment to and belief in the requirements of a good neighborly style, reinforced by the restraints traditional to the institution of diplomacy.

In these circumstances, it can hardly be considered odd that when Hull desired in July to send a note on agrarian expropriations, he entrusted it to Castillo Nájera rather than to Daniels and published it immediately. Later notes of August 22 and November 9, on the agrarian expropriations, were also addressed to the Mexican Ambassador. There is no positive evidence that Daniels was no longer chosen as a messenger because of the "misunderstanding" about the March 26 note, although the inference was drawn by at least one journalist.[39]

In his unique and unorthodox fashion, Daniels had imposed on the Department of State his own judgment of the way the United States should deal with Mexico as a Good Neighbor. In doing so, he had lost, as an ambassador, the confidence of Hull and Welles, but only after, as he put it, the "highest hurdle" had been twice vaulted.

It may be doubted that what had occurred was owing merely to a misunderstanding, as Daniels and Hull had said in July, or that Daniels was justified in recalling that he had been a "good messenger." He had had ample opportunity in March to say that he had used the term "not received" in talking with Hay; he did not do so, although he recalled it readily enough in July. In March, Daniels's policy aims were satisfied without his having to tell the full story of the note's "delivery"; in July, his policy aims were satisfied only because, by telling the full story, he could say that publication of the news that the note had been sent would constitute a breach of faith with the Mexican government. The misunderstanding existed only in Washington and not with Daniels, for Daniels knew what he was accomplishing by delay and obfuscation to make the Good Neighbor appear a better neighbor in Mexico than if, as ambassador, he had done what he was aware his Secretary of State desired. Daniels's action was nearly unique in the modern annals of United States diplomacy in the Americas; its justification may, however, be found in its results. Daniels was in a class apart among United States diplomats to Latin American states. He seems to have assumed the role of the apostle of the idea of the Good Neighbor and would probably have taken issue with President Roosevelt himself on the duties of a Good Neighbor had the occasion arisen. As Roosevelt's former "chief," he was unrecallable, and he made the most of his independence.

Ramón Beteta has asserted that Mexico would have broken diplomatic relations with the United States had Daniels officially presented the note of March 26 to Hay and that both countries owed "a heavy debt to the Ambassador's willingness to endanger his career in the furtherance of the Good Neighbor policy." [40] When Daniels retired, Roosevelt paid him a warm tribute that befitted a man who may be regarded as one of the most consistent exponents of the ideals of good neighborly conduct: "Of all the people in the last eight years who have been in foreign posts in Central and South America—Mexico—I think that Mr. Daniels probably has done more to encourage and live up to the Good Neighbor policy than anybody else I know." [41]

This was not quite the last to be heard of the March 26 note. On February 1, 1939, H. R. Knickerbocker published an article in newspapers in the United States, based on an interview with Cárdenas, claiming that a note had been sent to Mexico in March. Senator Styles Bridges wrote to Welles, inquiring about the existence of "a very mysterious or secret note." Welles, seizing the opening naively offered by Bridges's adjective, referred to the two notes on the agrarian claims which had been published and stated that he could assure him "that neither have there been any 'mysterious' communications despatched by the government of the United States to the government of Mexico nor has there been any need of despatching any 'mysterious' communication of any character whatsoever to the government of Mexico." All messages to Mexico were consistent with the position taken in the agrarian notes, and Welles said he was sure that Bridges would concede that it would not be "compatible with the public interest or consistent with the successful conduct of our foreign relations" to make public the texts of all communications exchanged in such negotiations.[42]

Force Is Not the Way of a Good Neighbor

Hull's acceptance of Daniels's "now-you-see-it-and-now-you-don't" technique with the note of March 26 was certainly not that of a man with any bellicose inclinations, and there is no evidence that at any time during the oil controversy any consideration was given in the White House or Department of State to the use of force against Mexico, except to reject any hints that it should be used. The oil companies themselves do not appear to have proposed the use of force to the Department of State, or to have supported any revolutionary movements in Mexico. A few instances, however, may be cited to show some of the ways the question was brought to the attention of the Department.

A flurry of excitement was caused in May, 1938, when, during an unsuccessful revolt by General Saturnino Cedillo, President Cárdenas went to San Luis Potosí and made a speech charging that the oil companies had gone to that state before and after the expropriation, "hoping to find traitors." The companies denied that they had helped Cedillo in any way, and the Mexican government produced no evidence that they had done so. It seems probable that Cárdenas had made use of the popularity of the expropriation as a means of rallying support for his government against the rebel leader.

General Cedillo had purchased two airplanes from a private company in the United States; these were illegally delivered to him without an export license. The evidence produced at the trial of Floyd Clevenger, the pilot who had delivered the planes, failed to indicate that any oil company was involved. *El Nacional* on June 17, 1938, published a report, quoted from the *Midwest Daily Record* (Chicago) that W. T. Brownell, general manager of the Howard Aircraft Corporation, had declared that Clevenger had "acted for some American oil companies who were supporting Cedillo." This allegation, however, was not admitted by Clevenger or upheld by other evidence.

The incident was closed, so far as the Mexican government was concerned, when Cárdenas on May 27 stated that he had no knowledge that foreign companies had given aid in any form to Cedillo.[43] This statement was not verbally inconsistent with Cárdenas's speech in San Luis Potosí, and its issuance fortified the interpretation that his vague expression in that speech was intended principally as a propaganda appeal to the people in Cedillo's area of operations, rather than as a serious charge against the oil companies.

In a talk with Donald Richberg, who represented the oil companies in negotiations with the Mexican government, Welles got the impression that the companies intended to break off negotiations in the late summer of 1939. Welles warned Richberg that it was already being said in Mexico that the companies wanted to wait in the hope that General J. A. Almazán would defeat General Manuel Avila Camacho in the Mexican elections of 1940, and that they "could make a deal with him" for the restoration of the oil properties. If the companies now ended the negotiations, they would be charged with "mixing directly in Mexican political affairs." Such a controversy in Mexico "would prejudice . . . not only every American interest in Mexico, but also very definitely relations between the two countries." He told Richberg that the companies "should exercise the utmost amount of patience in the present negotiations and should not close the doors until every effort had been made to try and find an equitable solution" that would satisfy them and also "prevent the issue from becoming one of a violent, political nature in Mexico." [44]

It seems unlikely that the Mexican government was greatly concerned about intervention—at least not after March 30, 1938. Although Castillo Nájera states that Mexicans "on more than one occasion feared for the fate of the country," he also told a New York financier, who suggested that the United States would intervene, that "Roosevelt would not commit such an attack, both because of his personal sentiments, and because of the international pledge of the Non-Intervention Protocol." [45]

The view of the Department was expressed privately by Assistant Secretary of State, Adolf A. Berle, Jr., when he was sounded out by a United States citizen as to the probable attitude of the Department of State toward recognition of a possible revolutionary movement against the Cárdenas government. Berle said he thought that such a movement would be "an extremely dangerous mistake," and he personally would have no sympathy with it. To a suggestion that the Department "need know nothing about it," and that a "purely institutional benevolence might do," Berle replied that:

we tried to be frank about these things; that we did not care for the left-handed variety of action; that we had a pledge not to intervene in the internal affairs of other countries and that we meant it; that our own attempt to resolve the Mexican difficulty through reason and common sense was a longer and far more difficult way of going at things but that the results were more nearly permanent. Any other result . . . probably meant warfare, which even if temporary could yield only a temporary solution. . . . The only way out was that of careful and painstaking negotiation looking toward an ultimate meeting of minds.[46]

Laurence Duggan took a like position in responding to a letter that referred to the oil dispute, noted the difficulties of investing in Latin America, and concluded that the situation could not be corrected without "an extremely firm position on the part of Washington, even to the extent of being prepared for final extreme action if all other methods fail." Duggan merely replied to the suggestion "that force be used" with quotations from the non-intervention pledges signed at Montevideo and at Buenos Aires.[47]

The same attitude was maintained at the White House in response to a remarkable inquiry from George Creel, a journalist and holder of a minor political office in the Roosevelt administration, that appeared to indicate that a revolution against the Mexican government depended only on a word of encouragement from Washington. This provocative letter to Marvin McIntyre, Roosevelt's appointments secretary, deserves full quotation:

I wish you could send me some guarded word about the Mexican business. It seems *so vital* to me. From all accounts, Almazán seems determined to go ahead, and is absolutely confident. I differ. If we favor him, shutting our eyes to border activities, he can win easily and immediately. If, on the other hand, we take a stand against him, he's whipped before he starts and thousands of lives will be lost needlessly.

Can't you give me a bit as to our attitude. If it's against him, I'll make an effort to see him—wherever he is—and try to persuade him to accept a compromise. They stand ready to give him any thing. The trouble has been that he refuses to trust them until they throw out a bunch of Nazi-Communist leaders. I have friends on both sides and am sure I can handle it.

To this conspiratorial missive, McIntyre telegraphed: "My advice is hands off. Best regards." [48]

Roosevelt's position was made crystal clear when, in November, 1940, it was announced that Vice-President-elect Henry A. Wallace would attend the inauguration of President Manuel Avila Camacho. The defeated candidate, Almazán, who had been "visiting" in the United States, shortly afterward returned to Mexico and announced that he had no further ambitions to be president of Mexico.

Reprisals and Boycotts Are Not Ways of a Good Neighbor

Even if force was not to be used, nevertheless, the Department of State did not hesitate to try to exert economic pressure on Mexico. In its first effort, relating to the suspension of the silver purchase arrangement announced on March 27, 1938, as noted above, Herbert Feis, economic adviser of the Department, urged Secretary of Treasury Henry Morgenthau not only to terminate the 1936 agreement with Mexico to purchase 5,000,000 ounces of its silver each month at a price slightly above the world price of about forty-five cents an ounce, but also to reduce the Treasury's price, the principal factor in keeping the world price at that level. This proposal was resisted by Morgenthau who did not wish to bring such pressure on Mexico or to be responsible for it. However, he agreed to Feis's proposal, which was also Hull's, when he did not gain any support from President Roosevelt in his resistance to it.[49]

The Mexican government benefited from its silver production in two ways: it received revenue from an export tax on silver of about $150,000 a year, and the silver exports were an important source of dollar exchange. In addition, silver was no less important than oil to the Mexican economy, not alone because it was the basis of the monetary system, but also because its value in terms of total production was greater than that of petroleum, and silver exports produced almost as many dollars as those of oil. One complicating factor from the point of view of the United States was that while United States companies controlled about 40 percent of oil production, about 70 percent of the silver came from mines owned by United States nationals. A second complicating factor was that, if Treasury purchases of Mexican silver should be stopped, the capacity of Mexico to make compensation for both agricultural and petroleum expropriations would be seriously reduced.

Before the oil expropriation, when a movement of capital from Mexico caused a deterioration in the country's exchange position, the United States Treasury agreed in neighborly fashion to an immediate, special purchase of 35,000,000 ounces of silver at forty-five cents an ounce, at the request of Finance Minister Eduardo Suárez. The monthly purchase arrangements were continued on the same basis. The special purchase of silver was not enough to ease the foreign exchange stringency, and at the beginning of January, 1938, Mexico established a new tariff schedule, which soon resulted in substantial decreases of imports, particularly from the United States. This action, of course, displeased the Department of State, which had been endeavoring through the trade agreement program to secure mutual tariff reductions.

In talking with Suárez, Secretary Morgenthau suggested at the end of 1937 that Mexico's exchange problem would only be solved "upon the creation of conditions under which private capital would feel secure in staying in Mexico." He then drew a parallel between Mexico and the United States, in saying that

In the United States, as in Mexico, it would be possible to carry forward on the progressive and reformist aims which the two countries had in common, such as the distribution of land ownership, the check on unsound concentration of wealth, the creation of decent housing, roads, et cetera; the questions of method and of timing, however, must be carefully observed.

Suárez expressed agreement with these views.[50]

The day before these friendly talks were completed, Beteta told Daniels that he felt that Mexico was "acting under pressure applied by our government" with respect to its own dealings with the oil companies in the wage dispute.[51] This news brought from Hull the word that he was "amazed" at Beteta's remark in view of the silver negotiations with Suárez and the latter's expressions of appreciation "of the friendly attitude of this government and of this practical evidence of its desire to act as a good neighbor in its relations with Mexico." Hull mentioned Daniels's report to Suárez, who replied that there was "no ground whatever for any such impression," and that he had "made it especially and entirely clear" to Cárdenas and Hay that "far from there being any pressure applied by the government of the United States, the position assumed

by this government was entirely friendly and very understanding." [52]

It was in the afterglow of this amicable negotiation that the
black smoke of the expropriation appeared, and, while Morgenthau
agreed to "defer continuation of the monthly silver purchase arrangement," [53] "his ire knew no bounds" when Hull intimated that
the Treasury was responsible for the decision.[54]

If the hopes of Feis and Hull were that strong pressure would be
brought to bear on Mexico, Morgenthau largely frustrated them,
since the Treasury continued to purchase silver in Mexico at the
world price, but not above it. In effect, the Treasury, in the three
weeks following March 18, bought a total of only about 500,000
ounces of foreign silver, and then resumed the purchase of silver
in New York at approximately the pre-March 18 volume at the
world price, without any discrimination against silver from Mexico. This was a day-to-day policy, so that Mexico did not any
longer have its month-to-month arrangement, but Treasury purchases from Mexico remained at about the same level during 1938.[55]
When informed of the plans of the Treasury, Feis stated that he
believed the Department would find them "satisfactory, i.e., the
avoidance of discrimination against Mexican silver offered in a
customary way for spot delivery on world markets." [56]

The announcement of the ending of the silver purchase arrangement caused "some antagonism" in Mexico. Beteta told Daniels
that "the United States government was being most unfriendly
and was attempting to coerce Mexico." Daniels was reported as
being "greatly disturbed" by the silver announcement, and he
wrote Roosevelt that it was "the end of the Good Neighbor policy." Duggan authorized Counselor Boal to indicate to Mexican
officials that "the Administration's attitude with regard to further
purchases of silver would be influenced by the assurances that Mexico gave in connection with compensation for expropriations." [57]

It is possible that this word reached Cárdenas in time to influence
his pledge of March 31 that Mexico would "know how to honor
its obligations."

Although Hay told Daniels that the termination of the silver agreement "at the time it was made hurt psychologically, economically, and financially," [58] the Mexican government at no time made any formal protest against the action. The actual economic and financial "hurt" was in fact a small one, but the uncertainty of the situation was a source of concern to Mexican officials, and may have had some slight effect on their later attitude on the question of compensation for expropriated properties. At the end of 1939, Beteta asked Daniels about rumors that the Treasury intended to stop purchases of foreign silver. In response to an inquiry from Daniels, a memorandum written in the Department stated that the day-to-day policy on silver purchases had been in effect "for many months," and the Department could not furnish information about the future policies of the Treasury, nor "predict whether the Congress [might] amend existing legislation." [59]

On balance, no great pressure was exerted on Mexico through the silver purchase policy. It had been accepted calmly by Cárdenas, partly because Castillo Nájera had been assured by "the Department of State" that neither this action, nor that of suspending existing claims negotiations, "partook of the character of reprisals." [60] The Mexican officials also presumably understood the Department's need to take some positive measure to satisfy sectors of Congress and the public. Indeed, since the Department of State acquiesced so readily in Morgenthau's policy, which was to continue silver purchases despite the discontinuation of the formal arrangement, the action taken seems to have been intended to impress more the United States Congress than the Mexican government. The Treasury had, in the silver purchase policy, a means of reprisal which could have been imposed immediately and easily. That it did not use it was owing partly to the complicating factors mentioned above and partly to Morgenthau's desire to reach a settlement of the oil dispute without damage to the friendly relations between the two governments.[61]

Daniels alone seems to have referred to the Good Neighbor policy in connection with the silver purchase policy; neither Hull nor Feis seems to have asserted they were making proposals in conformity with its precepts, nor does Morgenthau seem to have made any accusations, but neither does his effective frustration of their aims seem to have aroused any protests by them.

For a time after the announcement of the ineffective action on silver purchases, the Department of State took no further positive measures to exert pressure on the Mexican government. However, the Department was presented with some pretty problems about the conduct of a Good Neighbor in consequence of efforts on the part of the oil companies to prevent Mexico from operating the oil fields economically or from exporting oil. If such efforts were effective, the Mexican government might then invite the companies to return to Mexico to administer the oil fields, on terms which would be acceptable to the companies. In addition, even if Mexico could produce a substantial quantity of oil, exports of oil might be seriously curtailed, and Mexico might have so little foreign exchange that compensation demanded by the United States could not be paid in any reasonable period of time. The development of such a situation might provide the companies with opportunities for reopening the entire expropriation issue.

The oil companies did their best to prevent the sale of Mexican oil abroad. They worked together to try to bar Mexico from obtaining oil tankers, although this effort was not entirely successful. They were able to influence the makers of oil drilling equipment in the United States to refuse to sell machinery and pipe to the Mexican government.[62] They tried, again without complete success, to get other oil companies in the United States to refuse to import Mexican oil or to refine it for export. They brought suits in United States and European courts, attaching cargoes of oil from Mexico, alleging that the oil had been illegally taken by the Mexican government. They won a few of these cases at first, but in later cases decisions favored the Mexican government. It was difficult to prove that a given cargo of oil came from expropriated properties, since not all the foreign companies operating in Mexico had been expropriated, and some courts did not accept the claim that the action of Mexico was illegal, particularly after the Mexican Supreme Court had held the expropriation decree constitutional.

In the United States, federal courts in New York and Alabama held that the Eastern States Oil Company could not be prevented from selling Mexican oil in the United States, and that an oil tanker, formerly owned by a British company affected by the expropriation decree, could not be regained by the company when the ship was attached in Mobile, where it had gone for repairs. In both cases, the actions of the courts were based principally on the ground that the expropriation was the act of a sovereign government and could not be questioned by a United States court. Concerning the second case, the Mexican legation in Argentina issued a bulletin in May, 1939, in which it was stated that the release of the tanker, then named "18 de Marzo," "speaks very highly of the quality of the North American courts." [63]

The Department of State took no position whatever concerning any legal proceedings initiated by the oil companies in the United States or abroad. It did not attempt to block the entry of Mexican oil into the United States, which was freely permitted on payment of the established tariff. It did not feel that it could take any action to try to restrain attendants at gasoline stations in Texas from advising tourists that they should not visit Mexico.[64]

Ramón Beteta told Daniels that United States manufacturers of oil equipment, by refusing to sell to Mexico, "throw us into the arms of Germany, where we can swap oil for this machinery, etc., that we need," and he complained that the Standard Oil Company was selling oil to Germany, Italy, and Japan, with the consent of the government of the United States. Beteta and other Mexicans said they would have preferred not to sell oil to these countries, but they felt that they had "no alternative but to trade where we can." [65]

Daniels does not record that he protested against the Mexican government's selling oil to Germany, and the United States government did not make any representations to Mexico on this question, aside from Welles's pointing out to Castillo Nájera that Mexico might "be forced to dump the oil which it might produce into the hands of Japan, Germany, or Italy, which were the very governments that the Mexican government had consistently and openly opposed on the grounds of national policy." [66] This suggestion did not affect Mexican policy, and Mexico was aided in trading with the Axis powers by an American oil man and promoter named William Rhodes Davis, who contracted to sell and transport Mexican oil to Germany. Davis was reported to control seventeen tankers and was able to charter a few others not controlled by other oil companies or by shipping firms cooperating with them. Daniels may have exaggerated in saying that "the expropriation would fail" without markets for Mexican oil, but there is little doubt that the Mexican economic situation would have been considerably worse in 1938–40 without the substantial exports which Davis made possible.[67] Davis's role may even have been of critical importance immediately after expropriation, when Mexico most needed not only exports but also hope that the oil companies' efforts to prevent exports could be defeated. By the end of 1938, principally with the aid of the Axis markets developed by Davis, Pemex was reported to have realized that it had "almost oversold its export capacity." [68]

Hull talked with Davis on August 18, 1938, and the Secretary told Castillo Nájera that he had told Davis of the Department's position of upholding the principles of "just compensation" and the accompaniment of expropriation by "satisfactory arrangements as to payment," and that he had added that any individual was "left free to pursue his own course in the light of this position of this government." [69]

A month later, a Departmental memorandum advised Hull that there had been suggestions from outside the Department proposing that action should be taken against Davis under the Trading with the Enemy Act of 1917. The position was taken, however, that such a move would be unwise since the implication would be that the United States would prosecute "dealers in products expropriated without compensation from Americans throughout the world if these are the subject of diplomatic negotiation. This seems like a very large order." [70]

Just before the outbreak of World War II, Finance Minister Suárez told Daniels that Mexico was earning about $1,200,000 a month from petroleum sales abroad. Of this amount, Davis was providing about $300,000; the remainder was accounted for by

$400,000 from a barter deal with Italy for rayon yarn, $360,000 from oil being refined in the United States by Eastern States Petroleum Company, and about $200,000 from sales to other countries in Europe and the Americas. Suárez said he would be happy to see an investigation of Davis's activities by the United States Senate, because "the American people have been led to believe by newspapers that Mexico could not have survived without him." [71] Suárez was then speaking of the situation a year and a half after expropriation, which was quite different from that in early 1938 when Davis began operations.

To individuals who came to the Department to inquire whether they should complete a proposed purchase of oil from Mexico, the Department took the position that it would not give them any advice except to say, in what became standard terminology, that if they made a contract with the Mexican government, they "would be fishing in troubled waters" and "must take any risks attendant on such action." [72] In some cases, this mild warning caused businessmen to withdraw from negotiations with Mexico. The Eastern States Oil Company, which does not appear to have requested the advice of the Department, may have known the Department's views, but proceeded without interference to import Mexican crude oil, refine it, and export it in other forms. William Rhodes Davis was also told that he was "fishing in troubled waters," but he was not the kind of angler who would be disturbed by Departmental warnings either of possible seasickness or of hooking something that might pull him in.

Department of State officials were not pleased that United States citizens were helping to relieve Mexico from economic pressures at a time when they were insisting that Mexico make prompt compensation to the oil companies. In their helplessness under existing legislation, they may well have envied the British government, which was apparently able to handle its nationals more efficiently when individual enterprise was at odds with governmental policy. Francis W. Rickett, a British oilman who was no less adventurous than Davis, was reported to have reached an agreement with the Mexican government to purchase 15,000,000 barrels of oil at world market prices, but he stopped negotiating and left the scene shortly after the first British note of protest was presented in Mexico City. One view of this incident was that "the British Foreign Office has not been in sympathy with Mr. Rickett's negotiations and it is considered likely that he was asked to drop them." [73] Whatever the means of influence exerted from London —and it would be instructive to know what they were—the assumption may be made that Rickett was less "free to pursue his own course" than was his American competitor Davis.

This point is of some interest since it suggests, when set alongside the close collaboration of the British Embassy and British oil companies in Venezuela, the existence of a real difference between the two countries in the degree of freedom enjoyed by their citizens in actions affecting foreign policy. The British Foreign Office, corporations, and individual Britons followed what seemed from without to be a solidary line of policy in these cases. Whether or not such unity was secured by formal or informal techniques, it could hardly have been maintained without some form of governmental guidance. The Department of State, operating in a more fragmented political system, had never developed a comparable tradition of acceptance of its leadership by business firms or individuals.

In a related line of policy, it was reported that "British pressure has been put on friendly Scandinavian governments to restrain their large numbers of independent tankers from coming to Mexico." [74] For its part, the Mexican government made strenuous attempts to sell oil to other American countries. Antonio Rivero Osuna toured Central America seeking oil markets, and no less a literary light than Alfonso Reyes, then Mexican ambassador to Argentina, went to Rio de Janeiro as "petroleum commissioner at large" to promote sales of this product. [75]

The Department of State took some measures that may have had the effect of reducing the capacity of Mexico to export oil, although they do not appear to have caused the Mexican government any serious difficulties.

It is not possible to do more than speculate about activities of the United States government intended either to emulate in America the "pressure" of the British government in Scandinavia or to counter the Mexican trade drive in the Western Hemisphere by urging that other American states refrain from purchasing oil from properties expropriated by the Mexican government. It appears that oil companies in the United States had asked the Department of State "to take steps to prevent the sale and movement in international trade of oil and products from the seized properties on the ground that any sale of oil taken from the properties would be without title." [76] It would seem likely that in the mood prevailing in the spring of 1938, the Department would have responded affirmatively to this request, but it remains obscure whether or not the Department saw fit to espouse this view in communications to other governments in Latin America or elsewhere.

The Department did go so far in May, 1939, as to assert that it was "undesirable" for purchases of Mexican oil to be made by entities of the United States government, and the Department of State "encouraged Latin American governments to take a similar stand against Mexican oil." [77] Such encouragement was presumably not inconsistent with the Department's prevailing conception of the principles of the Good Neighbor, but it had little if any effect on Mexican policy.

Despite the sales promotion campaign of the Mexican government in Latin America, its petroleum exports to this area were not great. British and United States companies engaged in the oil trade met Mexican competition by lowering their prices, and this action was almost certainly more important than any activities of the Department of State aimed at limiting Mexican oil exports.

This moderate position of the Department was exemplified when in the autumn of 1940, the Navy rejected a low bid for fuel oil from the Eastern States Petroleum Company on the ground that it had come from expropriated properties. The next lowest bid was that of the Sinclair Oil Company, and it was rejected for the same reason. Patrick J. Hurley, representing Sinclair, said that Secretary of Navy Frank Knox had told him that the Navy would have nothing to do with "stolen oil." Hurley pointed out to the Department of State that the oil offered by Sinclair was not "stolen" but was received in compensation for Sinclair's acceptance of its expropriation, and that the Department had made no objection to Sinclair's settlement with Mexico.[78] Hull agreed with Hurley, and a letter was sent to Knox, recalling that, on May 2, 1939, he had written to the Navy Department expressing opposition to the purchase of expropriated oil by government agencies as mentioned above. However, the Sinclair arrangement with Mexico rested on the consent of the parties, and the position of the Department of State was, therefore, that oil deriving from properties covered by that arrangement would not be regarded as "confiscated," and on grounds of policy its purchase would not be opposed by the Department of State.[79] The Department's objections to the purchase of oil from other expropriated properties was completely removed shortly after the entry of the United States into World War II.[80]

It should be noted that governmental lending agencies in the United States did not make any loans to Mexico between August, 1937, and November, 1941. When Daniels inquired in 1939 if the Export-Import Bank would make a loan to Mexico to purchase vessels equipped for shrimp fishing, the Department replied that it knew of no agency that would provide such a loan.[81] Such action applied the principle of discrimination to Mexico as it had been applied to Bolivia. However, the refusal of loans, while effective in securing a change in Bolivia's policy toward the Standard Oil Company, had no effect in Mexico, where the government was both stronger and more determined in its course.

The Department of State did not attempt to take drastic economic measures since, in contrast to the British government, it did not assert that the expropriation was illegal, nor had it demanded that the oil properties be returned to the companies. Such influence as it wished to exert on the Mexican government had as its purposes either aiding a settlement between the oil companies and Mexico, or speeding payment of adequate compensation. These were lesser, and less urgent, objectives, and toward them the limited efforts of the Department were appropriate.

CHAPTER IX

The Principle of Accommodation: Mexico II

Arbitration Is Not the Way of a Good Neighbor

THE RESOLUTION of differences with Mexico over expropriation of oil properties by an impartial tribunal that would apply the principles of international law was strongly and consistently proposed by the British and Dutch governments and by all the oil companies concerned, except those represented by Harry F. Sinclair. With equal consistency, such arbitral procedures were opposed by the Mexican government, either as affecting the right of expropriation itself or the amount of compensation to be paid. The government of the United States at first requested arbitral settlements for both farm and oil properties and defended them as consistent with the Good Neighbor policy, but finally, in practice if not in principle, it relinquished these requests, abandoned the position upheld by the oil companies, and accommodated itself to the Mexican demand for determination of compensation by a commission on which each government had one member and from which there was no appeal.

The general problem of the use of arbitration in cases involving protection of nationals cannot be considered here, but the fundamental positions of Mexico and the United States may be exemplified by the following statements.

Speaking for Mexico in 1923, Foreign Minister A. J. Pani said:

Despoiled of their lands by the Spanish . . . plundered during three centuries of colonial regime, gun fodder for another century of civil wars and struggles for independence, and those of three foreign wars—two with France and one with the United States—the poor native population, as if the suffering from all these calamities had not been enough, also suffered . . . the consequences of the complete absorption of the small landholdings by the large estates which, in accordance with the immoral policy of favoritism of those Few Above at the expense of the Many Below, was developed by the Díaz oligarchy. It is not at all strange, then, that the aspiration of the people to recover the lands may have been . . . the most vigorous and persistent of all those which moved the popular Mexican spirit during the last revolution to the point of being rendered into radical laws.[1]

Speaking for the United States, Richard Flournoy, of the Legal Division of the Department of State, maintained:

Our country and Latin American countries alike subscribe to the universal doctrine of just compensation or its equivalent. In applying this principle some of the Latin American countries announce a policy of providing compensation to alien owners on not less than the same basis that payments are made to the nationals of the country making the expropriation. This government, in common with most others, has been quite willing to subscribe to this rule so far as it goes, but with the definite and express understanding that if the amount offered the nationals of the foreign country is *manifestly and substantially less than reasonable, fair, or just compensation, or if nothing at all is offered*, this government cannot leave its nationals to the mercy of debtor countries contrary to reason, the holdings of all international agencies and tribunals and the principles of long-established international law. . . .

The subject is now of increasing importance, due to the fact that so many nations are coming under the control of dictators who are able to change overnight their domestic laws pertaining to private property.[2]

In support of the Mexican position, Pani had appealed for the consideration of the issues "a little from the human and not solely from the legal and somewhat commercial standpoint, as it appears to have been considered abroad, without regard to its deep influencing historical causes and the interests of the country itself." The "systematic resistance" of the United States was said to be "worthy of a better cause."[3]

Beginning as early as the mission of Dwight Morrow in 1927, the "systematic resistance" of Washington gradually diminished, and by the affirmation of policy, if not by the repudiation of legal positions, the human standpoint came to be given precedence in the policy of the United States.[4]

The concomitant separation of the Good Neighbor policy from the procedures of international law freed the Department of State from the legal straitjacket that for decades had impeded political settlements and friendly relationships with Mexico and other Latin American countries, but the process was long and slow, and notable progress was not achieved until after Hull and Welles had made fruitless efforts against an unyielding Mexican as well as Bolivian resistance. Indeed, it is probable that once the fear of intervention was removed, the principal purpose of both the Bolivian and Mexican governments was to prevent the use of the procedures of arbitration in the settlement of their disputes, for it was through the imposition of these procedures by intervention that the international standard of justice had been applied in many previous cases. It was therefore for these countries a corollary of the renunciation of intervention that the procedure of arbitration also disappear in settlement of cases involving the protection of foreign nationals.

On the part of the Department of State, the effort to apply the procedures of arbitration was stoutly maintained both for farm and for oil lands before and after 1938 and down into 1940. At first, Welles emphasized that the Good Neighbor policy itself rested on principles of international law, although this theme gradually faded away and died out about the end of 1941.

Starting off, however, Welles wrote that the Good Neighbor policy

implies a community of neighbors, in which all are conducting themselves on a common plane of mutual confidence and fair dealing. My government has endeavored to hew strictly to the line of that policy, to respect its own obligations, and to be neighborly in rendering assistance where it could do so. It is entitled to expect in return respect for the obligations due it under international law, which, of course, include respect for obligations due its citizens. Other governments have recognized the inherently reciprocal character of the Good Neighbor policy and have formulated their policies accordingly.

Calling attention "to the inherent reciprocal character of the Good Neighbor policy," Welles said his government believed that "it has exhibited patience and forbearance, and has shown to the Mexican government all possible indulgence." However, it must insist that "expropriation and satisfaction of the obligation to pay go hand in hand." Otherwise, the United States would not "forward the Good Neighbor policy," but "would inevitably destroy that policy, by impairing the integrity of the principles upon which it rests." [5]

This statement is perhaps the strongest official declaration ever made that the Good Neighbor policy was founded on the principles of international law. In accordance with this position, the United States initiated on July 21, 1938, a series of notes with Mexico on agrarian claims that was fruitful only in the demonstration of its futility.[6] Hull did not want to send his second note, that of August 22. He told Castillo Nájera just after giving it to him to read, that "it has made me sick at heart for this government and Mexico to come upon differences of views which are very serious." He appealed to the Ambassador to ask his government to withdraw its note of August 3; if it did so, the United States would not "feel obliged" to send its second note. Castillo Nájera, however, said that Mexico would not withdraw its note, particularly since it had been published, and he was unwilling to convey Hull's proposal to his government.[7] In concluding this interview, Hull said that President Roosevelt had "thoroughly approved" the notes to Mexico of July 21 and August 22.

In its reply, the Mexican government, on September 1st, compared its expropriation to what it called the "indirect" expropriation of the property of foreign nationals by the United States government in requiring the exchange of gold and gold certificates for "depreciated" money. Still rejecting arbitration, it indicated a willingness to approve the establishment of a commission for the determination of the value of expropriated lands and of the method of paying for them.[8]

Hull at first told Castillo Nájera that he would have to reply to the note of September 1 because it was necessary to "leave no doubt in anyone's mind" about the United States position on the principle of just compensation.[9] However, Hull later decided not to send such a note. He told Castillo Nájera that he "had prepared elaborate data in connection with a note of considerable length, with a view to continuing the hammer and tongs discussions but also with the strong conviction that they would soon estrange our two countries in every important way." He said he would be glad to "discontinue these long drawn out notes, for the reason that they hurt both countries, but, in [his] opinion, hurt Mexico most," in favor of oral discussions.[10]

Apparently, Daniels had once more reduced the stridency of the diplomatic notes. Having vainly appealed to Hull for greater patience, he wrote directly to Roosevelt to stop the "further exchange of notes for the public, which get us nowhere." This letter of September 15 reached Roosevelt in time for him to tell Hull to try another method of negotiation.[11]

Private talks were accordingly entered upon. The United States laid down the hammer, and Mexico dropped the tongs, although each still clutched its favorite law books. After lengthy conversations an agrarian commission was established in November, 1938, that ultimately arranged for the payment of compensation.[12] In effect, the Mexican mode of settlement was accepted by the United States.

The dispute over the method of settling claims for the oil expropriation followed an essentially similar course. After the failure of direct negotiations between Donald R. Richberg, representing the oil companies (except the Sinclair Oil Company which employed Patrick J. Hurley for separate talks), and the Mexican government,[13] the government of the United States formally proposed arbitration as the means for determining the compensation due the oil companies. Curiously enough, in view of the outcome of the farm land dispute, Roosevelt himself took the initiative by proposing in a letter to Cárdenas in August, 1939, that the question of oil compensation "be submitted to the decision of impartial arbitrators" as "an admirable example of how with good will the governments and peoples of two neighboring countries can in a peaceful, friendly, and satisfactory way resolve their differences." [14] This offer, like all other offers of arbitration of any aspect of the controversy, was rejected by the Mexican government.

It is unlikely that this letter, which was probably drafted in the Department of State, expressed Roosevelt's own convictions, particularly in view of his part in the abandonment of arbitration for agrarian claims. In the light of subsequent events, this letter may be viewed as the first gesture in an elaborate ritual, fully understood in Mexico from the beginning and perhaps only later in the Department of State, that had to be staged before realistic negotiations could begin.

Although, after the Mexican Supreme Court on December 2, 1939, had unanimously upheld the constitutionality of the expropriation decree, the British government continued to demand the restoration to the oil companies of control over their former properties, the United States did not question the validity of the expropriation; it contented itself with renewing the proposal of arbitration on the limited question of the amount of compensation. Shortly after the start of World War II, the Netherlands Minister hoped that Hull "would stand firm in insisting on the rights of our nationals" in Mexico, and Hull replied:

I hoped the present situation, which leaves Mexico without an oil market, would encourage her to offer reasonable settlement with our oil owners; that, of course, my government had overlooked no word or act from the beginning that would be helpful in promoting a settlement; that it went without saying that this government "is standing firm," to use the Minister's expression, and doing all possible.[15]

The United States was standing firm, but the question as to whether or not it was on the same ground chosen by the Netherlands was left up in the air; certainly it was not on the ground selected by the British government.[16]

The Department of State persisted in its intention to propose arbitration, despite opposition to it by Cárdenas, voiced in reply to a pamphlet by Richberg. Welles knew of these, but he told Castillo Nájera that he "could not conceive of either one of our two governments being unwilling to submit to an impartial arbitration" differences which could not be settled diplomatically or through resort to the Mexican courts.[17]

Hull asked Castillo Nájera about Cárdenas's opposition to arbitration, and the Ambassador said Mexico would agree to that procedure only after all possibilities of negotiation were exhausted.

He added that two developments were taking place simultaneously: the companies had refused to participate in an appraisal of the value of their physical properties, and the Mexican government was proceeding to make its own appraisals; and negotiations he was carrying on with Patrick J. Hurley on behalf of the Sinclair Oil Company were going very well. In the Sinclair talks, the Company was not demanding compensation for its subsoil rights, and a stage had been reached where Mexico had offered to pay $9,000,000 in cash, plus oil to the value of $5,000,000 over a period of five years.[18] Sinclair was thus breaking the previously solid front of the oil companies, and Mexico was of course interested in completing an agreement with Sinclair in order to demonstrate that a form of settlement other than arbitration was feasible. Castillo Nájera told Hull that, if the Standard Oil Company wanted a settlement, it would have to accept terms comparable to those offered Sinclair; he added that the oil companies would have the right to raise questions about the Mexican appraisals in the Mexican courts. It does not appear, either at this or any other time, that the Department of State attempted to dissuade the Sinclair Oil Company from entering into a separate agreement with the Mexican government.

After reporting this conversation to Cárdenas, Castillo Nájera was ordered home to discuss the oil question, particularly with regard to Hull's mention of arbitration. Before he left, he talked with Hull, who said that "he preferred—and he thought this also would be the desire of President Cárdenas—to ascertain the President's position on arbitration through an oral and informal exchange of views rather than through an exchange of notes that might result in long arguments." The Secretary added that "he would like this information to help him in deciding what he should do with respect to the interests that were in touch with him." What he wanted to know, in effect, "was whether the Mexican government would agree to an arbitration of the petroleum controversy under an arrangement which would contain guarantees for the fulfillment of the award" and whether Mexico would treat United States and other oil companies as a unit in such an arbitration.[19]

Castillo Nájera replied that he had talked with Cárdenas by telephone, and he understood that the President would oppose an arbitration, since he wished to try further negotiations along the lines of those under way with Sinclair.[20] Castillo Nájera added that, if oil were delivered to Sinclair, he hoped that Mexico would be able to receive an increased quota for oil exports to the United States under the terms of the recently concluded trade agreement with Venezuela. Hull said he did not think an increase would be possible because of protests from other countries. The Mexican quota was not raised, partly for this reason and partly because it was thought inadvisable to relax the pressures of "natural economic forces" which Mexico was feeling as a result of the loss of its German markets. Such an affirmative action by the Department, it was thought, would reverse the Department's existing policy and would, in effect, be of assistance to Mexico in making a settlement only with Sinclair, apart from the other companies.[21]

On Castillo Nájera's return from Mexico on March 16, he gave Hull a memorandum answering Hull's questions whether Mexico "was willing to arbitrate (*a*) before any tribunal (American or European) and (*b*) with all the oil interests, domestic and foreign." [22] The memorandum asserted that the "right of expropriation is beyond discussion." That issue was thus not ripe for arbitration, but neither was that of the amount of compensation, since the two governments had not yet "expressed their respective points of view as to what should constitute a prompt, equitable, and adequate indemnity to compensate the American oil companies." The decision of the Mexican courts on the amount of the indemnity should be awaited, but, in the meantime, Mexico would be willing to accept the good offices of the United States in order to discuss "a prompt, equitable, and adequate compensation" with the companies. If such good offices were refused, Mexico proposed that a report on the appropriate compensation should be made by experts appointed by the two governments.[23]

The Mexican memorandum did not satisfy the Department of State. The Counselor of the Department, R. Walton Moore, wrote that, unless Mexico "desires to limit the effort of this government to obtain a full recognition of the legal rights of its nationals . . .

it is my belief that that government will promptly agree that the only method of disposing of the controversy is by the creation of an impartial arbitration tribunal." [24] Despite his realization that Mexico would reject an arbitration, Hull decided that it would be wise to put the Mexican government's position on the public record. He may also have wished to demonstrate to the oil companies the futility of a request for arbitration.

Hull's plans were carried through, and on April 3 Welles handed to Castillo Nájera a note formally proposing arbitration. Welles said that the note "provided an honorable and friendly way" to settle the controversy, and then the two countries could proceed "to a friendly adjustment" of all outstanding problems. However, he could not hold out hope for any constructive steps "unless Mexico were willing to pass through the open door" offered in the note.[25]

The note was not published immediately, but its existence became known, and denunciations of "intervention" were made in the Mexican press. Welles asked Castillo Nájera "why a constructive, friendly, and courteously worded note on the part of this government, calling attention to the just grievances of our citizens and proposing an impartial arbitration . . . should be regarded as aggressive." He had heard that certain Latin American diplomatic representatives in Mexico City had tendered their "good offices" to Mexico in the dispute, and Welles remarked that "this was the first time [he] had ever heard of good offices being tendered when one country proposed to another a solution of their dispute by recourse to friendly and impartial arbitration." However, Welles felt that the situation demanded immediate publication of the text of the note, and it was released to the press on April 9.[26]

Later, Welles told Castillo Nájera that "he had been afforded a great deal of amusement by reading pamphlets which had been circulated broadcast throughout some of the other American republics by Señor [Vicente] Lombardo Toledano, alleging that the note of the United States Government constituted an act 'of imperialistic aggression' and an evidence of 'direct intervention in the affairs of Mexico.'" Welles said he "wondered whether this kind of propaganda was able to delude many people," since he believed that an overwhelming majority of citizens in the other American republics were perfectly well aware of what the word arbitration meant and were equally well aware of the fact that arbitration was exactly the way in which "imperialistic aggression" and "intervention" were avoided when disputes arose between two countries.[27]

Whatever may have been thought elsewhere, there was little doubt about Mexican views. *El Universal*, for example, claimed that the Department of State, by the proposal for arbitration, had decided to "intervene" as an agent of the "plutocrats of petroleum," and that the Good Neighbor policy appeared to be reverting to that of the "Big Stick." [28]

In view of the surrounding circumstances, it appears that the note of April 3 was intended, not so much to influence the policy of the Mexican government, as to give some satisfaction to the "interests that were in touch" with Hull. Those interests, of course, were the oil companies. The note would go into the record to show that the Department of State had proposed arbitration, and Hull could thus demonstrate to the companies that he had tried to meet their request for the maintenance of the traditional methods of protection of nationals through international law. Hull could also anticipate that the Mexican government would feel that his note did not exert pressure on it, in view of the nature of his talk with Castillo Nájera on March 2. It seems highly probable that Hull would have made the proposal for arbitration in any case, in order to quiet domestic criticism. If Mexico had flatly rejected arbitration, instead of saying merely that it was premature, the only difference might have been a frostier degree of friendliness in the phrasing of the note.

The situation was similarly interpreted in some Mexican circles outside the government. An editorial in the weekly *Hoy* (Mexico City, April 13, 1940) anticipated that Hull would give up his request for an arbitral tribunal, and, declaring flatly that Washington knew that Mexico would not accept arbitration, added, with what well may have been officially informed prescience, that "the important note is not that which Castillo Nájera has just received, but the note which he will receive later, in response to the negative reply of Mexico to the first one." That note was never written.

The Mexican reply to the April 3 note, dated May 1, was negative, but it was conciliatory in tone. It asserted that the oil controversy was a domestic one and therefore not suitable for submission to arbitration. Hay stated generously and without overt resentment, in reply to Hull's remark that it was not "by any means reassuring" to be told that "the decision of the Mexican courts should be awaited," that he assumed this "is only meant to allude to the length of time that the progress of the valuation proceedings would be delayed." [29] Hay observed, no doubt with pleasure, that in view of negotiations under way with the Sinclair Oil Company, the oil controversy "is near solution," and so struck a shrewd blow at Hull's statement that "complete failure" had attended negotiations between Mexico and the companies.

Hay's positive proposal was that the other United States companies should follow the example of Sinclair, since Mexico was entirely willing to come to terms with them on the same basis. [30]

The Mexican position was strongly bolstered only a week later with the announcement of an agreement with Sinclair, in which the company accepted $8,500,000 in compensation for its expropriated properties, to be paid in cash within three years, and a five-year arrangement for the purchase of an unannounced amount of oil at less than the market price. Finance Minister Eduardo Suárez proudly proclaimed that the agreement "demonstrated that Mexico could arrive at an agreement with the oil companies, and that Mexico desired, and was capable of, indemnifying the companies in an equitable, prompt, and adequate manner for their former properties." [31]

These were very nearly Hull's own words from the note of March 26, 1938, that Suárez was flinging back at Washington. It was recognized in the Department of State that the Sinclair agreement "would greatly strengthen the Mexican position" and that it was a "very positive accomplishment." However, Duggan noted: "I see nothing to be done," when the suggestion was made that observations on the publication of the agreement might be made to the Mexican Embassy. [32]

Although there may have been some embarrassment in the Department that the arbitration proposal, already privately relinquished, had been publicly destroyed by the Sinclair agreement, it was later realized that Sinclair had, after all, done independently what the Department had been urging all the oil companies to do jointly.

The United States made no reply to the Mexican note of May 1. The proposal for arbitration had been made. The Mexican rejection was accepted, if not expressly, then quietly by default. To an inquiry by British Ambassador Lothian whether the United States would reply, Welles said: "For the time being we were letting the matter rest, although at some more suitable opportunity a reply would, of course, be made." [33] When after seven weeks, the Department of State had sent no note to Mexico, it received a letter from W. S. Farish, president of the Standard Oil Company of New Jersey. The letter pointed out that

in the numerous cases of confiscation which have occurred in American diplomatic history, the Department of State, taking its stand upon and upholding international law, has uniformly interposed to prevent confiscation or to obtain prompt redress; and where redress was not promptly obtainable the issue has been submitted to international arbitration.

Farish noted that the companies had never asked the Department of State to take "any drastic action with respect to Mexico . . . Certainly a proposal of arbitration can hardly be considered otherwise than as an attempt to maintain friendly relations and cannot be considered, as Mexico suggests, as a disturbance of trade relations or as an attempt to create international ill-feeling."

In reply, Welles wrote: "It is the intention of the government of the United States to follow up at the appropriate time the communications which have been exchanged by the two governments," but "in view of circumstances presently impending, I do not feel that it is immediately expedient to continue discussion of this matter with the Mexican government." [34] The appropriate time never arrived, and arbitration disappeared as an issue.

It was also in the spring of 1940 that the proposal for arbitration in the oil controversy with Bolivia was finally rejected by La Paz. Here again the rejection was accepted by the United States. Arbitration, which Welles had called "exactly the way in which 'imperialistic aggression' and 'intervention' were avoided," had in fact proven to be unusable in these two important disputes. Bolivia and Mexico felt that arbitration, under the existing principles of international law, would result in decisions harmful to their interests. The United States did not wish in either case to do more than earnestly urge the resort to arbitration—a measure of solicitation that Washington was fully aware would be disregarded.

One feature of this exchange of notes, from which the Mexican eagle emerged with fewest feathers in disarray, was a significant disagreement about one phase of the idea of continental solidarity. Hull had asserted that "there exists at this time a complete solidarity on the part of all the American republics in upholding the principle that international differences of a justiciable character, which it has not been found possible to adjust by diplomacy, shall be submitted to arbitration. I think that the questions here involved fall within this category." In reply, Hay noted that Mexico and "a large group of American countries" had made reservations to the Arbitration Treaty of 1929, excluding "differences of a domestic character" from arbitration. In consequence, he declared that "the unanimous will of the continent has been exhibited in the sense that international action in favor of foreigners is only proper when, domestic legal recourses having been exhausted, a case of denial of justice can be shown." Hay listed eight Latin American states, in addition to Mexico, which had excepted disputes of a domestic character from arbitration, and thereby effectively contested Hull's invocation of continental solidarity in defense of the position of the United States. By not replying to Hay's note and by not claiming a denial of justice, Hull may be considered to have contributed to a stiffening of continental solidarity on the side of the Mexican government.

It is an illuminating commentary on the changed diplomatic atmosphere in United States–Mexican relations that, in the "war scare" of 1927, approval of arbitration by a resolution of the United States Senate was regarded as a victory for Mexico, whereas, in 1940, rejection of arbitration by Mexico was equally regarded as a victory for Mexico. In 1927 the United States government was leading from strength; in 1940 it was pleading from Good Neighborliness. In 1927 arbitration was regarded as the easing of pressure on Mexico; in 1940 an arbitration proposal meant an increase of pressure. Thus far had the policy of the United States government changed, and thus far had its sympathy with the Mexican government grown. Henceforth, the Department turned its attention from proposing that Mexico arbitrate to suggesting that the Standard Oil Company approve other methods of settlement acceptable to Mexico. The Company resisted these suggestions, and the Department finally accepted a Mexican plan for determining compensation by a two-man commission, as outlined in the following section.

A Joint Commission Is a Good Neighborly Way of Settlement

The abandonment of arbitration by the United States government was not proclaimed from Washington in explicit terms. The new policy was not to be understood by reading the note of April 3, but by the gradual realization that the Department of State would make no reply to the Mexican rejection of arbitration.

When Welles referred to "circumstances presently impending" in his letter to Farish of July 10, 1940, he probably meant, beyond the great circumstance of the defeat of France in Europe, the proposals by Mexico of March 16, renewed on June 4, for the appointment by the two governments of a commission of experts to agree upon a valuation of the expropriated properties of companies other than the Sinclair Oil Company. Welles told Castillo Nájera that consideration would be given the proposal, although the United States was concerned about avoiding long delays and also about the undesirable effects of a failure of the commission to reach a decision. Castillo Nájera said that Cárdenas was willing to fix a period as short as two months for the deliberations and also to agree that, if the commissioners remained at odds, to leave the decision to an umpire.[35]

Although this proposal from Mexico ultimately provided the formula for the solution of the controversy, it took more than a year for the Department of State to decide to accept it. The Standard Oil Company resisted the plan to the end, and there were also important differences of opinion within the Department of State.

It can hardly be maintained that the Department was heedless of the Standard Oil Company's position, for a remarkable feature of the next seventeen months' negotiations was the Department's continuing solicitude that the Company either follow Sinclair's lead or approve the final method of settlement. As late as December, 1940, the Department of State made a further attempt to bring about a direct settlement between Mexico and the Standard Oil Company. Welles arranged a meeting between Castillo Nájera and Farish, because, as Welles told Farish: "The Standard Oil Company of New Jersey was placing the Department of State in an impossible position by refusing to discuss directly with the representatives of the Mexican Government the solution of the expropriation dispute." [36]

Farish talked with Castillo Nájera, who said that any settlement with Standard must, like that with Sinclair, exclude compensation for subsoil rights, and that Standard could not, except in an advisory capacity, take part in the management of its former oil properties. Farish informed the Department that he saw in these conditions no possibility of reaching agreement with Mexico, and he concluded with the statement: "We trust that the Department will renew and insist upon its proposal of arbitration." Such arbitration should include the following questions: (1) Was the expropriation legal? (2) If so, the tribunal should prescribe guarantees for compensation it considered to be due the companies. (3) If not, the companies should return to the management of their properties.[37] The Department's reply was that the question would be further explored.[38]

Following the failure of this conference, Department officials proceeded to discuss the Mexican proposal with Castillo Nájera. They could not accept Farish's suggestion, since the Department had already publicly admitted the legality of the expropriation. In effect, what they began to do was to arrange for an intergovernmental determination of the value of the properties of the oil companies and for ways of assuring that compensation would be paid by Mexico. In general, the Department proposed to answer the second of Farish's three questions, since it concurred with the Mexican government on the answer to the first and, therefore, the third. However, the method for determining the value of the properties, as favored by Mexico, was by a commission on which each government would have equal representation and not through an arbitral tribunal where a decision would be handed down by an impartial third party.

The adoption of the commission procedure was accepted only after long consideration in the Department of State that involved the resolution of differences of opinion among high officers of the Department. On one side were Daniels, who in the spring of 1940 had proposed a general settlement with Mexico, and Duggan, who at about the same time had noted that an unfriendly Mexico could create serious problems for the United States in time of war.[39] Expressive of this point of view was the following argument of one official of the Department:

In the event the United States is attacked and must enter the war, Mexico's oil resources might be of importance from the point of view of national and even hemispheric defense. For this reason it seems to be desirable not only that the controversy be settled but that steps should soon be taken with a view to insuring that the industry in Mexico is sufficiently equipped to produce, without danger of breakdown, at least the minimum quantity of oil it would be necessary to buy for defense purposes.[40]

Illustrative of arguments against a settlement of the oil dispute along the lines of the Mexican proposal were those of Herbert Feis and Max W. Thornburg, the economic and petroleum advisers of the Department. As late as the early autumn of 1941, Feis preferred to defer a settlement until the need for foreign investment was sufficiently great to induce Mexico to come to terms with the oil companies, and he joined Thornburg in maintaining that acceptance of the Mexican proposal would create an "unfortunate precedent" with respect to other countries.[41]

In this difference of opinion, the ultimately decisive factors were those related to the defense of the United States and of the Western Hemisphere. As in the case of the Bolivian oil controversy, the national interest was finally seen by the Department of State as being different from that of the oil companies and as superior to it. On its face this is not a surprising conclusion, but it is one that may be emphasized because of the length of time

required, from June 1940 to November 1941, before this conclusion received its necessary, formal validation in an agreement
with Mexico.

The connection between the security interests of the United
States and the interests of the Mexican government in an oil settle-
ment on its terms were clearly presented on June 11, 1940 in a
talk between Department of State officials and officers of the
United States Army and Navy, and Ambassador Castillo Nájera.
The Ambassador declared that Mexico was prepared to cooperate
unreservedly in plans for "the common defense," a subject that
had been explored with him on the initiative of the Department of
State in the previous few days. He went so far as to specify that
Mexico was "prepared to develop air and naval bases 'at places to
be chosen strategically, not only from the purely national point of
view but from the broader point of view of hemisphere defense.' "
However, the Ambassador combined this alluring prospect with
the significant condition that "the necessary basis of joint military
action in an emergency was a general political agreement between
the two countries." [42]

This was a clear enough allusion to the expropriation problem.
The knowledge that the United States desired bases in Mexico
must have encouraged the Mexicans to feel that their views as to
the appropriate method for settlement of the oil dispute would
prevail in Washington, and the increasing need for bases must have
made Hull and Welles regard insistence on arbitration of the dispute as more and more unrealistic.

Technical conversations between military officers of the two
countries followed the meeting with Castillo Nájera, but it was
found difficult to arrange any specific understandings. For example, in July, 1940, when Brigadier General Tomás Sánchez
Hernández was "asked point-blank whether Mexico would permit
the use of its airfields for movements to Panama . . . and whether
Mexico could guarantee the security of the airfields, he replied
that he was not authorized to say 'yes,' but his opinion was that the
President of Mexico would extend 'full and sincere cooperation.' " [43]

One reason for delay in securing precise arrangements for
military collaboration was the Mexican election in July, 1940,

when Manuel Avila Camacho was elected to succeed President Cárdenas. Avila Camacho did not take office, however, until December, and it was not until early in 1941 that new military and political initiatives by the United States began their intimately connected course toward the high measure of collaboration achieved in agreements made public less than two weeks before the Japanese attack on Pearl Harbor.

On the military side, Avila Camacho apparently decided to give positive if only partial evidence of his desire to collaborate in defense matters. Responding to an inquiry from the United States about establishing a joint defense commission, Foreign Minister Ezequiel Padilla approved the commencement of preliminary talks between military representatives. The commission was not established until March, 1942, but an important result of these early talks was the preparation of the draft of an agreement providing for the use of Mexican airfields by Panama-bound military planes of the United States. The draft agreement was completed on March 11 and approved by Avila Camacho on March 25. It became effective on April 25, 1941, when ratifications were exchanged.[44]

This was rapid action on both sides, and it was the most important agreement between the two governments since the silver purchase agreement of 1937, apart, perhaps, from the general understandings reached at the inter-American conferences of Panama and Havana. When the Mexican government approved the flight agreement, it presented at the same time, although not as a condition, a request for military materials. Unmentioned in the agreement, but almost certainly in the minds of officials of both governments, was the conviction that the time had come for a final settlement of the oil controversy. The flight agreement was limited to planes in transit and did not provide for the use of Mexican airfields as operating bases for United States planes, but it did prove Mexico's willingness to take one substantial, requested step toward collaboration. Further, its timing was important, since it was approved in Mexico shortly after Welles, having learned of the failure of Farish's visit to Mexico, began serious talks with Castillo Nájera about an intergovernmental settlement of the oil controversy "which they believe to be practicable and equitable." [45] Such a settlement would provide some compensation to the oil companies, but it could be carried out whether or not they approved either the amount of compensation or the procedure by which it might be determined.

Having determined to reach an intergovernmental settlement, because larger political and military considerations were regarded as making a disposition of the dispute imperative and because there was no longer any hope that Mexico and Standard could come to terms, the Department made a first step by obtaining an estimate of the value of the physical properties of the oil companies, excluding Sinclair. The estimate was made by experts of the Department of Interior, on the basis of figures furnished by the Mexican government. Their evaluation of the assets as being of the order of $13,000,000 was regarded by the Department of State as too low and as capable of successful challenge by the oil companies.[46] The report was not used in formal negotiations by the Department, but its conclusions may have been of influence in giving an idea of the order of magnitude of the final appraisal. Duggan estimated that the value of the companies' properties was "roughly" $25,000,000, and he proposed that this sum was probably within Mexico's capacity to pay by a plan involving about $9,000,000 in cash and the remainder in oil over a period of ten years. In view of the desire of Mexico to export more oil, he thought the companies should be asked to agree to sell outside Mexico perhaps 45–50 percent of the annual Mexican production. Summing up, he thought the aim of the Department should be to obtain for the companies at least $25,000,000 "but as much more as the Mexican Government will readily accede to." [47]

Encouraged by knowledge of these developments, Castillo Nájera again proposed the formation of a commission of two experts, with advisers to appraise the oil companies' properties. He thought they could complete their task in two months, and he proposed a down payment by Mexico of $1,000,000. The only problem raised by Duggan was that the down payment should be higher, and the Ambassador raised his offer to $3,000,000, which Duggan said was still too low.[48]

The discussions now reached a stage where a draft note to

Mexico, embodying an agreement for evaluation by a commission, was prepared in the Department and approved by President Roosevelt. The draft was presented to Castillo Nájera for transmission to Mexico City on August 21. The Ambassador requested a larger quota for the importation of Mexican oil into the United States, but he was told that this was possible only as part of a new trade agreement.[49]

The importance of this draft note is underlined by the delays that had accompanied both implementation of the flight agreement of April, 1941, and any further collaboration by Mexico, especially with regard to the offering of operational bases. From the military side it was apparent that

> one of the major stumbling blocks to a hard and fast defense agreement . . . was the continued failure of the two countries to settle the claims controversy. . . . Little progress, if any, could be discerned until mid-summer of 1941, when the two governments approved a tentative formula of settlement. Almost simultaneously, the course of military collaboration became smoother.[50]

The urgency of the War Department's desire to secure the use of air bases in Mexico in the spring of 1941 appears to have been the crucial, final factor in Washington's acceptance of the Mexican demand that the compensation for the oil companies be fixed by a commission rather than by an arbitral tribunal. There does not seem to have been any overt bargaining; the Mexican position was fully appreciated by the Department of State, and the Mexicans were content to wait at this time, without wishing to induce any undignified haste on the part of the United States.

It would be less than a fair appraisal of the controversy as a whole to charge that the Mexican government had taken advantage of the war crisis to press its claims, or that Roosevelt, Hull, and Welles regarded the settlement as one to which they were driven only by the requirements of national defense and which they would later try to modify. Once the Mexican rejection of arbitration had been accepted in 1940, the dispute could be dealt with only by way of a commission, an agreement between the companies and Mexico, or by letting the dispute drag on with no prospects for a settlement in the visible future. Since the recalcitrance of the Standard Oil Company showed no fissures and post-ponement of a settlement would mean no further military collaboration from Mexico, settlement by way of a commission was regarded as essential.

The Mexican government did not augment its demands with the coming of the war crisis, nor does it appear to have threatened to do so. Its basically anti-Axis orientation was manifest, so that the sources of concern in Washington for a rapid settlement in 1941 were not created by Mexican policy. Further, the controversy had originated in March, 1938, out of a domestic situation, a year and a half before the outbreak of war in Europe.

These considerations suggest that it was primarily the timing of the agreement for settlement, rather than the nature of the settlement itself, that was affected by the war emergency. Had settlement been indefinitely deferred, a succeeding administration in Washington might have returned to an insistence on arbitration as the oil companies hoped; but, so far as the Roosevelt administration was concerned, the timing was relatively unimportant to the substance of the controversy, since it had in 1940 accepted the fundamentals of the Mexican position. The timing was important to the security of the United States, and the announcement of the formal agreement three weeks before the Japanese attack on Pearl Harbor was a political triumph so far as inter-American relations were concerned.

The Department informed the oil companies of the general character of its plans for a settlement with Mexico, and Farish protested to Hull that

compensation based on a confiscatory valuation is no solution of the Mexican problem and is a repudiation of the principles which you have said "must be maintained". . . . The only possibility of a successful operation of the properties for the benefit not only of Mexico but of the United States and all parties concerned is to reinstate company management under a long-term contract which will give to Mexico and her people that economic advantage which Mexico has sought.[51]

Within the Department, it was pointed out that the use of a commission of experts was a "fundamental departure from the Secretary's suggestion of 'impartial arbitration'" in the note of

April 3, 1940,[52] but these objections were not thought, at least by Hull, Welles, and Duggan, to outweigh the broad political and military advantages to be gained through a settlement of the oil dispute and the opening of what was hoped would be a new era in Mexican–United States relations.[53] Along with the negotiations on oil, talks had been proceeding on all pending issues between the two countries, and it was desired to still the echoes of all past controversies and let amity replace recrimination at a time when a common danger demanded common action.

The suggestion was made that the agreement should include some arrangement for eventual participation by foreign companies in the Mexican oil industry, but Duggan successfully held that this was not the opportune occasion to take up that question with Mexico.[54]

The agreement went through five drafts before it was presented to Castillo Nájera. After the receipt of a Mexican counterdraft, numerous additional changes were made, but it finally reached a form ready for presentation to officials of the oil companies. Secretary Hull made the presentation in person on September 27. He recalled "the world situation and the important role Mexico could play in cooperation with us," including the furnishing of naval bases, and he "stressed the Axis activities being conducted in Latin America" and the help Mexico had already given us in preventing strategic materials from going to Japan.[55]

Hull's appeal for "consideration of the oil settlement" met with a negative response from the oil company officers, who said they preferred to see the question unresolved, even if the properties were lost, rather than to sacrifice "the principle of property rights." [56]

This conference was followed by a letter from Farish to Hull, stating that the Company did not feel "at liberty to give our assent to the agreement," and declaring:

To turn the industry over to Mexico under the conditions proposed in the plan of agreement would sacrifice the material interests of every party concerned, to say nothing of the sacrifice of principles of international law by which the safety of foreign investments against confiscation is assured.

If the companies could not return to Mexico, arbitration should be again proposed, in Mr. Farish's view, and if this procedure were unacceptable, then he suggested that "the whole oil question be omitted entirely from any proposed arrangements with Mexico, leaving the situation open until a more propitious occasion may arise." Hull's reply, written after a second talk with Farish and Armstrong on October 28, stated that it was the aim of the Department "fully to protect the interests of the companies and it is our belief that the plan as drafted will go as far toward accomplishing this purpose as any formula that could be agreed upon." Still anxious not to proceed without the companies' approval, however, he suggested that if Farish wished, another conference could be arranged.[57]

There were no more conferences. Apparently the companies had decided not to change their position and had concluded that Hull's stand was immovable. Was the grip of the Mexican government equally firm? Two possibly tendentious reports from Mexico City in late October raised some questions on this point. One referred to alleged differences on oil policy in the Mexican cabinet and stated that President Avila Camacho and his brother were inclined toward making an operating agreement with the companies and that "informed quarters" said that Castillo Nájera and Finance Minister Eduardo Suárez might be replaced by negotiators more in accord with the asserted views of the President. The second despatch stated:

It is notable that even in official circles it is frankly recognized that the oil agreement cannot be made without the oil companies. . . . It has become increasingly clear, first, that no settlement was likely without the approval of the companies, and, second, that Washington would like to see Mexico get together with the companies . . . [which] are believed to be awaiting the right moment and the right men to open negotiations.[58]

Whatever the source of these stories, events demonstrated their insinuations to have no effect on policy, either in Mexico City or in Washington; their target was presumably the Department of State, for it would have been passing strange for Avila Camacho, at this moment, to have repudiated the arrangement that, following the lead of Cárdenas, he had been urging on Washington for several months.

For two weeks after Hull's letter of October 29 to Farish, the Department received no reply it regarded as final, but on November 14 the occasion for action arrived in the form of a letter from Farish, reiterating the arguments presented in his letter of October 8 and reaffirming his company's position that

in view of the fundamental principles involved in a confiscatory seizure by the Government of Mexico of the foreign-owned oil properties in that country, principles on which the United States and the other interested governments have consistently stood, we do not feel that we could, from any point of view, justify our sacrifice, expressly or otherwise, of the interests with which we are intrusted.[59]

This was the last word of the oil men, but Hull still delayed completion of the agreement, not because he disapproved of its terms but because he clung to the vain hope that the companies might accept them. It was at this point that Daniels seems once more to have influenced policy. On his way home from Mexico, he impressed on Roosevelt the importance attached to the agreement by Avila Camacho. Roosevelt agreed, but said that Hull had still to be convinced he could not get the companies' approval; Daniels then talked with Hull on November 18,[60] and on the next day public announcement was made of the exchange of notes that provided for an intergovernmental determination of the compensation to be paid to the oil companies, as well as of agreements providing for adjustment of agrarian and other claims, the purchase of Mexican silver by the United States Treasury, the provision of credits to Mexico by the Export-Import Bank, and for a stabilization of the Mexican currency.[61]

The Secretary of State hailed the agreements as of "outstanding importance," and as "a further concrete proof of the fact that problems existing between nations are capable of mutually satisfactory settlement when approached in a reciprocal spirit of good will, tolerance, and a desire to understand each other's points of view." Daniels wrote that November 19, 1941, "might go down in the annals of Mexico and the United States as the Day of Deliverance." [62]

In pursuance of the agreement of November 19, the two experts forming the evaluation commission, Morris L. Cooke [63] and Manuel J. Zevada, reported their agreement on April 17, 1942, that Mexico should pay to the remaining oil companies $23,995,991, plus interest at 3 percent from March 18, 1938, to September 30, 1947, which amounted to $5,141,709.84.

To the Standard Oil Company of New Jersey, $18,391,641 was awarded, and the award was ultimately accepted by the Company on October 1, 1943. The agreement did not refer to subsoil rights; it stated that the award covered "all elements of tangible and intangible value," but it was clear that the two commissioners had not considered that the companies retained, after expropriation, any property right to oil under ground.[64]

The presidents of the two countries exchanged congratulations on the settlement of the controversy. From Mexico, it was reported: "Enthusiasm for the agreement appears to be unanimous and to surpass to a considerable extent the warmth of the approval of the basic agreements last November." Mexicans appeared to feel that the amount of compensation was less than they had expected, but it was thought that "respect for and confidence in the Good Neighbor policy and in President Roosevelt have also been materially enhanced." [65]

A summary of editorial comment in the United States prepared for the Department of State showed that

newspapers from coast to coast had agreed three to one that the report of the experts was "hard on the companies" but of "vital importance to maintain and strengthen friendly relations with Latin America" in war times. Minority opinion was to the effect that it was a poor precedent, and that "unless Mexico is willing to do better than that . . . it is useless to expect to make 'Good Neighbors' of the Mexicans in any real sense of the term." The *Raleigh News and Observer* [Josephus Daniels's paper] stood alone in unconditionally praising the agreement.[66]

The London, Ontario, *Free Press* on April 25, 1942, pointed out that Mexico should have no difficulty in meeting the required payments since through Export-Import Bank credits

In effect the United States is furnishing Mexico with funds to pay for expropriated property. It is the price of continental harmony. It is assurance that the "Colossus of the North," as they used to regard the United States south of the Rio Grande, has adopted a more liberal and international outlook and is willing to pay the price of her "good-neighbor" policy.

This view was shared by the New York *Times* which stated editorially on April 22, 1942, that the United States was "furnishing Mexico with the funds to pay for the property it has expropriated. This is a dangerous precedent. The best that can be said for it is that it terminates a troublesome controversy with a neighboring country at a time when it is of vital importance to maintain and strengthen friendly relations with Latin America."

Details still had to be settled, but the Cooke-Zevada agreement ended the oil controversy. Even before it was announced, under the spur of war the two countries had formed a joint defense commission and had entered into new agreements for the establishment of basic industries in Mexico, for the development of Mexican railroads and shipbuilding, and, significantly, for the construction of a high-octane gasoline plant in Mexico when materials became available.[67] A new era had, indeed, dawned in Mexican–United States relations. Welles has written that he thought "that a high level of statesmanship was exhibited in the petroleum difficulty." [68] In view of the bitter memories from the past, the delicacy of the negotiations, and the strength of pressures on both governments, Welles may not have exaggerated overmuch, if it were understood that he included the contributions to "statesmanship" those that were made by Daniels, Morgenthau, and, by no means least, the representatives of the government of Mexico. It was this statesmanship that made possible the cordial and collaborative ties developed between the two countries during the war.

CHAPTER X

The Principle of Collaboration: Venezuela

THE DEATH OF Juan Vicente Gómez, who was absolute master of Venezuela from 1909 to 1935, opened an era of political and social reform in the country. The relations between the United States and the new government headed by Eleazar López Contreras, who had been Gómez's last Minister of War, were not formally affected by the change. However, the oil companies owned in Great Britain, the United States, and other countries, whose drilling rights had been established by concessions obtained from Gómez, suddenly felt their positions insecure. Their concessionary rights had been sources of substantial profit to them and steady income to the dictator and members of his entourage.

The companies, accustomed to deal with Gómez, did not immediately change either their representatives in Caracas or their political and economic policies when the new regime came to power. However, habituated to a concessionary security and an undemanding labor force provided by their cooperative arrangement with Gómez, they soon encountered new and strange opposition in the form of free labor unions and a Congress that passed legislation in the summer of 1936 providing for an eight-hour day and collective bargaining. No less important was a new constitutional provision permitting the imposition of export taxes.[1]

The oil companies were faced not only by a movement toward higher living standards for the Venezuelan people, but they enjoyed no sympathetic attitude on the part of Venezuelans. They had made insufficient preparation for dealing with a successor regime that might differ both in form and policy, and they had failed to cultivate friendly relations with individuals and groups outside the Gómez retinue.

When a Venezuelan official told an officer of the United States legation that the continued residence in Venezuela of the same representatives of the principal oil companies—Standard of New Jersey, Gulf, and Royal Dutch Shell—caused the same reaction among Venezuelans as though three members of the Gómez cabinet had remained in power, the Minister reported his view:

> Just as the country itself is undergoing a new deal, so would the affairs of the oil companies benefit by a new deal in personnel; in the opinion of the Legation such a change should also afford an opportunity of improving the standing of Americans and the reputation of the United States in Venezuela.[2]

This report raised to the political level the problem, which turned out to be enduring one, of the nature of the oil companies' representation. The question was asked of Sumner Welles whether a suggestion might be made to the companies concerned, but the Under Secretary considered that "under present conditions" such action would be undesirable, although he might mention the matter orally and informally at a later time.[3]

Despite their antagonism toward the oil companies, and despite bitter attacks against the companies in the newly liberated newspapers,[4] Venezuelan officials recognized that the economy of the country depended almost wholly on the exportation of petroleum. The López Contreras government did not attempt to gain control of the companies' properties; its labor and other legislation, while cutting into the companies' profits, did not cripple the production or export of petroleum. The government even granted new concessions in September, 1936, to the Socony Vacuum Oil Company and the Standard Oil Company of New Jersey.

This policy was attacked from the left and defended on the right. *Petróleo* (Maracaibo) on December 9, 1936, alleged that conservatives in Venezuela attempted to dishearten the workers in the oil fields by saying that "any movement against the oil companies" would mean intervention by the United States. This publication attempted to encourage the workers to continue their demands by assuring them that they had nothing to fear because the reelection of President Roosevelt amounted to a promise by the American people that the United States would not intervene in Latin American affairs. On the other hand, *El Heraldo* (Caracas) on November 24, 1936, attacked "Marxist dogmatism" that would bring about the ruin of Venezuela and favored a policy that, while recognizing the evils attending foreign economic influence, attempted to gain the greatest possible advantage from it for the people of Venezuela. The government of López Contreras in its initial years adopted policies in harmony with this latter view.

For their part, the oil companies conformed to the new legislation by raising wages and providing better facilities for their workers. In 1938, they were paying wages that were somewhat higher than those paid by some of the same companies in Mexico. The companies were slower to change their representatives in Caracas; only one of the companies had done so by June, 1938.

When the Mexican government expropriated foreign oil companies in March, 1938, some fear was expressed in the United States that Venezuela might follow the Mexican example. In fact, however, the Venezuelan government does not appear to have seriously entertained the idea of expropriation. The highest court of Venezuela, on April 4, 1938, handed down a decision requiring the Venezuela Gulf Oil Company and its successor, the Mene Grande Oil Company, to pay about $5,000,000 for having benefited from a tax reduction in 1925 which the court declared to have been illegal. That this decision was not part of a campaign against the companies was suggested by a decision by the same court on April 30, permitting the Lago Petroleum Corporation to continue to enjoy freedom from customs duties on certain equipment and materials.

The United States legation in Caracas had, of course, been studying the effect in Venezuela of the Mexican action, and it reported the conviction that "there is nothing in the situation today which could warrant a conclusion that expropriation is contemplated by the Government or is at all likely to occur in the predictable future." The government was opposed to expropriation and defined its policy "as one of partnership in a common enterprise in which the companies have a legitimate interest by virtue of their very large contributions in capital, organization, and technique." The government was expected to limit itself to "securing a larger return from the industry" and "collecting through legal means the legitimate claims which it may have against the companies by reason of any irregularities in their concessions." Minister Antonio C. Gonzalez stated that the government doubted that Mexico could maintain its pre-1938 level of production, and it therefore regarded the expropriation in Mexico "as favoring the greater development of the Venezuelan oil industry." The most influential newspapers opposed the expropriation, "and even *Ahora*, the outstanding leftist daily . . . has not proposed that Venezuela emulate Mexico in the matter of expropriation." [5]

The reasons for the policy of López Contreras may be found in several features that differentiated the Venezuelan from the Mexican situation. Venezuela did not go through a social revolution following the death of Gómez, as had Mexico after the fall of Porfirio Díaz. The constitution of 1936 was a liberal and not a socialist document, and it did not contain any article vesting subsoil rights in the nation comparable to article 27 of the Mexican Constitution of 1917. Venezuela was more dependent upon the oil industry than was Mexico, where oil exports in 1937 were second to exports of silver; in 1938 about 90 percent of the value of Venezuelan export trade was in petroleum products. The companies, having adapted themselves in 1936 and 1937 to the comparatively moderate Venezuelan legislation, opposed later changes in their status, but they refrained from the intransigence demonstrated in Mexico in 1938, when confronted by subsequent claims by the Venezuelan government. In this policy, the companies may have been influenced by the fact that their stake in Venezuela was several times greater than in Mexico, in terms of production, investment, and anticipated reserves of oil. The United States companies' investment, in physical properties in Venezuela, exclusive of tankers, was about $375,000,000 in 1940.

However, the fact that Venezuela did not expropriate the oil companies did not mean that relationships were those of an amicable partnership. The government seems to have considered that it could exploit the sensitivity created in the companies by the Mexican expropriation, and in 1938 and 1939 it sought by legislative and administrative means to gain larger revenues from the companies. The companies resisted these demands, employing all available legal tactics.

In the middle of 1939, the United States embassy expressed concern, not at the seriousness of the existing situation, but at the trend of developments. It was noted that Venezuelan officials in at least one case had ignored the decision of the Supreme Court on exemptions from customs. One of the companies protested directly to the President, who had questioned the responsible minister. The latter talked with the oil company's representative, who said that his company thought the issue so important that it might appeal to Washington for assistance. The minister replied: "And do you think your government will give you any assistance?" It was the view of the embassy that the Department of State should authorize the making of a statement to López Contreras, expressing the Department's concern at "the growing tendency to take hasty and unfair measures against the oil companies." [6]

This despatch was given serious consideration in Washington, where, however, the problem was viewed much more broadly. The new Ambassador to Venezuela, Frank P. Corrigan, was instructed to talk with oil company officials in New York before he went to Caracas, and consideration was given to inviting the officials to Washington "to emphasize the Department's desire to cooperate in every practicable way toward resolving difficulties which the oil companies may experience before they assume more important proportions, and to emphasize the importance of the oil companies having in Venezuela the best type of representation to maintain a consistently cooperative attitude in relation with the Venezuelan government and people." [7]

This was a new and an important development in the policy of the United States. It signified that the Department of State did not wish to see in Venezuela a repetition of the Mexican experience.

Further, the Department, in contrast to its policy of waiting for something to happen in Mexico in 1938, was now attempting in the early stages of a possible dispute to avert difficulties between a Latin American government and private corporations controlled from the United States. This action appears to have been taken after mature consideration of the situation in which many factors were involved. Venezuela was viewed by the Department as being in the process of taking steps to secure social reforms denied the Venezuelan people during Gómez's long dictatorship.[8]

The oil reserves of Venezuela were large, and it was at the time the world's leading exporter of petroleum products. Expropriation was a possibility if the relations between the government and the companies were allowed to drift from the existing situation into one where exorbitant demands might be made by the Venezuelan government that would be countered by last-ditch resistance by the oil companies. If expropriation in Mexico were followed by a similar action in Venezuela, other Latin American countries might well make comparable moves against United States companies in other types of enterprise. Further, if Great Britain should become embroiled in war, Venezuela would be its only secure source of petroleum. These and other considerations led to the preparation in the Department of State of a memorandum recommending that:

In order to avoid these difficulties, I believe this government must be prepared to go further than may be customary in advising the American petroleum companies in the course they should pursue. It must not be permitted them (as occurred in the case of the Mexican dispute) to jeopardize our entire Good Neighbor policy through obstinacy and short-sightedness. Our national interests as a whole far outweigh those of the petroleum companies. I think that it would be proper to inform the President of Venezuela or the Ambassador of Venezuela here that we should like to hear from them at any time of any wrongdoing they believe has been committed by the American companies, since we expect our companies to conduct themselves in full accord with the letter and spirit of the law just as we expect that they will be treated similarly.[9]

The memorandum then proposed the conversations with oil company representatives to which reference has been made.

Although no meeting was held in Washington at this time,

Ambassador Corrigan expressed to oil company officials in New York the essentials of the Department's position, and he reported that most of the officials received his suggestions favorably. On his arrival in Caracas, Corrigan reported that, while the oil industry had been providing high wages for its Venezuelan employees, "high wages in the oil industry have been the ruination of agriculture." The industry, because of its preeminent position, "finds itself shouldered with social problems that have little to do with business as it is usually considered," and it should give consideration to cooperation with the Venezuelan government's "plans for social betterment of the whole country." The companies should therefore help develop a program that would be larger than the separate local projects they were currently undertaking, such as the provision of schools, hospitals, and other facilities for their workers, which in themselves were praiseworthy activities. The present moment was propitious since relations between the government and the companies were still fairly friendly, but there were danger signs, and the possibility of expropriation as an outcome of continuous wrangling between them could not be ruled out.[10]

At the end of 1939, Corrigan noted that there was a continuation of the trend first commented upon by the embassy in June. The Venezuelan government felt that "since the companies play such a preponderant role in the life of the country they should be prepared to cooperate and contribute in a much greater manner than they have done in the past towards the budget of the Venezuelan government." The government, however, was not showing any tendency to be "unfriendly" or to "penalize" the oil industry. Nevertheless, "the situation has now developed into one in which the government keeps pressing to obtain more revenues while the companies keep fighting a bitter rear-guard action against what they feel are unfair attacks." Corrigan felt that it was possible that the "legal rights" of the companies "can be maintained over a period of years only if the companies adopt a parallel policy of generous and ready cooperation with the Venezuelan government in all worth while measures, particularly those of social and economic significance." One way of doing this would be to take an interest in the development of agriculture, in which President

López Contreras was deeply concerned, particularly through assisting in the revival of the livestock industry.[11] Shortly afterward, it was regarded as "encouraging" that the Gulf Oil Company had employed an agricultural expert to advise its Venezuelan subsidiary on the production of suitable food crops in eastern Venezuela for its employees.[12]

These actions provided evidence that the oil firms were beginning to recognize the need to adopt new measures to deal with the new situation in Venezuela. The difficulty was that their actions were taken individually and at intervals and were on too small a scale to appear to Venezuelans as more than reluctant concessions to the demands of the Venezuelan government. What was necessary was a broad reassessment of the whole position of the oil industry in Venezuela. This came to be insisted upon by Caracas, and was recognized in Washington, but was not accepted as inevitable in the New York offices of the oil companies until just in time to avert drastic action by the Venezuelan government.

The story of the revision of the status of the oil industry in Venezuela from 1939 to 1943 is of interest in the evolution of Good Neighbor concepts, for it involved the use of new methods of diplomacy by the Department of State in dealing with a Latin American government as well as with the most powerful of United States industries having investments abroad. The use of new methods, however, was but a reflection of the maturation of a new conception of great significance in inter-American relationships, namely, that the national interest of the United States was vitally interwoven with the development of the oil industry in the Western Hemisphere on terms that would, firstly, be satisfactory to Latin American governments and would, secondly, preserve the essentials of the position achieved by the oil companies. In the disputes with Bolivia and Mexico, the principal issues were the amount and method of payment of compensation for the confiscation or expropriation of oil properties. In the case of Venezuela, the issue was the avoidance of any conflict between Venezuela and the oil companies that would limit or diminish the production of petroleum in wartime and would embitter relationships between the United States and Venezuela and perhaps other Latin American countries as well. The Department of State felt that it could not simply be a bystander when Venezuela and the oil companies appeared to be on the way to a repetition of the Mexican experience. At a time when the struggle was only a sparring match, the Department began to take measures to head off an open break, and its officers were largely responsible for the amicable settlement that was ultimately reached. It should be recognized at the same time that the Venezuelan government did not imitate the abrupt actions of Bolivia or Mexico. Its running struggle with the oil companies developed in 1939 without early major crises, and the Department of State had time successfully to impress on the companies the imperative need for compromise on their part to avert possible expropriation.

Following Corrigan's talk with oil company officials in the autumn of 1939, the first action taken by the Department of State was to arrange, in June, 1940, a meeting in Washington with leading officers of four oil corporations. The attitude of the Department of State at the time was set forth in a memorandum prepared in the form of a statement to be made by Secretary Hull in the opening meeting. After suggesting that in the past it was possible that both the Department and the oil companies might justly be considered to have made mistakes in their inter-American dealings, the memorandum proposed that the Secretary say:

This Department and I personally have always wanted to do what is best to protect our American interests and we feel this duty very keenly. Our intentions in this regard are very definite, and in order to perform this duty which is incumbent upon us we must have your cooperation and we must have plans prepared to meet difficulties that are foreseeable. We want to work out arrangements to facilitate such cooperation. . . . I realize that you gentlemen are competitors, and we do not wish to interfere in any way with your advancing the legitimate interests of your own companies. But, we do hope that something may be done to bring about more rapid and effective consultation on influences which may affect the whole industry, and enable us to foresee complications and avoid them. Details of that mechanism will require careful study. I would like to have your opinions on this. In the past, you have had joint consultations after your interests have been endangered, which is all right in its way but not as constructive as would be a mechanism which would also foresee and prevent difficulties.[13]

This memorandum may be noted as making explicit two suggestions of major importance in the later course of this controversy; these were the suggestions that the companies regard themselves not as competitors but as an industry, and that "difficulties" should be prevented rather than allowed to become serious. It seems reasonable to assume that these hints to the companies derived from experience in the Bolivian and Mexican cases.

The meeting with company officials did not produce any immediate results, and the situation was allowed to drift until early in 1941 when an incident occurred that roused the Department to further action. The Venezuelan government informed the Mene Grande Oil Company, a subsidiary of the Gulf Oil Corporation, that it had a claim against the Company for some $15,000,000 in taxes which should have been paid between 1927 and 1931. The Company admitted that it owed back taxes but held that the government's demand exaggerated the amount. President López Contreras told Ambassador Corrigan that he was determined to carry the claim to the courts if necessary, but that he preferred to handle it by negotiation, and he added that the claim did not represent any change in the general policy toward the industry in Venezuela.[14]

Negotiations between the government and the Company broke down in March, and Corrigan was informed that the President intended to announce in his message to Congress on April 15 that public action would be taken in the courts.[15]

Welles reacted swiftly by asking Corrigan to request López Contreras to delay any public moves until the Department had the opportunity to "impress upon the president of the Gulf Oil Corporation here the necessity for bringing about an atmosphere which [would] permit the direct negotiations . . . to be resumed." Welles said the Department "feels strongly" the undesirability of "a public controversy" because of "international implications." [16]

The time available to Welles was short, because López Contreras was leaving office and was determined not to leave the Mene Grande case to his successor. At Welles's invitation the president of Gulf went to Washington, and in a few days a settlement providing for the payment by the Company of approximately $10,-000,000 was arranged with the assistance of Welles and was then approved by the Venezuelan cabinet. The Company's president wrote to Welles, expressing appreciation for his cooperation in the dispute and saying that the Company was gratified at the settlement, "especially, realizing, as we do, that much more was involved than merely the issue between the Venezuelan government and our company." [17] This remark presumably referred to the current British needs as well as to possible United States needs for petroleum in wartime.

On the broader issue of the position of the oil industry in Venezuela, talks were opened between Venezuela and the companies in the summer of 1941 when Attorney General Gustavo Manrique Pacanins came to the United States. The Department of State took no part in these early contacts, although it was anticipated in Washington that unless the Department played "an informal part in the negotiations, the oil companies and the government of Venezuela [might] reach an impasse." It was also felt that unless the negotiations were successful the result might be expropriation.[18]

The fundamental position of Venezuela in the negotiations was that the concessions obtained from Gómez should be revised in order that the government might not only secure larger income from oil exports, but also participate more extensively in the administration of the country's petroleum resources. The companies adopted a position of firm, although not extreme, resistance on both issues. From the point of view of the Department of State, the controversy was of nearly vital importance, if only because Great Britain was at this time obtaining the major part of its oil requirements from Venezuela. Every effort was necessary to avoid any curtailment of shipments from what had become an indispensable source of oil.

The Department of State had another interest in the situation: "From the long term point of view, we still have an opportunity to see whether large scale business, particularly the oil business, can so arrange its affairs in one of the other American republics to avoid serious troubles and possible expropriation." Even though the atmosphere for negotiation seemed auspicious, it was thought desirable for the Department to talk with the companies and suggest that a revision of Venezuelan legislation was inevitable and that the serious difficulties in the coming negotiations should be avoided. In addition, it was felt advisable to make it known to Venezuelan officials that the Department "was prepared to use . . . good offices in the arriving at any arrangement equitable for the companies as well as the government." [19]

The negotiations between Manrique Pacanins and oil company representatives were broken off in November, 1941, after the presentation by the companies of a project for new legislation that was regarded as unacceptable. The negotiations were terminated amicably, but the Venezuelans seemed to feel that the companies, by standing firmly on their legal position, were failing to give adequate consideration to the government's desire to make an entirely fresh start and find a new, post-Gómez basis for the status of the industry. During a second trip to the United States in the spring of 1942, Manrique Pacanins placed this situation before the Department of State and indicated that, while the Venezuelan government preferred not to initiate action against the companies in the courts, it might feel compelled to do so. If court action were taken, it was not impossible that the pressure of public opinion in Venezuela might make more drastic and unilateral action, such as expropriation, unavoidable.[20] In consequence, the Department of State again impressed upon oil company officials the necessity of their coming to terms with Venezuela and the desirability of arranging a new relationship by means of mutual discussions rather than having to accept drastic unilateral action by Venezuela. It was stated to the oil men that the Department felt that the maintenance of the flow of oil from Venezuela, which had become of vital importance after Pearl Harbor, could best be assured if the companies continued to operate their production facilities in Venezuela.[21]

Shortly after this conversation, the Standard Oil Company despatched a special representative to Venezuela to confer with the new President, Isaias Medina Angarita, and to report on the situation. Before this mission could bear fruit, however, Medina took the initiative by despatching Manrique Pacanins on another visit to the United States. He carried a letter to President Roosevelt to inform him that the Venezuelan government, "with the greatest firmness," was resolved to bring about "a revision of the petroleum policy followed by Venezuela," to allow it to "rectify illegitimate, illicit, or distressing conditions in order that Venezuela may receive a truly just share in the exploitation of the riches of its subsoil." It was noted that the companies "have continued systematically to oppose the Government through passive resistance," but his administration intended to carry through the revision "under the laws of Venezuela and under the general principles of justice and equity." [22] Accompanying the letter was a memorandum setting forth in greater detail the plans of the government of Venezuela and characterizing in stronger terms the "intransigent jealousy" and "obstinacy" of the oil companies in the preceding negotiations.

It would hardly be accurate to interpret this letter as threatening expropriation of the oil companies, but the possibility was envisaged indirectly in the accompanying memorandum:

The present situation, unfavorable for the country already, could some day become intolerable, bringing with it serious injury to the mutual interests of the nation and the oil companies. For this reason, there is an urgent need of correcting from this moment onward, what perhaps afterwards might be impracticable because it would be too late.

At the same time the memorandum stated that "there is no intention in any way of nationalizing the industry or likewise of despoiling from their concessions those who have acquired them legally." This initiative by President Medina inspired the Department of State to take an active role in subsequent negotiations between Venezuela and the oil companies.

President Roosevelt's reply, drafted by Adolf A. Berle, Jr., Assistant Secretary of State, expressed appreciation for Medina's letter, and stated:

This government will not claim for American companies doing business in other countries any undue or unreasonable privileges or rights and fully recognizes the Venezuelan interest in guiding its economic development in the best interest of its people. Since I understand it to be the policy of your government to deal fairly with American companies and to give full recognition to their legitimate rights, and [since your government] is fully aware of the need for maintaining production in the interest of both of our countries, I naturally feel confident that your government and the companies will shortly find a just and satisfactory settlement of all controversial questions.

The President pointed out the mutual interest of the two countries in the production of Venezuelan oil for purposes of mutual defense, and noted with approval Medina's statements that it was his purpose to guarantee "the longest and most stable possible future industrial peace, which will be as beneficial to the nation as to the petroleum concessionaires"; as well as to "avoid and prevent in this manner events which could prejudice these concessionaires in the future, as has happened in other countries."

Again expressing the hope that a mutually agreeable settlement could be reached, Roosevelt added, in terms of general policy: "This expression is in keeping with sound international relations and the principles of the Good Neighbor policy, to which your country and mine have wholeheartedly subscribed." [23]

The inter-presidential exchange of letters was of significance in itself, but it could have practical results only if supplemented by action by the Department of State. Manrique Pacanins also called at the Department to explain his mission, and he emphasized the urgency with which the Venezuelan government looked at the problem. He also exhibited photostatic copies of documents as evidence claimed by his government to prove that at least one oil company had bribed an official during the Gómez regime in order to obtain exemptions from legal limitations upon the company. Under Secretary Welles told his visitor:

If the government of Venezuela adopted the policy announced to me, namely strict observance of the tenets of international law, complete compliance with the terms of Venezuelan legislation, submission to the tribunals of any controversies which could not be solved by negotiations, and the determination to encourage the American companies to continue to do business in Venezuela, I felt sure that fair negotiations between the companies and the government could result in a just and satisfactory settlement. [To that end] the Department of State would do whatever it appropriately could to facilitate a friendly adjustment.[24]

Welles apparently felt that there was a good deal of justification for the Venezuelan position. In a letter to Roosevelt, he said that in view of several failures to revise the relations with the oil companies after the death of Gómez, the Venezuelan government "has felt that the efforts which it has made to work things out and particularly to insure to the government and people of the country a larger share of their natural resources have been unproductive and that the tactics of the companies have been characterized by delay and evasion." [25] Welles noted that in the past few years the Department had on several occasions

indicated to the oil companies operating in Venezuela the desirability of their acceding to the legitimate desire of the Venezuelan government to modernize the conditions under which the companies operate. I have personally long been of the opinion that the arrangements under which the oil industry got its start in Venezuela and the conditions then prevailing are no longer applicable to an established industry operating one of the richest and best proven oil fields in the world.

Shortly after the conversation between Welles and Manrique Pacanins on August 20, 1942, news of an impending move by President Medina came from Caracas. It was reported that the President was awaiting a report from a commission which he had appointed to make recommendations as to the kind of settlement that Venezuela would offer to the oil companies. The membership of the commission was unknown, as was the way in which Medina might present the plan to the companies.[26]

Spurred by this news, Welles invited several oil company officials to Washington for a conference, at which the seriousness of the situation was reemphasized in view of the imminence of determined and unilateral action by Medina's administration. The officials were urged to replace their representatives in Caracas with new men who had no connections with the Gómez regime, in the hope that they would have a more sensitive understanding of the existing situation.[27]

This time, however, the Department of State did not content itself with exhortations to each side in the dispute but adopted measures it had refrained from using in the Mexican case. Its adviser on petroleum policy, Max W. Thornburg, undertook informal conversations with both Manrique Pacanins and executives of the oil companies, in order to bring about a reconciliation of the positions of the two parties. Thornburg was notably successful both in Caracas and in New York, and his mediation led directly to a friendly settlement of the dispute, which had still, however, to pass through some critical stages.

Mr. Thornburg had established "very friendly personal relations" with Manrique Pacanins in August, and had proposed further discussions with oil company officials before final action was taken in Caracas. Shortly afterward, Manrique Pacanins "asked Mr. Thornburg to continue to be of assistance to him in a purely personal capacity." This request, which was clearly "a matter of some delicacy," was granted by Welles, and Thornburg then engaged in talks with oil men to see whether an agreement were possible.[28] Following these talks, one of the principal United States oil companies "reorganized its managerial organization in Venezuela in such a way as to eliminate persons who had ceased to be agreeable to the President of Venezuela and other leading Venezuelan officials." [29]

The final phase of the negotiations began on December 1, 1942, when President Medina granted individual interviews to special representatives of the oil companies who had gone to Caracas for the purpose of engaging in a new round of talks with Venezuelan officials. These negotiations were participated in by the officers of British and United States firms and by two oil experts from the United States, Arthur Curtice and Herbert Hoover, Jr., whose services as consultants had been engaged by the Venezuelan government. At the request of the Venezuelan government, Thornburg flew to Caracas. Although he did not take part in the formal meetings, he talked informally with government and company officials, and it is probable that the confidence in him that was shared by both negotiating groups enabled him to make suggestions that ultimately found nearly unanimous approval for incorporation into the proposed new petroleum law. The drafting of the law, once the general principles had been accepted by the oil companies, was undertaken by a commission established by President Medina; the President himself sat frequently with the commission to stress the importance he attached to its work.

When the draft law was completed, it was submitted to the oil companies for comments, and some changes were made before a bill was introduced into the Venezuelan legislature. With no significant modifications, the bill became law on March 13, 1943. Its principal provisions were: (1) an increase in royalties to the government from rates varying between 7½ and 11 percent to a uniform rate of 16⅔ percent; (2) the establishment of a new base on which the royalties were calculated which was more favorable to the government than the one used previously; (3) a reduction in the customs exemptions formerly enjoyed by the companies; (4) a reaffirmation of existing concessions with the inclusion of these and other changes.

The terms of the new law were very similar to the proposals made by Thornburg in a letter of October 30 to Manrique Pacanins, copies of which were sent to the oil firms concerned; for example, the 16⅔ percent royalty rate was identical, and Thornburg's proposal was that the liquidation value of royalties due by oil companies be determined "on a fair world market basis instead of on the arbitrary values heretofore used." Welles emphasized, in writing to Roosevelt, that "the proposals were in no sense binding either on Dr. Manrique Pacanins or on the Venezuelan government. They were merely an indication of the type of settlement which it might be possible to reach, should the Venezuelan government decide to enter into discussions directly with the oil companies instead of persisting in its intention of taking unilateral measures." At the same time, in Welles's opinion, the proposals "represented a very marked concession on the part of the major operating companies." It was his belief, he wrote, that "they went a good deal further than the companies had earlier believed would be necessary." [30]

One problem threatened for a time to disrupt the otherwise harmonious proceedings. President Medina desired the oil companies to agree to build future refineries in Venezuela, rather than on the Dutch islands of Aruba and Curaçao near the entrance to the Gulf of Venezuela. The oil companies had built some of the world's largest refineries on these islands, presumably because they felt that such valuable properties would be safer and more independently controlled if they were on Dutch rather than on Venezuelan territory. There were in 1940 three small refineries in

Venezuela, but these produced gasoline and other products for local consumption only. Because President Medina had publicly expressed his determination to have future refineries built in Venezuela, and because the companies refused to establish large installations in Venezuela, a way had to be found to meet the requirements of both sides. It was finally agreed that within five years after the end of World War II, the British and United States companies would build in Venezuela refineries having a daily capacity of a total of 80,000 barrels of refined products.

The outcome of the revision of the petroleum industry's position in Venezuela was regarded with great satisfaction by President Medina. He told Ambassador Corrigan that he was satisfied with "the cooperation that had been received from nearly all of the companies," and said that the Venezuelan government's "appreciation would be reflected in its future relations and that the oil companies who had agreed to convert their titles under the new law will find in the Venezuelan Government a first line of defense." [31]

The oil company officials were less enthusiastic about the new legislation; they had, however, finally come to realize that their continued operation in Venezuela was dependent on their acceptance of a new and less privileged status, without further resistance. Any other course by them had been opposed by the Department of State, principally because of its fear that absolutely essential oil supplies might be curtailed or cut off if an appeal to the Venezuelan courts were made by the companies. This argument of national interest in wartime prevailed, although it appears that an intense struggle went on within some of the oil companies, and one of the smaller United States operators refused to acquiesce in the course followed by the others.

The position of the Department of State was set forth as early as the end of 1942 in Welles's letter to President Roosevelt, cited above:

In my judgment it was of the highest importance to reach a settlement between the oil companies and the Venezuelan Government, subject of course to the approval of the Venezuelan Congress, which would enable the companies to continue operating on a satisfactory basis at the same time that the Government and people of the country would receive a more equitable share of the proceeds of the business. Obviously, anything which at this time would impair the efficient functioning of the oil companies and would lead to a state of public opinion in Venezuela contrary to foreign interests would be most prejudicial and would in effect threaten the availability of an asset vital to the successful conduct of the war.

Welles's emphasis on a more equitable share of proceeds from the oil industry for the Venezuelan people is so strong as to strike a new note of policy. In the Mexican controversy Hull had at first rather grudgingly given recognition to the social aims of the Mexican people, but Welles here came close to implying that the United States had a measure of responsibility for the welfare of Venezuelans. So far had Welles, at least, moved from a defense of the rights of foreign investors on grounds of the international legal obligations of an American government even though he had upheld them in the early phase of the Mexican oil dispute.

It seems fair to assume that the Venezuelan government, fully cognizant of Washington's policy toward the Mexican expropriation and aware that its oil was precious to the United Nations, took advantage of the war emergency in the expectation that the Department of State would bring effective pressure to bear on the oil companies.[32] Commenting later, as a political leader in exile, Rómulo Betancourt charged that the Venezuelan government "had missed the splendid opportunity offered by a world at war and avid for fuel, and by the presence of Roosevelt in the White House, a president who, in the face of the radical action taken by Mexico in a situation like that of Venezuela's, had adopted a circumspect policy." Betancourt attributed this alleged failure to the autocratic character of the government; it could not risk stronger demands on the oil companies, in his view, because "it had not held fair elections, honestly administered public funds, or adequately respected social needs."[33]

For their part, the oil companies may have held their ground as long as they did in the hope that Roosevelt would not be so "circumspect," as he had been in 1938–41 toward Mexico; in 1943 the United States was at war, and Venezuela was a far more important source of petroleum than Mexico. There was undoubtedly some jockeying for advantage in a critical situation, both by President Medina and by the companies. If the Department of State had been less alert, the contest might have endured so long as to explode into expropriation. In that case, assurance of access to Venezuelan oil would probably have required measures of an entirely different order. However, the timing of Welles, advised by Corrigan, was precise enough to prevent the hardening of public commitments on either side. Moreover, Roosevelt and Welles did not swerve from their determination that a peaceful compromise was not only the best way to keep the oil flowing but would also provide some satisfaction for the desires of the Venezuelan people for a higher standard of living, and would also furnish an exemplary demonstration of the continuity of the Good Neighbor policy.

A remark made by Ambassador Corrigan may be quoted as expressing a pardonable pride in the handling of this delicate controversy: "On the whole a new approach to a difficult problem can be recorded, and it may be said that sincere and competent men and a spirit of fair play determined the future of Venezuelan oil." [34]

The new approach had two main features. Firstly, it provided for the use of political negotiations in order to prevent expropriation, as distinct from reliance on juridical and political methods to defend the interests of foreign investors after their properties had been taken from them, as in the Bolivian and Mexican cases. Secondly, and again in contrast to those cases, the Department did not simply make weak and ineffectual appeals to the oil companies, or limit itself to suggesting they undertake independent negotiations with the government in question; it brought the full weight of its influence to bear with urgency and effectiveness, and it actively participated in the negotiations.

There is a good deal that we do not know about these important developments, so that little more than an outline can be offered here. For example, we do not know the exact nature of the arguments that Welles used to induce the Gulf Oil Company quickly to agree to the settlement of the Mene Grande case mentioned above. Further, we do not know what arguments Thornburg used to get the companies to send new men to Caracas and to decide they had no alternative but to accept the Venezuelan demands in large meas-ure. In any case, however, the Department showed less sympathy for the companies' position in 1943 than it showed in 1941 and earlier during the Mexican negotiations. The difference must be in part attributable to the entry of the United States into the war, but other factors were at work as is suggested by Welles's state-ment of the Department's position at the end of 1942 as quoted above. Further, in the Mexican and Bolivian cases, such moderate influence as the United States exerted was directed at those govern-ments and not at the oil companies, but in the Venezuelan affair the direction of pressure was against the companies and not Vene-zuela. It is of interest in this connection that Betancourt does not assert that Washington tried to get the Venezuelan government to change its policy; his complaint is that Caracas did not make more out of such a remarkable opportunity.

In this context it may be observed that officials in the Depart-ment of State were quicker than oil company officers to sense the danger of expropriation, and that they undertook, first, to im-press on the companies the need to realize their social responsibility in Venezuela, and, second, the need to accept sacrifices as part of the war effort. The executives of the companies, after some demur, responded adequately to the urgings and warnings of the Depart-ment of State, and the Venezuelan government refrained from press-ing its wartime advantage too far.

Perhaps as a result of its experience with Mexico, the Depart-ment of State relied only on political techniques and showed no tendency at any time to propose a juridical solution to the con-troversy. There was no talk of "denial of justice," no suggestion that "local remedies should be exhausted," nor any proposal of arbitration as the proper mode of settlement. The time was one of urgency because of the war, but there was more than that in the attitude of the Department of State and, ultimately, of the oil companies. There was also a recognition that what was referred to in the Department itself as "a legalistic approach" would not satisfy the founts of demand by the Venezuelans for a new order. And, beyond this, it was realized that a recourse to the courts, besides risking incalculable losses to the oil industry, would inevitably arouse antagonistic feelings in Venezuela, not only toward the companies but toward the government and perhaps the people of the United States as well. The political and economic stakes were too high to permit reliance on legal procedures; no "winner-takes-all" game could be played.

The impression is given by the performance of the Department of State in this instance that policy was guided by men who felt sure of their principles, and were swift in their appreciation of the needs of the situation. The dangerous possibilities were perceived early, the developments were closely watched and adequate preventive measures taken in time, even if only just in time.

The contrast with the handling of the Mexican expropriation was sharp. In 1938 the Department was surprised by Cárdenas's expropriation decree and thrown into confusion by a failure to clarify what Daniels had done in Mexico City. After inconclusive exchanges of notes Hull publicly and firmly proposed arbitration and then quietly accepted Mexico's quick rejection of arbitration. In the Venezuelan case open diplomacy was shunned, cooperation between the minister and the Department was close, and understanding complete. The actions of the officials were those of men who had grasped and ordered the objectives of their policy, and had attained a freedom from traditional methods that allowed them to make imaginative use of new techniques. There may have been some slight uncertainty about the new techniques, particularly with regard to Thornburg's role in the negotiations, for elaborate care was exercised to dissociate his activities from his official position. Nevertheless, official approval was given to his acceptance of what was a really extraordinary invitation from the Venezuelan government that he go to Caracas during the most critical stage of the negotiations.[35]

This was a new and mature diplomacy that combined the spirit of the Good Neighbor with methods that were novel and effective.[36] In the Mexican case, the interests of the oil companies had been ultimately subordinated to the requirements of the national policy of the United States, but only after their position in Mexico had been irretrievably lost as a result of their own independent action. In Venezuela the companies might again have been driven out had their dispute with the government been allowed to run its course, but their interests were again subordinated to national policy, this time before a possible expropriation. Such subordination, in the Department's view of the national interest, however, may well have been also in the best long-range interest of the companies, since they continue to operate in Venezuela, but not in Mexico.

PART THREE

The Transformation of

the Good Neighbor Policy

CHAPTER XI

Opportunities and Disabilities

THE THREE POLICIES with which this study has been primarily concerned may from one point of view be regarded as conditions for the acceptance of the United States into an American neighborhood; these were renunciations of the exercise of power that Latin American states regarded as essential before they could feel that their independence of the military and economic dominance of the United States had been achieved. Thenceforth the whole nature of inter-American discourse underwent a great change, for the problems of status had been settled in favor of formal equality and the problems remaining were those of accommodation in a comparatively free society that contained, of course, members differing greatly in culture, in technical development, and in wealth.

The United States did not rely only on its renunciatory policies in its search for reciprocity. Concomitantly with the signing of the nonintervention protocol at Montevideo, Secretary Hull commenced his assault on the Smoot-Hawley tariff. In this and in other ways positive policies were followed that were aimed at eliminating impediments to inter-American trade and at stimulating military collaboration among the American states.

The Reciprocal Trade Agreements Program

When Secretary Hull took office he recounts that he moved into the Latin American field "armed with the President's declaration of our Good Neighbor policy." [1] In addition to this untested weapon, Hull carried to the Montevideo Conference his intention to "introduce a comprehensive economic resolution calling for lower tariffs and the abolition of trade restrictions." [2] After a struggle with what he called the "nationalistic philosophy of the New Deal group about the President," Hull's desires were approved by Roosevelt, and Hull obtained the acceptance by the Conference of a resolution calling for the reduction of trade barriers and observance of equality of treatment in commercial policy.

Hull still had a battle to fight at home, but he won it with the passage of the Reciprocal Trade Agreement Act of 1934. Although Hull anticipated that the passage of this act would brighten the inter-American atmosphere,[3] his efforts to reduce tariffs were primarily based on the long-cherished convictions of a low-tariff man, who sought commercial advantages to the United States no less than those of a political character.

The first trade agreement was made with Cuba in August, 1934, and nine of the first twelve agreements were negotiated with countries in Latin America, including the five Central American states. It is beyond the scope of this study to give detailed consideration to economic foreign policy,[4] but it may be noted that the Trade Agreements Act gave to the Roosevelt administration a flexibility that the Smoot-Hawley Tariff Act had denied to the Hoover administration. It was now possible to arrange for mutual tariff reductions through a process of specific, limited, and clearly defined reciprocity. It is of interest to note that reciprocity in the economic field involved a perfectly respectable form of bargaining, a process that was regarded by statesmen as disreputable in the sphere of politics. Something akin to bargaining was carried on in political relationships, but the specification of "conditions" or *quid pro quo*'s was ordinarily avoided; the customs of inter-American diplomacy demanded that the process be hidden or euphemized. Economic diplomats might haggle, it seemed, but political diplomats could not descend below the level of negotiation.

Without endeavoring to trace the development of the trade agreements program, it is essential to recognize the great contribution made by that program to the development of that broader reciprocity with which this study is concerned. The lowering of trade barriers combined with the encouragement given to the improvement of communications by sea and air was hardly less important in the evocation of reciprocity than nonintervention and its fellow policies. Latin American expressions of support for the Good Neighbor policy frequently combined these two policy developments. As one example only, there may be quoted the remarks of Dr. Soto del Corral, foreign minister of Colombia, who expressed satisfaction at the first reelection of President Roosevelt, as an endorsement of the Good Neighbor policy, with its "new criterion in the diplomatic sphere, and commercial relations based on liberal principles which consecrate the operation of the most-favored-nation clause." [5]

The combination of the trade agreements program with an economic upturn in the United States after 1933 brought about a substantial increase of trade between the United States and nearly all the countries of Latin America, and certain countries, such as Cuba, whose export trade was almost wholly dependent upon the United States market, secured special concessions on sugar and other products.

The establishment of the Export-Import Bank in 1934 assisted individual United States exporters in transactions with Latin Americans, but its important role as a provider of credits to governments did not begin to be played until after the outbreak of war in 1939.

Limitations on a Good Neighbor

Beyond the negotiation of trade agreements, the Department of State also attempted to eliminate or reduce other impediments to inter-American commerce. In one outstanding case, that of the Sanitary Convention of 1935, which would have permitted the entry of chilled meats from areas where hoof-and-mouth disease was certified not to exist, the Department made valiant efforts to secure approval of the Convention by the Senate. It went so far as to carry on a national educational campaign, pointing to an anticipated increase in trade with Argentina, but the active opposition of cattle-raising interests that were politically strong in some twenty Western states proved a greater obstacle than the nearly voteless Department could surmount.

The substantial effort of the Department to secure adoption of the Convention demonstrated the political importance it attached to the cultivation of inter-American economic collaboration, but the Department's failure also demonstrated significant limitations on the scope of the Department's capacity to promote its conceptions of the Good Neighbor policy.

Although the Department had been able to bring about a fundamental change in traditional policies in connection with the oil disputes, this development was largely due to the combination of three circumstances: (1) the policy change could be determined upon and put into effect by the action of the executive branch of the government alone; (2) the outbreak of World War II provided compelling reasons for subordination of the oil companies' policies to the national interest as understood in the Department; and (3) the policy change did not arouse the opposition of solidary pressure groups in the United States capable of decisively affecting electoral contests in a substantial number of states.

These circumstances did not combine to favor the attempt of the Department of State to improve relations with Argentina by negotiating the Sanitary Convention, which in the Department's view was an application of the Good Neighbor policy. In this case, the Department's conception of the national interest was not shared by cowboys, feedlot owners, and ranchers, and they proved strong enough to prevent the Convention even from reaching the floor of the Senate.

The nature of a further limitation became clear when in 1937 the Department announced that an arrangement had been made to lease to Brazil for training purposes six World War I destroyers.[6] The announcement brought a protest from the British government, but this might have been dodged. The lethal blow to the plan was delivered by Carlos Saavedra Lamas, the Argentine foreign minister, who charged that it should not have been formulated except in consultation with other American states, and that it was out of harmony with the spirit of collaboration evoked by the Buenos

Aires conference of 1936.[7] The Department was unable to obtain support in the Senate, and the lease was not effected.

This affair demonstrated that, in addition to the domestic limitations mentioned above, the Department was dependent on the interpretation given to Good Neighborliness by Latin American states that could make a persuasive claim that they had an interest in a policy initiative on the part of the United States, even though they were not directly concerned. In this instance, the principal basis for the Argentine claim was that the lease of destroyers risked starting an armament race in South America.

The Department of State was thus most notably successful in carrying out those aspects of the Good Neighbor policy with which this study is mainly concerned when the effects were most strictly bilateral and intergovernmental; that is, when the United States and one other government were the principal actors and the subject of action offered little or no opportunity for protests by other countries, and when the necessary action could be taken by the executive branches of each government with little concern for domestic political consequences. Further, the Department of State was more successful, with respect to internal political pressures, when it was on the defensive than when it tried to initiate policies dependent on the generation of popular sympathy or action in the Congress; thus it was able to resist the effects of direct influence and propaganda of the oil companies but utterly failed to move the cattlemen or their Senators.

In the campaign for approval of the Sanitary Convention, the Department's arguments, based on improving foreign trade and developing good will with Argentina and other states, even when supported by the National Foreign Trade Council and the International Apple Growers' Association, were of no avail against the attitude of the most directly interested group. This was expressed, for example, by a livestock association official: "It is fine to assume the policy of brotherly love and affection for these South American republics but I believe in first recognizing the brother in the family and safeguarding his interests and one of our essential industries before carrying the policy across the seas."[8] On the defense, the Department was substantially sheltered by Roosevelt's popularity and his party leadership; on the offensive, however, Roosevelt was only lukewarm about the Sanitary Convention, and he did not wish to antagonize Senators whose votes he needed on greater issues by urging them strongly to accept this proposal.

In the course of the three oil controversies, the expression of public opinion, either directly or through the Congress, does not appear to have influenced officials in Washington to change any basic decisions. In the Venezuelan case, the negotiations were secret, and public opinion was uninformed. In the Bolivian case, the stakes were low, there was no history, or likelihood, of the use of force by the United States, and the public was uninterested. In the Mexican case, important sectors of the public were both interested and vocal, but policies were formulated primarily out of conceptions of the national interest of the United States, that were held in common, with minor differences, by Roosevelt, Hull, Welles, Daniels, and Duggan. A glimpse of some aspects of the role of United States public opinion during the controversy with Mexico may be of interest in this connection.

The Mexican government acted at no time as though it were afraid that the policy of the Roosevelt administration would be changed because of the pressure of Congress or public opinion in the United States. In so doing, the Mexican government was proven to be an accurate judge of Roosevelt's firmness of purpose in resisting Congressional and other attempts to change the course of policy toward Mexico. In 1939, several resolutions were presented in the Senate and House of Representatives, aimed at investigating the oil negotiations. Several of these were offered at the beginning of the year, and the attitude of the Department of State was expressed to Senator Key Pittman, chairman of the Foreign Relations Committee of the Senate. Hull wrote that while he was ready at any time to talk with members of the Committee, an investigation would have "unfortunate repercussions" on the oil dispute, at least until after the result of the negotiations between Mexico and the companies was known.[9] The Committee declined to act on any resolutions, as in July, when one was presented by Senator Styles Bridges.[10] After this time, the attention of legislators and the public was diverted to the war in Europe, and pressure from this source was eased.

Concerning the public at large, there seems to have been no time when public opinion was sufficiently unanimous or sufficiently influential to cause the Department of State even to reconsider its policies toward Mexico, much less to change them. Roosevelt had set the tone of the administration's attitude in his press conference on April 1, 1938; the note he struck then, one of sympathy only for the small United States farmers in Mexico, was in harmony with many of his domestic policies, and on the whole those who supported him in internal affairs also gave him their adherence in his policy toward Mexico. It would have taken an outburst of public opinion of unusual proportions to overcome a resistance to certain evidences of popular feeling which Welles had developed by 1938:

The Ambassador [Castillo Nájera] told me that President Cárdenas had said that he had been deluged with telegrams and letters from all elements within the United States supporting the stand he had taken with regard to the oil properties and urging him not to retreat. I remarked to the Ambassador that I was so familiar with the way in which artificial publicity was worked up during the past four years I could not construe this fact as being of any importance.[11]

Despite their determination to maintain their own course, however, the conjuration of the specter of an outraged public opinion was not disdained as an occasional diplomatic technique by United States officials, who on more than one occasion depicted themselves as on the verge of being forced to adopt a different policy by Congress or the public.

Welles told Castillo Nájera, with regard to agrarian claims, that the situation "had almost reached the point where an explosion of public indignation on the part of United States citizens was at hand," and Welles himself had begun to lose his own "innate optimism" about the settlement of the problem.[12] Similarly, Roosevelt had earlier said to Chargé Luis Quintanilla that, if an agreement were not reached with the oil companies, "public opinion in this country would be so incensed" that Congress would make it impossible for the Executive to buy any more Mexican silver.[13]

Ramón Beteta and Laurence Duggan had a talk in mid-1939 that was both illustrative of the relationships between their governments and of the types of pressures on the other that each thought might be effective. Beteta said he had found that the "atmosphere" in Washington was "very bad," if he interpreted the press correctly, and Duggan said the Washington press "had properly diagnosed the trend of thought." Duggan then summarized the course of the negotiations and the attitude of his government:

I said that the President and the Secretary were very concerned at the present status of the negotiations between Richberg and the Mexican Government; they had handled the oil situation from the day it occurred with the greatest deftness in an endeavor not to permit it to cast a blot over relations between the United States and Mexico; that they had assumed, on the basis of what President Cárdenas had publicly stated, that the Mexican Government intended to make good on the statements that it intended to make compensation; that they had been waiting for well over a year, but that it was only within the last few months that there had been any real effort to come to an agreement; that now the effort appeared on the verge of a breakdown so that naturally they were very much concerned.

Duggan concluded by warning Beteta that, if the oil companies did not get an agreement, they "would throw all their power, which was considerable, behind whatever presidential candidate in the 1940 elections [in the United States] they thought would bring about a settlement." Duggan said he would not forecast the outcome of the elections, but, "if an opposing administration were to come into office, a different policy might be pursued by the United States."

Beteta said he recognized that the United States "had within its power means of compelling Mexico to do whatever it wanted, even to the extent of requiring the return of the properties to the companies." Duggan pointed out that no such request had been made, but Beteta went on to express a warning of his own that, if the United States tried to "compel" Mexico to follow a particular policy, "this would mean the overthrow of the Cárdenas regime in Mexico, political and social chaos, probably continued civil strife, and very definite antagonism between the United States and Mexico." Finally, Beteta made what he may have felt was his strongest threat: "It would mean the end of the Good Neighbor policy, which would be completely unmasked as nothing more than crude imperialism. He added significantly that Mexico would take the steps to see that this was done."

This curious battle of public opinion, in which each man described to the other the dangerous consequences of the possible fall of his own government, ended with a strong defense by Duggan of the policy of restraint followed in Washington:

Señor Beteta said that he regretted it had become known by the press that the United States government was considering "taking strong action" against Mexico. I said that I did not think that the press had any idea of what measures the United States might be contemplating and that I wanted to make it clear to him that so far this government had taken not a single means of pressure to bring Mexico to an agreement.[14]

This was a remarkable conversation, and it probably gave Beteta the impression that the "atmosphere" in the higher reaches of the Department of State was cooler than in the editorial offices of the newspapers. At any rate, his government acted as though it did not fear that the United States would compel it to accept the proposal presented by Donald Richberg, acting for the oil companies. It answered a revised proposal by Richberg by presenting an arrangement that the companies thought would be "totally unacceptable." Welles told Chargé Luis Quintanilla that, if the negotiations now broke down, the Department could no longer "remain out of the picture," since it could not avoid interposing "its support in behalf of what we regarded as the legitimate and well-founded complaint" of the oil companies that Mexico was making "no effective effort whatever" to offer compensation. The companies were planning to issue a public statement of their case, and Welles emphasized "the very great disquiet" he felt at the prospects of publication.[15]

These examples of appeals to a higher, if less reasonable authority may have been in the category of empty threats, but there seems to have been at least one occasion when the Department of State was serious in its concern about its public image. Having found it impracticable to publish the note of March 26, 1938, Hull told Castillo Nájera that, unless Mexico proposed to offer a reasonable plan for compensation of the oil companies, it "would have the inevitable effect of destroying the Good Neighbor policy" and would place the United States in the impossible position of acquiescing in acts that are "contrary to law, equity, fair play, and fair dealing, and they would be so viewed by all civilized nations."[16]

Hull asked Daniels to see Cárdenas and to say that, while the

United States "has been endeavoring with patience and forbearance to arrive at some satisfactory understanding," Mexico seemed to have lost sight "of the fact that our government likewise has duties and responsibilities to its citizens of which it cannot divest itself." [17]

What Hull was most concerned about at this time was to receive from Mexico a plan of compensation sufficiently precise, and sufficiently feasible, so that he could announce it publicly and say that this seemed satisfactory to the Department of State. This would be used to counter the allegations from members of Congress and a part of the business community that the Department was not giving enough protection to the interests of United States citizens in Mexico. The Department was being bombarded by demands that its position be declared more clearly and firmly than Hull had done on March 30. The Department defended its policy by rejecting, among others, a remarkably unrealistic proposal by Senator William Gibbs McAdoo, of California, that the United States government pay Mexico $150,000,000 which Mexico would hand over to ex-propriated oil companies, on condition that Mexico cede to the United States Lower California, including the mouth of the Colorado River. Welles wrote to the Senator, saying that the plan would not only be rejected by Mexico, but its proposal by Washington would create such "resentment" in Mexico as to endanger the reaching of any settlement. In addition, such a suggestion would result in the loss of "much of the good will for the United States now existing" among other countries of the Americas.[18]

In Mexico, the government recognized that some satisfaction must be given to Hull. Taking a cue from Roosevelt's remarks to the press on April 1, Cárdenas on April 19 agreed to make monthly payments to former United States owners of small farms in the Yaqui Valley. He delayed, however, making plans to pay either the large landholders or the oil companies. Roosevelt had made it clear that he thought the oil companies were demanding more than they had invested in Mexico, and this statement was interpreted by some people in Mexico as meaning that Roosevelt actually approved the expropriation.[19]

Cárdenas's action did not fully satisfy the Department of State, but it opened negotiations for a settlement of agrarian claims that was reached before the end of 1938, and so may have alleviated some of the external pressures on the Department. Mexico thus showed its appreciation of the principle that friendly if disputatious governments must occasionally help each other, within limits, to appease or defy domestic opposition in order to reach a solution both governments desire.

In the instance of the United States note of April 3, 1940, that formally proposed arbitration to settle the oil dispute, it has been noted above that the Mexican public was told by certain well-informed press organs not to take the note seriously. In the United States, however, groups normally friendly to the Roosevelt administration wrote to the Department of State in protest. The Department was criticized for its "unfortunate" note of April 3 and asked in the future to place more emphasis "on the *Good* Neighbor policy." In reply, the Department defended arbitration as "a friendly way of settling disputes." [20] In May and June, the Department received protests from over a hundred labor unions of fishermen, agricultural laborers, ship scalers, and other workers in places on the Pacific Coast from Bellingham to Los Angeles. The majority of these protests took the form of a mimeographed resolution signed on behalf of different local unions. The resolution asserted that the "demand" on Mexico for arbitration was "in violation of international law" and asked that all "diplomatic, economic, and military pressure be removed from the Mexican government." The Department acknowledged the receipt of a few of these resolutions, but its policy was unaffected by them, for it had previously decided not to insist on arbitration.[21]

Similarly, the Department appears to have been uninfluenced by expressions of public opinion favoring the position of the oil companies. The Department received during the controversy several scores of letters from individuals holding oil company stock, or otherwise interested in the expropriation, most of which urged more effective action by the Department to change the position of the Mexican government. In addition, the oil companies took their case to the people of the United States through the press and other media.[22] Besides the usual legal arguments made to the Department of State, it was claimed that the Mexican action did not contribute to the welfare of the Mexican people. The Cárdenas regime was charged with harboring communists and, after September, 1939, of throwing Mexico "into the arms of the Soviet-Nazi combination." The Department of State acted as though it ignored these views.[23]

If public opinion limited the development of the Good Neighbor policy only in minor matters, there was one further limitation on action by the United States government in inter-American affairs that was inherent in the very name of the Good Neighbor, and is exemplified by Argentina's thwarting the desire of Brazil to purchase some 400,000 tons of wheat in the United States at a price lower than that on the world market because of an anticipated subsidy from the United States Department of Agriculture. In November, 1938, a Missouri grain dealer, Frank A. Theis, was reported to be going to Brazil to sell wheat to the Brazilian government, and it was known that he had previously talked with an official of the Department of Agriculture. The news created some excitement in Argentina, and *La Prensa* (Buenos Aires) charged that the purpose of the proposed wheat deal was "to dislodge Argentine producers from the market that we have secured and consolidated in our neighboring country." [24] The issue was sufficiently important to cause President Ortíz to remark to newsmen that "so long as the facts do not demonstrate the contrary, we presume that the Good Neighbor policy will continue to be fulfilled in accord with the intentions of President Roosevelt." [25]

Secretary Hull on this occasion did not require any prompting from Argentina. He had apparently not been consulted by Secretary of Agriculture Henry A. Wallace, and his opposition on general principles to governmental support of the sale of agricultural surpluses abroad was well known.[26] Hull went into action at once, and Wallace admitted in a press conference that he had had talks with Department of State officials. President Roosevelt made no comment on the affair, but Wallace visited the White House on November 12, and on the same day, Hull announced that there would be no participation by the United States government in any sale of wheat to Brazil.[27]

This flurry of chaff is less important in itself than as demonstrating that, when President Roosevelt dedicated his nation to the policy of the Good Neighbor, he set up a huge red, white, and blue target for the barbed shafts of his critics at home and abroad. He made use of a homely and familiar notion that invited the judgment of every man, and he left the way open to other governments to claim, not merely that some future Rooseveltian policy was unjust or immoral in universal terms but that it was violative of his own principles and aspirations. This was an opportunity that was used by individual critics in the United States, and, as has been indicated, by the governments of Argentina, Mexico, and other American states.

Roosevelt had in effect made application for friendly and dignified acceptance into the neighborhood of the Latin American countries, a rather disorderly precinct, united only in a notorious hostility to policemen. In so doing, he took the risk of having to accept his neighbors' definition of the sacrifices that would be required of the United States. At the same time, however, by labeling his policy as "good," he made a bid to gain popular support for his policies among his fellow citizens and to stir currents of cordiality in other countries. If on specific issues the United States government was occasionally forced to revise its own conception of the proper deportment of a Good Neighbor, there is also ground for considering that there may have been a real if immeasurable value in the employment of the phrase "Good Neighbor," particularly since the actions that accompanied the repetition of the phrase appeared on the whole to justify its implications. As two straws in the wind, it may be recalled that the Mexican government adopted the title "Good Friend policy" for its own moves toward rapprochement with Central American states in the late 1930s and that President Roberto M. Ortíz of Argentina, at the close of the Chaco Peace Conference, replied to expressions of thanks for his country's three years of hospitality to the Conference, by saying that Argentina had only been playing the part of a "Good Neighbor."

CHAPTER XII

Factors External to Policy

A GOOD NEIGHBOR is not regarded with sympathy unless his neighbors like the cut of his jib, as well as his formal deportment. The Latin American neighbors of the United States wanted to know whether they could believe in the sincerity and the enduring qualities of the new turn in policy symbolized by the nonintervention resolution of the Montevideo Conference. Their attitude at the time was mistrustful but not without an expectation of changes they regarded as desirable.[1]

In preparation for the Montevideo Conference of 1933, the Department of State requested its missions in Latin America to "prepare a carefully thought out study of the attitude toward the United States of the Government and the people of each of the other American republics." [2] This instruction and others issued in 1932 and 1933 brought a series of responses varying considerably from country to country but having certain common characteristics. Of most importance was the widespread fear of, and hostility toward, intervention by the United States, and the continuation of the Nicaraguan intervention was frequently cited.[3] This view was not universal, however; President Gómez of Venezuela was reported as having said that "the United States never intervened in a country which was governed," and one Uruguayan newspaper sarcastically commented in regard to the "rallying cry" of "Yankee imperialism" that "it would not be surprised to hear 'Yankee imperialism' blamed for the bad weather." [4] Allied with this attitude was a more generalized fear that the United States sought economic and political domination of the American continent, partly through "economic penetration" by business firms supported by Washington.

A third attitude relating to the policy of the United States was dissatisfaction over the passage of the Smoot-Hawley tariff, which was held partly responsible for the great decline in the export trade of many Latin American countries during the depression.

In relationships that were outside the field of policy, the diplomatic reports commented on the existence of a dislike of "Anglo-Saxon culture" and a concern for preventing the "Americanization" of the local culture. Factors in this feeling were tactlessness and a "contemptuous attitude" on the part of citizens of both the United States and Great Britain and anxiety lest Latin American youth be influenced in various undesired ways by motion pictures from the United States.[5] Much of the local knowledge about life in the United States was reported to be derived from despatches issued by press associations in the United States, and the nature of these despatches was generally deplored not only because they reported such phenomena as gangland killings, but also criticism within the United States of the government's Latin American policies.[6]

An unfavorable opinion of the United States was also thought to be fostered by word-of-mouth as well as by newspaper propaganda by European businessmen and officials.[7]

On other points there was greater difference of opinion. In some countries United States businessmen were highly regarded; in others, it was suggested that the quality of business representatives could be improved and business policies modified. One of the most severe indictments of the behavior of United States businessmen in Latin America was made by Ambassador Jefferson Caffery, then in Colombia, who reported:

The best efforts of the Department of State and our diplomatic missions abroad may be almost nullified by prejudicial activities of American business concerns. . . . I do not believe that [Latin American] hostility will cease until some way is found to have American business concerns understand that it is imperative for them to act towards the Governments and peoples south of the Río Grande in the same manner as they act towards people and concerns in the United States;

and we are only deceiving ourselves if we pretend that the majority of American concerns act in these countries as they do at home.[8]

Caffery here raised two important issues; the first was that of the hostility created in Latin America by the policies of United States enterprises, and the second was the lack of coordination between the Department of State and business firms operating in Latin America, where activities might in some cases be at cross purposes.

As to hostility in Latin America, certain oil companies, as we have seen, changed their policies in Venezuela and elsewhere following their expropriation in Mexico, and other enterprises have in various ways and for various reasons sought to reduce antagonism against them.[9]

As to coordination between the Department of State and United States enterprises in Latin America, some light on the nature of the problem may be shed by the previous discussion of the three oil controversies. These issues, raised in one form in 1931 by Caffery, are permanent issues so long as direct investment in Latin America continues. They will be handled in different ways in different countries of Latin America, by different companies, and by different generations of officials in the Department of State. In the 1930s the Department of State, against the stubborn resistance of the oil companies, achieved some success in mitigating hostility toward the government of the United States. In so doing, at least in Venezuela, it may also have reduced hostility against the companies themselves.

In such action the role of the Department of State has nowhere been more clearly depicted than in a remark by President Eduardo Santos of Colombia:

The honest, practical Good Neighbor policy was so effective that where previously American companies were accustomed to threaten the government [of Colombia] by saying an appeal would be made to Washington, the picture was reversed, and it now was the government who made or threatened to make the appeals to Washington.[10]

The opinion was fairly general that exchanges of students and teachers was desirable, but a warning was issued against "good will tours" and against the use of the term "good will": "Almost without exception in the wake of these so-called 'good will' tours one finds rancor and bitterness over the uncouth, rude, and vulgar attitude of one or more of the party." [11] On the other hand, it was noted that there was great appreciation in Brazil for the work of the Rockefeller Foundation in helping to eradicate yellow fever. In general, the Brazilian attitude seemed to be unique; there were no old sores such as those that festered in Peru because of the alleged United States responsibility for the Tacna-Arica settlement and the Salomón-Lozano treaty, and many Brazilians seemed to feel a kinship with the United States in a similar isolation from the Spanish American countries.[12]

By the beginning of 1933, although other features of antagonism toward the United States continued to be noted, it was reported that in some countries a more favorable judgment was forming because of the nonintervention policy of the Hoover administration.[13]

By and large, the policy sources of antipathy to the United States listed in this survey were eliminated before the United States entered World War II. The sources of antagonism attributed to factors external to policy continued to influence the attitudes of individuals in Latin America, although governmental attitudes, which depended mainly upon policy developments, underwent profound changes, as exemplified by the outcomes of the controversies with Bolivia and Mexico.

The Department of State could do almost nothing to improve the standards of personal behavior of United States citizens touring or residing in Latin America, and it could exert no influence over the judgment of such agencies as the Associated Press and the United Press about what should go to Latin American subscribers. Similarly, no political censorship could be imposed on motion picture exporters to reduce the reportedly unfavorable effects of films on United States prestige in Latin America, even if it were possible to identify the offending footage. The best the United States government could manage in this sphere was to apologize occasionally in individual cases of outrageous conduct. Thus President Roosevelt made a public apology for what he called a "disgusting lie" that appeared in the weekly magazine *Time* and quoted the United States Ambassador in Chile as commenting: "This is another illustration of how some American papers and writers by such methods are stocking the arsenals of propaganda of the Nazis to be used against us." [14]

This incident was not at all typical, and Roosevelt remarked that this was the first time in eight and one-half years that he had felt it necessary to take such action. On balance, the newspapers and magazines of the United States favored the Good Neighbor policy and demonstrated reasonable restraint in their comments on Latin American developments.

The nonpolicy factors affecting the reputation of the United States were, however, by no means entirely antagonistic to its ambitions to be a Good Neighbor. One of the most important favorable factors was the economic and social policy of the Roosevelt administration in domestic affairs. In several Latin American countries, notably Uruguay and Colombia, the measures taken by Roosevelt to bring an end to the depression and to improve standards of living appear to have been of great importance in giving to officials and private citizens alike a sense of common cause with the government and people of the United States.[15] In Mexico, the only Latin American state that had carried through a social revolution, a similar feeling existed in governmental circles. President P. E. Calles wrote that he thought:

[Roosevelt's policy] coincides in general terms with the policy which we have sought to carry out in Mexico. You may be sure that we particularly appreciate and admire the magnanimous work of your administration in favor of the unemployed, the workers, and the forgotten man in general.[16]

In other countries, where the governments were less desirous of social reform, official comments of this type were not made nor were criticisms offered. Even in these countries, however, if there existed a measure of freedom of the press, opposition parties, probably with an eye to local politics, occasionally commented favorably on Roosevelt's domestic policies.

Another nonpolicy factor of major importance was the emergence of militarism and aggression on the part of Germany, Italy, and Japan. The contrast between the policies of these countries and that of the United States was most keenly appreciated in Latin America after the Italian invasion of Ethiopia in 1935, although some observers drew the distinction earlier. Carlos Dávila, a former Chilean ambassador in Washington, making no distinctions of time or party, upheld the record of the United States as a whole in the Americas:

If we examine every century's history in Europe and in Asia, it will be realized that the United States, in the present and the immediate past, with comparatively greater power than that of any of the countries that dominate in those continents, has maintained a much more decorous and worthy attitude in its treatment of the weakest nations of this continent.[17]

The Buenos Aires Conference of 1936 was the occasion for the expression of a major shift in public opinion and official attitudes in many countries of Latin America. Although some of the Latin American governments had regarded their membership in the League of Nations as a way of maintaining political contacts with Europe and as a source of support against possible expansionist moves by the United States,[18] the tendency was general to regard the League as a failure by 1936 and to look favorably, if cautiously, on Roosevelt's proposals that aimed at stronger institutions for the maintenance of intra-American peace. Roosevelt's initiatives were not approved in their original forms by the Conference, but the acceptance of the principle of consultation was a major step that gave evidence not only of growing confidence in intimate political association with the United States, but also of a feeling that the American states, in and of themselves, possessed the capacity to offer a political example to Europe.

A leading Chilean newspaper spoke with pride:

America is at peace and must defend its peace at any cost against disputes between American republics or with countries of other continents. . . . This continent of ours has in the future a destiny that each day becomes clearer—it is to receive and preserve the inheritance of Western civilization, now so gravely menaced in Europe.[19]

The Committee on Foreign Relations of the Colombian Senate recommended the ratification of the Buenos Aires Conference agreements and stated that the group of accords "places our Continent, not only at the head of the crusade for peace, but also makes it the only refuge of peace in an era when those peoples who are not suffering the ravages of war are afflicted by anxieties and tortures that are no less devastating than war itself." [20]

The alienation of Latin American governments from the League, where their delegates had come to feel they were little more than balcony observers in the Ethiopian affair, and from the mounting crisis in European politics did not escape European commentators. A Swedish newspaper remarked that "the world has witnessed the unusual event of a Pan American conference that has had a message for the Old World," namely, that of safeguarding peace and free institutions.[21]

The creation of a new sense of hope for a larger role of Latin Americans in the future of America and the world was brought to Roosevelt by Fred Morris Dearing, the ambassador in Peru:

The European tradition is strong in this part of the world, but one can almost see a new orientation taking place from day to day as the center of interest shifts to our own country, and in a most notable degree to yourself. There has been a tremendous disillusionment on account of what is taking place in the dictatorships in Europe and in Asia, and a more liberal and democratic existence, which now becomes so imminent and great a reality, and which is too precious a thing to lose, absorbs all minds. Peruvians feel—but in no overweening way—that Europe can now learn something from our Western world.[22]

A third significant source of sympathy for the Good Neighbor policy was the personality and background of its leading United States advocates. When Cordell Hull of Tennessee went from hotel room to hotel room calling on the chiefs of the Latin American delegations to the Montevideo Conference, he opened a new era of warm personal relationships that contrasted sharply with the coldness and hostility prevailing at the preceding conferences at Santiago and Havana, and tended to ease negotiations and predispose diplomats, foreign ministers, and heads of state to take up problems with the United States in a friendly rather than antagonistic spirit. President Roosevelt was personally less close to Latin Americans, but he inspired confidence in both public opinion leaders and officials in Latin America, and he had an immense popular success during his visit to Brazil, Uruguay, and Argentina in 1936. Sumner Welles, after a handicapped start due to his activity in Cuba in 1933, appears to have won the respect and esteem of the Latin Americans with whom he dealt, and it was he, rather than Hull or Roosevelt, who bore the major share of the day-by-day responsibility for carrying negotiations forward. Tall, austere, and aloof almost to the point of imperiousness, Welles would seem to have had little of the geniality and warmth of manner likely to attract the friendship of Latin Americans. Yet, the advice given to his successor by one of Welles's close colleagues in the Department of State in preparation for a first talk to Latin American members of the diplomatic corps was:

Practically all of these representatives were and are close personal friends and admirers of Mr. Welles. All of them feel a definite sense of personal loss at his removal from the work to which he contributed so much for so many years. I am sure that you will take this into account and that you will feel both the desirability and the propriety of your paying a tribute to your distinguished predecessor, expressing at the same time your hope that you can establish with each of your hearers the same relations of friendship, understanding, and confidence which he was able to achieve.[23]

To these personal qualities was added the fact that these men were not associated, in the minds of Latin Americans, with the Nicaraguan intervention, with governmental support for United States business enterprise in Latin America, or with the policies of United States bankers and investment houses that had been brought to public view in congressional investigations. Consequently, there existed a willingness to believe in the sincerity of Roosevelt and his colleagues that had not existed for a decade and a half; history could not be erased, but recriminations became stale as hope grew in a fresh start with a spirit exuberantly expressed by new men who were untrammeled by the past.

The Department of State established in mid-1938 a Division of Cultural Relations intended principally to promote educational exchanges with Latin America. It was not, however, until after the outbreak of World War II that a substantial program of cultural relations with Latin America was carried out by the expansion of the work of the Division and the establishment of the Office of the Coordinator of Inter-American Affairs.[24] The unofficial contacts through press, films, tourism, and a limited interchange of students and teachers do not appear to have changed markedly in the five years following the Montevideo Conference. The assessment of the importance of these factors in Latin American attitudes toward the United States, which has been mentioned above, seems, however, to have undergone a change. In 1933, the export of scandal-laden news reports and motion pictures thought to be damaging to the prestige of the United States had loomed large, because they were combined with interventions and protective tariffs to provide a nearly unrelieved picture of antagonism to the United States. By 1939, however, the changes in policy had created such sympathy with the United States that these irritants seemed relatively unimportant.

The contrast between the attitudes of Latin Americans early in 1939 and those in 1933 is outlined in two paragraphs of the report of a two-months' visit to the countries of the Caribbean area by one of Welles's closest associates in the Department of State:

> It is sufficient to say that at no time since the United States took the lead in recognizing the independent existence of the American republics has there existed more genuine warmth of feeling for the United States in the other American nations. While the day has been carried by the principles, the objectives, and the methods of the Good Neighbor policy, the general philosophy of the President and his principal achievements in domestic politics have had an enormous appeal and have inspired confidence in the execution of his foreign policies.
>
> There is one element of danger in this trusting friendship. In the smaller countries visited, there is an apparently implicit confidence that with one wave of his hand, President Roosevelt can solve all of their difficulties and open up new vistas before them. They have little appreciation of the difficulties, delays, and obstacles that our government must contend with under a truly democratic process.[25]

This was the judgment of a partisan observer, but it was no friend of the United States who reported that "it cannot be denied that Roosevelt has achieved extraordinary results in South America generally and also in Uruguay with his Good Neighbor policy." [26]

The shift of sympathy, which cannot be attributed entirely to changes in policy, is nevertheless of capital significance in inter-American relations. It was, of course, far from universal, and its strength differed from country to country. It was not shared by permanent political enemies of the United States, such as communists and fascists, nor by significant groups, such as those who feared that emulation in their own countries of the social reforms in the United States would be accompanied by an infiltration of the allegedly materialistic culture of a nation predominantly Protestant in religion and racially different from Latin Americans.[27]

These are broad categories of people who resisted or welcomed the Good Neighborly advances of the United States, and it is difficult to distinguish among more clearly defined groups. There are, however, occasional reactions that are like flashes into the ordinarily impenetrable depths of the minds and feelings of distant neighbors. Latin American newspapers sometimes commented didactically, and probably with an eye on their own domestic politics, that their citizens would do well to follow the good example set by the operations of democratic processes in the United States.[28] More impressive, however, are comments that seem to spring from surprise rather than from calculation. Such, for example, was the previously quoted praise for the independence of a United States court in freeing a tanker carrying Mexican oil.[29] Such also may have been the appreciation by an Ecuadoran newspaper of the reprimand issued to General George S. Patton on the occasion of the General's having struck one of his soldiers, and the General's subsequent apology:

Here is an incident of war that is worth more than a battle, that elevates the reputation of the North American soldier, that holds dear human dignity. Men go to war to fulfill a duty, but they do not renounce their rights as men, and the officers are made to respect the individual. It is a magnificent lesson.[30]

It is possible, also, that Latin Americans may have felt a shift in the attitudes of North Americans away from feelings of superiority, or at least away from public expression of them. Franklin D. Roosevelt discarded the attitude implied by a remark made early in his career that "we are in a very true sense the big brother of these little republics," [31] and the New York *Times* has adopted its own advice on relations with Latin Americans: "Even if we cannot escape feeling in our own hearts vastly superior to them, it is neither wise nor profitable to treat them as if they were acknowledged inferiors." [32] Similarly, a term such as "ignorant masses" that was used by Sumner Welles in reports from Cuba in 1933 has become increasingly rare in diplomatic reporting from Latin

America. Manners and modes of speech, no less than legal relationships, have shown a trend toward giving reality to the ideal of equality in the Americas, and these may both reflect and have an influence on underlying values.[33]

On balance, these policy and nonpolicy elements combined to create sympathy and good will toward the United States, and toward the conception of continental solidarity that took shape as supplementary to the Good Neighbor policy when World War II drew near. Among Latin American states only Argentina remained apart, and the other governments appeared in this regard to be representative of the attitudes of the majority of their peoples.

CHAPTER XIII

The Evocation of Reciprocity

THE IDEA OF the anticipation of reciprocity, which has been suggested as the basic conception of the United States government from 1933 onward in its relations with Latin America, was supplemented in 1939 and afterward by an idea that may be called the evocation of reciprocity.

The "old" Good Neighbor policy anticipated that, in response to the policies of nonintervention and noninterference and a more liberal trade policy, the Latin American governments would make friendly compromises with the policy concerns of the United States. Chief among those concerns was protection of the property of its nationals in Latin America, and the experience of the United States was that reciprocity on this issue was not provided by Latin America to the satisfaction of Washington. However, a satisfactory compromise on this issue might have been ultimately worked out through the slow processes of anticipating reciprocity had it been possible to continue them in the peaceful circumstances prevailing in the Americas when the Bolivian and Mexican controversies began.

The combination of the policies of the United States government, and of the factors external to policy that have been reviewed, brought about significant changes in the political climate of inter-American relations in 1939. Latin American governments and peoples provided evidence both of a marked increase in good will and sympathy toward the United States, and of a recognition that their interests would be furthered by a close association with the United States and not by partiality toward or association with the Axis powers in the developing world conflict.

These political changes were solid and significant achievements of the application of the theory of the anticipation of reciprocity, although they were insufficient in themselves, in the short period before the threat of world conflict became a serious one, to bring about a mutually agreeable adjustment of differences on the issue of the protection of property, and specifically on the status of oil companies in Bolivia and Mexico. For the renunciation of domination by the United States the Latin American countries gave a generalized and abstract response in the form of good will. A hint of the nature of this response is offered by Eduardo Villaseñor: "The policy of the Good Neighbor can be only this: from his neighbor who has everything, he who has nothing should accept things courteously, so that friendship may be solidly established." [1]

However, when the United States gave to reciprocity the specific meaning of its view of appropriate treatment for business enterprises of its citizens in Latin America, the specific responses of Bolivia and Mexico were diametrically opposed to the desires of the United States. As has been suggested, these differences might well have been composed in time; but the influences exerted in inter-American relationships, first by United States fear of involvement in World War II, and later by fears for the security of the United States itself, induced policy moves by the United States that evoked rather than merely anticipated reciprocity.

The effects of the threat to American security presented by the early advances of the Axis powers were so great as to suggest that, beginning in August, 1939, the "old" Good Neighbor policy commenced to change so radically that the bases of a new policy, new in name as well as in theory, were established. The principal objective of the new policy displaced that of the old; for the protection of property on traditional terms there was substituted the defense of the United States and of the hemisphere. At the same time, new policy techniques had to be devised. In a crisis involving security, rapid action was necessary, and there was no time for reliance on the slow processes of the anticipation of reciprocity —reciprocity had to be evoked by specific measures.

The application of the theory of the evocation of reciprocity is observable in both the Bolivian and Mexican oil disputes. The refusal of economic assistance to Bolivia was primarily responsible for the eagerness of La Paz, after September, 1939, to reach a settlement with the Standard Oil Company that general good will toward the United States had not generated in the previous two years. In the case of the Mexican expropriation, the refusal of loans or economic assistance was ineffective because the Mexican government was more determined to maintain its course, and its economy was strong enough so that its leaders felt no compelling need to compromise on the oil issue in order to secure financial aid from the United States. On the contrary, it was the United States that made the specific concession of accepting the Mexican position on the method of settlement of the issue with the Standard Oil Company in order to secure the use of Mexican air bases.

The use of these specific inducements to gain specific objectives was a reflection of the shift in policy objectives that meant the subordination of the interests of private corporations to the public interest in the security of the United States, as defined by the Department of State.

The application of the theory of the evocation of reciprocity may also be observed in the enlargement of the functions of the Export-Import Bank in 1939 so as to become a lender to Latin American governments as well as to United States exporters. When Sumner Welles went to the Panama Conference of foreign ministers in September, 1939, he carried with him not only the good will earned by a Good Neighbor, but also the authority to negotiate economic agreements, and financial assistance of various types was initiated at this time with more than half of the Latin American countries. That the new situation was understood in Latin America as well as in Washington is illustrated by the remark of a Cuban commentator that, although the purpose of the Panama Conference was to consider general issues of neutrality and security, "the majority of the Cuban delegation was composed of sugar experts." [2] Welles was ready to meet the sugar experts on their own ground, so far had Washington's idea of reciprocity quickly changed from vague generalizations about a "two-way street" to concrete arrangements for economic assistance to accompany and support the political collaboration that nearly all the American governments desired as a result of the Good Neighbor policy.

This change amounted to a transformation of the conception of reciprocity as the central idea of the Good Neighbor policy. The idea of the anticipation of reciprocity had done its work well without, however, achieving all the changing objectives set for it by the Department of State. It had significantly affected the general political orientation and attitudes of Latin American governments toward the United States, and occasionally, as in the case of Mexico's refusal to sell oil to Japan in 1941, it had affected their policies. There were also cases where policies were not affected. Latin American governments realized that their commercial opportunities were expanding in the late 1930s as the rivalry between great powers became more intense, and some of them were quick to take advantage of the situation. An incident in relations with traditionally friendly Brazil offers a nice example of the width of the gap between the Department of State's generalized anticipation of reciprocity and specific performance by a Latin American country in 1938:

The members of the Brazilian Mission who were in Washington last summer were particularly anxious to ascertain whether retaliatory measures could be expected from the United States in case Brazil continued her compensation mark trade with Germany. As the members of the Mission received the distinct impression that retaliatory measures were not to be expected, they have been since that time impervious to blandishment or argument and have, thus far at any rate demonstrated only faint interest in the point of view set out in the Department's various telegrams on the subject.[3]

When World War II broke out, it was considered in Washington that good will alone could not be expected to produce the measures of close collaboration desired for the defense of the United States and the hemisphere. Therefore it was necessary to supplement the theory and practice of anticipating reciprocity and adopt new ideas and new techniques more appropriate to the unprecedented demands of World War II.

One source of Welles's financial operations at the Panama Conference may be observed as early as April 14, 1939, when in a speech to the Board of Governors of the Pan American Union, Roosevelt foresaw possible wartime problems and said that the United States would "give economic support, so that no American nation need surrender any fraction of its sovereign freedom to maintain its economic welfare." It has been suggested that this statement was made because Roosevelt and his advisers "realized that all hope of political solidarity would be illusory unless supported by adequate financial and trade arrangements." [4]

This realization, it may be assumed, expressed a judgment that reciprocity, in the form of collaboration from Latin America that the United States might desire for its national security, could not be anticipated solely as a response to the policies followed by the aspirant Good Neighbor during the previous seven years.

It is not intended here to suggest that the acceptance by the Latin American countries of the political proposals of the United States for cooperation in neutrality and hemisphere defense was conditional upon economic assistance by the United States. The interesting question of the sources of solidarity among the American states during World War II is a complex one, and the issues involved may be stated in many different ways. It is beyond the scope of this study to try to analyze these issues, but they are far less simple than is intimated either by those commentators who have charged that the Latin American governments "blackmailed" the United States in 1939 and after or by those who have taken a position suggesting that solidarity sprang from outraged democracies "in celestial panoply all arm'd." Some broad aspects of this question will be outlined in the succeeding chapters.

The main political achievement of the "old" Good Neighbor policy, designed only for peacetime requirements, was to predispose nearly all the Latin American governments to accept the leadership of the United States in wartime, that is, to collaborate in the quite different requirements of coalition politics. This achievement was not lost when the aims and methods of policy were transformed by the exigencies of war. Its pervasive influence mediated the differences that inevitably arose in circumstances when relationships were both closer and more far-reaching, and when the urgency of speedy action was intensified.

From the time of the Panama Conference, official statements gave less attention to reciprocity and even to the Good Neighbor policy, and more emphasis was placed on the idea of continental solidarity. However, continental solidarity was not created at the Panama Conference or at the Rio de Janeiro Conference in 1942; rather, the satisfaction of preconditions for solidarity in the six years before 1939 had made those conferences possible. Continental solidarity was at first little more than a euphemistic, collective term for reciprocity. All the American states were menaced from abroad, and it was therefore desirable to introduce a term expressing mutual concern, rather than those, like reciprocity or the Good Neighbor, that would have suggested that the Latin American states were merely conforming or reacting to the wishes of the United States. This purpose was well expressed by Sumner Welles in rejecting a proposal that the United States government should publish "a comprehensive list of the specific assets of the Good Neighbor policy":

It has always been my view that the proper concept of the Good Neighbor policy is one of mutuality of interests based upon the self-respect and sovereignty of each of the twenty-one American republics. While many concrete advantages may be derived, and in fact have been derived, by all of these countries from the application of this broad principle of joint interest, such gains should properly be considered, I think, as growing out of this broad basis of inter-American cooperation, rather than as a specific exchange of favors. The important thought, in my opinion, is not that any one country has benefited in particular from the Good Neighbor policy, but that the economic and cultural advancement of all the American republics will be greatly enhanced by cooperation and fair dealing among themselves.[5]

The idea of the mutuality of interests that Welles viewed in 1942 as the "proper concept" of the Good Neighbor policy is another term for continental solidarity in time of war, but its implications are less defensive, and so the term may be more adaptable to long-range usage in times of peace. The following chapter delineates some Latin American estimates of the advances made toward agreement on the mutuality of interests among neighbors.

CHAPTER XIV

Latin America Appraises the Good Neighbor

SINCE, in trying to be a Good Neighbor, the United States appealed to its neighbors for their judgment of its eligibility, it is fitting that they should have a hearing in a study that has attempted to understand the policy of the United States. Latin American judgments of the Good Neighbor policies, so far as can be gauged from a wide if unsystematic sampling of its press comment, was given an opportunity for expression as a result of a political attack on the policy during the course of World War II. Attention is here given to expressions of these judgments, not only because they are relevant to an assessment of the efforts of the United States to be regarded as a Good Neighbor, but also because they throw some light on the nature of policy problems, including that of the sources of continental solidarity.

Throughout its first ten years, the Good Neighbor policy had been generally acclaimed in the press and in the Congress of the United States. There had been criticism of specific actions, particularly in the case of the Mexican oil expropriation, but the policy itself had not been seriously attacked. The oil companies had preferred to avoid a general onslaught on the policy, although they did criticize the Mexican government for misunderstanding the Good Neighbor policy. On the other side, criticism had been leveled at the Department of State for failing to live up to the Good Neighbor policy in making its demand that the dispute with Mexico be arbitrated.

In 1943, however, a direct attack was made on the Good Neighbor policy by Republican Senator Hugh A. Butler of Nebraska, in an article in the *Reader's Digest*.[1] Unlike many of the articles in this monthly, Senator Butler's article was not a condensation of a contribution to another magazine, and, unlike most Senators engaging in journeys abroad, Senator Butler was accompanied by a member of the staff of the *Reader's Digest*, Maurice K. Mumford. Mr. Mumford's presence was commented on unfavorably both in Latin America[2] and in the United States.

The attack was a sensational one because of the extravagance of its charges,[3] although it does not appear to have had any great influence on the public in general or on responsible opinion in either the Democratic or Republican party. Its importance lies rather in the attention given it by the Department of State and especially in the nature of the reaction in the Latin American press.

Senator Butler said he had returned from twenty thousand miles of inquiring travel in twenty Latin American countries "astonished and appalled that our Good Neighbor policy—backed by *six thousand million* U.S. dollars—has widely become a hemispheric handout that is neither good nor neighborly." He listed examples of spending he regarded as absurd, such as subsidizing the stocking of Venezuelan streams and lakes with game fish,[4] the rehabilitation of El Oro province in Ecuador, which had been invaded by the Peruvian army in 1941, and the compilation of bibliographies of Latin American music. The Senator alleged that the United States was treating the Latin Americans as "mendicants" and was trying to "seduce them with boondoggles." He concluded that the answer to what he called a "handout," the nature of which was being kept from the United States public, was "not to scrap the Good Neighbor policy," but "to make it authentically Good Neighbor." Having said that Latin American states were making almost no reciprocal contributions to United States "handouts," he proposed that "we should insist that, according to their ability to pay, what we do for the nations of Latin America is matched, dollar for dollar, by what Latin America does for itself."

The article signed by Senator Butler was the journalistic statement of a report made by him shortly afterward to the Senate.[5] A reply both to the report and the article was made by a senator from Secretary Hull's home state of Tennessee, Kenneth McKellar (Democrat). In fact, if not in form,[6] Senator McKellar's speech may be considered as having been the presentation of the case for the Good Neighbor policy on behalf of the Department of State.[7]

Condemnation of Butler's charges and support for the Good Neighbor policy by Herbert Hoover, Thomas A. Dewey, Wendell Willkie, Henry L. Stimson, Alfred M. Landon, Robert A. Taft, and other prominent Republicans left Butler a lonely, isolated figure, and the appearance of a second article in the *Reader's Digest*, replying to some of his critics, did not noticeably strengthen his position.[8]

The reaction in Latin America to the Butler articles is of especial interest as evidence of Latin American attitudes toward the Good Neighbor policy on one of the rare occasions when it was openly criticized by a man prominent in public life in the United States. In general, the views expressed by the Latin American press were heartening to the Department of State and to all those who placed a high value on continental solidarity in wartime. In Cuba, for example, it was reported:

The reaction provoked by the address of Senator Butler . . . has been extremely and unanimously unfavorable [to Butler's point of view]. Conservatives, Liberals, and Communists alike have expressed their dissatisfaction in a manner similar in concept and differing only in style, and have formed in this respect what might almost be defined as a unified national front.[9]

The Latin American press was not, however, entirely antagonistic to Senator Butler's views. In Argentina, the Nazi-subsidized paper *El Pampero* (Buenos Aires) on November 26, 29, 1943, used Senator Butler's article as a basis for sarcastic comments and as evidence that the Good Neighbor policy had "failed." Some independent papers expressed approval of two references made by Senator Butler. It was admitted that some money was being wasted in Latin America by United States governmental agencies and that some lend-lease funds were being misused by Latin American government officials,[10] although these considerations were not regarded as serious enough to cast doubt on the wisdom of the lend-lease program as a whole.

In the second place, a few papers admitted the accuracy of Senator Butler's remark that there were only three democracies among the Latin American states. *Hoy* (Mexico City), December 4, 1943, made a bitter attack on "the majority of our [Latin American] presidents, [who] are assassins, thieves, and infamous men," and thanked Senator Butler for providing an opportunity to point out that the United States, by indiscriminately distributing lend-lease funds in Latin America, was strengthening dictators and damaging the cause of democracy.[11] On the other hand, *El Popular* (Mexico City), November 30, 1943, took the view that, granted the existence of undesirable dictatorships, the nonintervention policy of President Roosevelt allowed Latin Americans to rid themselves of tyrants. If, however, "the circles that Senator Butler represents in the United States should attain political power, it is certain that dictators would become stronger and would multiply throughout the Continent."

One unexpected result of Senator Butler's declarations was the stimulation of some soul-searching by Latin American newspapermen. An editorial in *El Día* (Quito) on November 27, 1943, for example, while calling the Senator's statements "unjust and outrageous," pointed out that the opportunity should be seized to examine some failings of the Ecuadoran people:

We have sometimes the feeling that we are not, or do not represent a respectable nation . . . . not because we are poor, but because we are disorganized. . . . With a politics of ambush and of permanent mistrust, one for the other, we cannot do otherwise than create ruin and destruction in the national soul; this kind of politics has wasted our energies and made us weak. . . . We cannot properly organize a republic in this way, and without organization we cannot merit or attain respect from other nations.[12]

The bulk of Latin American comment expressed three types of hostility to Senator Butler's views: attempts to discredit the Senator; resentment at his slurs on Latin America; and praise for the Good Neighbor policy. Many editorials showed coolness and sophistication by commenting that Senator Butler was attacking

not the Good Neighbor policy so much as the Roosevelt administration, and by pointing out that 1944 was a presidential election
year.[13]

Senator Butler's trip, it was noted, was a flying one, made with
"a velocity comparable only with the levity of the observer." [14]
The tour of the twenty countries was made in fifty-five days
during July and August, 1943, and within this period stops were
also made in the Guianas and Puerto Rico.

Confidence was expressed by several Latin American commentators that Senator Butler did not represent the people of the
United States or any great part of them.[15] *El Comercio* (Quito),
November 25, 1943, said that Butler's charges would be dishearten-
ing if recognition were not given to the nature of political opposition in all countries, which demonstrates "the Samsonian attitude of
desiring death if only that of one's enemies is simultaneously en-
compassed." Sadly, and perhaps in some surprise that this incident
had occurred in the United States, this paper commented: "Political passion is mean in all countries; it lacks loftiness, principles, and
justice." A few papers went so far as to assert that some of Senator
Butler's charges could only be made by one harboring sympathy
for the Axis powers.[16] Such assertions were unjustifiable attacks
on Senator Butler's patriotism. He had been imprudent, perhaps,
in failing to realize either the dismay and discouragement that his
words would arouse in Latin America or the opportunity his
charges would give to German propagandists, but these were
almost certainly unintended side-effects of an action aimed at
domestic political objectives.

Doubts about the continuity of the Good Neighbor policy
were raised in some minds by the evidence that the Republican
party was not solidly in its favor. These doubts were not entirely
set at rest by affirmations of support by Herbert Hoover and other
party leaders.[17] *El Popular* (Mexico City) editorially stated on
November 29, 1943, that the Senator's words "make us think, not
of the civilized North American, a lover of democracy and peace,
understanding of the aspirations of his own and other peoples, but
of the North American filibusterer and unscrupulous exploiter
whom the Mexican people have characterized derogatively with

the insulting term of 'gringo.'" The editorial expressed the belief that any attempt by Senator Butler and those who shared his attitudes to change United States policy toward Latin America would be defeated by the strength of North American democracy, "the power of a great people that loves liberty and peace."

The keenest resentment among Latin Americans was felt at the Senator's implication that they were begging favors from the United States. They also understood him as suggesting that their cooperation in the war effort was being purchased. Butler was called "ignorant," and his assertions "infamous." [18] The Latin American defense of the acceptance of loans, grants, and war materials from the United States took several forms. The most important argument was that there was no connection between cooperation by Latin America and any so-called "alms-giving" from Washington. The United States had not tried "to buy friends at the lowest prices," [19] and any attempt to do so would have been indignantly rejected in Latin America. One paper wrote:

Without the courage of the Latin American States, the security of the hemisphere would not have been enhanced by Mr. Butler's counting up of nickels, dimes, and dollars. Money would not have been enough to pay for a base at Natal, if there were lacking in the spirit of the Brazilians their faithfulness to the principles of Pan Americanism.[20]

A bitter response was evoked in Ecuador by Butler's statement that certain private yachts had been fitted out as naval vessels "and shipped, gratis, to Ecuador." [21] The use of the word "gratis" was denounced as suggesting that Latin America had provided no assistance to the United States following Pearl Harbor. "It is impossible to establish in monetary terms the value of our prompt, loyal, and disinterested cooperation."

The reciprocal character of the relationships between the United States and Latin America was stressed in several instances. Senator Butler should have known that "the expenditures of the United States are not gratuitous concessions, but constitute a form of aid that is appreciated, in the first place, and is well utilized and reciprocated, in the second place." Not only would the United States gain in the form of future trade and investments, but "there is in Latin America a sense of loyal collaboration and of true friendship which never could be bought at the cost of all the millions in the world." [22] Similarly, in *El Universal* (Mexico City) on December 1, 1943, Deputy Carlos Madrazo enumerated the mutual gains from the Good Neighbor policy. Latin America gained the elimination of old aggressive policies of the United States; military aid via lend-lease; a more equal trade balance; and substantial investments in Latin American industry. On the other hand, the United States gained from the same policy the desire of Latin Americans to build a new organization of the Americas; resources for the war effort; labor from Mexico and other countries; a diminution of resentment against the United States; and friendly fields for capital investment. [23]

However, the value of the Latin American contribution could not be measured in monetary terms. Latin America readily sold its raw materials for the war effort, and "if the prices were fixed in accord with the magnitude of the services provided to the United States in this life and death struggle, money enough could not be found to pay for the materials," such as tin, copper, and oil. [24] How could the value of Mexico's support be weighed in dollars? "Mexico did not hesitate for a moment in helping protect the United States by preventing the Japanese, after their traitorous aggression, from making use of Mexican territory either for espionage or for belligerent actions." [25]

The relationship of money to policy was given a curious twist by a remark by Representative Jessie Sumner of Illinois (Republican). She told her colleagues in the House that the administration was "having a lot of trouble with Argentina right now. That is the only country they have not been able to reach with a checkbook." [26] This comment was seized upon with delight by the pro-Axis press in Argentina and elsewhere. *El Pampero* said that in the kind of heated discussion from which truth often emerges, "this stupendous judgment had come from the country most concerned." [27]

Furthermore, Latin Americans regarded as outrageous Butler's suggestion that their support for the United States in the war might be less enthusiastic if loans and grants should cease. A Chilean paper stated:

Our collaboration can be priced neither by a monetary standard nor by material benefits, first, because the sacrifices that have been made have exceeded the benefits received; and, second, because for free nations, brought up in the old democratic school, it is little less than an insult to try to obtain by means of money what already exists in our nature as an original characteristic of our spirituality.[28]

Or, as *El Imparcial* (Guatemala City), November 27, 1943, put it: "The Latin Americans have made sacrifices affecting their welfare, their progress, their lives and lands, simply out of the recognition of the need for solidary action and of the desire to promote the dearest ideals of the individual and of peoples—liberty and justice."

Beyond denunciation of Senator Butler and his ideas, the most encouraging aspect of the Butler affair from the viewpoint of the United States government was the strong and specific support for the Good Neighbor policy expressed by nearly all sectors of the Latin American press. There was close continental solidarity in the defense of that policy on the part of editorial writers, and their testimony was all the more heartening because unsolicited. Senator Butler and those whose point of view he was felt to represent were regarded as enemies of Latin America no less than of the Roosevelt administration. A few examples demonstrate the warmth of the Latin American response. "The Good Neighbor policy, already part of American international law, inspires in the minds of all people on this side of the Atlantic the sentiment of solidarity." [29] *La Esfera* (Caracas) on December 1, 1943, stated:

Neither Butler nor the few who, chorusing him in nostalgia for the hard times of Coolidge's imperialism, can change the Rooseveltian line of policy which is firmly devoted to the creation in this hemisphere of a climate of mutual understanding, of progress, and of disinterested justice in which all American states might find freedom and protection to enjoy in peace the fruits of their labor, their principles and their intelligence. . . . [The result of the Roosevelt policy] has been a complete reversal in the sentiments of the Spanish American peoples who today look on the United States as a senior comrade, strong and just.[30]

A contrast between the Good Neighbor policy, which was almost universally identified with President Roosevelt, and the policy followed by the Republican party between 1921 and 1933 was frequently emphasized.

We have always distinguished between the idealistic United States of Roosevelt and the other, we do not wish to say realistic, but commercial and perhaps egoistic United States which was repudiated by Latin America. The great merit of Roosevelt (and of Sumner Welles) consisted in substituting in international affairs, the America of the Good Neighbor for this America of yesterday.[31]

Roosevelt was quoted as having said, "handsomely, that he himself, if he had been a Latin American in the last twenty-five years, 'could not have been anything but an enemy of the United States.' "[32]

President Roosevelt, in the eyes of *Excelsior* (Mexico City), November 29, 1943, "recognized as early as 1933 that the interest of his country lay in a policy of good neighborhood, of mutual cooperation with the other American countries, in order to form with them a single political, economic, and even military unit in the midst of a world then at the gates of war." The paper considered that out of the Butler affair there might come a tightening of the ties among the American states: "This was an opportunity for the Latin American peoples to learn to recognize their friends and to beware of those who still consider the Latin Americans as factory fodder and imperialist prey."[33] The Good Neighbor policy was not an opportunistic one, based on an expectation of conflict, according to Abelardo Bonilla in *Diario de Costa Rica* (San José), December 1, 1943. He pointed out that the policy was not only initiated years before the war, but "its finest and most effective feature is not of a material kind, but of a cultural order."

A common theme, adopted perhaps as encouragement to the Roosevelt administration, was that the Good Neighbor policy had become firmly established as part of United States foreign policy. *El Mundo* (Havana) on January 28, 1944, for example, stated editorially that the Good Neighbor policy had been "transformed into a fixed direction for the foreign policy of the United States . . . as demonstrated by repeated and affirmative actions." The magistral *La Prensa* (Buenos Aires), December 13, 1943, stated that "when all is said, the Good Neighbor policy is not a simple verbal formula, but the expression of a deeply rooted sentiment, which, carried into practice, has been translated into deeds impossible to deny." [34]

One of the greatest of these deeds was that Roosevelt had established "a climate of justice in which our peoples are coming to have a consciousness of their dignity, and are acquiring control of the techniques of exploitation of their own resources. . . . It is fitting, therefore, for in this we have much to gain or to lose, that we should contribute in every way at our disposal to the failure of the sinister enterprise of Senator Butler and those who are making use of him." [35]

In the United States, Secretary Hull bided his time until he had ample evidence of a reaction favorable to the Department of State both in Latin America and at home. He issued on December 14 a formal statement declaring that "the unfair attack recently made on the good-neighbor policy by Senator Butler was a matter of general astonishment throughout the Western Hemisphere." Hull said that it was "imperative" that the charges be answered "in the national interest," because of their "inaccuracies . . . fallacies . . . and misstatements." He noted that Senator Butler had disclaimed any intention of injuring the Good Neighbor policy, but that the manner and implication of the report "were such as to constitute a most unfair and unfounded attack calculated to injure the whole policy." The Secretary briefly recounted features of Latin American solidarity with the United States, emphasizing that nineteen of the countries had declared war on the Axis or had broken diplomatic relations. He recounted how they had opened their ports to United States vessels, "welcomed and quartered our troops on their soil," produced materials of war, "rounded up Axis spies and saboteurs," stopped trade with the Axis powers—all with the result that "without this cooperation the course of the war in highly essential strategic areas might have been different." [36]

The Department of State followed Hull's statement with a memorandum refuting specific statements in Senator Butler's report. This memorandum abounded in paragraphs like the following:

The Senator includes in his computation of United States expenditures in Latin America $570,000,000 in aid to Puerto Rico from the United States government.

Puerto Rico is a Territory of the United States, not a foreign country.[37]

Senator Butler issued a reply to Hull's declaration, saying, with regard to the statement, that "it was a tribute to the good sense of the people of the Americas . . . that these gross misrepresentations were not generally believed," that it was to be anticipated that Latin American newspapers would comment unfavorably on his charges because "none of us expects the child to attack Santa Claus." Stirred by this remark, the *Star & Herald* (Panama), December 16, 1943, called this "a nasty and unwarranted crack" and stated that it had never received anything from Washington other than publicity material like that issued by all countries. The only ways in which the newspaper had been helped were that it had received courteous and considerate treatment in obtaining export licenses for newsprint, and that one of its editors had been enabled to visit the United States at the expense of the Coordinator of Inter-American Affairs. Otherwise no government agency in Washington "played Santa Claus to our paper. They have not even influenced advertising coming to our paper." It was this newspaper's opinion that "the same condition prevails insofar as the great majority of newspapers in Latin America are concerned."

The *Star & Herald* here touched on a point of some importance. The Department of State, both before and during the war, was scrupulously careful to avoid any actions in the nature of inspiring articles in Latin American newspapers, and nothing in the way of subsidizing Latin American newspapers was attempted, nor does it appear even to have been seriously considered in Washington.

The Department of State could take comfort from the information that the majority of the press in the United States had criticized Senator Butler's article as inaccurate and exaggerated in its claims, and that this majority had increased after the statements by Senator McKellar and Secretary Hull. Perhaps as large a proportion as a fifth of the total number of United States newspapers, however, continued to support Senator Butler after the Department of State had answered him. A larger proportion considered that it was likely that there had been some financial waste in Latin America, and that Butler's attack might be useful in limiting extravagant expenditures in the future.[38]

There appeared to be, however, no significant tendency in United States papers to support Senator Butler's attack on the Good Neighbor policy as a whole, whatever doubts may have existed as to the utility of some projects for which money had been spent. The view that the Butler incident had "closed with a net gain" and had "served to clear the atmosphere and clarify thinking generally on the subject throughout the Hemisphere" [39] was one that was echoed in Latin America. *El Tiempo* (Bogotá) on December 18, 1943, declared that Senator Butler's efforts had served to demonstrate "the solidity of the Good Neighbor policy and provided an occasion for its affirmation as a national policy above party struggles in the United States." Such affirmation was earnestly desired, not only by *El Tiempo*, but by almost the whole of the press of Latin America, which may be assumed on this occasion to have represented the views both of politically significant elements of public opinion, and of all the governments, except that of Argentina.

Without speculating about Senator Butler's motives, it is possible to say something about his possible objectives. If he had intended, as Senator McKellar suggested, to "bring about distrust and division among the American republics," he had signally failed. If his purpose had been to create a political issue for the 1944 presidential election, he was unable to find a single supporter among the leaders of the Republican party. If he had hoped to make the policy of the United States, as he said, "authentically Good Neighbors," he discovered that there was general satisfaction throughout America with the current direction of the policy. His charges of wastefulness, which might have been substantiated in some measure, were forgotten in the uproar over his exaggerated claims. The principal outcome of the affair was that it provided the occasion for the firmest and most spontaneous expression of Latin American confidence in the policy of the United States in the recent history of inter-American relations.

CHAPTER XV

The Good Neighbors

Understandings among Good Neighbors

THE EXPRESSION "Good Neighbor" has been used in the preceding pages both to denote an attitude on the part of the United States government and to describe the several policies that experience demonstrated to be necessary before a Good Neighborly attitude was accorded credence in Latin America. Such credence was essential to Latin American willingness to adopt satisfactorily reciprocal policies, and, without such reciprocity for the great power's relinquishment of force, that always retractable concession might have been withdrawn.

If the Good Neighborly attitude and policies of the United States required Latin American credence before they produced a reciprocity deemed adequate in Washington, then there is reason to add a third dimension to the meaning of the Good Neighbor, by viewing it as including the existence of a set of relationships or understandings that transcended the notions of attitude or policy on the part of the United States alone and involved the interactions of attitudes and policies of the governments of Latin America as well. In this light, it may be said that, while the attitude was initiated and the policy worked out in the United States, the establishment of relationships or understandings was the result of a political process shared in by the governments and peoples of Latin America.

It is difficult to give these relationships, so amorphous yet so real, a characterization such as "society" or "community," much less "organization." The American states possessed institutions in the Pan American Union and the inter-American conferences, and these institutions played a role in maintaining formal contacts among the American states that were different from those of ordinary diplomatic intercourse. The conferences occasionally were important as opportunities for the concentrations of joint Latin American diplomatic pressures upon the United States and, at Lima and afterward, for Washington's mobilization of majority support for its policy toward the world crisis. For example, Hull did not go to Montevideo expecting to sign a protocol on non-intervention, either with or without reservations; it appears that he overrode his advisers on this point after sensing the strength of feeling on the part of Latin American statesmen. This institutional structure has been given little attention in the present study, however, since the policies here reviewed were worked out principally in bilateral negotiations; the conferences largely, although not entirely, reflected the collaborative drive engendered by policy created elsewhere. For example, the Mexican Foreign Minister, Ezequiel Padilla, made an eloquent speech, at the Rio de Janeiro Conference in 1942, in support of Latin American solidarity with the United States, but his resonant voice was not raised simply because the Conference was held a month after the Japanese attack on Hawaii; what would he have said about "the spirit of self-sacrifice" of the United States, had the expropriation controversy not been settled by the agreement of November 19, 1941?

The considerable significance of the conferences in establishing legal obligations, setting up organizational arrangements, and creating visible symbols of inter-American cooperation should, however, be given due recognition, and their achievements have been reviewed in other publications.[1]

Alfonso Reyes, the Mexican diplomat and man of letters, has written: "Cooperation is the contribution of America to international affairs. In contrast to the systems of universal domination and of the balance of power, there was conceived and developed in America the system of cooperation that is based upon common action, mutual aid and mutual respect."[2]

There existed before 1933 a system of relationships based on the general rules of international law, including the right of intervention or at least interposition for purposes of maintaining an international standard of protection of nationals engaged in business abroad. When the right of intervention was relinquished by the United States, the international standard of protection of nationals, as interpreted by the great powers, began to be changed in two important ways so far as Latin America was concerned. Firstly, the right of expropriation was admitted by the United States in principle and by Great Britain in practice. The British government, in the Mexican case, held that expropriation would be justified only if it were in the interests of the Mexican people, and it denied that this was so. However, Britain could no longer coerce a Latin American country by force, so the Mexican position could not, except in principle, be challenged; and British oil companies ultimately accepted settlements comparable to those accorded by Mexico to the United States companies. In the second place, the terms of compensation would not be determined by judicial, arbitral, or coercive methods, but by negotiations in which the expropriator was on formally equal terms with the government representing the protesting corporations.

In addition, of course, the United States gave up the right to intervene by force in Latin American countries for any other reason, on the basis either of international law or of a treaty, as in the instances of Cuba and Panama.

One significant difference between these two abandonments was that, with regard to the second, the United States government had concluded as early as the Montevideo Conference of 1933 that it did not wish to become embroiled again, *à la* Cuba or Nicaragua, in the domestic politics of its neighbors. However, as late as the Buenos Aires Conference in 1936, it had not realized the implications of the nonintervention protocol with respect to the protection of United States enterprises abroad, nor did it at first wish to go so far as it ultimately did in giving up the measure of protection to American business that it had customarily afforded.

If, then, an old order began to change in 1933 or even a little earlier,[3] the shape of a new order was by no means immediately apparent. The prohibition of intermeddling that might lead to intervention was not a policy of the Department of State until 1936, and the full requirements of the policy of pacific protection were not appreciated by Welles until the end of 1942, in the Venezuelan oil case. Those requirements were, in Welles's judgment, "the exercise of vision and foresight . . . coupled with an abandonment of an exaggeratedly legalistic position." [4] Welles was here referring to what "a solution of the Venezuelan problem" demanded of the oil companies. For the Department, it may be reasonably asserted that, as a result of its Mexican experience, it had abandoned an excessively legalistic position in the field of protection, and, further, that Welles's actions in the Venezuelan case demonstrated wisdom and foresight in sufficient degree for the issue at hand.

To these elements of policy and in place of coercion, the United States added the theory of the anticipation of reciprocity. The full content of reciprocity does not seem to have been defined by the Department of State, even to itself, but at first it certainly included the expectation that United States enterprises would continue to receive consideration in Latin America identical, or closely similar, to that which they had enjoyed when intervention was imminent. This expectation went unfulfilled.

In 1933 the Department of State seems to have been under the impression that the single desire of those Latin American states that had seen United States troops on their territory was to secure the pledge to abstain from intervention in order to gain freedom to conduct their domestic political affairs as they wished. After 1936, however, it was apparent that another freedom from intervention was cherished no less—the freedom to treat foreign corporations as the Latin American governments thought best. This freedom was revealed, as a direct consequence of nonintervention, as the single strongest desire of certain Latin American governments. Indeed, one of the chief, unanticipated political functions of the adoption of the policy of nonintervention was the demonstration of the nature of this major Latin American objective in relations with the United States. That this objective was immediately sought only by Bolivia, Mexico, and Venezuela did not mean that other states would not later seek to secure it. The action of these three was a warning to the United States that the issue would be an enduring one.

The extent of the enjoyment of this freedom was not clarified until the end of 1942, and not until then may it be said that agreement as to the nature of the new understanding had been reached. Not until then was there an appreciation on both sides that the values held by each were sufficiently alike so that amicable settlements could be counted on when differences appeared. The United States accepted the right of expropriation, and Bolivia and Mexico, at least in practice, admitted that they should make compensation. Further, there was mutual agreement that the timing, amount, and other criteria of compensation would be negotiated as among equals, which meant, again in practice, that judicial means of settlement were discarded. The issues were regarded as political and not as legal, for by 1942 these governments were neighbors who thought out-of-court adjustments were necessary conditions for mutually satisfactory settlements.

Such satisfactory settlements could be reached, of course, only if both the United States and Latin American governments exhibited restraint and moderation in the substance of demands and in the style of negotiation. Since the focus of this study has been on political relationships among governments, attention has been concentrated on evidences of restraint and moderation rather than on the sources of these general attributes of policy. No serious attempt has been made, for example, to analyze the reasons for Cárdenas's willingness to offer compensation or for Medina's willingness to accept terms for revising concessions that Betancourt regarded as less than Venezuela's bargaining position warranted. The foreign policies of these and other Latin American countries have been little studied, especially in terms of their domestic origins, and they have been considered here primarily from an external viewpoint.

Some conclusions may be drawn from policies adopted in the oil controversies about changing conceptions of "the national interest" as viewed over a period of years by statesmen in the several countries, but specific references to the national interest are infrequent in inter-American diplomacy. When they are made, they ordinarily take a negative form, rather than a positive one that would attempt a definition of the term. Nevertheless, American statesmen, like those elsewhere, held sets of interrelated ideas

and attitudes about foreign policies of the governments they represented that provided the sources of their decisions, and it is to these
sets of views and attitudes, visible and invisible, changing and permanent, that the term national interest is here applied.

In this sense, the national interests of the United States and of
certain Latin American governments were compatible in the era of
the Good Neighbors. The adjustments in relationships during the
oil controversies, both in detail and in principle, were made to
further national interests as conceived in each country. In the case
of all governments, inference from policy actions is the principal
guide to conceptions of the national interest. In the case of the
United States, greater light is occasionally provided at the verbal
level, as in the previously quoted memorandum of June 26, 1939:
"Our national interests as a whole far outweigh those of the
petroleum companies." [5]

That such a statement was made at all is suggestive not only of
controversy within the Department of State and of the importance
of the issues at stake, but it is also descriptive of the general line
of policy that the United States adopted in the oil controversies.
After 1937, the advancement of the national interest of the United
States in the Americas was seen in Washington as giving high value
to Latin American collaboration in case of a major war. In view
of the intensity of Latin American drives against the positions of
the oil companies, and the consequent threat to collaboration,
there was found no alternative to an accommodation to Latin
American demands. This accommodation was made at the expense
of United States business enterprises, which suffered in status,
property, and revenues. Some of the corporations had become
powerful and bold enough to deal with Latin American states on
nearly equal terms, as though they too were sovereign entities.
Indeed, so long as the companies had been able to count on en-
joined arbitration of their controversies with Latin American
governments there was good reason for the remark, said by Mexicans to have been made by an oil company official, that Cárdenas
would not dare to expropriate. The companies were no quicker
than the Department of State to recognize the implications of the
nonintervention pledge, nor were their policies or attitudes rapidly
modified when governments emerged that determined to reduce

the power and profits the companies received as the result of contracts made with previous regimes that were less concerned with social welfare than those of Cárdenas or Medina.

The companies lost their position as having indirect benefits under international law when the Department of State refused to claim that Bolivia or Mexico had violated international law and so did not elevate the controversy from the political to the legal plane. They also lost all, or nearly all, of such sympathy as the Roosevelt administration harbored toward them in consequence of their obstinacy in maintaining what Welles called an "exaggeratedly legalistic position."

Unable to count on support from Washington that Latin American governments would regard as having weighty consequences, the companies ultimately found it necessary to review their policies in a novel situation where they were almost wholly subject to local law and local courts. The actual position of the companies differed from country to country, depending on the nature of the local regimes, the relative financial power of the companies and of their hosts, and other factors. The policies of the companies were in some cases changed so as to improve wages and working conditions. The question whether these changes were due to the Mexican settlement is perhaps an open one, for there were other elements involved, but it may be said that the Mexican settlement was one important contributor to the development of a new climate of opinion on the part of some United States businesses with regard to the attitudes they expressed and the actions they felt able to take in conditions when local laws were controlling.[6] In addition, the experience of the companies, especially in the Mexican and Venezuelan controversies, gave them ample reason for recognizing that their Latin American operations could not be conducted without a sense of responsibility to the national interests of the United States. As one of their officials remarked, he realized that "much more was involved than merely the issue between the Venezuelan Government and our company."[7] This admission was an acceptance of the Department of State's position about the superiority of the national interest, whatever the precise nature of that elusive concept. The concept would be given life and meaning in specific cases, and it should be remembered that the main business of United States diplomats in Latin America before 1939 was the defense of the economic interests of their co-citizens.

The companies were not entirely deserted by the Department of State, and it is in connection with the limited, pacific protection afforded them that an additional feature of the new order comes into view. The Department not only took the firm stand that compensation must be paid in cases of expropriation, but, in the Bolivian case, it brought pressure to bear by the refusal of loans and technical assistance until compensation was forthcoming. The United States had forsworn military action, but it was able to offer or withhold economic rewards, and this capacity, which it alone possessed among the American states in adequate measure, underlined the fact that the "system" comprised one wealthy power and twenty states of varying, but vastly lower, levels of economic resources. The discovery of the potentialities of the rewards technique was itself novel in inter-American affairs, for loans, grants, and technical assistance to Latin American governments by governmental agencies in Washington began to be offered on any significant scale only in 1939, and from the beginning they had a political tinge. The exploration of the possibilities and limitations of the technique became a continuous process when its potentialities were realized.

Just before the Japanese attack on Pearl Harbor, then, it may be said that the United States had established, with the assistance of certain Latin American states, an unprecedented set of relationships productive of a nearly solidary American attitude toward threats from without. The basis for this relationship had been laid before the hemisphere was seen to be threatened and was originally unconnected with any security concern on the part of the United States. The weak countries of Latin America, needing a protector, were satisfied to support the United States in that role in 1939 and through the war because they had both formal and informal reason to believe that they were then safe, both from their powerful protector and from other powerful states.

The nature of reciprocity to be accorded the United States, after being whittled down by Bolivia and Mexico, was never fully defined. The relative shift of power in favor of Latin American states that followed the nonintervention pledge amounted to a compromise in principle by the United States government and a sacrifice in substance by some corporations and individuals with interests in Latin America. The ponderable if immeasurable good will subsequently demonstrated on the part of Latin American states was regarded, in the Department of State at least, as sufficient compensation with respect to the interests of the United States as a whole. It was in this sense, rather than in identifiable acts of reciprocity, that the Latin American response was evaluated. Such an evaluation on the national level by the Department of State was probably a wise one, for the tendency was strong in Latin America to regard the Good Neighbor policy as little more than the righting of wrongs done either by the United States government or by foreign business enterprises in collaboration with dictators like Díaz and Gómez.

The characterization of the process of reaching these new inter-American relationships is rather more than a matter of taste. We have earlier called it bargaining on a grand scale, but this expression would be shunned by statesmen, who, with reason, do not wish to employ any term suggestive of barter in a description of compromises that involve major acts of sovereign states. There is a level of diplomatic manners above obvious hypocrisy and still above the blatantly hortatory where governments desiring to avoid acrimonious bickering strive to pitch their understandings. President Roosevelt was assuming too much at the moment he wrote to President Medina of Venezuela, that "your country and mine have wholeheartedly subscribed" to the Good Neighbor policy.[8] Sumner Welles, on the other hand, may have come close to the right note in saying that no one country had "benefitted in particular from the Good Neighbor policy, but that the economic and cultural advancement of all the American republics will be greatly enhanced by cooperation and fair dealing among themselves."[9] This view of the spirit of the era of the Good Neighbors very nearly matches that expressed by Alfonso Reyes, as quoted above, and it exemplifies that nice blend of description, mutual congratulation, and aspiration that is found when, at its most civilized limit, diplomacy engenders joint action toward similar aims.

A System of Reciprocity?

Viewed in terms of institutions, these understandings of the Good Neighbor era formed a primitive political order indeed. In terms of its principles, however, this combination of relinquishment of force and anticipation of reciprocity was a sophisticated arrangement.

A review of substantive understandings between the United States and certain Latin American countries has suggested to some observers that by the end of 1941 there existed such measure of mutual acceptance of common values as to justify the use of the term "system of reciprocity" to describe the relationship.[10] One of the most explicit statements of these understandings was that made by President Peñaranda of Bolivia, as quoted above. There were other influential elements of understanding, of course, but those mentioned appear to have been most strenuously sought by Latin Americans.

However, before the use of so comprehensive a term as "system of reciprocity" could be justified, it would be necessary to look into two additional features of inter-American relationships existing at about the time of the entry of the United States into World War II. These features were the dynamic elements in the relationships, as distinct from the above substantive understandings, and the prospects for continuity of both.

The principal dynamic elements were three abilities demonstrated by the government of the United States. The first of these was the ability to perceive and accept the minimum demands of certain Latin American countries for treatment of United States business firms. The second was the capacity to exert pressures, both by refusing to provide loans or other economic benefits to states it identified as nonreciprocating, and by offering financial and other assistance to encourage cooperation. The third dynamic element was the ability, demonstrated in the Venezuelan case, to respond to early warnings of impending crises, and to take preventive or evasive action by exerting influence on United States businessmen as well as on Latin American governments. As the initiator of the policy, and as its principal single beneficiary, the United States could not escape the responsibility for vigilance in maintaining balance among these dynamic elements.

It was the use of these elements that constituted the process of the evocation of reciprocity. The nature of the reciprocity evoked varied from country to country and from time to time; the Bolivians agreed to make compensation, for example, and possible expropriation by Venezuela was averted. These were direct results of specific actions by the United States. The great indirect result of the slow weaving of a web of many strands of policy was the co-operative reception given to United States initiatives during World War II.

The reception varied from warm to cool on the part of several governments, and it would be misleading to speak of Latin America as an entity in this and many other connections. Indeed, experience under these reciprocal arrangements suggests that in comparable relationships between a great and several lesser powers there will probably exist at least one pole of resistance or obstruction to the policies of the leading power. Elements of opposition will probably be present in some measure within all the lesser states, and, when they possess leadership in the form of a Saavedra Lamas or a Cantilo, one dissenting government, such as Argentina, can be expected to endeavor to rally other governments to its support.

The techniques of application of these dynamic elements required, on the part of the United States, competent reporting by diplomatic missions, finesse and a sympathetic style of application,[11] and a nice sense of timing. Further, an easy and informal atmosphere of communication between governments was required; the social distance between sovereignties needed to be short. This did not mean only the raising of legations to embassies; it meant also the growth of cordiality and respect among individuals. Such relationships were not, of course, universal, but they were established in many cases, and the long tenure of office of Roosevelt, Hull, and Welles cultivated their warmth. Duggan's advice to Stettinius on the position Welles had attained is illustrative of the significance of this intangible relationship.[12]

The procedures of consultation initiated at the Buenos Aires

Conference in 1936 have not been considered in this discussion, because they were only indirectly contributory to the growth of reciprocity and were not used in the oil controversies. Those procedures were designed to be used in case of war between American states or international conflict elsewhere that might menace the peace of the American republics.[13] The American states referred to there were only the Latin American states, since none of them would attack the United States, and the latter had agreed not to intervene. The occurrence of war elsewhere created issues that were, of course, external to the system of reciprocity. These consultative procedures were not used in the case of the Peruvian invasion of Ecuador in 1941, but were employed for the three meetings of foreign ministers after the outbreak of World War II. The fact that these meetings were held, and the approval there given to the leadership of the United States, were generally regarded in the United States as fruits of the Good Neighbor policy. In one important respect, however, these meetings enhanced the confidence in the Good Neighborly intentions of the United States that other elements of policy had already created. The meetings of foreign ministers gave to the governments of all Latin American countries a sense of participation in the framing of certain decisions affecting the hemisphere as a whole. The range of these decisions was not restricted to neutrality or security measures alone but included plans for trusteeships for colonies of European countries and for collaboration in economic affairs, involving both commercial relations and what came later to be called economic development.

A sense of participation had also been encouraged by the Department of State in the course of its collaboration with Latin American governments in the settlement of the Chaco, Leticia, and Marañón disputes. The United States had refrained from unilateral efforts to bring the contending governments to terms and had amply demonstrated its adherence to the principle that the pacific solution of intra-American conflicts should be sought on a multilateral basis.[14]

Consultation with Latin American governments in these affairs of concern to all American states tended to reinforce confidence in the moderation of the policy of the United States that was generated by the growth of an appreciation of the meaning of reciprocity through bilateral arrangements and the unilateral renunciation of intervention. It is probably impossible to distinguish the precise effects of interaction between these several policy lines, but there is little question that they were mutually productive of the intimate cooperation achieved in 1939 and through the war years.

Acceptance of the idea of reciprocity was not gained through consultation among the American governments, but rather through a series of bilateral settlements with Cuba, Panama, Mexico, and other countries. As these settlements were completed and made public, their cumulative effect was to cultivate a willingness in Latin America to reciprocate in some of the ways desired by the United States. The resultant wartime cooperation might be regarded as the multilateral phase of the Good Neighborhood, but the term continental solidarity was preferred at the time.[15]

President Roosevelt once expressed the opinion that the Good Neighbor policy "can never be merely unilateral. In stressing it the American republics appreciate, I am confident, that it is bilateral and multilateral and that the fair dealing which it implies must be reciprocated."[16] Formal multilateral arrangements were few indeed, however, and it remained for the American states to register the level of their multilateral response to the Good Neighbor policy, and to wartime developments, by creating the Organization of American States at the Bogotá Conference in 1948.

In terms both of substance and of process, the idea of reciprocity possessed viability by 1942, since there existed an appreciation of the limits of policy on both sides, together with a capacity for restorative and preventive action by the United States. The capacity to evoke reciprocity was of fundamental importance; because it was centrally controlled and not subject to veto, it could generate action and dissolve stalemates. Used with discretion and imagination, as it was in different but consistent ways in the three oil cases, this capacity was at once the motive power and the regulator for understandings that otherwise would have offered meager prospects of being workable.

There remains to be examined the prospects for continuity in the application of the idea of reciprocity in order to appraise the aptness of the characterization "system of reciprocity." The durability of the relationships depended on three principal factors: continuity in the policy of the United States; moderation in the policy of Latin American states toward United States investors; and mutual resistance to certain types of incursions from outside.

For continuity of United States policy, the Mexicans and others counted on the nonintervention protocol and the "personal sentiments" of Roosevelt. Although Roosevelt's sentiments about the status of foreign corporations in Mexico and elsewhere were stable enough, it was a matter of constant concern to Latin Americans both how long Roosevelt would remain in office and whether his point of view would be shared by his successors. Although Welles has stated that under Roosevelt's "guidance and . . . inspiration the Good Neighbor policy became a living thing," [17] the transformation of sentiments into policy was performed in the Department of State. This had meant, in effect, that Hull, Welles, and Duggan were almost exclusively responsible for the building of policy over a period of ten years. Welles dominated the day-to-day policy decisions relating to Latin America, and he was not a man who made his decisions in council. His practice was to make decisions based on information provided by his subordinates, but he rarely invited them to comment on what should be done. It may have been in part for this reason that the minuting of despatches was a less common procedure in the American republics area of the Department than in certain other divisions.[18] Consequently, very few officials other than Hull, Welles, and Duggan were in a position to gain an overview of Latin American affairs and to appreciate the intricacy of the rules of the game that these three gradually learned.

Beyond this, however, full comprehension of the good neighborly understandings does not seem to have been shared equally by Roosevelt, Hull, Welles, and Duggan, especially in the early stages of policy growth. The creation of policy and, consequently, the formation of the idea of reciprocity, were gradual constructions, unillumined by blueprints or by doctrine, and guided by sympathy rather than strategy. In the Cuban affair, Hull disagreed with Welles's proposal for "limited intervention" and persuaded Roosevelt to reject it. Similarly, the noninterference policy was determined upon only after differences of views between Welles and Duggan, and an understanding of the policy of pacific protection was gained gradually with the aid of the skillful parries of Mexican diplomacy and Daniels's independent activities.

The Department of State never developed an instrument comparable to a War Plan Orange for the conduct of good neighborly operations. Major policy decisions resulted from spasmodic discussions among these and a very few other officials, whose minds gradually came to move more and more harmoniously on the surface of common assumptions derived from common experiences. However, it appears that these occasional discussions were crucial to the consistency of policy, for they alone compensated for the lack of an explicit statement of the articulation of the several policy lines on which the Good Neighborhood was based. The spirit of the Good Neighbor was not enough for a policy guide, and, in the absence of an explicit theory, the congruity of policy actions with policy aims depended at critical moments on checks and correctives provided by others than those immediately engaged in negotiations. In this connection, the roles of Latin American statesmen, such as Cárdenas, Castillo Nájera, and even Saavedra Lamas, should not be forgotten. Policy was in constant course of evolution through interaction within a small group of officials related to each other less significantly by the hierarchy of office than by their need for joint exploration of policy terrain which they had not reconnoitered by preliminary planning for alternative contingencies.

There are two significant attributes of this small group of officials that are worthy of note. In the first place, they remained in office together for more than ten years; there was time to conceive, test, understand and put into effect a coherent line of policy. In the second place, Roosevelt and Hull were professional politicians, and Welles (formerly) and Duggan (in 1933) were career officers in the Department of State. None of them entered office in 1933 on leave from positions in law firms or business enterprises, and it is unlikely that any of them anticipated going to such positions at the end of their public service. These factors, it is suggested, may have had an important bearing on their decisions about the nature of the national interest of the United States with respect to Latin America, particularly in the oil controversies. It is not meant to imply that this combination of factors was an absolute requirement for the development of the policies of the Good Neighbor, but it may well have been an influential circumstance that responsibility for policy toward Latin America in the decade following 1933 rested with men whose experience and orientation inclined them to give primacy to the national as against any lesser interests.

The breakup of this team would not necessarily entail fundamental changes in policy. Continuity would, however, depend on two conditions which were difficult to satisfy. Firstly, continuity would demand adherence to the substantive principles of the relationships that have been outlined above. Secondly, continuity would require a policy testament of some sort so that new men in the government in Washington would be acquainted with the requirements for maintaining reciprocity.

These considerations emphasize the scope of the Good Neighbor as comprising a set of relationships as well as a policy of the United States. The nature and limits of the relationships had been learned, by Welles and Duggan, over a period of ten years, if not as the only alternative to the use of force, at least as one which was feasible and was regarded with satisfaction by nearly all the governments concerned. These relationships were more than a policy because, to use Reyes's terms, their existence depended on "common action, mutual aid, and mutual respect." Unless the full implications of these essential features were understood by those who made decisions in the Department of State, the relationships would break down.

Perhaps the chief problem affecting continuity was that of transferring an understanding of the new relationships from the men who created them to their successors. Public understanding of the principles of the Good Neighbor appears to have been largely limited to the recognition that the use of force had been renounced. Statements to the effect that nonintervention was the "essence of the Good Neighbor policy" were frequently made by commentators, and declarations of oil company representatives that the Mexicans misinterpreted the Good Neighbor policy, and even some remarks by Hull and Roosevelt, could be taken as assumptions that the United States government had no more concessions to make after its nonintervention pledge.

The policy of pacific protection as worked out in the oil cases appears to have been given little attention as a policy, and its significance to the Good Neighbor relationship as a whole was not generally recognized. Since this policy was developed in a period of great events in other parts of the world, and since the Department of State emphasized the facts of the Bolivian and Mexican agreements rather than their policy background, the lack of recognition of the importance of the cases is understandable. In the case of the Venezuelan settlement, the role of the Department of State has remained largely unknown; the arrangement was, of course, between the Venezuelan government and the companies and so was different from the other two which were concluded by intergovernmental agreements. The Department did not make public its role at the time, and it is of interest that the negotiations at the end of 1942 appear to have escaped notice by the newspaper press.[19] Thus, the vital part played by the Department in identifying the issue and in taking measures to prevent a crisis of expropriation seems to have gone almost entirely unnoticed outside the Department and, of course, the companies concerned. Consequently, the systemic elements of foresight and prevention of crises, and the idea that the Department would not hesitate to bring its influence to bear on private enterprises in the United States to demand that they revise their policies in Latin America, were not brought to public view and may even have escaped due appreciation in the Department itself.

The conception of the Good Neighbor policy as a set of relationships was probably held, in 1943, by no more than a few individuals apart from Welles, Duggan, Hull, and Roosevelt. Welles resigned suddenly in the summer of 1943, and the other principals were no longer on the scene two years later. None of them left what could be called a policy testament about the Good Neighbor;

its nearest substitute was a series of newspaper articles written by Welles after he left office. Welles did speak of an "inter-American system," but his description was in such broad terms as to be of little aid to political analysis.[20]

In its Latin American policy, the Department of State did occasionally pull together some of its experiences and make judgments about cause and effect relationships among them. The outstanding example of this infrequent activity was the drawing of the conclusion that interference should be given up because it was likely to lead to intervention. However, comparable recapitulation of experience with respect to the policy of pacific protection does not appear to have been made. It is, of course, easier to discern and proclaim a policy of complete abstention than one that must necessarily be based on judgments about the scope and speed of adjustment. In the Mexican case, for example, Welles and Hull ultimately realized the extent of accommodation to Mexican demands before reciprocity in terms of wartime collaboration from Mexico could be secured. This, however, seems to have been regarded as a unique case, as was that of Bolivia, and each was different from the Venezuelan situation.

Neither Welles nor Hull, nor Roosevelt, appears to have considered following a policy of nonprotection of United States business enterprise in Latin America. Although, as has been indicated, Welles once referred privately to "national policy" as taking precedence over protection of the interests of oil companies, the Roosevelt administration did not go so far as to make such an assertion in terms of principle, nor did Welles explicitly distinguish national policy from a lower level of policy that would provide protection to property of United States nationals in foreign countries. By the time Welles left office in 1943, he seems fully to have accepted the conclusion that the protection of business enterprise abroad was no longer a matter of "national" or "high" policy for the United States. Since force would not be used and arbitration could not otherwise be employed, political negotiations alone remained, supplemented by such mild economic pressures as might seem in a particular instance to be justified. The protection of the property rights of corporations or individuals was, in these circumstances, regarded as of secondary importance, and property losses by corporations and individuals were an unavoidable price of the policy of nonintervention. This did not mean that Welles or Hull reached conclusions of this order easily either in their own minds or with respect to domestic pressures on them by oil companies or other groups. The course of the Mexican oil negotiations indicates that their final decision was long delayed and was reached only after avenues to other solutions had been fully explored.[21]

It may have been in part for this reason that the experience of the oil cases was not explicitly linked to the nonintervention pledge, as was the policy of noninterference. Further, it may have appeared unwise, if the question had been considered at all, to have made any public statement of the new policy in general terms. There would have been, in 1938 and later, political risks in debates at the level of general principles of policy, for the gulf between leaders of the oil industry and perhaps others, and the position gradually assumed by Welles and Hull was wide indeed, as was demonstrated by the following stand taken in an editorial in the *Oil and Gas Journal:*

Oil is where you find it, and where Americans find it they should be supported by their government in rightful disposition of it. American companies have gone into the most remote and inaccessible parts of the globe to find oil and have thereby greatly strengthened their country's position in world commerce.

Unless relationships are to be reduced to brigandage, as in the old world today, and treaties, agreements and concessions are to be regarded as mere "scraps of paper" the governments of this hemisphere must take a stand for mutual respect of their obligations.[22]

Although in the Venezuelan case, Welles was willing to go so far as to encourage his petroleum adviser to persuade oil officials to adopt a conciliatory position in advance of a possible expropriation, he did not elevate to the level of explicit principle his working knowledge of how far he had found it necessary to go both in withdrawing protection from business firms in Latin America, and in demanding that they change their policies and even reassign their personnel.[23] It would have been bold and even foolhardy to have given official and public expression in wartime to so controversial an issue, and for a time after the war the issue was dormant and there were by then no custodians of the policy to assert it. However, from the foregoing review of the Good Neighbor policy, it is difficult to avoid the conclusion that the policy of pacific protection, no less than the policy of noninterference, was a direct consequence of the policy of nonintervention. It was not a "corollary" of that policy in the sense that it was a logical derivation from doctrine, like the Roosevelt Corollary, and it would raise irrelevant argument to describe it as a "necessary" consequence. It was, rather, the set of policies that the government of the United States over a period of some seven years of transition from peace to war settled upon as the most satisfactory among alternative lines of action in a complicated situation involving pressures upon it from Latin America, from the Axis powers, and from its own citizens.

In its most general terms, the fundamental principle of the policy of pacific protection was that the national interest of the United States was superior to the interests of private enterprise in relations with Latin American states. On its face, this principle may seem both simple and banal, but its application in policy struggles is complex, and that it is no truism is demonstrated by the policies of the oil companies and, as indicated above, by the apparent surprise of one oil company official on realizing that there was more involved in the Venezuelan dispute than the interests of his company.

This line of discussion raises some interesting questions about the degree to which, in the United States, the interests of business enterprise abroad should and could be subordinated to the general foreign policy concerns of the United States as understood by the national government, but further consideration of these questions is beyond the scope of the present study. It may be added, however, that, in relations with Latin America, the lack of express enunciation both of the fundamental principle of the policy of pacific protection, and of its consequential linkage to the policy of nonintervention, made uncertain the continuity of the policy of pacific protection. The continuity of the policy of the Good Neighbor as a whole was therefore uncertain, since the policy of pacific protection was regarded in Latin America, and not alone in Mexico, as an absolute requirement for that reciprocity by Latin American countries that was asserted by Washington to be essential to the policy of the Good Neighbor. This was the case in time of war at least, since, as has been indicated, Mexican military assistance would not otherwise have been provided; and the strength of the desire demonstrated by Latin American countries to revise the status of foreign enterprises in their jurisdictions promised to present new cases comparable to those of the oil controversies, when in time of peace the urgency of the continuation of the policy of pacific protection might be less apparent.

The problem of continuity was not a new one and it may seem strange that little or nothing was done about it. When Hull succeeded Stimson in 1933, he does not seem to have acted with the caution he would have used had he been aware of Stimson's difficulties in Nicaragua and the character of Stimson's concern about involvements in the maze of Cuban politics. When Welles resigned, he left behind an intellectual transfer problem even more complicated than Hull had encountered in 1933, and he did not convey to a successor at his administrative level an understanding of the relationships with Latin America that he had done so much to establish.

If there was doubtful continuity in the Department of State, there is no reason to suppose that there was not continuity in the policies of the business enterprises that felt themselves adversely affected by the Good Neighbor policy, or in the foreign offices of Latin American states inspired by the examples of Mexico, Bolivia, and Venezuela. Officials of oil companies might prefer to sit and simmer and lose their properties, as one of them said, rather than to retreat by so much as a comma from their adherence to the principles of prompt, adequate, and equitable compensation to which they had been previously accustomed. The compromises they had accepted had been compromises in practice only, and they had been made expressly as contributions to the war effort. The companies could therefore be expected to maintain their principles and exert on the Department of State such influence as they possessed if at a later time the Washington climate should become more propitious to their cause. More single-minded, treasuring at least as keen a concern for the past, and possessing at least as stable a career system in higher echelons as the Department of State, the companies would probably return to the lists. On the other hand, it was equally probable that the examples given by Bolivia, Mexico, and Venezuela would be followed by other Latin American countries seeking to obtain advantages by changing the status of United States companies within their jurisdictions. It was in the Department of State that these durable sources of influence would be appraised and the policy of the Good Neighbor tested.

The continuity of reciprocity depended, in the second place, upon less than absolute policies by Latin American governments, particularly in the treatment of United States corporations. This was an area in which Mexico had found a solution acceptable to the Roosevelt administration, a way ultimately accepted by Bolivia. This, however, was a way marked by crises of expropriation and confiscation, and the question remained open whether moderation on the part of Latin American governments and prevision on the part of the United States could in future prevent crises and discover satisfactory compromises. This area was critical because it was the principal sphere where the Latin American states could assert their power and freedom of action. Their capacity for exerting influence outside their own territories was negligible, but they could inflict serious damage upon foreign interests within their jurisdictions, even if at substantial cost to themselves. Further, because one or a few corporations held dominant positions in the economies of a number of countries of Latin America, their status was of vital importance to governments, and the latter were often more deeply concerned with their relationships to the companies than with broad issues of continental solidarity that were of primary significance to the government of the United States.

In other words, the big problem for these smaller powers, the status of powerful foreign-owned corporations, was one that directly concerned them, and for which they could, unaided, provide at least a partial solution. After the United States renounced intervention, these countries still saw imperialism existing in the power wielded in their territories by foreign business enterprises, and they could not feel entirely free until, like Mexico, on March 18, 1938, they had achieved their own economic independence day. On the other hand, the big problem for the United States after 1938 was that of meeting the German and Japanese challenges. Bolivia and Mexico could join in attacking this problem only after their own demands for control of their petroleum resources had been realized through their adoption, ultimately, of less than extremist policies that were matched by political and financial adjustments by the United States.

These considerations lead into an additional requirement for the continuity of reciprocity—resistance to external threats. The foundations of the closely linked policies of nonintervention, noninterference, and pacific protection were laid before the outbreak of World War II, and it is impossible to say how the policies would have developed in other circumstances. It is highly probable, however, that, if most of the Latin American countries had not responded to Washington's changing interpretations of the substance of reciprocity, the group of policies developed in the 1930s would have been strained to the breaking point, and perhaps beyond it. If the government of a state in the Caribbean area had obstructed measures on its territory that the United States deemed essential to the protection of the Panama Canal, would the United States have shrunk from the use of force to install a more cooperative regime? If the government of such a state were likely to fall under the domination of pro-Axis groups, would the United States have refrained from interfering even had the government not asked for aid?

These are not simply rhetorical questions. As early as the spring of 1938, Roosevelt declared that if

European governments were to do in Mexico what they did in Spain. . . . Do you think that the United States could stand idly by and have this European menace right on our own borders? Of course not. You could not stand for it. . . . We probably all agree that we could not stand for a foreign nation doing that under the guise of a Mexican flag.[24]

The issue of the nonintervention policy was not specifically raised on this occasion, but it seemed clear that Roosevelt was prepared to protect the United States in Mexico against what he would regard as European intervention, whether or not the government of Mexico requested assistance from Washington.

The question was considered with greater seriousness and formality in 1941 when William S. Paley addressed a memorandum to Roosevelt, emphasizing the desirability of considering "a policy under which the Americas will not tolerate the control of any American republic by a foreign nation, irrespective of the methods used to gain and maintain such control. Nothing would so discourage the Latin American Trojan horses as such a policy, once adopted." [25]

Paley's memorandum was sent by the President to Sumner Welles, who replied that he did not think that Paley gave sufficient importance "to the danger which would result to the whole structure of inter-American cooperation if the United States undertook to determine for itself whether or not the government of some other American republic were subservient to Nazi or Fascist influence and, should it be determined that such government was in fact operating under alien influence, undertook to intervene directly in order to correct that situation. If we adopted such a policy we would, as you realize better than anyone else, afford exactly the opportunity which the Nazi propagandists are seeking to raise the old charge of Yankee imperialism." Welles felt that if such a "danger spot" should appear, "our neighbors would join with us to remove it," and the less the possibility were discussed publicly the less chance there would be for such a situation to arise.[26]

The expression of these views raised a question that had no reality before 1938: What were the limits of the renunciation of the use of force by the great power? The question acquired reality because of an external menace. Welles, confident of the solidity of the relationships he had nurtured so carefully, had faith that any external threat could be handled collectively, and he feared that the growth of reciprocity would be destroyed by the unilateral use of force by the United States. Paley, while admitting that "it is most important that we do not brandish the 'big stick,'" thought it was "equally important that we remain strong" in the eyes of

Latin Americans, for otherwise "our influence will lessen and our opponents will be encouraged." [27] Paley, who had no intimate connection with the development of Latin American policy, and even Roosevelt, who was better informed if only occasionally interested, were apparently willing to contemplate the use of force as an arm of policy far more readily than was Welles.

The great power could, of course, always employ force at its discretion, a capacity that was not shared by any other state in the Americas. The great power was bound by formal pledge not to intervene, and it had adopted policies designed to avert any chain of events that might tempt it to intervene. However, the great power was not a monolithic entity. A few men in the Department of State understood the concept of reciprocity and were willing to rely heavily on that concept to serve the national security of the United States. Other men who were influential in high governmental circles and who did not appreciate the concept or did not share Welles's faith in it, or both, were understandably attracted to consideration of forcible solutions for situations posing threats to the United States.

Here, then, was the combination of external menace and lack of faith in reciprocity that presented the greatest danger to the continuity of the era of the Good Neighbor. So long as Welles directed policy toward Latin America, confidence would be placed in the sympathy of Latin American governments and peoples with the cause of the United States, and in their collaboration with it to resist any infiltration or attack from outside the hemisphere. However, if Welles were the principal bulwark of the concept of reciprocity, the "system" was weak indeed. Otherwise, the principles of reciprocity had not been firmly adopted as national policy, and reliance on them by Latin American governments would not be fully tested. If Paley's proposals for easy and ready recourse to "strength" were accepted by Welles's successors, the hopes that Welles placed in reciprocity would be shattered without a profound probing of the tenacity and resilience of the relationships so carefully nurtured.

In view of these several considerations, there does not seem to be sufficient reason to assert that the relationships established by the policies of the Good Neighbor by the end of 1942 constituted a "system of reciprocity." The understandings among statesmen in office at the time were clear enough to them, but inadequate provision was made for continuity of the understandings in changing and unforeseeable circumstances. The elements of a theoretical system were present, but, except for the principle of nonintervention, they lacked the official adoption and widespread comprehension that were essential for translation into enduring policy that a political system of relationships would require.

On the other hand, however, it may be said that, by the end of 1942 the Roosevelt administration had worked out for itself a new synthesis of purposes and techniques of policy toward Latin America. This synthesis supplanted the older order of inter-American relationships and was sufficient in 1939 for the immediate purposes of gaining the association of Latin American states with the United States during World War II. In view of the condition of inter-American affairs as recently as 1932, this was a significant achievement, even though the new synthesis might be precariously balanced. This synthesis included, of course, new purposes and techniques of policy not only toward Latin America, but also toward United States oil corporations, which displayed such independence in dealings with their own government that the development of policy by the Department of State may be viewed as a double system of negotiations, one with sovereign and one with quasi-sovereign powers.

The rise of the power of the Axis after 1936 was of course viewed in different ways by Latin American governments, but the continuity of reciprocity during World War II was assured since all of them, except Argentina, accepted the cause of the United Nations as their own. Continuity depended on their perceiving the Axis threat as a real one to them as well as to the United States in the sense that a victory for the Axis would alter to their disadvantage the many types of respect for the dignity of small states and the welfare of their peoples that the United States government had gradually learned to observe as the concept of reciprocity was sympathetically, if gropingly, explored. The reactions of representative organs of the Latin American press to Senator Butler's attack on the Good Neighbor policy give evidence of the values seen as furthered by close association with the United States.

It is of some importance in this connection to recall the timing of developments in the Good Neighbor policy. The main actions that were publicly appreciated came early; these included the nonintervention pledges of 1933 and 1936, the abrogation of the Platt Amendment in 1934, and the rapidly succeeding trade agreements. These important policy changes by the United States were unrelated to any immediate concern for national security. The no less significant shifts in policy in the oil cases, on the other hand, were intimately related to the desire of Washington to secure the cooperation of Bolivia, Mexico, and Venezuela, and other countries in World War II. The Good Neighborly intent of the United States had thus been demonstrated before the external threat arose, and Washington's actions under pressure in the oil cases were consistent with the reputation it had earlier gained. Such timing and consistency, it seems reasonable to assume, were mutually reinforcing in the formation of Latin American attitudes that distinguished the United States favorably from the Axis powers.

However, here as elsewhere, generalizations are qualified by exceptions demonstrated by attitudes of certain countries and by difficult negotiations where the requirements of the idea of reciprocity were severely strained. One example of such exceptions, apart from the oil cases, is offered by the resistance of the government of Panama in 1940 and 1941 to the building of the Río Hato air base, which the government of the United States considered necessary for protection of the Panama Canal. The government of President Arnulfo Arias proved so racalcitrant that by the end of 1940 "it seemed that Washington was headed for a showdown with the government of Panama. . . . The administration was confronted with a real emergency 'in which practical considerations should prevail over theoretical ones.' "[28] In other words, defense requirements as viewed by the War Department might reluctantly have to be given primacy over the principles of the Good Neighbor as cherished by the Department of State. The crisis was essentially resolved in April, 1941, when Arias, who was strongly suspected in Washington of having sympathies with the Axis powers, authorized

United States forces to make use of the base sites while leaving for further negotiations the amount of compensation and other questions. When Arias left the country in the autumn of 1941, and a new government was formed, charges were made that the United States government had participated in these developments, but Hull denied any "connection, direct or indirect, with the recent governmental changes in the Republic of Panama." [29]

In principle, the maintenance of reciprocity in situations where the United States government believed that its national defense was vitally involved required on its part a maximum reliance on the confidence and good will engendered by the whole course of the Good Neighbor policy, in order to obtain from Latin American countries the measures of collaboration it deemed essential to its own security. On the part of Latin American countries, the maintenance of reciprocity demanded sufficient appreciation that the measures essential to the security of the United States were also so essential to their own defense against a common enemy that they would accept the great power's definition of minimum demands upon them. This did not mean that all Latin American states responded with equal enthusiasm or efficiency to measures initiated by the United States, nor that all of them even gave lip service to resolutions of solidarity. The extent of Argentina's wartime alienation is convincing evidence of the low level of regimentation within the scope of the concept of reciprocity.

The United States was not limited, however, to recounting the concessions it had made in the past and to exhortations in support of reciprocity. It began in 1939 to offer, and to refuse, loans and other forms of economic aid to the other American republics. It was this policy line, attacked as extravagant by Senator Butler, that raised the question whether Latin American collaboration in wartime had been dependent upon financial assistance from the United States. This was an implication that Latin Americans indignantly and nearly unanimously denied, and it does not appear that United States officials regarded the economic measures initiated at the Panama Conference in 1939 as more than supplementary to the measure of collaboration secured in consequence of their earlier policies. For example, Roosevelt wrote to the Secretary of the Navy:

Because markets for forty percent of the normal exports of Latin America have been lost due to the war, there is grave danger that in some of these countries economic and political deterioration may proceed to a point where defense of the Western Hemisphere would be rendered much more difficult and costly. In the interest of hemispheric solidarity and as Good Neighbors, the United States government must do what it reasonably can to prevent any such development.

He then suggested "priority of consideration" for Latin American sources of supply in buying materials abroad for the Navy.[30] It seems reasonable to conclude that the total course of policy followed by the United States since 1933 made it possible to minimize the political significance of financial aid to Latin America in 1939 and after.

In this connection and others throughout the course of the Good Neighbor policy, diplomats of all participating countries made every effort to avoid any suggestion of bargaining in their political relationships. "Reciprocity" and "mutual advantage" were the usual terms employed to suggest that each side expected negotiations to result in equality of sacrifices. Men who in trade agreements talks saw no difficulty in offering tit for tat, or rice for sugar, ostentatiously shied away from either admitting or claiming that compensation for expropriation was a possible price for nonintervention, or indeed, that any of their political moves were dependent on those of another state. The adoption of the policy of nonintervention by the United States made obsolete the respectable bow to *force majeure*, and regard for the principle of equality of states placed a premium on the avoidance of pressures or haggling in the political realm.[31] Consequently, ingenuity in the formulation of well-regarded general concepts became an essential part of reciprocal arrangements. The words "Monroe Doctrine," for example, almost disappeared from inter-American diplomatic usage in the 1930s, and even "Good Neighbor" was driven out of circulation as "continental solidarity" and "America" gained favor.[32] One political advantage of making these terms current was that governments were able to justify to their peoples and to the world at large actions that, otherwise open to criticism, could be upheld as contributions to the causes the concepts portrayed.

This is of course a partial, and perhaps a cynical, view of one of the most subtle and difficult of questions—the relationship of policy to ideology. A similar view, however, has been expressed by a former Assistant Secretary of State for Inter-American Affairs:

> We want good relations with our sister republics. We want to cooperate with them. We want peace and democracy and continental solidarity and due process of law and sovereign equality and mutual assistance against aggression. Amid such noble sentiments and overflowing good will my job ought to be easy—but it isn't. For these lovely phrases conceal but do not destroy a great many hard, ugly facts which make it difficult to attain our objectives in this hemisphere. . . .
> One of the difficulties of diplomacy is that in public we must generally deal in mellifluous phrases but in our work we must deal with hard facts.[33]

However, somewhere between the granitic fact and the honeyed phrase there must be, for each government, an amalgam of desires, fears, and estimates of capabilities that solidifies in the minds of one or a few men when a decision to take some form of action is reached. In any given case, a decision may appear to be capricious, but in many cases, over a period of time, recurrent themes or traces of consistency may be observed that permit both an ordering of facts and a judgment as to the relevance of that order to public protestations of intent. It is in this shadowy region that policy may be sought and sometimes discerned. In this sense we may regard policy as principled action, demonstrating in promise and in behavior over a period of time such evidence of continuity that assumptions of stability may with confidence be based upon it.

But how explicit are the assumptions on which policy actions are taken? When Jefferson Caffery retired, he was asked for a definition of "old-style diplomacy" of which he was reputed to be an examplar. His reply was: "Getting things done. That's about all it amounts to. How is it done? You just play it by ear." [34] In contrast, a retired British diplomat, Sir Ivone Kirkpatrick, asserts: "The art of diplomacy, like the art of war, has two ingredients. First comes the formulation of policy, which corresponds to the strategic plan; second comes the execution of that policy, corresponding to the conduct of battles by generals in the field." [35]

The foreign policy of the United States is not always quite so naive as Caffery suggests, nor does it appear that British policy is quite so sophisticated as Sir Ivone would have us believe, but the element of strategy in the Good Neighbor policy played a small role indeed until the summer of 1941. It was then, as involvement in the war progressed, that the threads of policy began to be woven into a coherent pattern, one that achieved its maximum balance and harmony with the Venezuelan oil settlement. It is difficult to overemphasize the importance of the Venezuelan settlement in theory, although it was easy to do so in practice because its significant implications were shielded in secrecy. Early appreciation of the potentialities of the dispute, close cooperation between the Department and the mission in Caracas, strong pressure upon the home offices of the oil companies, intimate relationships with Venezuelan officials—these and other factors combined to provide a model for emulation in comparable situations in time of peace if the vital importance of the dynamic initiative of the Department of State was to be fully appreciated.

It was during the course of the Venezuelan affair that the glimmering of some new policy ideas became visible. One of these was Welles's conviction that the utmost use should be made of the resources of consultation and common action by all of the American republics. The policy implications of this conviction are glimpsed in his response to Paley's views, as mentioned above, and, more clearly, in his insistence at the Rio de Janeiro Conference that no resolution on breaking diplomatic relations with the Axis should be adopted without the concurrence of Chile and Argentina.

Another and no less important idea is suggested by a sentence in Welles's letter to Roosevelt about the part played by Max Thornburg in the Venezuelan affair. He wrote:

It was of the highest importance to reach a settlement between the oil companies and the Venezuelan government . . . which would enable the companies to continue operating on a satisfactory basis at the same time that the government and people of the country would receive a more equitable share of the proceeds of the business.[36]

At about the same time, Welles expressed himself more explicitly in similar vein:

The last ten years of the Good Neighbor policy should have been convincing proof . . . that this government reflects in its foreign policy the objective of its domestic policy, namely, improvement in the standard of living in which all elements will participate, but particularly those heretofore ill-clothed, badly housed, and poorly fed.[37]

When it is recalled that in 1933 Welles had referred slightingly to "ignorant masses" as supporting the Grau San Martín government in Cuba, the above statements suggest a noteworthy shift of attitude on his part, even granting that, as an able advocate, Welles was in each case supporting a position to which he was already committed. Welles was here expressing policy ideas that are still being explored. To what extent is the improvement of the economic and social welfare of the peoples of other American countries a matter of interest to the government and people of the United States?

In this area of discourse, Welles was dealing with an idea that opened policy vistas far wider than the concept of reciprocity, whether the latter be regarded narrowly as a mere euphemism for bargaining or, more generously, as the expression of a helpful neighborliness.[38] The Good Neighbor policies, at least until 1939, were largely negative in the sense that they had constituted the discovery of the implications of nonintervention. They had made wartime cooperation possible, but they did not themselves provide ideas about the nature of such cooperation either during the war or after. Nevertheless, it was entirely consistent to move from nonintervention toward collaboration, so that the transition from the practices of mutual respect to those of mutual assistance was not a difficult one.

Welles, however, does not seem to have gone so far into policy implications of these ideas as did Roosevelt. The President, in 1940, told members of the National Conference of Business Paper Editors that when he had visited Rio de Janeiro in 1936, President Getulio Vargas had told him that the bus lines in the capital were owned in Montreal and Toronto, and had asked: "What would the people of New York City do if the subways were all owned in Canada?" Roosevelt's reply had been: "Why, there would be a revolution." The President went on to say that he thought that, when foreign capital went into a Latin American country, the country should gain control of the utility or other business after the investment had been paid off in a period that might be set at twenty-five or thirty years. Thus, the country could look forward to gaining ultimate control of utilities and perhaps other foreign-financed corporations through having what Roosevelt called "an option on the equity." The President concluded: "That is a new approach that I am talking about to these South American things. Give them a share. They think they are just as good as we are and many of them are." [39]

These suggestions were, of course, no more than hints of attitudes, but they indicated that the slant of thinking of the two men was toward a concern for the well-being of the people of Latin America, as distinct from an exclusive attention to relations among governments and corporations.

Evaluations of the Good Neighbor policies will depend on the points of view taken by different observers; these points of view are multifarious and no effort will be made here to assess them in comprehensive fashion. The range of judgment is wide. The Latin American response to Senator Butler's charges was generally favorable, and this judgment was, on the whole, echoed in the United States, where Latin American collaboration during the war was regarded as the satisfying test of policy. [40]

However, there are other criteria. "The 'Good Neighbour' policy of the United States in Latin America is not the antithesis, but the continuation and consequence, of 'Yankee Imperialism'; for it is only the strongest who can both maintain their supremacy and remain 'Good Neighbours.'" [41] This view would have seemed strange to Sumner Welles, who had once been surprised at charges that the United States government was "imperialistic" in seeking to arbitrate the oil controversy with Mexico. Could a great power not divest itself of "imperialism" by renouncing force, by permitting weaker states to make drastic modifications of the position of corporations owned by its citizens, and by bringing successful influence to bear on those corporations to accept financially disadvantageous changes in agreements formerly considered legally valid? In one sense, the answer to this question is in the negative, since political antipathy, whatever its origin, may be readily expressed through a term that is both rich in opprobrious connotations and possessed of a measure of historical justification. In another sense, however, it is at least of some theoretical interest to observe that a great power—a great capitalist power—in the course of two decades when it knew depression and prosperity, in a period when it felt both safe and, later, insecure, did not act in accord with mechanistic predictions of domination by "finance capital"; it behaved in ways peculiarly its own, curbed its finance capital, and experimented with a policy reliance on its neighbors' moderation and political judgment.

Even though intervention was given up in theory and in practice, the United States could not divest itself of its vast margin of political and economic power over any and all of its neighbors. Further, in many countries United States business enterprises were unaffected by expropriations elsewhere, and in these countries the policy of pacific protection did not have immediate or directly appreciated consequences. To the extent that "imperialism" was associated in Latin America, not with the presence of Marines, but with the presence of utilities, mines, and other enterprises owned by citizens of the United States, the Good Neighbor policies did not exorcise that enduring complex of attitudes. In a number of countries, the governments welcomed foreign enterprise, although in each of them there were opposition groups calling for various types of economic emancipation. The activity of these groups could be predicted to continue, and the policy of pacific protection would be tested again if they should obtain control of their governments.

Within the United States there were influential groups that did not approve of the policy of pacific protection, and the important problem of the role of private enterprise as affecting the foreign policy of the United States government in dealings with Latin American countries could be expected to reappear in various forms as these groups sought to reassert themselves in Washington. At the same time, there were other influential groups that took pride in the Good Neighbor policies as a whole because they felt that those policies provided a rare amalgam of moral elevation and political achievement. It was, presumably, this combination of peace with prizes that was largely responsible for the claims made by leaders in each major political party that their party should have credit for originating the Good Neighbor idea. If, however, the great power had some reason for satisfaction at gaining its essential policy goals at a critical period with the warm support of its neighbors, the responsiveness of the lesser powers should be recognized as essential to the relationship achieved at the beginning of World War II. By renouncing domination the United States had won a sympathy that accorded it wartime leadership acknowledged by nearly all the Latin American states. There would be new challenges to the policy and its future was not clear, but in its time it provided a promising demonstration of the desire of Americans to strive in good will to forget an often bitter past and, with mutual respect, to find amicable ways both to adjust differences of interest and to unite in furthering common aims.

Note on Sources

THE PRINCIPAL SOURCES on which this study is based are published and unpublished documents of the Department of State and documents in the Franklin D. Roosevelt Library.

Of published documents, the main collection is that entitled *Foreign Relations of the United States,* and documents in this collection have been cited wherever possible.

The author is indebted to the Committee on the Use of Departmental Records of the Department of State for the opportunity to consult unpublished documents. The Department of State did not restrict access to materials, but quotations from and citations to documents required the approval of the Department before use could be made of them in published form.

Such approval may be obtained in two ways by one who is interested in the study of what has been called "contemporary history." One way is to take notes on documents in verbatim or paraphrased form and to submit the notes for clearance by officers of the Department of State. A second way is to prepare a manuscript incorporating quotations from and citations to documents and to submit the manuscript for clearance.

In the present study the second method for securing clearance was followed. Either method, of course, involves restrictions on complete freedom in the use of source materials, but these restrictions must be accepted by those whose curiosities center about foreign policy developments within the past thirty years. Even so, students of the foreign policy of the United States are more favored than are those of most countries; in Great Britain the fifty-year rule is generally applied, and elsewhere, notably in Latin America, one is fortunate indeed to secure even limited access to foreign office documents in any period since 1830.

In presenting this manuscript to the Department of State for clearance there were included direct quotations from, and citations to, every document regarded as relevant to my primary concern for outlining the ideas that would illuminate what seemed to me to be significant aspects of the Good Neighbor policy. The Department of State requested that a substantial number of changes in the manuscript be made, and these suggestions were almost wholly concerned with two types of references. The first of these related to the naming of officials of foreign governments, and the second related to direct quotations of the texts of notes or other documents prepared by other governments or statements attributed to diplomats of foreign countries in memoranda of conversations made by officials of the Department of State. At no point were suggestions made for the modification of interpretations offered in the manuscript.

These requests seemed to me to be reasonable ones on the whole, particularly in view of my primary concern with the nature of policy ideas rather than with their specific sources, and I saw no difficulty in complying with them, even though some narrative color was thereby lost.

In some instances, the Department of State accepted my protests against its preliminary exclusion of references to certain documents, and in only one case where, in my view, a significant policy action by the United States required documentary support, did the Department refuse to allow citations to the relevant materials. In this case, it was suggested that other sources be found, either in published comments or in interviews, and, failing these, I was invited to speculate, an invitation that was accepted.

The files of the Department of State contain a large number of clippings from Latin American newspapers, and most of the citations from such papers made in this study derive from this source.

With regard to materials available in the Franklin D. Roosevelt Library, notes may be made freely and permission to publish quotations from them is generously approved. In one instance, at the suggestion of the Library, permission to quote was obtained from the author of a memorandum.

The memoirs of statesmen and diplomats of the United States are peculiarly barren insofar as they touch upon relations with Latin America since 1920, and little more can be said of their counterparts in the states of Latin America themselves. There is a fair number of diplomatic memoirs, but, with an occasional disgruntled exception, these are mostly of the "fair land between the mountains and the sea" variety; few of them contain serious critical and detailed discussions of policy problems. Latin American revolutions are rarely of the kind that give rise to the orderly publication of the diplomatic or other records of previous administrations, and political catastrophes, those founts of frank recrimination, were happily infrequent between the two World Wars.

Similarly, biographical studies have not provided substantial enlightenment in this period. In Latin America, the reputations of public men, and especially of diplomats, are more tenderly handled in formal published works than in the United States, and biographies of statesmen of the past two generations, other than eulogies, are not often written. This may be in part owing to the nonavailability of diplomatic and other official correspondence, but it seems also to be related to differing intensities of respect for personal dignity and family pride, and to varying concepts of the degree to which an individual's performance as office holder should be open to contemporary public scrutiny.

In the United States few biographical studies have been written that are relevant to inter-American affairs in the 1930s. The Hull papers are not yet fully available for research purposes, and the many books on Roosevelt and other figures understandably concentrate on issues of World War II that have little to do with Latin America. Further, since the Good Neighbor policy was generally regarded as both "good" and "successful" there has been little controversy about it in the United States; consequently efforts to understand it have not had the benefit of specialized documentary publications of a defensive or explanatory nature, such as *United States Relations with China* (Washington, D.C., Department of State, 1949).

There are, of course, exceptions to these general remarks, and two outstanding ones are Josephus Daniels's *Shirt-Sleeve Diplomat*, among memoirs, and E. David Cronon's *Josephus Daniels in Mexico*, among biographies, both of which have been extensively cited in the present study. These two books illustrate some interesting opportunities for diplomats and for scholars to give subtance and a sense of reality to relationships among the American states.

Abbreviations

DS   U.S. Department of State unpublished documents. E.g., 812. 6363/3337. 812 is the country number for Mexico; 6363 is the subject number for the oil expropriation; 3337 is the serial number for a specific document, to which may be attached other documents or papers, including newspaper clippings.

FDRL   Franklin D. Roosevelt Library, Hyde Park, New York.

FR   *Foreign Relations of the United States*, Washington, D.C., U.S. Government Printing Office, 1 to 5 vols. annually, at present, through 1939, for "The American Republics."

Notes

Introduction (*pages 3–10*)

1. Captain Harry Alanson Ellsworth, *One Hundred Eighty Landings of United States Marines, 1800–1934.* (Washington, 1934.) 2 vols., mimeographed, Library of the Department of the Navy. To the nineteen Caribbean landings listed in this work may be added the pursuit of Pancho Villa into Mexico by the United States Army in 1916.

2. Telegram 14 to the Commissioner in the Dominican Republic (Sumner Welles), April 8, 1924. FR, 1924, 300.

3. Referring to the Mexican oil dispute, Castle said: "In all this miserable story of despoliation the American Government still continues to turn the other cheek—until one wonders how many cheeks it has." Quoted in New York *Times*, December 8, 1938.

1. The Nicaraguan Experience (*pages 13–47*)

1. Henry L. Stimson, *American Policy in Nicaragua* (N.Y., Scribners, 1927).

2. Instruction to the Delegates to the Seventh International Conference of American States, Montevideo. FR, 1933, IV, 44.

3. The outlook of the Department of State is thus described in what may well have been an inspired article by John Carter in New York *Times*, February 20, 1927. Apart from treaties such as that with Panama concerning defense installations, "The actual interests of this country abroad . . . consist of our citizens, our trade and our investments. It is the duty of this country to protect its citizens in their just rights, wherever they may be. . . . In short, we claim that an American citizen has the right to his life, to his business, and to his property and that he should not be discriminated against by foreign powers or laws. This is the basic foreign policy of every nation and is the basis of our foreign affairs."

4. Quoted in New York *Times*, February 21, 1927. Official opinion, at least, would not have followed Borah's additional view that "it is not war between the great powers but spoliation of the weak nations which seems most vital and imminent in international affairs at this time."

5. For descriptions of the background and course of the revolution see, among others, *The United States and Nicaragua: A Survey of the Relations from 1909 to 1932*, Department of State, Latin American Series, No. 6 (Washington, U.S. Government Printing Office, 1932); Dana G. Munro, *The United States and the Caribbean Area* (Boston, World Peace Foundation, 1934); Isaac Joslin Cox, *Nicaragua and the United States, 1909–1927* (Boston, World Peace Foundation, 1927); Charles P. Howland, *Survey of American Foreign Relations* (New Haven, Yale University Press, 1929), pp. 167–98.

6. The Minister in Costa Rica (Roy T. Davis) to the Secretary of State, San José, October 29, 1926. Despatch 831, DS, 712.13/2. It may be noted that, to Jiménez and to the dictator Jorge Ubico in Guatemala, it was probably less the Mexican "savages" that worried them than the Mexican social revolutionaries that threatened to upset the old order in the Central American countries to the south. They turned to the United States for support, since the United States was at the time resisting the radical expressions of the Mexican revolution in so far as they affected the property of foreigners in Mexico.

7. Memorandum by Stokeley W. Morgan, assistant chief, Division of Latin American Affairs, December 2, 1926. DS, 817.00/4170. A Mexican historian has suggested that the Mexican government supported the Sacasa revolution by stating that President P. E. Calles "carried out a bold policy of counter-revolution in Nicaragua." Francisco Cuevas Cancino, *Roosevelt y la Buena Vecindad* (Mexico, Fondo de Cultura Económica, 1954), p. 163. This well-documented study has been based on extensive research in the Franklin D. Roosevelt Library.

8. Stimson, *American Policy in Nicaragua*, p. 26.

9. This term was used in a report that the "Mexican Minister financiered gun runner 'Tropical' that attempted to deliver arms and ammunition Nicaraguan rebels short time ago." The consul in Mazatlán, Mexico, to the Secretary of State, December 15, 1926. DS, 817.00/4258.

10. The Minister in Nicaragua (Charles C. Eberhardt) to the Secretary of State, Managua, December 13, 1926. Telegram 237. DS, 817.00/4243.

11. November 18, 1926.

12. *Literary Digest*, December 4, 1926, p. 14, and New York *Times*, January 4, 1927.

13. New York *Times*, February 3, 1927.

14. Opposition had become so strong by the first of the year that President Coolidge appealed to the press to support the position of his administration on the Nicaraguan situation; he called for " 'correct' representation of the situation—the 'American attitude,' he characterized it." New York *Times*, January 1, 1927. This appeal was generally ignored.

15. New York *Times*, January 5, 6, 7, 8, 11, 1927, and President

Coolidge's message to Congress, January 10, 1927. FR, 1927, III, 288–98.

16. Editorial, January 11, 1927. In this connection, see the article by Arthur Warner, "The Eagle and the Red Bird: A Fable," *The Nation*, January 26, 1927, pp. 86–87.

17. Quoted by New York *Times*, December 25, 1926. In an editorial on the 27th, the *Times* disagreed with Borah, but showed its concern by stating "that Mexico contemplates sending out military expeditions to dominate all Central America is too wild a supposition. . . . It is impossible to believe that President Coolidge would tolerate the thought of a 'little war.'" It should be noted, however, that the *Literary Digest*, December 4, 1926, quoted both the New York *Herald Tribune* and the Washington *Post* as seriously concerned about the danger to the Panama Canal from Bolshevism and Mexico.

18. Text in FR, 1927, III, 288–98.

19. The New York *Times*, January 11, 1927, stated editorially that, while Coolidge and Kellogg were "as far as possible from being Jingoes" and "they would never rush light-heartedly into war," nevertheless "in the statements which they have made and in the acts which they have ordered are evident the possibilities of unpleasant consequences." Similar views were repeated in this paper on January 12; Coolidge, it was said, "is the last man to imagine cherishing the thought of riding through slaughter to a throne."

20. Issues of the *Bulletin* of the National Council for Prevention of War, published during this period, contain a detailed account of the Council's activities. Correspondence and other related material may be found in the Council's files, in the Friends' Library, Swarthmore College.

21. Editorial, New York *Times*, January 16, 1927.

22. Quoted from text in New York *Times*, January 19, 1927. A few days before this statement, President Calles of Mexico had said he would be willing to submit the dispute to arbitration if that were necessary in order to avoid greater difficulties, although he had added: "We know from painful experience, and history confirms this, that arbitration courts adopt the viewpoints of the strong nations, which always dominate." Quoted in New York *Times*, January 20, 1927. Apparently acting on the Kellogg statement, the Mexican foreign minister announced on January 20 that his government accepted arbitration of the dispute in principle. *Ibid.*, January 21, 1927.

23. *Ibid.*, January 22, 1927.

24. It seemed to be thought at the time, and this may have been the case, that Coolidge's statement implied the maintenance of an intransigent attitude toward Mexico. However, in his speech of April 25, 1927, in which he still opposed arbitration because he did not desire any questioning of the principle that "property is not to be confiscated," he said he thought a settlement was more likely to be reached through negotiation. This last conciliatory note was missing from the comments he made in the January crisis.

25. Text in New York *Times*, January 26, 1927.

26. *Ibid.*, January 16, 1927. On the same day, former Secretary of

State Charles Evans Hughes was quoted as saying that the Latin American states were neighbors and should be treated in a neighborly fashion. On the 18th, the *Times* expressed pleasure that the Department of State was trying "at least by a new tone and less threatening gestures, to undo the mischief which apparently to its own surprise, it has discovered that it set brewing."

27. *Ibid.*, editorial, January 23, 1927.

28. *Daily News* (London), and *Times* (London), as quoted in New York *Times*, January 12, 1927. The *Times* stated, presumably in reply to the New York *Times*'s editorial of December 29: "The United States may not be willing to be numbered among the 'imperialist' nations, but their pioneers of commerce have created American interests in neighboring undeveloped countries whose natural resources offer profitable markets to the overflow of national wealth."

29. The Chargé in Argentina (P. L. Cable) to the Secretary of State. Buenos Aires, January 14, 1927. Telegram 7. DS, 817.00/4413.

30. New York *Times*, January 23, 1927. For expressions of opinion in support of the administration, see the *Literary Digest*, January 22, 1927. See also the New York *Times* editorial, January 26, 1927, stating that "resentment" created by our government in Latin America "might easily tip the balance in favor of European exporters," for "there is such a thing as sentiment even in international business." The United States should deal in a "prudent and conciliatory spirit" with the Latin American states, for "even if we cannot escape feeling in our own hearts vastly superior to them, it is neither wise nor profitable to treat them as if they were acknowledged inferiors."

31. Morrow's instructions were only "to keep us out of war with Mexico." Quoted in Harold Nicolson, *Dwight Morrow* (N.Y., Harcourt, Brace, 1935), pp. 313–14.

32. Stimson, *American Policy in Nicaragua*, p. 42. This action was taken despite earlier reports that criticism from Congress "seems to have made President Coolidge set his jaws upon a more determined policy with reference to Nicaragua." R. V. Oulahan in New York *Times*, February 22, 1927.

33. Stimson, *American Policy in Nicaragua*, p. 43.

34. Telegram 105, from Managua, April 20, 1927. FR, 1927, III, 324.

35. Telegram 107, from Managua, April 23, 1927. *Ibid.*, III, 327.

36. For the details of these negotiations, see Stimson, *American Policy in Nicaragua*, Chap. II, and FR, 1927, III. On May 4, 1927 at his conference with General Moncada "under a large blackthorn tree" at Tipitapa, Stimson found it necessary to state in writing that the completion of his term by President Díaz "will be insisted upon" by the United States. The New York *Times* (Editorial, May 9, 1927), did not believe that Stimson threatened to make war on the Liberals in Nicaragua during the Tipitapa negotiations; it did, however, consider that the administration by "awkward words and still more awkward actions" had "sowed a crop of dislike and suspicion of the United States throughout all Central and South America." Uncle Sam did not think of himself as an imperialist, "but too

many South Americans do. He knows that his own intentions are excellent; he feels that his heart is kind; he only wishes that the Spanish-Americans, confound them, would understand him and love him. But they do not. The fault is partly his—a fault largely of blundering method."

37. Telegram 10, to Santo Domingo, February 26, 1930. FR, 1930, II, 704.

38. Memorandum quoting Woodward's report, January 27, 1933. FR, 1932, V, 832.

39. One measure, inconclusive but suggestive, of the importance of Nicaraguan affairs in this period, is given by the fact that in *Foreign Relations*, 1927–32, 883 pages are devoted to Nicaragua, while only 494 are given over to relations with Mexico.

40. Stimson's own conclusions about his early Nicaraguan experience should not be omitted from this summary: "To Stimson himself the big lesson of his Nicaraguan experience was a simple one: if a man was frank and friendly, and if he treated them as the equals they most certainly were, he could talk turkey with the politicians and other leaders of Latin America as he could with his own American colleagues. And they would not let him down." Henry L. Stimson and McGeorge Bundy, *On Active Service in Peace and War* (N.Y., Harpers, 1947), p. 116.

41. Instruction 127, to Managua, February 15, 1924. FR, 1924, II, 488.

42. Instruction 102, to Managua, October 8, 1923. FR, 1923, II, 608.

43. The New York *Times*, for example (Editorial, April 9, 1927), was pleased with this move, because if successful it would "refute the charge, so widely echoed in South America and in Europe, that the sending of our marines to Nicaragua was a sinister development of 'American Imperialism.'"

44. Stimson, *American Policy in Nicaragua*, pp. 112ff. This revival of the Roosevelt Corollary is of especial interest because, when the British government sent the cruiser "Colombo" to Corinto to guarantee the safety of British nationals in Nicaragua, this action was not regarded in Washington "as a step in contravention of the Monroe Doctrine nor, in fact, in opposition to American policy in Central America." New York *Times*, February 25, 1927. This record of the Washington opinion of the time was apparently forgotten by R. V. Oulahan later when he reported that the "Colombo's" visit "gave impetus to the United States intervention in Nicaragua." *Ibid.*, April 18, 1931.

45. Stimson, *American Policy in Nicaragua*, pp. 117–18. See also the article by Dana G. Munro, "American Intervention in the Caribbean," *Current History*, September, 1927, pp. 857–61. Munro declared that no Secretary of State could free himself from responsibility because the influence of the United States "even if it is not consciously exercised, is always a dominant factor in the affairs of small Caribbean countries. . . . It is obviously better that our tremendous moral influence should be consciously and intelligently directed than that we should attempt or pretend to close our eyes to its existence."

46. It is worthy of note that it was in this same speech that Coolidge expressed sympathy with Mexican desires to break up large landholdings, and said that "it will surely be possible to reach an amicable adjustment"

in the Mexican controversy. Text in New York *Times*, April 26, 1927.

47. *American Policy in Nicaragua*, p. 129. For a sample of the bitterness of attacks on the administration see Senator Henrik Shipstead, " 'Dollar Diplomacy' in Latin America," *Current History*, September, 1927, pp. 882–87.

48. For a brief historical account see Dana G. Munro, *The United States and the Caribbean Area*, Student ed. (Boston, World Peace Foundation, 1934), pp. 227–75.

49. Telegram 381, from Managua, December 22, 1927. FR, 1927, III, 388.

50. Telegram 105, from Managua, March 2, 1928. FR, 1928, III, 472. In the final vote, which was 24 to 18 against passage, it turned out that Cuadra Pasos had not succeeded in changing more than two votes.

51. Telegram 119, from Managua, March 14, 1928. FR, 1928, III, 477.

52. Telegrams 93, 96, from Managua, April 8, 11, 1929. FR, 1929, III, 590–91. When the Nicaraguan minister in Washington told Stimson that in the case of one arrest, Moncada did not feel that he could interfere "in view of the separation of the executive and judicial functions under the Constitution," Stimson stated that "Presidential action was not called for but perhaps a Presidential whisper would be sufficient." Memorandum of conversation, May 2, 1929. *Ibid.*, III, 594.

53. Instruction 591, to Managua, November 9, 1929. FR, 1929, III, 605.

54. *Ibid.*, 1929. III, 601–7.

55. Instruction 108, to Managua, January 3, 1931. FR, 1930, III, 708. In justifying this second deportation order, Moncada implied in a message to Congress that the United States was to blame for his fear of being assassinated. He asserted that his political opponents, who could not "for fear of the North American cooperation . . . resort to civil war to attain power, think on occasions of another shorter and more decisive method." Despatch 270, from Managua, December 16, 1930. *Ibid.*, III, 703. This suggests that Nicaraguan devotion to the ballot box was not, as Stimson apparently assumed, the necessary consequence of the prevention of revolutionary disturbances. It should be recognized that Moncada was not entirely without provocation by the Conservatives, for there was a long tradition of political violence in Nicaragua, and Emiliano Chamorro, one of the Conservative leaders, was publicly named by Moncada as being a "habitual revolutionist." Telegram 241, from Managua, October 1, 1929. FR, 1929, III, 600.

56. Instruction 583, to Managua, October 29, 1929. FR, 1929, III, 604.

57. The Department maintained that objections to the constitutionality of the proposed law were "absolutely untenable as a proposition of constitutional law." Telegram 10, to Managua, January 10, 1928. FR, 1928, III, 418–20.

58. Telegram 58, to Managua, June 27, 1930. FR, 1930, III, 640.

59. Letter to Stimson, January 22, 1932. FR, 1932, V, 768.

60. Telegram 216, to Managua, December 6, 1927. FR, 1927, III, 385. Munro was authorized to express these views to Díaz.

61. Telegram 36, from Managua, January 20, 1928. FR, 1928, III, 442.

62. Telegram 114, to Managua, May 18, 1928. *Ibid.*, III, 492. Kellogg instructed Eberhardt: "You should make it plain that the Conservatives are expected to get together and solve their own difficulties in their own way." Telegram 117, to Managua, May 22, 1928. *Ibid.*, III, 493.

63. Telegram 100, to Managua, October 5, 1932. FR, 1932, V, 826–28.

64. Telegram 226, to Managua, December 22, 1928. FR, 1928, III, 522.

65. For example, that appointments of some provincial party chiefs were within the powers of General Moncada, according to the Tipitapa agreement, but not appointments of police officers or collectors of internal revenue. Telegram 142, from Managua, May 31, 1927. FR, 1927, III, 399. Similarly, a Conservative judge was "removed at the Legation's request," after he had ordered 348 Liberals imprisoned as a means of disfranchising them. Telegram 98, from Managua, February 28, 1928. FR, 1928, III, 567.

66. After a raid on a mine and a pitched battle with an outpost of Marines and "Guardia" at Ocotal in Nueva Segovia province, Kellogg wired Eberhardt that the Department and the public were "much disturbed" by reports of fighting in Nicaragua, particularly since "the Department has been led to believe that armed opposition to the present program would speedily disappear, and that it need anticipate no serious complications on this account." Telegram 117, to Managua, July 27, 1927. FR, 1927, III, 442.

67. Address by Walter C. Thurston, chief, Division of Latin American Affairs, to the American Academy of Political and Social Science, Philadelphia, April 18, 1931. Press release, April 17, 1931.

68. *Ibid.*

69. Telegrams 336 and 388, from Managua, November 17, December 26, 1927. FR, 1927, III, 450, 451. Chamorro might have been aiding "Conservative bandits" as well.

70. *Ibid.*

71. Telegram 41, to Tegucigalpa, December 28, 1927. FR, 1927, III, 452.

72. Instruction 305, to Tegucigalpa, and Telegram 58 in reply, July 1, 10, 1932. FR, 1932, V, 926–29. In making this suggestion the Department may have recalled that in 1928 "secret advance permission was obtained" from Mejía Colindres's predecessor, President Paz, for an attack "by Marine airplanes on Sandino's encampment a few miles above the mouth of the Patuca river, far within Honduran territory." Despatch 579, from Tegucigalpa, July 30, 1932. *Ibid.*, V, 932.

73. Despatch 579, from Tegucigalpa, July 30, 1932. FR, 1932, V, 931–36.

74. Despatch 599, from Tegucigalpa, and Telegram 40 in reply, August 19, September 2, 1932. FR, 1932, V, 937, 939. Lay said that he had told Mejía Colindres that it was difficult for him to understand how arms stolen from the arsenals could be obtained by Sandino, and he commented: "This observation seemed to impress the President," who said he would try to intercept a truckload of rifles that Lay was able to inform him was near the town of Danlí.

75. Despatch 1008, from Managua, May 24, 1929, and Telegram 85,

to Managua, June 10, 1929. FR, 1929, III, 568–69, 574–75. Stimson did not change his position even when Hanna brought the cost down to $25,000 a month, and reported that General Dion Williams of the Marines believed that it would be "in the interest of economy" for the United States itself to construct certain roads, both because present transport costs were high, and because it would have a pacifying effect "by giving work to unemployed, many of whom are potential bandits." Telegram 160, from Managua, June 12, 1929. *Ibid.*, III, 576.

76. Telegram 19, from Managua, and Telegram 13, in reply, January 11, 13, 1928. FR, 1928, III, 560, 561.

77. Telegram 8, from Managua, January 15, 1930. FR, 1931, II, 861. Beaulac later reported that Moncada agreed with the Department as to the "inefficiency of the courts" in Nicaragua. However, it would be unconstitutional to try bandits by civil courts under martial law, as Moncada had once proposed to the Supreme Court. Despatch 1290, from Managua, January 21, 1930. *Ibid.*, II, 863. Beaulac made some efforts to encourage Moncada to bring about an appropriate amendment to the constitution, but the project bogged down, and the Department finally admitted defeat on this point. Despatch 511, from Managua, and Instruction 245, in reply, September 24 and October 12, 1931. FR, 1931, II, 571–73.

78. Memorandum from General D. C. McDougal, commander of the "Guardia," to Beaulac, Managua, January 18, 1930. FR, 1931, II, 864–65.

79. When the Sandino "campaign" began, the New York *Times* (Editorial, July 20, 1927), commented that the plans of the administration had miscarried and expectations had been frustrated; "the lot of an international policeman on foreign soil is distinctly not a happy one. . . . Exactly the kind of thing has happened which Republicans charged upon President Wilson in 1920."

80. Early in 1929, Moncada told Hanna that he realized the Marines had to operate under limitations that kept them from "adopting measures which might be resorted to if Nicaraguan forces under the command of Nicaraguan officers were responsible for the character of the operations." Moncada said he felt that Nicaraguan troops, with lighter equipment, knowledge of the country, "greater endurance under the special conditions," and for other reasons, were better adapted for close pursuit of bandits during the rainy season than were the Marines. Despatch 1008, from Managua, May 24, 1929. FR, 1929, III, 567.

81. Telegram 202, from Managua, November 23, 1931. FR, 1931, II, 825.

82. Telegram 12, from Managua, January 14, 1931. *Ibid.*, II, 836–37.

83. Despatch 1008, from Managua, May 24, 1929. FR, 1929, III, 568.

84. Memorandum by General McDougal, January 18, 1930, cited in FR, 1931, II, 864.

85. Memorandum, May 6, 1929. FR, 1929, III, 564–66.

86. Telegram 200, from Managua, July 23, 1929. FR, 1929, III, 577–78. A series of bandit raids in the north in November caused "considerable apprehension among the foreign and native coffee growers" near Mata-

galpa, no more than 80 airline miles from Managua. Despatch 1246, from Managua, December 6, 1929. *Ibid.*, III, 580.

87. Telegram 80, to Managua, April 16, 1931. FR, 1931, II, 808. Stimson here expressed dissatisfaction with the inability of the Guardia to send forces quickly to the east coast and complained that the appearance of bandits in areas they had not previously entered showed "a serious lack in the leadership of the Guardia."

88. Text in Telegram 81, to Managua, April 16, 1931. FR, 1931, II, 808.

89. Cf. his contradictory, privately expressed view above, note 87.

90. Stimson added: "The events of this last week have pretty thoroughly torn the mask off the character of the mythical patriot Sandino." FR, 1931, II, 814–16.

91. Memorandum of the press conference, Wednesday, April 15, 1931. DS, 817.00 Bandit Activities, 1931/55. A correspondent had raised the issue by quoting Admiral Pratt as saying that "the Navy did not consider it its job to protect property," but that it was engaged only in protecting lives and preparing for evacuation.

92. Stimson may have had in mind the possible inconsistency of the use of Marines in Nicaragua with the terms of the Kellogg-Briand Pact; such inconsistency had been alleged to exist by Latin American newspapers as early as 1929.

93. Quoted in Stimson's diary, April 15, 1931, Stimson and Bundy, *On Active Service in Peace and War*, p. 182. "Our recent policy with respect to Nicaragua was one which merely faced the facts of the difficulties of attempting to extend physical protection to Americans in the interior of a country in disorder." Statement by Thurston in conversation with a United States businessman, Memorandum, April 22, 1931. DS, 817.00 Bandit Activities. 1931/129.

94. Statement in Chicago *Tribune*, May 8, 1914, quoted in E. David Cronon, *Josephus Daniels in Mexico* (Madison, Wis., University of Wisconsin Press, 1960), p. 11.

95. New York *Times*, April 18, 1931.

96. Despatch from Washington, and Department of State press release, New York *Times*, April 19, 1931.

97. Editorial, April 20, 1931. Cf. *The Times* (London), April 21, 1931: "A reversal of the methods and theories of the Coolidge period is under way," although Stimson "was under the polite obligation to justify the change without implied criticism of the Coolidge Administration and its adventure in coercive intervention in 1926–27"; an action that "deceived nobody." The New York *Herald Tribune*, April 18, 1931, said that "Americans . . . would resent and indignantly reject any abandonment of the historic policy of protecting American lives abroad," thus challenging the Department's assertions of continuity in policy. *El Universal*, (Mexico City) regarded the Stimson doctrine as a policy reversal and hailed Sandino as deserving credit for bringing it about and demonstrating that "it is not always extreme repression which gives results in dealing with a nation such as Nicaragua." Quoted in New York *Times*, April 18, 1931.

98. Text of statement issued on February 13, 1931 in FR, 1931, II, 844–45. Stimson's hopes, expressed here, for the reduction of the Marines to five hundred by June, 1931 were not carried out because of the east coast raids in April.

99. This opinion was independently shared by certain Latin American observers. Nemesio García Naranjo, the New York correspondent of *La Nación* (Buenos Aires), May 12, 1931, remarked that when the last Marines left Central America their co-citizens would begin to live in peace in Nicaragua. He noted that United States citizens had not been molested in the recent revolutions in Peru, Argentina, and Brazil. "The best protection that Washington can offer its citizens abroad is to withdraw its troops from the nations they have invaded." Similar views were expressed by the *Panama American*, May 7, 1931.

100. Letter to Stimson from W. J. Hawkins, June 10, 1931. DS, 817.00 Bandit Activities of 1931/171. It is worthy of note that a similar claim that less, rather than more, protection for foreign settlers resulted from attempts by Marines to suppress banditry, had been made by Dugal McPhail, a British manager of a sugar plantation in the Dominican Republic during the United States occupation of that country. This claim was the subject of an energetic counter-argument by Secretary Hughes. FR, 1924, I, 686–91.

101. New York *Times*, April 18, 1928. By the spring of 1931 over one hundred Marines had lost their lives in Nicaragua. *Ibid.*, April 26, 1931.

102. Letter from the Assistant Secretary of State, Francis White, to the Chargé in Managua, Willard L. Beaulac, March 30, 1932. FR, 1932, V, 795.

103. Telegram 49, to Managua, May 24, 1932. FR, 1932, V, 802.

104. Memorandum of electoral organization plans, April 29, 1932. FR, 1932, V, 799.

105. Diary, March 7, 1932, quoted in Stimson and Bundy, *On Active Service in Peace and War*, p. 182.

106. Telegram 225, from Managua, September 3, 1927. FR, 1927, III, 446. Sandino was reported at that time to be "an erratic Nicaraguan about 30 years of age with wild Communist ideas acquired largely in Mexico." Telegram 175, from Managua, July 20, 1927. *Ibid.*, III, 441.

107. Memorandum, November 16, 1931. DS, 711.17/253.

108. Press release, January 2, 1933. FR, 1933, V, 848–49.

II. The Cuban Experience I (pages 48–80)

1. Sumner Welles, *Relations Between the United States and Cuba*, Department of State, Latin American Series, No. 7 (Washington, U.S. Government Printing Office, 1934), p. 6. As early as 1928, the Chargé in Cuba reported that President Gerardo Machado y Morales had "developed into a Latin-American dictator of a type not far removed from the worst." Despatch 474, from Havana, October 29, 1928. DS, 837.00/2714.

2. William M. Malloy, *Treaties, Conventions, International Acts,*

Protocols and Agreements between the United States of America and Other Powers (Washington, D.C., Government Printing Office, 1910), I, 364.

3. Memorandum of conference by the Secretary of State with the press on October 2, 1930. Quoted in FR, 1930, II, 663.

4. Telegram to Havana, June 14, 1912. FR, 1912, pp. 265–66.

5. Despatch 1970, from Havana, April 16, 1927. DS, 837.00/2646.

6. Memorandum by Stokeley W. Morgan, chief of the Division of Latin American Affairs, April 11, 1927, quoted in undated memorandum by Laurence Duggan, about December, 1935. DS, 837.011/128.

7. Memorandum of conversation, April 23, 1927. FR, 1927, II, 527.

8. Memorandum by Laurence Duggan, see above, note 6.

9. Colonel Carlos Mendieta, leader of the National Union party, suggested to Ambassador Harry F. Guggenheim that in view of what he believed would be a serious situation, the United States should "intervene in Cuban affairs to restore constitutional government." The ambassador rejected this suggestion, and also a proposal that he should mediate between the opposition parties and Machado, "so that Cuba might regain her lost political liberties they believe the United States had an obligation to protect." Despatch 221, from Havana, May 28, 1930. DS, 837.00/2808.

10. Letter from Acting Secretary of State Joseph P. Cotton to Senator Burton K. Wheeler, March 5, 1930. DS, 837.00/2791.

11. "In Cuba Stimson repeatedly refused to intervene under the Platt Amendment; whatever the need for such intervention in the past, he believed that 'the situation in Cuba ought to so develop that less and less pressure would be necessary on the part of the United States to keep matters straight.' (Diary, September 18, 1930)." Stimson, Henry L. and McGeorge Bundy, *On Active Service in Peace and War* (N.Y., Harpers, 1947), p. 183.

12. It may be noted, however, that Knox had stated that "in case intervention becomes necessary . . . the United States will be at liberty in the event of intervention to take such steps as may be appropriate and necessary to undo and redress any wrongs which the Cuban people may have suffered at the hands of the Cuban Government." Despatch 123, to Havana, August 15, 1912. FR, 1912, 315.

13. See, for example, Carleton Beals, *The Crime of Cuba* (Philadelphia, Lippincott, 1933), for a bitter attack on Stimson and Guggenheim.

14. Despatch 337, from Havana, August 15, 1930, and copy of attached letter from Pacheco of December 30, 1929. DS, 837.00/2825.

15. Telegram 38, from Havana, February 13, 1931. FR, 1931, II, 47–48.

16. Memoranda, February 20, March 26, 1931. DS, 837.00/2990, and 837.00/3016–1/2.

17. Memorandum of conversation, written by Francis White, approved by Stimson. FR, 1931, II, 51–54.

18. Letter from the Secretary of State to the Postmaster General, July 5, 1932. DS, 837.00/3454.

19. Memorandum of conversation, October 27, 1932. DS, 837.00/3382.

20. Telegram 1, from Havana, January 5, 1933. FR, 1933, V, 270.

21. Despatch 1532, from Havana, February 28, 1933. *Ibid.*, V, 273.

22. Memorandum of conversation, January 10, 1933. FR, 1933, V, 272. See also FR, 1932, V, 559–60, for similar protests to Ferrara, then Secretary of State.

23. *The Memoirs of Cordell Hull* (N.Y., Macmillan, 1948), I, 308.

24. Instruction 1 to the appointed ambassador in Cuba (Welles), Washington, May 1, 1933. FR, 1933, V, 279–86.

25. *The Memoirs of Cordell Hull*, I, 309, 312–13. Hull quotes a letter from Josephus Daniels, the ambassador in Mexico, as stating that he was cheered to hear Hull's voice on the phone, saying: "I would rather walk from here to the South Pole than to have to intervene." *Ibid.*, p. 316.

26. Letter, January 20, 1928. FDRL, Group 14.

27. *Foreign Affairs*, July, 1931, pp. 551–52. This article was written by Davis at Roosevelt's request, following receipt of a letter from Welles criticizing Stimson's defense of his policies. Letter to Welles, February 23, 1931, in *F.D.R., His Personal Letters, 1928–1945*, I, 177.

28. Memorandum for the President from Hull, May 27, 1933. FDRL.

29. Press conference No. 28, June 9, 1933. FDRL.

30. Letter, June 9, 1933. FDRL, OF 470. On June 24 he again wrote Welles to say that he was "proud" of Welles's accomplishments in Havana, but because of the European situation, he had done nothing more than read Welles's despatches "and dismiss them from my mind for the very good reason that you seemed to be getting the situation under control and to have the confidence of the people who count." FDRL, OF 470.

31. FR, 1933, V, 325ff, and Department of State, Press release, No. 166, July 28, 1933.

32. Details of the negotiations are set forth in FR, 1933, V, 287–334.

33. Telegram 129, from Havana, August 7, 1933. FR, 1933, V, 336–37.

34. FR, 1933, V, 323–35, 338. It is not entirely clear whether Roosevelt realized that Welles had threatened Machado with intervention, although the general character of Welles's policy had been faithfully reported.

35. Telegram 133, from Havana, August 8, 1933. FR, 1933, V, 339–40.

36. Telegram 66, to Havana, August 9, 1933. FR, 1933, V, 347–48; and Press conference No. 42. FDRL.

37. Welles's new role did not go unremarked at the time. *El Nacional* (Mexico City), August 13, 1933, said: "Our good wishes would go to the Cuban people with the deep emotion of those who regard the liberation of a sister country as a personal cause for rejoicing did we not see in the center of the revolutionary movement under discussion the decisive influence of a foreign ambassador: Mr. Sumner Welles, first, as a mediator between the belligerent parties and later as an arbiter of the political destinies of Cuba." The paper added: "In view of the activities of Mr. Welles in Cuba, it is necessary to await the development of future events to give force to the 'good neighbor' policy nobly announced by President Roosevelt."

38. Telegrams 134, 135, from Havana, August 8, 9, 1933. FR, 1933, V, 340–45.

39. Telegram 70, to Havana, August 11, 1933. *Ibid.*, V, 354.

40. Telegram 69, to Havana, August 10, 1933. *Ibid.*, V, 352–53; and memorandum of conversation, August 10, 1933. DS, 837.00/3628.

41. Quoted in Telegram 69, to Havana, August 10, 1933. FR, 1933, V, 353.

42. Telegram 149, from Havana, August 11, 1933, 3 P.M., received in Washington 8:35 P.M. *Ibid.*, V, 355–56.

43. Telegram 150, from Havana, August 11, 1933, 8 P.M., received in Washington 11:40 P.M. *Ibid.*, V, 356–57.

44. Telegram 152, from Havana, August 12, 1933. *Ibid.*, V, 358–59. Welles cleared this arrangement with Assistant Secretary of State Jefferson Caffery, and asked for permission to "enter into official relations with the new government" immediately on Céspedes's assumption of office.

45. Telegram 73, to Havana, August 12, 1933. *Ibid.*, V, 360.

46. Telegram 152, from Havana, August 12, 1933. *Ibid.*, V, 359.

47. Ramón Padilla, Mexican chargé, inquired of Laurence Duggan "whether it was true that Mr. Welles had asked for President Machado's resignation." Duggan replied that Welles, "as mediator had transmitted to President Machado a proposal supported by the Conservative and Popular parties, as well as by prominent leaders in the Liberal party, which Mr. Welles considered a fair and just solution, and that the President felt that he could accept only part of the proposal." Memorandum of conservation, August 10, 1933. DS, 837.00/3713.

48. Telegram 152, August 12, 1933. FR, 1933, V, 358–59.

49. Telegram 69, from Havana, June 2, 1933. *Ibid.*, V, 299.

50. Telegram 129, from Havana, August 7, 1933. *Ibid.*, V, 336.

51. Letter from Machado, Montreal, September 5, 1933, and reply by Roosevelt, drafted in the Department of State, September 26, 1933. FDRL, OF 159.

52. Arthur Krock, New York *Times*, August 17, 1933.

53. Telegram 149, from Havana, August 11, 1933. FR, 1933, V, 356.

54. *Ibid.*

55. New York *Times*, August 13, 1933.

56. The first of these terms, perhaps a slightly embarrassing one, was used along with "fine skill" by Arthur Krock, in praising Welles as having "manoeuvered Machado out of office," New York *Times*, August 17, 1933. The second appeared in a laudatory editorial in the New York *Herald Tribune*, August 14, 1933.

57. New York *Times*, August 13, 1933, reported that relieved State Department officials said that Welles at forty-one had "brought off a difficult job with the aplomb of a veteran"; his "success" was of the kind "rarely falling to the lot of a young diplomat." Washington had been so concerned over the apparent impasse between Welles and Machado that plans for a military occupation had reportedly been made by "army and

navy chiefs." However, the defection of the Cuban army showed that Welles's "efforts had borne more fruit than was realized" in Washington.

58. Telegram 172, from Havana, August 19, 1933. FR, 1933, V, 367–69. Welles also wished to return to Washington to help make plans for United States participation in the Montevideo Conference of American states.

59. Telegram 77, to Havana, August 21, 1933. *Ibid.*, V, 369.

60. It might also be suggested that his sense of the future was close to the uncanny, since he wished it announced immediately that he would leave Cuba about September 1. However, there seems to be no sufficient reason to believe that he calculated that the Céspedes government would have a short period of life.

61. Telegram 158, from Havana, August 14, 1933, 3 A.M. FR, 1933, V, 363. It appears that Welles requested the despatch of the destroyers. Hull told correspondents at a news conference that it had been felt that the risk of "conditions of anarchy" was too great to be run without "a little sobering influence" represented by the "moral effect" of the destroyers. Memorandum of the press conference, Monday, August 14, 1933. DS, 837.00/3661. Concerning the usefulness of sending warships, the memorandum of the press conference, September 7, 1933, reported: "In order to throw a little sidelight on the psychology of the situation, the Secretary said that there had been no disorders at Santiago since the arrival of the destroyer 'Sturtevant.' As soon as this little vessel dropped anchor at Santiago, the people came to the realization that if they should plunge into anarchy the vessel was there to cooperate with the law-abiding elements, as far as the lives and safety of Americans are concerned." DS, 837.00/3931.

62. Telegram 175, from Havana, August 20, 1933. DS, 837.00/3685.

63. Telegram 192, from Havana, September 5, 1933. FR, 1933, V, 381–83.

64. Telegram 195, from Havana, September 5, 1933. *Ibid.*, V, 384.

65. Text of this conversation of September 5, 1933, in FR, 1933, V, 385–86.

66. Memorandum of telephone conversation, September 5, 1933. *Ibid.*, V, 386–87.

67. Memorandum of telephone conversation, September 6, 1933. *Ibid.*, V, 389–90.

68. *The Secret Diary of Harold L. Ickes: The First Thousand Days, 1933–1936* (N.Y., Simon & Schuster, 1954), p. 87. Ickes notes that Roosevelt had earlier forbidden the Navy to land Marines or sailors to protect property only. Ickes's own position was that "even if there should accidentally be a loss of one or two American lives, still we should not intervene." (p. 93)

69. Telegram 206, from Havana, September 7, 1933. FR, 1933, V, 396–98.

70. *The Memoirs of Cordell Hull*, I, 315.

71. Telegram 90, to Havana, September 7, 1933. FR, 1933, V, 402.

72. Telegram 209, from Havana, September 7, 1933. *Ibid.*, V, 400–1.

73. Telegram 216, from Havana, September 8, 1933. *Ibid.*, V, 405–7.

74. Telegram 224, from Havana, September 10, 1933. *Ibid.*, V, 417–18.

75. In view of the subsequent conduct of the army under Batista, there was an element of exaggeration in Welles's description of it as "absolutely disorganized and demoralized" on September 8. He said the majority was "anxious to find any peaceful way out of the situation they have created for themselves," and "another group . . . in close touch with Communist leaders in Habana may resort to desperate measures if they become sufficiently drunk." Telegram 214, from Havana, September 8, 1933. *Ibid.*, V, 403–4.

76. Memorandum of the press conference, September 6, 1933. DS, 837.00/3859. A week later, speaking of warships sent to various Cuban ports, Hull said that the only test of whether they should be withdrawn was "whether American lives are liable on the shortest possible notice to become imminently in danger. If this test is applied, it can then be determined to what extent we should try to have a small vessel available somewhere to exercise ordinary diligence on our part. Not to do so would subject us to the condemnation of the public for being grossly negligent, if through a sudden outbreak a number of lives should be lost." Memorandum of the press conference, September 14, 1933. DS, 837.00/3948.

77. Telegram 261, from Havana, September 15, 1933. DS, 837.00/3896.

78. Memorandum of telephone conversation, September 22, 1933. DS, 837.00/4043. Welles replied that Hull's view was also that of the resident sugar managers, but that people with shorter experience in Cuba took a more alarmist position. However, Welles had earlier transmitted without comment a statement by the Board of Directors of the American Chamber of Commerce in Cuba that declared there had been a collapse of agencies of peace and order; that some property of United States citizens had already been destroyed; that the communist element was the best organized group in Cuba; and that the United States government should take "such steps as are necessary to protect American lives and property and maintain order, and further that these steps be taken immediately and be decisive." Telegram 196, from Havana, September 5, 1933. DS, 837.00/3755.

79. Telegram 330, from Havana, October 2, 1933. FR, 1933, V, 463.

80. *La Mañana* (Montevideo), September 8, 1933, commented: "It is certain that the mobilization of thirty ships of war around the Island could be interpreted as a measure of excessive prudence."

81. Press conferences, September 8, 13, 1933. FDRL.

82. New York *Times*, October 4, 1933.   83. See above, note 61.

84. Memorandum of the Press conference, September 6, 1933. DS, 837.00/3859. Later, Hull said that "naturally we could not keep our vessels anchored in our own ports until anarchy broke out and with just a sergeant, wholly inexperienced in government, in chief command of everything on the island. We knew that, because of this, anarchy was all the more possible and that, if we kept our vessels at anchor in home ports until this condition actually occurred, we would then have been

censured for not having taken reasonable precautions that would enable us on very short notice to safeguard the lives of our nationals." Memorandum of the Press conference, September 7, 1933. DS, 837.00/3931.

85. One, and perhaps the only, exception to this statement was the charge made by a prominent Argentine senator during the brief period when Welles stayed at the National Hotel at the same time as ousted Cuban army officers, that this was evidence of the desire of the United States to bring about intervention. Asked about this by reporters, Hull retorted that "this is part of all those fantastic and absurd rumors and suspicions that are picked up, peddled out, repeated, and seized upon, sometimes even by credulous statesmen." Memorandum of the Press conference, September 11, 1933. DS, 837.00/3965.

86. Memorandum written by Roosevelt aboard the yacht "Nourmahal," 8:30 A.M., September 5, 1933. DS, 837.00/3762. Italics in original.

87. Memorandum of the Press conference, September 8, 1933. DS, 837.00/3932.

88. Memorandum, September 8, 1933. DS, 837.00/3930. The only other action by a Navy officer appears to have been the granting of an interview by Admiral Charles S. Freeman to Havana journalists, in which he said that, so far as he could see, peace and quiet prevailed in the city. Welles cabled the Department of State that he preferred that interviews should be given only by himself; otherwise statements made by persons not having complete information would only complicate the situation. Telegram 243, from Havana, September 12, 1933. DS, 837.00/3849. At about the same time, Welles himself had emphasized to Washington the "possibilities of danger" in Havana due to "an absolutely disorganized and demoralized army of some 2,000 men." Telegram 214, from Havana, September 8, 1933. FR, 1933, V, 403.

89. Telephone conversation between Hull and Welles, October 2, 1933. DS, 837.00/4171. At the time of the November revolt, the "Wyoming" was given similar orders. Telegram 444, from Havana, November 9, 1933. DS, 837.00/4364.

90. Memorandum of telephone conversation between Welles and Hull, September 9, 1933. DS, 837.00/3939.

91. Telegram 356, from Havana, October 12, 1933. DS, 837.00/4187.

III. The Cuban Experience II *(pages 81–117)*

1. Memorandum of telephone conversation, September 6, 1933. FR, 1933, V, 390.

2. Telegram 202, from Havana, September 6, 1933. *Ibid.*, V, 392.

3. Telegram 233, from Havana, September 11, 1933. *Ibid.*, V, 423.

4. Circular telegram from Hull, September 11, 1933. *Ibid.*, V, 422.

5. Memorandum of telephone conversation, September 8, 1933. *Ibid.*, V, 410.

6. Telegram 96, to Havana, September 11, 1933. *Ibid.*, V, 424.

7. Telegram 224, from Havana, September 10, 1933. *Ibid.*, V, 417.

8. New York *Times*, September 17, 1933.

9. Telegram 5, from Havana, January 10, 1934. FR, 1934, V, 95.

10. Telegram 86, from Havana, March 14, 1934. DS, 837.00/4929. Similarly, Russell Porter had earlier written that, besides the army, "only the radical ABC's, other small radical secret societies, some independent professional men, some radical University of Havana professors and the lowest economic and social groups support the government." New York *Times*, September 28, 1933.

11. *Relations Between the United States and Cuba*, Department of State, Latin American Series, No. 7 (Washington, U.S. Government Printing Office, 1934), p. 10.

12. Quoted in interview in New York *Times*, September 22, 1933.

13. Memorandum of the press conference, September 7, 1933. DS, 837.00/3931.

14. Memorandum of telephone conversation, September 16, 1933. FR, 1933, V, 439–40.

15. Press conference, September 27, 1933. FDRL. Roosevelt's press conferences were only infrequently the occasions for serious discussion of Latin American affairs; the transcripts of these conferences, however, in the absence of memoranda of his talks with Hull and Welles which unfortunately seem never to have been made, are one of the principal pieces of evidence available of his informal and private opinions.

16. Memorandum of telephone conversation, October 2, 1933. DS, 837.00/4171.

17. Telegram 216, from Havana, September 8, 1933. FR, 1933, V, 406.

18. Quoted in New York *Times*, September 22, 1933.

19. Telegram 340, from Havana, October 4, 1933. FR, 1933, V, 469–72.

20. Telegram 113, to Havana, October 5, 1933. *Ibid.*, V, 472. Hull also referred here to a memorandum received from "the Cuban representative" in Washington. This message asserted that the National Hotel affray showed that the Grau government "disposes of sufficient force to maintain its authority," stated that cabinet changes were to be made, and offered other evidence designed to make a case for recognition. Memorandum, October 4, 1933. DS, 837.00/4162.

21. See above, p. 82; and Telegram 341, from Havana, October 5, and Telegram 117, to Havana, October 10, 1933. FR, 1933, V, 473–74, 482.

22. Telegram 367, from Havana, October 16, 1933. *Ibid.*, V, 487–91. By this time, only Mexico, Uruguay, and Panama of the Latin American states, had recognized the Grau regime. Argentina proposed joint recognition to Brazil, but the government in Rio de Janeiro had rejected the proposal. *Ibid.*, V, 491.

23. Response to a questionnaire submitted to Grau by Russell Porter, New York *Times*, October 29, 1933. The charge of intervention was also made to the Montevideo Conference by Angel Alberto Giraudy, but the Cuban delegate spoke at an inopportune moment, and the Latin American delegates were apparently more impressed by Giraudy's lack of diplomatic finesse than by the nature of his allegations.

24. Telegrams 366 and 393, from Havana, October 16, 24, 1933. DS, 837.00/4204, and 837.00/4268.

25. Telegram 392, from Havana, October 24, 1933. FR, 1933, V, 498.
26. Telegram 376, from Havana, October 19, 1933. DS, 837.00/4235. See also Welles's account of an earlier occasion when Grau announced at a meeting with opposition representatives that he intended to resign. When Grau started to rise after making this statement, "Escalona, one of the leaders of the students who was standing behind him forced him back into his chair by physical force and told him that he was going to remain as President as long as the students desired him to, whether he wished to or not. Varona, another of the student leaders, was so incensed by Grau San Martín's statement that he showed his displeasure by breaking several pieces of furniture in the room where they were sitting." Telegram 279, from Havana, September 19, 1933. FR, 1933, V, 449.
27. Telegram 273, from Havana, September 17, 1933. *Ibid.*, V, 446.
28. Telegram 410, from Havana, October 29, 1933. *Ibid.*, V, 502.
29. Telegrams 431 and 455, from Havana, November 6, 13, 1933. *Ibid.*, V, 515, 520–21. It appears that no record of this telephone talk with Phillips on November 6 was kept in the Department. Shortly before leaving for his talk with Roosevelt, Welles reported that he had been visited by representatives of several Cuban real estate, engineering, and business groups, who had told him that "under no conditions" should recognition be given to Grau. All of them said that "none of the productive interests of Cuba, upon which the business life of Cuba depends, had or could have confidence in the stability or policy of the present government and that recognition . . . 'would prolong the agony of the Cuban people.' " Telegram 468, from Havana, November 17, 1933. DS, 837.01/44.
30. Telegram 439, from Havana, November 8, 1933. DS, 837.00/4352.
31. President Grau announced in Havana on November 17 that he had asked President Roosevelt to replace Welles, whose "presence in Cuba tends to maintain conspiracy, fratricidal warfare, and public disorders which greatly injure American business interests here." New York *Times*, November 18, 1933. However, "the White House emphatically denied [November 17] that any request had been received from the Cuban Government for the withdrawal of Sumner Welles."
32. Telegram from Acting Secretary of State Phillips to President Roosevelt, November 23, 1933. FR, 1933, V, 525–26.
33. Roosevelt's announcement was praised by the New York *Times*, November 25, 1933, which also lauded "prudence and tact" of Welles, who, "in the swift procession of unexpected events, by no fault of his own and largely as the result of propaganda and myth . . . became *persona non grata* to the Grau San Martín regime." On the next day, the New York *Herald Tribune* also supported the President's statement, although with some reluctance, while criticizing Welles and the previous course of policy toward Cuba.
34. Press conference, November 24, 1933. FDRL.
35. Telegram 475, from Havana, November 21, 1933. DS, 837.00/4436. Ambassador Hugh Gibson reported that Brazil had been under pressure from other Latin American governments to recognize, but it had not

done so in deference to United States policy. Telegram 116, from Rio de Janeiro, November 24, 1933. DS, 837.00/4449. The Department of State had received word that the British government planned to recognize Grau in the near future. Memorandum of conversation, November 23, 1933. DS, 837.00/4473. The Italian minister in Cuba told Welles that he had advised Rome that "there was no possible basis" for recognizing Grau's regime and that he understood that London, Paris, and Rome all intended to follow the lead of the United States, although the British minister in Cuba had recommended recognition. Telegram 488, from Havana, December 2, 1933. FR, 1933, V, 529.

36. Telegram 24, to Secretary Hull, on board SS. "American Legion," November 28, 1933. FR, 1933, V, 527–28.

37. Telegram 341, from Havana, October 5, 1933. *Ibid.*, V, 474.

38. Speech at fifth meeting of the Second Committee, December 19, 1933. *Seventh International Conference of American States, Minutes and Antecedents* (Montevideo, 1933), pp. 111–12.

39. Speech, December 6, 1937, in the Atheneum of Arts and Sciences of Mexico. Despatch 6009, from Mexico City, January 18, 1938. DS, 710. Peace. Non-Intervention/22. It should be noted that Sumner Welles's formal public account of his mission in Cuba offers interpretations that differ at some points from those presented above. See *The Time for Decision* (N.Y., Harper, 1944), pp. 193–200.

40. Telegram 517, from Havana, December 14, 1933. FR, 1933, V, 541–43.

41. Despatch 278, from Havana, December 28, 1933. DS, 837.00/4571.

42. Telegram 527, from Havana, December 21, 1933. FR, 1933, V, 544.

43. Report of a conversation with a Foreign Office official, Telegram 7, from London, January 6, 1934. DS, 837.01/60.

44. Telegram 4, from Havana, January 6, and Instruction 6, to Havana, January 8, 1934. DS, 837.01/59.

45. Roberto Esquenazi Mayo, "Cuba en la VII Conferencia Panamericana," *Revista Bimestre Cubana*, July–December, 1949, pp. 42–43. Hull had apparently asked Portell Vilá to call, in the hope of persuading him not to attack the United States in a speech on the following day. Portell Vilá refused to change his prepared text.

46. Telegram 9, from Havana, January 13, 1934. FR, 1934, V, 97.

47. "After four months Sergeant Colonel Fulgencio Batista, who headed Grau's military backers, saw that it was hopeless for Cuba, whose life depended on a restored sugar market in the United States, to buck our disapproval. He dislodged Grau and substituted a conservative president whom the United States immediately recognized." Laurence Duggan, *The Americas: The Search for Hemispheric Security* (N.Y., Holt, 1949), p. 62. Hull says merely that, during his return to Washington from Montevideo, the Grau government "had faded out." *The Memoirs of Cordell Hull*, I, 342. A one-time member of the Student Directorate later charged that the Grau government had fallen because Batista deserted it and came to terms with Caffery and Mendieta. Interview with José Antonio Rubio Padilla in *La Opinión* (Santiago, Chile), February 12, 1934. Russell Porter

said that Grau's fall "followed the realization that [he] could never get recognition from the United States," and he noted that January 15 was the date "Cubans generally had set as the deadline on which the political situation had to be settled if Cuba was to be able to make a sugar crop this winter." New York *Times,* January 17, 1934.

48. Telegram 5, from Havana, January 10, 1934. FR, 1934, V, 95–96.

49. Telegrams 9 and 12, from Havana, January 13, 14, 1934. *Ibid.,* V, 97–98.

50. Quoted in Telegram 12, to Havana, January 14, 1934. *Ibid.,* V, 100. Caffery replied: "Of course the President's position is understood. I made the suggestion regarding Mendieta in view of his well-known vacillating tendency and reluctance to assume responsibility." Telegram 20, from Havana, January 15, 1934. *Ibid.,* V, 100.

51. Interview published in *El País-Información* (Havana), November 8, 1934. Grau also stated that his principal difference of opinion with Batista had resulted from his attempts to prevent Batista from engaging in conversations at the United States Embassy.

52. Support for Machado is not, however, entirely lacking; a junior member of his civilian staff has written an account of Machado's fall, in which the author charges that Welles was directly responsible for the revolt of the army against Machado on August 11. Alberto Lamar Schweyer, *Como Cayó El Presidente Machado,* 2d ed. (Havana, Montalvo Cárdenas, 1934).

53. Telegram 36, from Havana, January 17, 1934. FR, 1934, V, 103. Caffery had previously cabled that, despite the opposition of the navy, "Batista would probably be prepared to go ahead with Mendieta if I recommend it, but I do not feel that I can do so partly because Mendieta desires definite previous assurance from us which we cannot give." Telegram 21, from Havana, January 15, 1934. *Ibid.,* V, 101.

54. As Caffery reported at one o'clock in the morning on January 18, everything was ready for Mendieta to become President: "The plan (if he does not back out) is for all matters connected with the transmission of powers to be handled exclusively by civilians, no military to participate." Telegram 42, from Havana, January 18, 1934. *Ibid.,* V, 104.

55. Telegram 49, from Havana, January 18, 1934. *Ibid.,* V, 105.

56. Memorandum of the press conference, January 18, 1934. DS, 837.00/4699.

57. Telegram from U.S.S. "Richmond," January 19, 1934. DS, 837.00/4645.

58. Telegram 60, from Havana, January 22, 1934. FR, 1934, V, 106. Hull states that, after the talk with Caffery, he cabled Roosevelt in support of recognizing Mendieta. *The Memoirs of Cordell Hull,* I, 342.

59. Roosevelt was reported to have said to the diplomats: "Our information indicated that the Mendieta government was maintaining order and performing the normal functions of government, and that it enjoyed the support of the great majority of the Cuban people and of the organized political groups; that in view of this situation we intended to recognize Mendieta tomorrow afternoon or Wednesday morning." Memorandum

from E. C. Wilson to Welles, January 22, 1934. DS, 837.01/77. It may be noted that Roosevelt's phrases were very similar to those regularly used by Welles.

60. Department of State Press release 225, January 27, 1934. Laurence Duggan states that "Latin Americans remarked that the new regime had less 'popular support' than Grau, whatever support it may have had among the landowning and commercial classes." *The Americas*, p. 62.

61. Memorandum of the press conference, January 22, 1934. DS, 837.00/4703.

62. *Excelsior* (Mexico City), January 25, 1934. *El Universal* (Mexico City), January 26, 1934, also commented caustically on the timing of the recognition of Mendieta and declared that United States policy was not in accord with that of the "good neighbor" and so had given strength to Latin American suspicions that no great change in Washington's Latin American policy had taken place.

63. "While recognition alone would greatly strengthen the hand of the new President [Mendieta], his ability to maintain his post, it is admitted in official circles, will depend in the long run largely on the negotiation of favorable treatment in United States markets for Cuban sugar and tobacco." New York *Times*, January 19, 1934.

64. Telegram 64, from Havana, January 23, 1934, and Telegram 16, to Havana, January 23, 1934. DS, 837.00/4670.

65. Despatch 434, from Havana, February 1, 1934. DS, 837.00/4730. A month later, when the Navy Department suggested the desirability of the withdrawal of the "Richmond," Caffery took the view that it was not necessary to keep a large ship in Havana indefinitely, "but, in view of the existing communistic menace here," he did not wish to fix any definite date for the cruiser's departure. He also desired that a force of Marines should be maintained not farther away than Florida until the "Richmond" left. Despatch 18, from Havana, March 5, 1934. DS, 837.00/4881.

66. Telegram 111, from Havana, February 5, 1934. DS, 837.00/4736.

67. Quoted in Havana *Post*, February 4, 1934.

68. Department of State Press release, June 30, 1934.

69. Russell H. Fitzgibbon, *Cuba and the United States, 1900–1935* (Menasha, Wis., Banta, 1935), p. 201.

70. Telegram 86, from Havana, March 14, 1934. DS, 837.00/4929.

71. Two weeks later, Caffery countered the charge that Mendieta was doing nothing constructive by cabling that the charge was unfair, since the government "has had to fight for its very existence against the united elements of disorder, from its inception up to within about ten days ago." Despatch 173, from Havana, March 31, 1934. DS, 837.00/4962.

72. Despatch 1559, from Havana, October 11, 1934. DS, 837.00/5577. Batista concerned himself mainly with army affairs and allowed the civil authorities to carry on normal governmental activities, although, as Caffery stated, "of course it remains a fact that no government, this or any other, could last a day if opposed by Batista." Despatch 181, from Havana, April 2, 1934. DS, 837.00/4964. Among Cubans of the "better classes" Caffery found a disposition to feel that the only solution to the situation

was for Batista to become a military dictator. "I, of course, state with equal
frankness that that is out of the question and impossible." These Cubans,
he added, were usually the same people who shortly before "were denouncing Batista as a bandit and a scoundrel." Despatch 732, from Havana,
June 25, 1934. DS, 837.00/5196.

73. Telegram 38, from Havana, March 7, 1935. DS, 837.00/6123.

74. Telegram 49, from Havana, March 10, 1935. DS, 837.00/6142.

75. Letter, October 26, 1935. DS, 837.00/6635. An example of an unsympathetic attitude toward policy in Cuba was given by an editorial in
the New York *Post*, May 16, 1936. Hull formally denied press reports that
the United States was "showing undue interest in the internal affairs of
Cuba," since the policy toward Cuba "is naturally absolutely impartial,
without any preference or prejudice toward any particular electoral candidate, political group, or party." He added that, if the United States had
had any intention of interfering in Cuba, "such a course might have been
considered" when the Platt Amendment had been removed. Press conference, December 30, 1935. DS, 837.00/6988.

76. Despatch 209, from Havana, April 7, 1934. DS, 837.00/4984.

77. This invitation was held by *La Prensa* (Buenos Aires), December
14, 1935, to be an "error" since the question of electoral procedure was not
a proper one for the use of foreign experts, and since it gave some basis for
charges by at least one Cuban party (the Auténticos) that the government was under the influence of the United States.

78. Telegram 78, from Lima, May 31, 1934. DS, 711.3711/6.

79. Hull recalls that Welles made "an earnest plea to be allowed the
privilege" of signing the treaty. Hull agreed that they would both sign,
since Welles had "taken a considerable part in the negotiations." *The
Memoirs of Cordell Hull*, I, 343.

80. Despatch 7825, from Havana, December 16, 1936. DS, 837.00/7759.

81. Memorandum, December 19, 1936. DS, 837.00/7770.

82. Telegram 74, to Havana, December 19, 1936. DS, 837.00/7770/B.

83. Telegram 51, from Havana, December 20, 1936. DS, 837.00/7769.

84. Memorandum of conversations, December 21, 1936. DS, 837.00/-
7787.

85. Telegram 53, from Havana, December 21, 1936. DS, 837.00/7774.

86. Batista's victory was interpreted by J. D. Phillips as evidence that
"the military clique is convinced that the United States Government dare
not intervene in any manner in Cuban affairs for fear of endangering the
Good Neighbor policy, and it is a fact on which they have gambled in
their fight for supremacy and power." New York *Times*, December 27,
1936.

87. Telegram 64, from Havana, December 28, 1936. DS, 837.00/7800.

88. Despatch 1062, from Havana, September 2, 1938. DS, 837.00/8304.
Beaulac also said that "we could take no step that might possibly be construed as interference in the internal politics in Cuba."

89. Memorandum of conversation, September 9, 1938. DS, 837.00/-
8313-1/2.

90. Despatch 1291, from Havana, November 2, 1938. DS, 837.00/8348.

91. As reported by R. Hart Phillips in New York *Times*, November 26, 1938.

92. *Ibid.*, November 30, 1938.

IV. Origins of the Good Neighbor Policy (pages 118–35)

1. Quoted in *Report of the Delegates of the United States of America to the Seventh International Conference of American States, Montevideo, Uruguay, December 3–26, 1933*, Department of State, Conference Series No. 19 (Washington, U.S. Government Printing Office, 1934), pp. 18–19.

2. *Ultimas Noticias* (Mexico City), December 15, 1936.

3. Memorandum given to Ambassador Daniels by Mexican Foreign Minister J. M. Puig Casauranc, October 6, 1933. DS, 710.G.1A/220.

4. *El Nacional* (Mexico City), June 3, 1936.

5. *La Nación* (Buenos Aires), December 24, 1936. This editorial added: "Those states of another continent [Europe] who live in constant anxiety will not fail to note the superb spectacle of the Americas, upholding the predominance of justice over force, the incompatibility of civilization with war, and the condemnation of war as a crime."

6. Hull gives little importance to this protocol, saying merely that "The conference implemented and somewhat strengthened the agreement we had reached at Montevideo in 1933 to refrain from intervening in the internal or external affairs of one another, by adding to it an agreement to consult among ourselves in the event of such intervention." *The Memoirs of Cordell Hull* (N.Y., Macmillan, 1948), I, 500.

7. *El Nacional* (Mexico City), February 8, 1937. Castillo Nájera quoted from a speech by Ramón Beteta, who stated: "And how could the members of the Mexican Delegation likewise fail to be proud and grateful for the unanimous and enthusiastic approval accorded by this Assembly to the additional Protocol of Non-Intervention, which Mexico proposed and which crystallizes ambitions and hopes of many years and evidences the sovereignty and the equality of all the peoples of America?"

8. Below, p. 221.

9. *Ultimas Noticias* (Mexico City), December 15, 1936, called the role of the Mexican delegation "brilliant."

10. *La Prensa* (Buenos Aires), December 23, 1936.

11. "Convention for the Maintenance, Preservation and Reestablishment of Peace," December 23, 1936, in *Report of the Delegation of the United States of America to the Inter-American Conference for the Maintenance of Peace, Buenos Aires, Argentina, December 1–23, 1936* (Washington, U.S. Government Printing Office, 1937), pp. 116–24.

12. "Declaration of the Principles of the Solidarity of America," December 24, 1938, in *Report of the Delegation of the United States of America to the Eighth International Conference of American States, 1938* (Washington, U.S. Government Printing Office, 1941), pp. 189–90.

13. "Hail Argentina," *Hoy* (Mexico City), January 14, 1939.

14. *The Memoirs of Herbert Hoover: the Cabinet and the Presidency,*

1920–1933 (N.Y., Macmillan, 1952), p. 334. Herbert Hoover, Jr., shortly after becoming Under Secretary of State in 1954, took the occasion of a visit to Brazil to say: "My father first enunciated the Good Neighbor policy when he visited South America in 1928." Department of State Press release No. 661, November 20, 1954.

15. On Hughes, his biographer entitles a chapter on Latin American policy "The Friendly Neighbor," quotes Hughes as employing the word "neighbors" in a speech, and claims that the Roosevelt-Welles policies toward Latin America were largely due to Welles's having worked in the Department of State under Hughes during the Harding administration. Merlo J. Pusey, *Charles Evans Hughes* (N.Y., Macmillan, 1951), II, 530–32.

16. This was "the first mention of 'Good Neighbor' in American relations," of which Hunter Miller, historical adviser to the Department of State, was aware in 1937. Memorandum to Sumner Welles, August 25, 1937. DS, 710.11/2154. On this point, see the comment in *Correio da Manha* (Rio de Janeiro), December 12, 1943, that Roosevelt had created by effective action, a "solid confidence" that was not previously achieved by the "protocolary cordiality" voiced by Elihu Root and Herbert Hoover in their references to the idea of the "good neighbor."

17. Alexander DeConde, *Herbert Hoover's Latin-American Policy* (Stanford, Calif., Stanford University Press, 1951), pp. 125–26. Further: "Hoover even before he was inaugurated applied the good neighbor ideal specifically to Latin America, whereas Roosevelt appropriated the same concept and gave it world-wide application. *As such things happen*, the term has become popularly associated with Roosevelt and inter-American relations" (p. 127). Italics added.

18. Julius W. Pratt, *A History of United States Foreign Policy* (N.Y., Prentice-Hall, 1933), p. 7.

19. Arthur P. Whitaker, *The Western Hemisphere Idea: its Rise and Decline* (Ithaca, N.Y., Cornell University Press, 1954), p. 135.

20. Samuel Flagg Bemis, *The Latin American Policy of the United States* (N.Y., Harcourt, Brace, 1943), p. 221.

21. For a balanced, pro-Rooseveltian view of the origins of the policy, see Francisco Cuevas Cancino, *Roosevelt y la Buena Vecindad* (Mexico, Fondo de Cultura Económica, 1954), pp. 159–62. See also Edward O. Guerrant, *Roosevelt's Good Neighbor Policy* (Albuquerque, N.M., University of New Mexico Press, 1950), and Sumner Welles, *The Time for Decision* (N.Y., Harper, 1944), in which it is asserted that Hoover failed to gain understanding and good will in Latin America because it was "scarcely possible" for people there "to believe that the policy of a President of the United States, who had served for eight years in the preceding cabinets, would be different from the policies of his predecessors" (p. 190).

22. Hoover's own statement, quoted in DeConde, *Herbert Hoover's Latin-American Policy*, p. 14. DeConde states that "Hoover saw the trip as a means of taking the first step in what was to be a reorientation of policy toward Latin America."

23. The Buenos Aires *Herald,* December 18, 1928, commented: "Our visitor's simplicity of manner, the total absence of 'side,' though with no lapse of personal dignity, and his unfailing tact on all occasions have made a decided impression on the Argentine."

24. Telegram 41, to Buenos Aires, December 21, 1928. DS, 033.1110. Hoover, Herbert/279.

25. Telegram 99, from Buenos Aires, December 22, 1928. DS, 033.1110. Hoover, Herbert/280.

26. Ambassador Henry P. Fletcher, who was with Hoover's party, cabled that Irigoyen had mentioned intervention to Hoover and that Hoover had replied that "the United States has no policy of intervention, but merely the policy of protecting the lives and property of its citizens from violence when unfortunate local conditions make this unfavorable." When Irigoyen asked if Hoover disagreed with Coolidge's policy, Hoover "replied emphatically that he did not disagree with it." Telegram from U.S.S. "Utah," December 22, 1928. DS, 033.1110. Hoover, Herbert/282.

27. Quoted in Hoover, *Memoirs,* p. 213. Italics in original.

28. *Ibid.,* p. 333. Italics in original. For Hoover's own statement of the "seven things" he did in respect to Latin America, see *ibid.,* p. 334.

29. *The Memoirs of Cordell Hull,* I, 308. Looking back, the editor of *El Mercurio* (Santiago, Chile), March 10, 1934, expressed pleasure at the "increase every day of confidence and faith in the United States in contrast with the profound animosity which existed when Mr. Roosevelt became President." Sumner Welles goes further than Hull: "It is an obvious fact that after four years of the Hoover Administration there was no country of the Western Hemisphere where the United States was, in even the most superficial sense of the word, regarded as a Good Neighbor." *The Time for Decision* (N.Y., Harper, 1944), pp. 190–91.

30. See for example the article by Julio Caro in *Revista del Banco de la República* (Bogotá), April 1933, which stated that "we have seen the termination of the administration of President Hoover, with sentiments of admiration and gratitude toward him." Especial appreciation was voiced for the "support" of the United States in Colombia's dispute with Peru over Leticia.

31. The Chargé in Chile expressed confidence that "the recent modifications in our Latin American practices with respect to recognition, intervention, and protection of nationals" have caused "thinking people" to realize "that we are sincerely endeavoring to remove as many irritants as possible from our Latin American diplomacy." Despatch 878, from Santiago, June 3, 1931. DS, 710.11/1639. See also the article by Gastón Nerval in *El Nuevo Diario* (Caracas), August 15, 1931. This well known critic of United States policy wrote: "A fundamental change in the policy of the United States toward Latin America is being brought about by President Hoover's administration. The new policy adopted in Nicaragua is a definitive proof of this change. . . . Those who took Hoover's visit to South America as the 'stepping stone' for Pan American understanding were not mistaken."

32. C. Bauer Aviles in *Nuestro Diario* (Guatemala City), January 22, 1935. This view was not that of the Republican party, as expressed by Hoover's remark that he asked Congress for "an official commission to examine the situation in Haiti and advise when and how we were to withdraw—in effect, how to extricate ourselves from the mess into which we had been plunged by the Wilson administration." *Memoirs*, p. 333. Compare the comment in *Diario del Plata* (Montevideo), November 29, 1928, that Latin American sympathies had been with the Democratic party in the 1928 election because the policy of President Coolidge "has justly made even the name of the Republican party of the United States hateful to Latin Americans." This paper considered that Hoover's visit could not dissipate "the invincible resistance which the policy of his predecessor has engendered in the soul of all America." Quoted in unnumbered Despatch from the Minister in Uruguay to the Secertary of State, Montevideo, December 15, 1928. DS, 033.1110. Hoover, Herbert/ 337.

33. It should be noted, however, that there was also recognition in Latin America that Wilson's idealism had not prevented him from intervening in Latin American countries. *La Razón* (Buenos Aires), November 4, 1936, commented that Roosevelt's policy after 1933 was a personal one and not necessarily that of the Democratic party, since Wilson, a "theorist and idealist," had intervened in Mexico and had also on more than one occasion adopted "severe measures" against the states of the Caribbean.

34. *La Prensa* (Buenos Aires), June 8, 1936, commented that the tariff policies of the Harding, Coolidge, and Hoover administrations had acquired a "prohibitionist" character. *El Cronista* (Tegucigalpa), November 21, 1936, charged that Hoover had made "insincere promises" during his good-will visit to that country, which had not been followed up by deeds.

35. January 25, 1928. FDRL, Group 14.

36. *Foreign Affairs*, July, 1928, pp. 573–86.

37. The original typescript of this document is not signed or initialed by Roosevelt, but it contains the notation by Stephen Early: "Dictated by the President for me. S.E." It is dated May 17, 1942. This statement was sent to Wallace on May 19. Wallace did not use any part of the text dictated by Roosevelt in his speech on June 8. See text of speech, which contains commonplace mellifluities about the Good Neighbor policy, in *The Churchman*, June 15, 1942, pp. 13–14. A part of the text of this statement appears in Spanish, in Cuevas Cancino, *Roosevelt y la Buena Vecindad*, pp. 45, 58. FDRL (PSF) Box 37, Henry A. Wallace folder.

38. *The Memoirs of Cordell Hull*, I, 308–10. Hull admits that Secretary Stimson had taken "two or three steps" toward "fair treatment of other American nations," one of which was the withdrawal of Marines from Nicaragua in January, 1933, but says that these steps were unfortunately not enough to "impress Latin America in our favor."

39. "Immediately after the Havana Conference, President Hoover inaugurated an era of better comprehension and cooperation between the

United States and Latin America." "La Conférence panaméricaine pour la consolidation de la paix et le nouveau Panaméricanisme," *Revue de Droit International et de Législation Comparée*, 1937, No. 4, p. 508.

40. Memorandum of conversation, November 7, 1945. DS, 710.11/11-745. Mr. Braden in this conversation said that the policy had actually started even before 1928.

41. See, for example, *Diario de la Marina* (Havana), July 19, 1936, which declared editorially that "Roosevelt changed the political direction of the United States, and an atmosphere of inter-American fraternity spread throughout the continent. Imperialist arms were converted into commercial agreements, and the tariffs of the United States were generously reduced to the advantage of all America." For a French comment, see *L'Action Française*, December 28, 1936. J. Delebecque declared that Hoover's tour in 1928 had failed to dissipate Latin American resentment, but Roosevelt's policies "far from weakening United States prestige, had the result of consolidating it, and assuring it . . . of gaining the precious sympathy in Latin America which had previously been withheld." In this fashion, Roosevelt had put an end to constant frictions and may well have "better served the general interests of his country" even at the cost of doing some damage to "private interests."

V. The Policy of Noninterference (pages 136–55)

1. The degree to which this statement may be considered too sweeping will be considered in Part Three.

2. Department of State, Press release, January 2, 1933. FR, 1933, V, 848–49. For text of the agreement on the Guardia, see FR, 1932, V, 887.

3. Instruction 7, December 28, 1933. FR, 1933, V, 849–51.

4. Shortly after the murder, Somoza admitted to Lane that the officers responsible had "acted under orders." Telegram 65, from Managua, February 23, 1934. FR, 1934, V, 535.

5. *Ibid.*, and Despatch 933, July 16, 1935. FR, 1935, IV, 866. At the time Lane reported that "Since the events of last night, however, I have less confidence in his [Somoza's] assurances than formerly." Telegram 58, from Managua, February 22, 1934. FR, 1934, V, 532. Lane also stated that Somoza "had even gone so far in Granada as to admit responsibility for the assassination of Sandino." Despatch 933, July 16, 1935. FR, 1935, IV, 865.

6. Telegram 65, from Managua, February 23, 1934. FR, 1934, V, 535.

7. See Despatch 273, from Managua, June 14, 1934. FR, 1934, V, 555. The charges that Washington favored the Guardia as against the government were based on the following points: (1) the Guardia was created by the United States; (2) Lane's close association with Somoza; (3) official silence in Washington on recognition policy; (4) the feeling that the "elimination" of Sandino had the approval of the United States government; (5) conspiratorial assumptions about Lane's having lunched with General Moncada on February 21, 1934. FR, 1934, V, 542 and 555.

8. Despatch 829, from Managua, May 14, 1935. FR, 1935, V, 858–59.

9. The Department of State entirely approved Lane's rejection of concerted diplomatic action. Instructions 256 and 266, May 13, 31, 1935. *Ibid.*, V, 855, 862.

10. See above, p. 139.

11. Telegrams, from Managua, March 21, 1934, and from Washington, March 22, 1934. FR, 1934, V, 549–50. Rather than having misunderstood Hull, Argüello was probably just making one more attempt to induce the Department to favor a reorganization.

12. Despatch 147, from Managua, March 26, 1934. FR, 1934, V, 550.

13. Despatch 192, from Managua, May 4, and Instruction 78, May 21, 1934. FR, 1934, V, 554.

14. Telegram 29, from Managua, April 25, 1935. FR, 1935, IV, 851–53. On this occasion Lane reported that he had spoken to Somoza "personally as a friend," but had intimated that violent action on Somoza's part would be "distasteful" to the United States. He considered that his "good offices on behalf of peace and the constituted authorities was justified and necessary."

15. Instruction 256, May 13, 1935. FR, 1935, IV, 854–55.

16. Memorandum of conversation, October 1, 1935. FR, 1935, IV, 877–79.

17. Memorandum of conversation, October 16, 1935. FR, 1935, IV, 885.

18. Telegram 83, from Managua, September 26, 1935. FR, 1935, IV, 873.

19. Despatch 561, from San Salvador, January 21, 1936. FR, 1936, V, 126.

20. Telegrams 18 and 19, from Managua, February 11, 1936. FR, 1936, V, 815–16.

21. Telegram 57, from Washington, March 28, 1936. FR, 1936, V, 817–18. Whether or not Long replaced Lane because of Washington's dissatisfaction with Lane's activities in Nicaragua is not clear; it is highly probable, however, that Hull thought that, in view of Lane's close personal relationships to Nicaraguan politicians, he would not be a satisfactory exponent of a policy of strict noninterference.

22. Memorandum of March 17, 1936, to Laurence Duggan. FR, 1936, V, 127–28.

23. Memorandum of March 25, 1936, to Welles. FR, 1936, V, 128–30. It is difficult to avoid the impression that Duggan here had the Nicaraguan situation in mind. He may have recalled also the embarrassment to the Department caused by a failure to communicate with Minister Matthew E. Hanna in Guatemala in 1935, when it was reported that President Jorge Ubico was planning illegally to perpetuate himself in office. In this instance, the Department expressed itself ambiguously, Hanna did not interpret aright what the Department had in mind, and Welles found it necessary to direct Hanna to correct Ubico's erroneous impression that the Department "did not desire him to continue in the Presidency." What Welles had said was: "This Government has no attitude, either of sympathy or lack of sympathy," about an alleged "popular movement" of support for Ubico's candidacy. The position of "no attitude" was looked upon by Hanna as "a precise definition of our attitude"

and "in complete harmony with the 'good neighbor' policy." Despatches 645 and 669, from Guatemala City, May 11, June 3, 1935, and Instruction 129, May 24, 1935. FR, 1935, IV, 625, 631, 634.

24. Memorandum of March 26, 1936, to Duggan. FR, 1936, V, 130–31.

25. The treaty, in article II, provided for nonrecognition of certain Central American regimes coming to power through revolution. Text in *Conference on Central American Affairs, Washington, December 4, 1922–February 7, 1923* (Washington, Government Printing Office, 1923). The United States was not a signatory to the treaty, but it subsequently based its recognition policy in Central America upon article II.

26. Instruction of April 30, 1936. FR, 1936, V, 134–36. Italics added. Concerning international relations among the Central American states, the Department would issue instructions on reports from ministers. Three weeks before this instruction, Minister Leo J. Keena, fearing civil war in Honduras, suggested that a United States naval vessel be sent to cruise "in the vicinity of Honduras" for two weeks. Secretary Hull replied that, if Keena had meant that the vessel might "afford protection to our citizens, this Government considers that the responsibility for the maintenance of order and the protection of foreigners rests squarely on the Government of Honduras." Keena quickly retreated by saying that his suggestion "was based on the belief that the moral effect would be good" if a naval vessel cruised near Honduras; his suggestion was not carried out. Telegrams 39, 41, from Tegucigalpa, April 11, 15, 1936, and Telegram 22, from Washington, April 14, 1936. FR, 1936, V, 689–90.

27. Despatch 684, from San Salvador, May 14, 1936. DS, 817.00/8416. Corrigan faithfully carried out the new policy, although he expressed in this despatch the view that "the moral influence" of the Department had been "prematurely removed." He felt that "such influence is expected and, if prudently exerted, is not looked upon with such hostility as was evoked in the past by impolitic pressure and actual armed intervention." This opinion did not cause the Department to vary from its new course.

28. Memorandum of conversation, May 5, 1936. FR, 1936, V, 819–20.

29. Telegram 66, to Managua, May 8, 1936. FR, 1936, V, 821.

30. Letter from Sumner Welles to Minister Boaz W. Long in Managua, May 19, 1936. FR, 1936, V, 821–22. This quotation is from a cable Welles decided not to send to Long because the situation did not appear urgent; however, the portion quoted here was given orally to the Salvadoran Minister in Washington.

31. Above, p. 143.

32. Despatch 1073, from San Salvador, July 29, 1937. FR, 1937, V, 522–25.

33. Instruction 325, August 13, 1937. FR, 1937, V, 525. It may be recalled that Welles, when he called for the landing of Marines in Cuba, also pleaded the desirability of upholding the prestige of the United States.

34. For example, Minister William H. Hornibrook in Costa Rica was asked by an envoy from a group of Nicaraguan refugees for some indication of the attitude the United States might take toward a possible revolution against Somoza. The Minister refused to become involved even

to the extent of expressing any personal views. Despatch 952, from San José, November 6, 1939. DS, 817.00 Revolutions/22.

35. Quoted in *The Times* (London), August 22, 1936.

36. Letter to President Roosevelt, March 17, 1941. DS, 710.11/2669–1/2.

37. Press conference, with members of the Associated Church Press, April 20, 1938. *The Public Papers and Addresses of Franklin D. Roosevelt, 1938* (N.Y., Macmillan, 1941), pp. 255–56.

38. Press conference 667, August 6, 1940, FDRL, Press Conferences, XVI, 97.

39. See article by Frank L. Kluckhohn, New York *Times*, May 14, 1939.

40. Above, p. 141.

41. Memorandum of conversation, July 11, 1939, between Trujillo and Laurence Duggan. FR, 1939, V, 579.

42. Letter from Welles to Roosevelt, October 19, 1937, enclosing copy of Despatch 16, from Ciudad Trujillo, October 11, 1937. FDRL, PSF, Box 20. See also New York *Times*, November 7 and 9, 1937.

VI. The Evolution of a New Policy (pages 159–67)

1. Ambassador Fred Dearing interpreted this statement in terms that appear to have been typical of the views of United States diplomats at the time: "I do not understand good neighbor to mean that our Government is making public a self-denying ordinance, but rather that, being a good neighbor and intending to remain so, our Government expects other nations to be good neighbors too and will be as little disposed as ever to look with favor upon a bad neighbor who is doing things that are illegal and improper." Despatch 2818, from Lima, May 11, 1933. DS, 721.23/1759.

2. Commenting on an editorial in *Crónica* (La Paz), April 17, 1937, which stated that "the intervention of the American Government in favor of the Standard Oil Company has been discarded, completely and forever," Minister Norweb remarked that the statement "is typical of the assumption, too frequently encountered, that 'good neighbor' does not necessarily imply some measure of mutual obligation." Despatch 208, from La Paz, April 23, 1937. DS, 710.11/2130. It may be added that the claim made in the editorial was shortly proven to be erroneous.

3. Circular telegram, April 1, 1938. DS, 812.6363/3273A. See also Hull's remarks to the Mexican Ambassador, January 22, 1938. FR, 1938, V, 776ff.

4. To a question about the Mexican view of the Good Neighbor policy, in view of charges in the United States that expropriation and the resulting dispute was evidence of the "failure" of the policy, President Cárdenas told H. R. Knickerbocker: "I think that the American people, which has always shown itself to be sensible, will not consider that Mexico has ceased being a good neighbor merely because it demanded that the petroleum companies respect our laws, and I am sure that despite the campaign being waged by the press of the neighboring country, the people of the United States will not be prejudiced against our country." Quoted in *El Universal* (Mexico City), February 8, 1939.

5. *Report of the Delegation of the United States of America to the Inter-American Conference for the Maintenance of Peace, Buenos Aires, Argentina, December 1–23, 1936* (Washington, U.S. Government Printing Office, 1937), pp. 232–34.

6. A copy of this speech, given on December 6, 1937, in the Atheneum of Arts and Sciences, Mexico City, was given by Córdoba to Ambassador Josephus Daniels. Text attached to Despatch 6009, from Mexico City, January 18, 1938. DS, 710 Peace Non-Intervention/22. Italics added.

7. In 1938, the Ecuadoran government desired to secure revisions in the contract of a North American enterprise in that country. The Department of State expressed the hope that the company might be given "a reasonable period of time" to consider the proposal, and this request was granted. However, the Ecuadoran government issued a press statement claiming that the Department of State had acted "officiously" and had "intervened in the domestic affairs of Ecuador." Welles wrote that this statement had caused surprise and disappointment "because of the well-known and well-established policy of this Administration not to intervene in the internal and external affairs of any nation." He added that the "informal and friendly actions" of the Department were "in complete harmony and conformity with the Good Neighbor policy," which sought "to prevent the development of situations that might adversely affect the cordial relations among the American Republics." Memorandum given to the Ambassador of Ecuador, February 9, 1938. DS, 822.6341 South American Development Co./67a.

8. Letter from Daniels to Hull, Mexico City, October 29, 1937, and Letter from Hull to Daniels, Washington, November 17, 1937. DS, 812.5045/587.

9. Letter from Daniels to Welles, Mexico City, March 24, 1939, and Memorandum by Welles, April 24, 1939. DS, 812.6363/5675.

10. Eduardo Rodríguez Larreta declared that Secretary Hull had stated "almost publicly" when asked at the Montevideo Conference to "intervene with American bankers" to prevent them from continuing their demands for payment of the Uruguayan debt, that "the American Government was not the lawyer of the American bankers and that their fate did not interest it fundamentally." This statement, said Rodríguez Larreta, "produced, naturally, in the Uruguayan Government, the decision . . . to pay them not more than half of their interest, after such a reply. The abuse of this declaration by the Uruguayan dictatorship in its first year of functioning should not interest us. What does interest us is the evolution of the ideas of the American Government which is no longer the advocate of American bankers." From an unidentified Uruguayan newspaper, Montevideo, August 17, 1936, quoted in Despatch 323, from Montevideo, September 9, 1936. DS, 710 Peace/769.

VII. The Principle of Discrimination: Bolivia (pages 168–202)

1. Text in FR, 1937, V, 277–78.
2. Telegram 12, from La Paz, March 16, 1937. *Ibid.,* V, 279. Norweb

thought the government was "glad to have a pretext to seize the property of the company without necessity of indemnification."

3. Despatch 221, from La Paz, May 8, 1937. *Ibid.*, V, 286–88.

4. Despatch 174, from La Paz, March 19, 1937. *Ibid.*, V, 280–81. Norweb here reported an informant as saying that the latter had told Finot that in this way "what the Argentine had failed to obtain through the efforts of the Paraguayan Army during the Chaco War, the Argentine would be obtaining diplomatically." Finot later told Norweb that "Bolivia simply has to play up to Argentine imperialism in order to obtain an acceptable settlement in the Chaco." Despatch 221, frcm La Paz, May 8, 1937. *Ibid.*, V, 287.

5. It was soon after rumored that "if the Argentine obtains advantages in this matter and the Bolivian Government expropriates the fields held by the Standard Oil Company and allows their purchase by the 'Yacimientos Petrolíferos Argentinos,' the Argentine will guarantee that Paraguay will not again go to war with Bolivia." Despatch 117, from La Paz, January 14, 1937. *Ibid.*, V, 275–76.

6. Despatch 181, from La Paz, March 22, 1937. DS, 824.6363 St2/87. Norweb added that the government "must have . . . decided . . . that the petroleum at stake was worth the risk of diplomatic complications, of dampening our enthusiasm in the Chaco, and of killing the prospective tin negotiations."

7. Telegram 10, to La Paz, April 26, 1937. FR, 1937, V, 281–82. After listening to Norweb, Finot sarcastically commented that "the least any government could do under the circumstances would be to hope for an equitable settlement." Despatch 214, from La Paz, April 27, 1937. *Ibid.*, V, 282. Norweb's mild statement of the Department's position was communicated to the Standard Oil Company. In a note to Welles, suggesting that such communication be made, Duggan wrote that, so far as the Company was concerned, "It will be cold comfort." DS, 824.6363 St2/113.

8. Quoted in Telegram 27, from La Paz, May 4, 1937. FR, 1937, V, 284.

9. Despatch 220, from La Paz, May 5, 1937. DS, 824.6363 St2/133.

10. Telegram 14, to La Paz, May 7, and Telegram 14, to La Paz, May 7, 1937. FR, 1937, V, 284–85, and DS, 824.6363 St2/126a. This message, and Finot's reply were published in La Paz in 1941, when copies were made available by Foreign Minister Ostria Gutiérrez during legislative debates on the question of authorizing the government to negotiate a settlement with the Standard Oil Company.

11. Despatch 221, from La Paz, May 8, 1937. FR, 1937, V, 286–88.

12. Text of message from Finot to Hull, May 12, 1937. DS, 824.6363 St2/137.

13. Despatches 235 and 244, from La Paz, May 24 and June 4, 1937. FR, 1937, V, 290–92.

14. Despatch 263, from La Paz, June 28, 1937. *Ibid.*, V, 292–94. Muccio added that he thought it would be wise for the Company to send to La Paz "a competent American representative" who might be able to reopen direct negotiations. It was not until October 9 that such a representative arrived, and in the meantime the YPFB had become firmly

established in the business of operating the Company's former wells, and the officials of that agency had become both politically influential and determined to hold on to their new positions.

15. Telegram 63, from La Paz, October 26, 1937. *Ibid.*, V, 302.

16. Telegram 30 to La Paz, November 13, and Telegram 83, from La Paz, December 18, 1937. *Ibid.*, V, 303, 311.

17. Despatch 73, from La Paz, November 17, 1937. *Ibid.*, V, 305.

18. Telegram 70, from La Paz, December 3, 1937. *Ibid.*, V, 308–9.

19. It may be noted that a memorandum prepared in the Legal Division following the deportation, expressed the view that "there may be sufficient grounds now for taking the position that the American interests in question have suffered a denial of justice. Whether this stand should be taken at the present time, however, appears to be largely a question of policy, and I understand that it is deemed expedient to avoid doing so until all possible efforts toward effecting a direct settlement shall have been exhausted." December 6, 1937. DS, 824.6363 St2/201.

20. Cited in Memorandum of September 7, 1937. DS, 824.6363 St2/172.

21. Telegram 29, to La Paz, October 28, 1937. FR, 1937, V, 302–3.

22. Instruction 31, to La Paz, December 6, 1937. *Ibid.*, V, 309–10. Welles took a similar position in a letter to T. R. Armstrong of the Standard Oil Company of New Jersey, in which he pointed out that the Department did not wish to request arbitration of the dispute since the Company had not resorted to the Bolivian courts, and since the Bolivian government had expressed a willingness to enter into exploratory conversations despite the decree of October 22. Letter of November 15, 1937. *Ibid.*, V, 304.

23. Despatch 134, from La Paz, February 1, 1938. DS, 824.6363 St2/225.

24. Despatch 1717, from Buenos Aires, August 25, 1937. DS, 624.3531/17. The agreement with Brazil dealt only with the exportation of oil, via a projected line from the Brazilian railhead at Corumbá westward toward Santa Cruz de la Sierra.

25. Memorandum of conversation, December 6, 1937. DS, 624.3531/27.

26. Memorandum of conversation, February 2, 1938. DS, 811.6354/373.

27. Despatch 171, from La Paz, March 11, 1938. DS, 824.6363 St2/240.

28. Letter from H. A. Metzger to Foreign Minister Diez de Medina, March 22, 1938. FR, 1938, V, 325. The protest was based on the short time allowed to file the suit, the confiscation itself, and on "the unconstitutional and irregular organization of the present Supreme Court, also by a decree of the Executive who should not intervene in the matter, by which the previous court constitutionally established was suppressed." The Company had requested Caldwell to accompany Metzger when he called on Diez de Medina to deliver his letter of protest, but the Department refused to allow Caldwell to go so far as to lend his presence to the occasion.

29. Memorandum, March 16, 1938. DS, 824.6363 St2/242. A Calvo Clause provided that a company agreed not to invoke its government's protection in a dispute regarding its concession or contract.

30. Memorandum of conversation, March 17, 1938. DS, 824.6363 St2/246.

31. Letter from T. R. Armstrong, to Welles, November 7, and Reply by Welles, November 15, 1938. DS, 824.6363 St2/289. Welles added: "I believe that the foregoing statement gives a clear indication of the Department's attitude and action in the case."

32. Quoted in *Crónica* (La Paz), March 29, 1938.

33. Letter from Welles to T. R. Armstrong, May 14, 1938. DS, 824.6363 St2/255. This letter was written in response to a request from Armstrong that the Department try to get the dispute submitted to international arbitration before the Court's decision was rendered. The Department, however, maintained its position that it would take no further action in this direction until the verdict of the Supreme Court was known. Letter from Duggan to Armstrong, July 12, 1938. DS, 824.6363 St2/268.

34. *Ultima Hora* (La Paz), July 19, 1938. The same paper on July 1 claimed that the Company was financing a new purchase of planes by Paraguay in order to obtain revenge on Bolivia.

35. *La Calle* (La Paz), November 15, 1938. This article included an attack on the personal character of the Company's representative in Bolivia as a "black pope" and a man who politely distributed bribes by losing at poker.

36. *La Noche* (La Paz), July 18, 1938.

37. Memorandum, April 11, and Memorandum of conversation, April 11, 1939. DS, 824.6363 St2/336.

38. Memorandum, April 24, 1939. DS, 824.6363 St2/373.

39. Memorandum of conversation, April 28, 1939. DS, 824.6363 St2/375.

40. Memorandum of conversation, May 31, 1939. FR, 1939, V, 328–30.

41. Memorandum of conversation, June 15, 1939. *Ibid.*, V, 330–32. Welles's emphasis on the unofficial character of his action was a resolution of a difference of view among United States officials about the role of the Department. One view was that the Department should not be "drawn into the position of a negotiator between the two parties"; it should do what it could to be helpful in getting an agreement in principle, but changes in the draft should be made directly by Guachalla and Company officers. On the other hand, the opinion was expressed that "we have a duty to try to bring about a fair settlement." Memorandum and Comment, June 14, 1939. DS, 824.6363 St2/384-1/2. This difference of view, which occurred in other instances, is of some significance as indicating a distinction in attitude on the part of those concerned with the principles of the Good Neighbor policy and of those concerned with the principles of international law. On the legal side, the view was given that "it would be very unfortunate for this Government to acquiesce in the refusal of the Bolivian Government to arbitrate. Such acquiescence would have the effect of seriously injuring legitimate American interests." Memorandum, September 8, 1939. DS, 824.6363 St2/414-1/2. The later acquiescence of the Department in the final rejection of arbitration by Bolivia demonstrated the victory of political over legal considerations.

42. Memorandum of conversation, June 26, 1939. FR, 1939, V, 334-35. Guachalla did not wish, as he later told Duggan, to send anything to La Paz until it was in a form which he himself could support and recommend. Memorandum of conversation, August 14, 1939. *Ibid.*, V, 337-38.

43. Memorandum of conversation between Duggan and Guachalla, August 14, 1939. *Ibid.*, V, 337-38. Text of the proposal in *Ibid.*, V, 338-40.

44. When the question of "a friendly arbitration" was suggested by the Bolivian Minister of Mines, Foianini, to H. A. Metzger, the Company's representative expressed interest, and the Company consistently favored an international arbitration as the best means of defending its claims. The Company had informally stated that it hoped it would have the support of the Department "in demanding that the neutral member of the arbitral tribunal should not be a Latin American." However, Welles stated: "I am entirely unwilling to agree in principle or in practice that the Department of State is justified in excluding Latin American jurisconsults as arbitrators in cases arising either between the United States and some other American republic, or between some private American interest, such as the Standard Oil Company, and the Government of some other American republic." Memorandum of conversation, March 8, 1939, and Memorandum by Welles, March 9, 1939. DS, 824.6363 St2/325. This view was accepted by the Company.

45. Despatch 259, from La Paz, June 19, 1940. DS, 824.6363 St2/473.

46. The United Press despatch was too well-informed to have been based on mere speculation. Department of State officials regarded its publication as "highly unfortunate," and they were without any clues as to its origin. Memoranda attached to Despatch 159, from La Paz, March 20, 1940. DS, 824.6363 St2/451. It is not impossible that Guachalla himself had come to the conclusion that any plan for arbitration would be rejected in Bolivia, and that this was the best way to terminate the negotiations so that he would not be held responsible for having appeared to favor an arbitral settlement.

47. The contract of the Company gave it the capacity to make explorations and to extract petroleum from Bolivian territory. In Mexico, the oil companies, at least before 1937, were the owners of certain areas from which oil was obtained. The Bolivian government declared the Company's concession void on the ground that the contract had been violated, and Bolivia did not admit that the Company was entitled to compensation. In the Mexican case, however, the government admitted that compensation was due to the oil companies and declared its intention, as early as two weeks after the expropriation, to pay it.

48. Despatch 516, from La Paz, May 12, 1939. DS, 824.6363 St2/364.

49. Memorandum of conversation with Pablo M. Insfrán, September 13, 1939. DS, 834.6363/50.

50. Instruction 282, to Buenos Aires, June 14, 1940. DS, 724.35/78.

51. Despatch 696, from Buenos Aires, May 21, 1940. DS, 724.35/79.

52. Despatch 1263, from Buenos Aires, September 17, 1940. DS, 824.6363 St2/493.

53. *La Razón* (Buenos Aires), October 29, 1940.

54. Letter from T. R. Armstrong to the Secretary of State, November 29, 1940, and Letter to Armstrong, December 11, 1940. DS, 824.6363 St2/496.

55. See below, p. 232.

56. Memorandum of conversation, August 7, 1939. FR, 1939, V, 313. Duggan informed Guachalla that "it appeared to me very doubtful whether this government would wish to extend credits to the Bolivian government until that government had taken steps to clear up certain well known differences with American citizens."

57. Welles would have preferred to make a loan to Bolivia, but Hull, concerned about Congressional and public criticism, did not favor a loan unless La Paz showed willingness to be reasonable about compensation to the Standard Oil Company. See Telegram 38, to Panama, September 30, 1939, and Welles's reply, October 3, 1939. FR, 1939, V, 320–21, 321–22.

58. Despatch 200, from La Paz, April 25, 1940. DS, 824.6363 St2/460.

59. Memorandum, January 29, 1940. DS, 824.51/1009.

60. Quoted in Telegram 38, to Panama, September 30, 1939. FR, 1939, V, 320.

61. Memorandum, written about June 5, 1940. DS, 824.51/1114.

62. The Minister of Finance, Edmundo Vásquez, was reported in *La Nación* (La Paz), June 14, 1940, as saying that one obstacle to Bolivia's obtaining capital from the United States was the situation with regard to the Standard Oil Company. Minister Jenkins stated that so far as he knew this was the first time that a high Bolivian official had "publicly admitted this self-evident truth although many naturally do so privately." Despatch 253, from La Paz, June 14, 1940. DS, 811.6354/622. Jenkins later reported that sentiment in the government was "overwhelmingly" in favor of making some kind of settlement. Despatch 520, from La Paz, December 11, 1940. DS, 824.6363 St2/504.

63. Letter from T. R. Armstrong to the Secretary of State, November 13, 1940. DS, 824.6363 St2/495. The Company evidently had in mind the Mexican expropriations.

64. Letter to W. S. Farish, November 28, 1940. DS, 824.6363 St2/495.

65. Memorandum of conversation between Long and C. W. Wright and Glen M. Ruby, February 25, 1941, and Memorandum from Long to Welles, February 25, 1941. DS, 824.6363 St2/537.

66. Despatch 788, from La Paz, April 28, 1941. DS, 824.6363 St2/542. Jenkins quoted the Foreign Minister as saying he was going to ask the Department of State "to put the Standard Oil case aside for the present so that the Government here would be in a better position to strengthen its relations with the United States." Jenkins also pointed out that the opposition to the government was being "encouraged and assisted in every possible way by the Germans who are bent on destroying American influence in this part of the world, if they can."

67. Minister Jenkins, who had previously supported the Department's decision to refuse loans until the dispute was settled, now modified his opinion and proposed that "while the policy of discouraging ordinary

loans is continued, it may be a good idea to look with favor upon loans for the construction of certain highways and also perhaps to assist the Army in the purchase of equipment." Despatch 801, from La Paz, May 5, 1941. DS, 824.6363 St2/543.

68. Memorandum, undated, probably written about September, 1941. DS, 824.6363 St2/607.

69. *Ibid.*

70. Telegram 18, from Rio de Janeiro, January 16, 1942. DS, 824.6363 St2/558.

71. Telegram 50, to Welles in Rio de Janeiro, January 21, 1942. DS, 824.6363 St2/559. The Company also expressed the hope that criminal indictments pending in Bolivian courts against officers of the Company for allegedly having furnished oil to Paraguay during the Chaco War be dropped if an agreement were reached, and this was subsequently done.

72. Text in Department of State *Bulletin,* February 21, 1942, pp. 172–73.

73. Memorandum from Duggan to Hull, January 20, 1942. DS, 824.6363 St2/298. Duggan said that the proposal from Anze Matienzo might be "an unusual opportunity to bring about a quick settlement of this long-standing dispute, that . . . would be of course very desirable from the viewpoint of relations between Bolivia and the United States." In reviewing the course of the dispute he said that on the one hand while there "seems to be no doubt but that a disinterested arbitrator of the matter would consider the action of the Bolivian Government unwarranted on any legal basis," on the other, "in exaggerated fairness to the Bolivian Government," it should be stated that the Standard Oil Company, "while it had invested large sums (claimed to be $17,000,000) in oil exploration and exploitation in Bolivia, had nevertheless considerably relaxed its efforts to develop Bolivian oil because it had found oil in fields in Venezuela and other countries which was much more plentiful and much more accessible to tidewater."

74. Memorandum from Duggan to Bonsal, January 27, 1942. *Ibid.*

75. Spanish text attached to Despatch 1770, from La Paz, February 26, 1942. DS, 824.6363 St2/577. Commenting on the linking of the agreement and the Export-Import Bank credit in the decree, Dawson remarked: "This feature of the decree, which to us sounds unfortunate, will not appear gauche to Bolivians—instead of seeing any impropriety in officially coupling the Standard Oil settlement and the Export-Import Bank credit, the latter is to their minds the reason for the former and it is fitting that this should be made clear."

76. Despatch 1794, from La Paz, March 2, 1942. DS, 824.6363 St2/580.

77. Despatch 1803, from La Paz, March 5, 1942. DS, 824.6363 St2/582.

78. Legation translation of speech attached to Despatch 998, from La Paz, December 17, 1942. DS, 824.6363 St2/628.

VIII. The Principle of Accommodation: Mexico I (pages 203–33)

1. Despatch 6318, from Mexico, March 22, 1938. DS, 812.6363/3141.

2. Francisco Castillo Nájera, *El Petróleo en la Industria Moderna: las*

Compañías Petroleras y los Gobiernos de México (Mexico, Cámara Nacional de Las Industrias de Transformación, 1949), p. 40. He quotes Thomas R. Armstrong, a director of Standard Oil Company of New Jersey, as saying that "Cárdenas would not dare to expropriate us" (p. 41). This attributed remark has become well known in Mexico. See, for example, the references (pp. 150–51) in the prize-winning novel, *El Alba en las Cimas,* by José Mancisidor (Mexico, América Nueva, 1955), a book about the expropriation that is of interest in reflecting the character and intensity of some Mexican attitudes about Cárdenas, Roosevelt, and oil company officials.

3. Despatch 6015, from Mexico, January 21, 1938. DS, 812.5045/636. Harlow S. Person in *Mexican Oil* (N.Y., Harper, 1942), p. 52, claims that Cárdenas preferred to avoid expropriation and implies that the President of Mexico did not make up his mind until just before the decision was announced. However, Samuel Flagg Bemis in *The Latin American Policy of the United States* (N.Y., Harcourt, Brace, 1943), pp. 346–47, asserts that "the actual program for driving out the foreign petroleum companies took the shape of most burdensome labor legislation."

4. Memorandum of conversation, February 25, 1938. DS, 812.5405/707. Welles said he did not think "that the course of events would be such as to make this government feel that it was desirable for it to interpose," and added that he did not consider that charges that the Mexican court was under pressure from the Mexican president could be substantiated.

5. Despatch 6300, from Mexico, March 20, 1938. DS, 812.6363/3108.

6. E. David Cronon, *Josephus Daniels in Mexico* (Madison, Wis., University of Wisconsin Press, 1960), p. 184. The source for this statement is given as a private admission by "an American oil man, one of the leaders of the old Petroleum Producers Association in Mexico."

7. A substantial account of the oil controversy based largely on unpublished documents in the Daniels Papers and Department of State archives is provided in Cronon, *Josephus Daniels in Mexico,* Chaps. VII–X.

8. Memorandum of conversation, March 21, 1938. FR, 1938, V, 729–33.

9. Josephus Daniels, *Shirt-Sleeve Diplomat* (Chapel Hill, N.C., University of North Carolina Press, 1947), p. 246.

10. *The Memoirs of Cordell Hull* (N.Y., Macmillan, 1948), I, 610.

11. Memorandum of telephone conversation with the Counselor of Embassy in Mexico (Pierre Boal), March 21, 1938. DS, 812.6363/3146.

12. Daniels to Hull, March 22, 1938. Cronon, *Josephus Daniels in Mexico,* p. 189, citing the Daniels Papers.

13. Telegram 57, from Mexico, March 19, 1938. DS, 812.6363/3093.

14. Memorandum of telephone conversation between the Counselor of Embassy in Mexico and Laurence Duggan, March 21, 1938. DS, 812.6363/3146.

15. See Cronon, *Josephus Daniels in Mexico,* Chaps. VII–VIII *passim.*

16. Telegram 68, from Mexico, March 22, 1938. FR, 1938, V, 733.

17. Text of the note in *Shirt-Sleeve Diplomat,* pp. 232–35. Text of the statement on silver purchases in FR, 1938, V, 735. The text of the note of March 26 appears never to have been published officially by either

government concerned, but there is no reason to doubt the accuracy of the text as given by Daniels.

18. *Shirt-Sleeve Diplomat*, p. 231.

19. Telegram 76, from Mexico, March 27, 1938. DS, 812.6363/3167.

20. Telegram 47, to Mexico, March 27, 1938. DS, 812.6363/3190B, and Cronon, *Josephus Daniels in Mexico*, pp. 194–95.

21. *Shirt-Sleeve Diplomat*, p. 235.

22. Telegram 81, from Mexico, March 27, 1938. FR, 1938, V, 736.

23. *Shirt-Sleeve Diplomat*, p. 235. For Cárdenas's assurances see above, p. 209.

24. Telegram 83, from Mexico, March 29, 1938. DS, 812.6363/3203.

25. Memorandum of telephone conversation, March 29, 1938. DS, 812.6363/3270.

26. Duggan told Boal that the modification of the silver purchase agreement had been made because, otherwise, "there would have been a hue and cry in the Congress which would have aired Mexico's policies in a way that would have been much more detrimental to Mexico." Résumé of telephone conversation with the Counselor of Embassy in Mexico, March 29, 1938, DS, 812.6363/3415.

27. Text in FR, 1938, V, 662.

28. Text in Telegram 93, from Mexico, March 31, 1938. *Ibid.*, V, 740. This statement was a public reaffirmation, in presidential language, of a note of March 30, given to Daniels by Hay that asserted that Mexico was able to pay compensation and would discuss indemnities with the oil companies for the "irrevocable expropriation" of their properties. Telegram 87, from Mexico, March 30, 1938. DS, 812.6363/3215; Daniels, *Shirt-Sleeve Diplomat*, p. 236.

29. New York *Times*, April 2, 1938; see also Cronon, *Josephus Daniels in Mexico*, pp. 200–1, for details on Roosevelt's press conference.

30. Telegram 98, from Mexico, April 2, 1938. DS, 812.52/2643.

31. Telegram 140, to Mexico, July 20, 1938. FR, 1938, V, 756.

32. Telegram 315, from Mexico, July 20, 1938. DS, 812.6363/4415.

33. Memorandum of telephone conversation, July 21, 1938. DS, 812.6363/4490.

34. Memorandum of conversation, July 21, 1938. DS, 812.52/2942.

35. Memoranda of telephone conversations, July 21, 1938. DS, 812.6363/4491; 812.52/2968.

36. Memorandum of the press conference, July 22, 1938. DS, 812.6363/4532.

37. Text in Daniels, *Shirt-Sleeve Diplomat*, p. 237. This instruction was presumably sent about July 23, 1938.

38. Quoted in Allan Seymour Everest, *Morgenthau, the New Deal, and Silver* (N.Y., King's Crown Press, 1950), p. 91.

39. Frank L. Kluckhohn in *The Mexican Challenge* (N.Y., Doubleday, 1939), p. 124, reported that Daniels did not know the contents of the August 22 note until six days after it was delivered, which appeared "to offer at least circumstantial evidence that Mr. Hull felt that delivery of the oil note had been botched."

40. Cronon, *Josephus Daniels in Mexico*, p. 198, citing letter from Beteta to Cronon, June 23, 1953. See also *Ultimas Noticias* (Mexico City), February 7–8, 1939.

41. Press conference 780, October 31, 1941. FDRL, Press Conferences, XVIII, 267. In a letter to Daniels of the same date, Roosevelt said: "Our relations with our southern neighbor have, largely because of you, become relations for understanding and real friendship." FDRL, PSF, Box 12.

42. Letters of February 3, 7, 1939, DS, 812.6363/5446.

43. *Novedades* (Mexico City), May 28, 1938.

44. Memorandum of conversation, August 2, 1939. DS, 812.6363/6078.

45. Castillo Nájera, *El Petróleo en la Industria Moderna*, p. 71, 48. This talk took place in June, 1938. The protocol was that signed at the Buenos Aires Conference of 1936.

46. Memorandum of conversation, April 17, 1939. DS, 812.00 Revolutions/468.

47. Letter of September 11, 1939. DS, 812.6363/3146. A rejoinder from Duggan's correspondent, urging that the above agreements should not be construed "as shielding aggression and unwarranted exercise of force on the part of any nation against reprisal by injured parties," does not seem to have been answered. DS, 812.6363/6154.

48. Letter of September 11, 1940, and Telegram of September 21, 1940. FDRL, OF 146 (Mexico) Box 1. J. A. Almazán had been defeated in the Mexican presidential elections of July, 1940, by Manuel Avila Camacho, the government candidate. See also Cronon, *Josephus Daniels in Mexico*, pp. 212, 256–57.

49. See Cronon, *Josephus Daniels in Mexico*, pp. 190–92.

50. Memorandum of conversation between Morgenthau and Suárez, by the Adviser on International Economic Affairs of the Department of State, December 31, 1937. DS, 812.51/2255.

51. Telegram 328, from Mexico, December 30, 1937. DS, 812.5045/611; FR, 1937, V, 676.

52. Telegrams 251 and 253, December 31, 1937. FR, 1937, V, 676–77. Suárez said that Beteta's impression that "pressure" was being exerted "could only have been received from the Chairman of the Labor Board."

53. Text in announcement by Department of State, March 27, 1938. FR, 1938, V, 735.

54. Everest, *Morgenthau, the New Deal, and Silver*, p. 89.

55. In 1937, the Treasury bought 88,152,000 ounces of Mexican silver, but this included a special purchase of 35,000,000 ounces to aid Mexico's foreign exchange position. In 1938, 1939, 1940, and 1941 Treasury purchases were 43,933,000, 25,395,000, 13,420,000 and 500,000 ounces, respectively. Treasury purchases from other silver suppliers also declined in these years. The reason for the low purchase in 1941 is that, in order to assist United States commercial silver users, the Treasury price was reduced to thirty-five cents an ounce, which meant that Mexico sold its silver elsewhere. See Everest, *Morgenthau, the New Deal, and Silver*, pp. 177–78.

56. Memorandum, March 29, 1938. DS, 811.515 Silver/154.

57. Memorandum of telephone conversation, March 29, 1938. DS, 812.6363/3415. See, on Daniels, Cronon, *Josephus Daniels in Mexico*, pp. 198–99.

58. Despatch 6432, from Mexico, April 7, 1938. DS, 811.515 Silver/162.

59. Memorandum, December 16, 1939, and Telegram 306, to Mexico, December 20, 1939. DS, 812.51/2415. In the summer of 1939, a determined effort was made in Congress through the so-called Townsend Amendment to cut off all purchases of silver from abroad. President Roosevelt opposed the amendment, and his influence was sufficient to cause the defeat of the amendment in the House after its passage in the Senate. The amendment appears to have been motivated by the desire of United States miners to raise their sales, as well as by a desire to bring pressure on Mexico in connection with the oil expropriations.

60. Castillo Nájera, *El Petróleo en la Industria Moderna*, p. 42. Daniels, however, cabled Hull that the action on silver "would be regarded by Mexico and all the world in the nature of a reprisal." Telegram 77, from Mexico, March 27, 1938. FR, 1938, V, 735.

61. Cronon in *Josephus Daniels in Mexico*, p. 192, states that "the silver boycott was only one phase of the State Department's offensive against the errant Cárdenas regime." The term "boycott" would be applicable only if silver purchases had actually been terminated.

62. Daniels records that he "wrote home" in October, 1938, that Beteta told him that the Mexican oil corporation (Pemex) had been refused pumps and other equipment, even for cash, which was regarded in Mexico as a "boycott by American manufacturers." *Shirt-Sleeve Diplomat*, pp. 248–49.

63. Text in Despatch 2589, from Buenos Aires, June 2, 1939. DS, 812.6363/5814.

64. Note of August 23, 1938, from Hay, and reply of September 30, the latter in FR, 1938, V, 760.

65. Quoted in Daniels, *Shirt-Sleeve Diplomat*, p. 249.

66. Memorandum of conversation, March 21, 1938. FR, 1938, V, 732. At the time of this talk, Welles had some vague hope that the expropriation decree might be canceled; he does not appear to have raised this question later when expropriation was seen to be irrevocable.

67. See Daniels's characterization of Davis in *Shirt-Sleeve Diplomat*, pp. 251–53.

68. Memorandum from the Vice-Consul at Tampico, December 14, 1938. DS, 812.6363 Davis and Company/159.

69. Memorandum of conversation with the Mexican Ambassador, August 22, 1938. DS, 812.52/3178. Castillo Nájera thanked the Secretary for this information.

70. Memorandum, September 23, 1938. DS, 812.6363/4879.

71. Despatch 8911, from Mexico, August 8, 1939. DS, 812.6363 Davis and Company/194.

72. Memorandum, September 16, 1938. DS, 812.6363/4773.

73. New York *Times*, April 13, 1938; *The Times* (London), April 20, 1938.

74. Frank L. Kluckhohn, New York *Times*, May 22, 1938.

75. *Ibid.*, September 4, October 30, 1938. The Brazilian private firm of Correa & Castro announced an $18,000,000 purchase of petroleum from Pemex in mid-1939. *Ibid.*, July 5, 1939. Mexican oil was by then being exported in small amounts to Guatemala, Costa Rica, Nicaragua, and Uruguay, as well as to Australia, Germany, Italy, and other European countries. The Mexican government announced: "The boycott some imperialistic entities attempted to declare against our products has been a failure." *Ibid.*, July 15, 1939.

76. Henry D. Rolph and H. Stanley Norman, "Mexican Situation Presenting New Series of Complications," *Oil and Gas Journal*, April 7, 1938, p. 13. Three months after noting the oil companies' request, this publication asserted editorially that President Cárdenas had called on other Latin American countries to follow the lead of Mexico, and it inquired: "Is it not the immediate duty of Washington to put its 'good neighbor' policy into practical application so that not only will rights of its own nationals be protected according to international law but that at the same time the real interests of its neighbors shall be protected to the end that they can continue to improve their standard of living made possible largely through foreign enterprises? Failure to offer our good offices in an attempt to secure a settlement makes farcical our claims regarding the fostering of good feeling with our neighbors to the south." "Bankrupt Policy," *ibid.*, July 14, 1938, p. 23.

77. Cronon, *Josephus Daniels in Mexico*, p. 208.

78. See below, p. 244.

79. Letter from Hull to Knox, October 14, 1940. DS, 812.6363/7123A, and Memoranda October 10, October 11, 1940. DS, 812.6363/7159–60. It was pointed out that assisting a boycott on the Sinclair oil would only increase the difficulty of settling the controversy.

80. Letter from Hull to Knox, February 11, 1942. DS, 812.6363/7486. That the ban had not been lifted earlier was owing to the desire to avoid resentment on the part of the Standard Oil Company during the proceedings of the Cooke-Zevada commission. Memorandum, December 31, 1941. DS, 812.6363/7621.

81. Despatch 8936, from Mexico, August 11, 1939, and Instruction 2619, August 28, 1939. DS, 812.628/537. Daniels had reported that, if Mexico could obtain the boats, Japanese vessels then shrimping in Mexican waters would be ordered out.

IX. The Principle of Accommodation: Mexico II (pages 234–59)

1. Note of March 31, 1923. FR, 1923, II, 529.

2. Memorandum for the President, March 26, 1937. FDRL, PSF, Box 20. This statement was made in response to a suggestion from Roosevelt that United States policy toward expropriation should be to expect "prompt and effective compensation to be paid to the owners on not less than the same basis that payments are made to the nationals of the country making the expropriation." See Cronon, *Josephus Daniels in*

Mexico (Madison, Wis., University of Wisconsin Press, 1960), pp. 146–47.

3. Note of March 31, 1923. FR, 1923, II, 524, 531.

4. Roosevelt's sympathy for the "real hardship cases" of the small farmers and his unsympathetic attitude toward United States citizens with large landholdings in Mexico illustrate this change of emphasis. See above, p. 214.

5. Letter to Castillo Nájera, June 29, 1938. FR, 1938, V, 668.

6. Notes of July 21, August 3 (Mexico), August 22, September 1 (Mexico). FR, 1938, V, 674, 679, 685, 696.

7. Memorandum of conversation, August 22, 1928. DS, 812.52/3178.

8. Note of September 1, 1938. FR, 1938, V, 696.

9. Memorandum of conversation, September 10, 1938. FR, 1938, V, 706.

10. Memorandum of conversation, September 20, 1938. *Ibid.*, V, 708.

11. See the discussion of this important move by Daniels, with quotations from Daniels's letters of September 3 and 15, 1938 to Hull and Roosevelt, in Cronon, *Josephus Daniels in Mexico*, pp. 224–27. Characteristically, there seems to be no record of any talk between the President and the Secretary.

12. Note of November 9, to the Mexican Ambassador, and Note of November 12, from Foreign Minister Hay to Ambassador Daniels. FR, 1938, V, 714, 717; also Cronon, *Josephus Daniels in Mexico*, pp. 228–29.

13. See Cronon, *Josephus Daniels in Mexico*, pp. 238ff and references there cited.

14. Letter of August 31, 1939. FR, 1939, V, 703–6.

15. Memorandum of conversation, October 6, 1939. FR, 1939, V, 709.

16. See *aide-mémoire* from the British Embassy, December 12, and Telegram 392, from Mexico, December 6, 1939. FR, 1939, V, 716–19, 713–14.

17. Memorandum of conversation, February 5, 1940. DS, 812.6363/6486. Richberg's pamphlet was entitled *The Mexican Oil Seizure* (New York, Arrow Press, 1940).

18. Memoranda of conversations, February 19, 1940. DS, 812.6363/6523 and 812.6363/6529.

19. These questions were given to the Ambassador in an informal memorandum for transmission to Cárdenas. Memorandum of Conversation, March 16, 1940. DS, 812.6363/6609.

20. Memorandum of conversation, March 2, 1940. DS, 812.6363/6595.

21. Memorandum, March 12, 1940. DS, 812.6363/6597.

22. Memorandum of conversation, March 16, 1940. DS, 812.6363/6609. Hull thanked the Ambassador "for his strenuous exertions in an effort to cooperate in this matter by flying to Mexico in bad weather."

23. Quotations from the memorandum are contained in the note from Hull to Castillo Nájera, April 3, 1940. Department of State *Bulletin*, April 13, 1940, pp. 380f. This memorandum, on oil, essentially restated the Mexican position on arbitration of land claims as given in the note of September 1, 1938. See above, p. 236 and note 6.

24. Memorandum, March 20, 1940. DS, 812.6363/6609–1/2.

25. Memorandum of conversation, April 3, 1940. DS, 812.6363/6651.

Text of the note in Department of State *Bulletin*, April 13, 1940, pp. 380–83.

26. Memorandum of conversation, April 9, 1940. DS, 812.52 Agrarian Commission/137.

27. Memorandum of conversation, April 23, 1940. DS, 812.6363/6800.

28. *El Universal* (Mexico City), April 8, 1940.

29. Hay's calmness of temper in referring to this remark was not fully shared by *El Nacional* (Mexico City), May 6, 1940, the semiofficial newspaper of the government. An editorial suggested that in Hull's statement there was hidden "an intimation offensive to the uprightness of the government of Mexico and of its Courts," which the paper energetically rejected.

30. Text in Department of State *Bulletin*, May 4, 1940, pp. 465–70.

31. Quoted in *Excelsior* (Mexico City), May 8, 1940.

32. Memorandum May 2, 1940. DS, 812.6363/6845; and Cronon, *Josephus Daniels in Mexico*, pp. 248–53.

33. Memorandum of conversation, May 21, 1941. DS, 812.6363/6911.

34. Letter from Farish to Secretary Hull, June 20, 1940, and Letter from Welles to Farish, July 10, 1940. DS, 812.6363/6981.

35. Memorandum of conversation, June 4, 1940. DS, 812.6363/6952.

36. Memorandum from Welles to Green H. Hackworth, February 5, 1941. DS, 812.6363/7218.

37. Letter from W. S. Farish to the Secretary of State, January 24, 1941. DS, 812.6363/7208.

38. Letter to W. S. Farish, January 29, 1941. *Ibid.*

39. Cronon, *Josephus Daniels in Mexico*, p. 258.

40. Memorandum, February 25, 1941. DS, 812.6363/7215–1/2.

41. Cronon, *Josephus Daniels in Mexico*, p. 264, citing Departmental memoranda of September 3 and October 4, 1941.

42. Stetson Conn and Byron Fairchild, *The Framework of Hemisphere Defense* (Washington, D.C., Office of the Chief of Military History, Department of the Army, 1960), p. 334.

43. *Ibid.*, pp. 334–35.

44. *Ibid.*, pp. 338, 344–45. Text of the flight agreement in United States *Treaty Series*, No. 971.

45. Welles to Roosevelt, January 10, 1941, quoted in Cronon, *Josephus Daniels in Mexico*, p. 260.

46. Text of report, dated May 1941. DS, 812.6363/7301–1/2; Memorandum, June 10, 1941. DS, 812.6363/7308–1/2. Information about this report reached the press, and *Newsweek* (August 25, 1941, p. 8) reported that H. J. Duncan, James L. Minehan, and R. W. Richards of the U.S. Geological Survey had valued the expropriated properties at "a figure so close to the Mexican one that Ambassador Nájera hastily approved it," and the Department of State was "pointing out that the proceedings were just exploratory," since the geologists' figure was less than one-twentieth of the companies' own valuation. See also Cronon, *Josephus Daniels in Mexico*, pp. 260–61.

47. Memorandum to Hull and Welles, June 12, 1941. DS, 812.6363/

7317–5/11. One reason for not accepting the Department of Interior's figures, said Duggan, was that they were based only on Mexican sources, and the companies had not been consulted. In addition, he thought it entirely likely that Mexico would be willing to pay more than the experts' estimate.

48. Memorandum of conversation with Duggan and others, July 5, 1941. DS, 812.6363/7317–1/11. At this talk Castillo Nájera said a third member of the commission, to resolve disagreements, would be acceptable, but he later stated that the Mexican government would insist on a two-man commission. Memorandum of conversation, July 14, 1941. DS, 812.6363/7317–8/11.

49. Memorandum of conversation, August 21, 1941. DS, 812.6363/7354–1/11.

50. Conn and Fairchild, *The Framework of Hemisphere Defense*, p. 337.

51. Letter, August 27, 1941. DS, 812.6363/7329. This letter was briefly acknowledged by the Department. The quotation is from Hull's note of July 21, 1938 to Mexico: "The right of prompt and just compensation for expropriated property . . . is a principle . . . which must be maintained."

52. Memorandum, September 22, 1941. DS, 812.6363/7365–8/21.

53. Roosevelt wrote to Daniels, March 28, 1941, that he agreed that Daniels should "refrain for the present from discussing the question of financing by the United States of Mexican defense construction works." However, he had been encouraged by "the friendly and cooperative attitude of the Mexican Government and of the Mexican Foreign Minister in particular in these matters of mutual interest. It does seem that Mexico realizes the sincerity of the United States in its Good Neighbor policy and is preparing to go as far as necessary with us along the paths of friendship and collaboration." Letter, March 28, 1941. FDRL, OF 237 (Josephus Daniels 1933–45) Box 2. This letter was drafted in the Department of State.

54. Memorandum, September 17, 1941. DS, 812.6363/7365–11/21.

55. In September, 1940, Finance Minister Suárez had told the commercial attaché in Mexico that Mexico had rejected Japanese requests to purchase oil from Mexico "in order not to antagonize American public opinion," although Suárez said he knew that British and United States companies were selling oil to Japan from Venezuelan sources, and that certain types of oil were still being sold directly from the United States to Japan. Memorandum, September 11, 1940. DS, 812.6363/7090–1/2. Later, Suárez said Mexico did not want to sell any oil to Japan, and he hoped the Japanese "would continue to make their purchases in the United States." Welles asked Daniels to express to Suárez the "Department's sincere appreciation of his attitude" on this issue. Despatch 11545, from Mexico, October 1, and Telegram 309, to Mexico, October 7, 1940. DS, 812.6363/7115. In January, 1941, it was reported that the Mexican government had canceled all oil contracts with Japan, and that these had

called for the shipment of between five and ten million barrels of crude oil, besides small quantities of lubricants and fuel oil. Telegram 46, from Mexico, January 25, 1941. DS, 812.6363/7204.

56. *The Memoirs of Cordell Hull* (N.Y., Macmillan, 1948), II, 1141.

57. Letter from Farish to Hull, October 8, 1941, and Letter from Hull to Farish, October 29, 1941. DS, 812.6363/7353.

58. New York *Times*, October 23, 26, 1941.

59. Letter from Farish to Hull, November 13, 1941. DS, 812.6363/7430.

60. Duggan apparently regarded this talk as important to Hull's decision. Cronon, *Josephus Daniels in Mexico*, p. 268. Hull merely records: "Knowing what I did about the dangerous status of our negotiations with Japan, I felt, and the President with me, that we could not wait longer." *The Memoirs of Cordell Hull*, II, 1141.

61. Texts of agreements in Department of State *Bulletin*, November 22, 1941, pp. 399–404.

62. Daniels *Shirt-Sleeve Diplomat* (Chapel Hill, N.C., University of North Carolina Press, 1947), p. 266. Cronon in *Josephus Daniels in Mexico*, p. 270, suggests that this "was in a real sense, Josephus Daniels' day."

63. Cooke was Roosevelt's personal choice, made from a list of several names presented to him by the Department of State; others on the list included Lloyd K. Garrison, I. L. Sharfman, and Isaiah Bowman. Cooke had been head of the Rural Electrification Administration, 1935–37, and an adviser to Roosevelt in Albany. Letter from Welles to Roosevelt, December 18, 1941, and Memorandum from Roosevelt of the same date. FDRL, OF 146 (Mexico) Box 2.

64. Text in Department of State *Bulletin*, April 18, 1942, pp. 351–53. On the subsoil issue, Cooke wrote to Welles: "The evidence is conclusive that at least something of the order of 90% of the oil originally available to the American companies in exploited areas had already been recovered at the time of expropriation and sold or otherwise disposed of. Therefore, except for highly speculative wildcat areas without proven production and which had little or no installations of physical facilities, the possible present value of the claimed investments of the American companies included in our settlement could neither logically or fairly be in excess of 10% of the maximum claimed investment [$200,000,000] or $20,000,000." Letter, May 13, 1942, quoted with permission of Morris L. Cooke.

65. Despatch 1051, from Mexico, April 22, 1942. DS, 412.11 Oil/116. Cooke later wrote Roosevelt: "It is almost impossible to convey to you the sense of gratitude of the Mexican people and their government for the manner in which you have changed the quality of the United States–Mexican relations." Letter, June 5, 1942. DS, 812.6363/7683. (Photostat).

66. Memorandum, May 12, 1942. DS, 812.6363/7682.

67. Executive order 9080, February 27, 1942, and joint statement by Welles and Mexican Foreign Minister Ezequiel Padilla, April 8, 1942. Department of State *Bulletin*, April 11, p. 325.

68. Letter to Morris L. Cooke, February 10, 1943. DS 812.6363/7868. Welles added that he was glad to see "that this is being generally acknowl-

edged." Cooke had sent Welles a copy of a favorable review of Harlow S. Person, *Mexican Oil* (N.Y., Harper, 1942), by Walton Hamilton in *The Progressive*, January 25, 1943.

X. The Principle of Collaboration: Venezuela (pages 260–82)

1. For descriptions of relations between the oil companies and Gómez see, e.g., Edwin Lieuwen, *Petroleum in Venezuela: a History* (Berkeley, University of California Press, 1954), and Rómulo Betancourt, *Venezuela: Política y petróleo* (México, Fondo de Cultura Económica, 1956).

2. Despatch 455, from Caracas, September 11, 1936. DS, 831.6363/913.

3. Memorandum of September 21, 1936. *Ibid.*

4. For example, *El País* (Maracaibo), August 11, 1936, after stating that Venezuela was just emerging from feudalism into a system of capitalist exploitation, charged that oil companies had been trying to incite separatism in the state of Zulia, which surrounds Lake Maracaibo.

5. Despatch 16, from Caracas, June 2, 1938. DS, 831.6363/1044.

6. Despatch 339, from Caracas, June 15, 1939. DS, 831.6363/1125.

7. Instruction 160, to Caracas, July 22, 1939. DS, 831.6363/1125.

8. This, of course, was an external view. Betancourt, in *Venezuela: Política y petróleo*, asserts that in 1938 the Venezuelan government gave in to the pressures exerted by the oil companies, and that the Supreme Court, whose justices had become "mineralized," acted as though it were serving the interests of the companies and not those of law and justice (pp. 104, 103). Betancourt compares the court unfavorably with those of Bolivia and Mexico which, in contrast, rendered decisions destructive to the claims of the oil companies.

9. Memorandum of June 26, 1939. DS, 831.6363/1141.

10. Despatch 68, from Caracas, October 9, 1939. DS, 831.6363/1155. Following this despatch, a recommendation was made to Welles that oil company officials should be asked to come to Washington for talks, and Welles suggested that Secretary Hull should issue the invitation. Memorandum. *Ibid.* Corrigan's analysis was supported by the report of a mission that had been sent to Venezuela by the Tariff Commission. Memorandum of conversation, November 22, 1939, and Memorandum, November 28, 1939. DS, 831.51A/54; DS, 831.6363/1164.

11. Despatch 163, from Caracas, December 30, 1939. DS, 831.6363/1165.

12. Memorandum, March 19, 1940. DS, 831.6363/1202–1/2. It was also reported that the Standard Oil Company planned to engage an economist to advise it on long-range policy questions.

13. Memorandum, June 7, 1940. DS, 831.6363/1207. This memorandum is quoted only as indicative of views held in the Department of State at this time; no memorandum of the discussion at this meeting appears to have been filed.

14. Despatch 669, from Caracas, January 9, 1941. DS, 831.6363/1219.

15. Telegram 57, from Caracas, March 30, 1941. DS, 831.6363/1226.

16. Telegram 65, to Caracas, April 2, 1941. DS, 831.6363/1226. Welles added that the Department did not desire to take a position on the merits

of the claim, "but merely [wished] to keep the discussions in friendly channels until every effort [had] been exhausted to reach a satisfactory solution."

17. Letter, May 2, 1941. DS, 831.6363/1240. The president told an officer of the Department that he and his executive committee had been "very much impressed" by Welles's statement "of the international aspect of the situation." Memorandum of conversation, April 19, 1941. DS, 831.6363/1238.

18. Memorandum, July 3, 1941. DS, 831.6363/1244.

19. Memorandum, August 12, 1941. DS, 831.6363/1249.

20. Memorandum of conversation, March 26, 1942. DS, 831.6363/1276. The force of this suggestion was supported by an editorial in *Acción Democrática* (Caracas), April 25, 1942: "We do not propose *immediate* nationalization of the oil industry by decree, but feasible means of financial and economic defense for the nation. We ask simply for the increase within just and equitable limits of national participation in petroleum resources." Quoted in Betancourt, *Venezuela: Política y petróleo*, p. 145. (Italics added.) This weekly publication was the organ of the party of the same name that came to power in 1945.

21. Memorandum of conversation, July 28, 1942. DS, 831.6363/1308.

22. Letter of August 3, 1942. FDRL, OF 535 (Venezuela).

23. Letter of September 14, 1942. FDRL, OF 535 (Venezuela). The insertion in the text of this letter is made at the suggestion of Herman Kahn, director, Franklin D. Roosevelt Library, to correct what he considers to have been a stenographic error in the original. Letter to the author, November 14, 1960.

24. Memorandum of conversation between Welles and Manrique Pacanins, and the Venezuelan Ambassador, August 20, 1942. DS, 831.6363/1311.

25. December 30, 1942. FDRL, OF 535 (Venezuela). This letter was written in response to a statement by Harold Ickes that the latter feared the development of a scandal of major magnitude in the course of negotiations with Venezuela.

26. Despatch 2981, from Caracas, September 4, 1942. DS, 831.6363/1314.

27. Memorandum of conversation, September 23, 1942. DS, 831.6363/1324.

28. Letter, Welles to Roosevelt, December 30, 1942. FDRL, OF 535 (Venezuela).

29. *Ibid.* After receiving this letter from Welles, Roosevelt sent it to Ickes with the notation: "Your turn." (January 1, 1943). No reply by Ickes was found among the Roosevelt papers. Welles presumably referred, among others, to Henry E. Linam, who was reported as having been replaced as president of Lago Petroleum Company and as general manager of the Standard Oil Company in Venezuela, because of his "unwillingness to revise contracts according to President Medina's wishes." New York *Times*, December 3, 1942.

30. Letter, Welles to Roosevelt, December 30, 1942. FDRL, OF 535 (Venezuela).

31. Despatch 4067, from Caracas, February 23, 1943. DS, 831.6363/1429. Corrigan added: "Foreign capital is as necessary for these countries as air to breathe is for a man."

32. This observation is not made without giving due account to the statement made in the memorandum accompanying Medina's letter to Roosevelt (above, p. 272) that the attitude of the Venezuelan government was not adopted "even remotely to take advantage of emergency conditions, but it is obliged to do so by the intransigent attitude of the companies exploiting petroleum in the republic."

33. Betancourt, *Venezuela: Política y petróleo*, pp. 147–48; see pp. 154ff for the case against the new law as argued at the time by deputy J. P. Pérez Alfonzo.

34. Despatch 4072, from Caracas, February 25, 1943. DS, 831.6363/1435.

35. At the end of 1943, Secretary Hull requested Thornburg's resignation on learning that he "still was connected with an American oil company," but this action was apparently unrelated to Thornburg's participation in the Venezuelan negotiations. *The Memoirs of Cordell Hull* (N.Y., Macmillan, 1948), II, 1517.

36. It is possible that the origin of the policy followed toward Venezuela may be found in the comment made by a Department official following a trip to northern South America: "Many of the United States companies are already alive to the necessity for improving the type of their executive personnel. Others are lagging. It is my belief that the Department cannot risk another Mexican oil expropriation merely because of inept handling or for any other reason and should be prepared to give more positive advice as to the best method of handling problems as they arise." Memorandum, March 17, 1939. DS, 710/118.

XI. Opportunities and Disabilities (*pages 285–97*)

1. *The Memoirs of Cordell Hull* (N.Y., Macmillan, 1948), I, 308.

2. *Ibid.*, I, 320.

3. Hull later wrote: "To me it seemed virtually impossible to develop friendly relations with other nations in the political sphere so long as we provoked their animosity in the economic sphere. How could we promote peace with them while waging war on them commercially?" *Ibid.*, I, 355.

4. The economic policy of the period 1933 to 1941 has been given extensive treatment. Among many useful studies may be mentioned: William Diebold, Jr., *New Directions in Our Trade Policy* (N.Y., Council on Foreign Relations, 1941); Francis B. Sayre, *The Way Forward: The American Trade Agreements Program* (N.Y., Macmillan, 1939).

5. *Unión Liberal* (Bogotá), November 6, 1936. Even though Latin Americans frequently commented that the trade agreements program was undertaken in the economic interest of the United States, they also frequently expressed satisfaction at the advantages thereby obtained by their own peoples. See *Diario de la Marina* (Havana), April 18, 1936.

6. For documents on this proposal and its aftermath, see FR, 1937, V, 149ff.

7. *La Prensa* (Buenos Aires), August 13, 1937.

8. Letter to Department of State, June 13, 1936. DS, 711.359 Sanitary/199.

9. Letter, February 7, 1939. DS, 812.6363/5388.

10. Senate Resolution 177, 76th Congress, 1st Session, July 31, 1939. This resolution noted the existence of allegations that "a certain official or officials" of the United States government had made statements in Mexico that the oil expropriation "was in accord with the social objectives of the New Deal"; it stated that the expropriation was "not compatible with the so-called Good Neighbor policy"; and it noted that the United States "aids and assists" Mexico by its silver purchases. The reference here was presumably to Daniels.

11. Memorandum of conversation, March 30, 1938. DS, 812.6363/3338.

12. Memorandum of conversation, December 11, 1939. FR, 1939, V, 714–15.

13. Quoted by Welles in Memorandum of conversation with Castillo Nájera, August 2, 1939. DS, 812.6363/6078.

14. Memorandum of conversation, June 19, 1939. FR, 1939, V, 680–83.

15. Letter from Castillo Nájera to Richberg, July 5, 1939. DS, 812.6363/5636–4/8, and Memorandum of conversation, July 20, 1939. FR, 1939, V, 686–87.

16. Memorandum of conversation, April 12, 1938. FR, 1938, V, 742.

17. Telegram 65, to Mexico, April 12, 1938. FR, 1938, V, 748.

18. Letter, April 21, 1938, in response to a letter of April 4, 1938. DS, 812.6363/3696.

19. A report that this was the "dominant opinion" in the consular district of Agua Prieta was made by the consul there on May 17, 1938. DS, 812.6363/3963.

20. Letter from Women's International League for Peace and Freedom, Berkeley, Calif., May 1, 1940. DS, 812.6363/6853.

21. Copies in DS, 812.6363/6807. The Alameda (California) County Industrial Union Council accompanied its resolution by a letter stating that the action of the Department of State was "indefensible and entirely out of keeping with the 'Good Neighbor' policy." Letter, May 8, 1940.

22. See *The Reply to Mexico: the Companies' Reply to the Mexican Document "The True Facts About the Expropriation of the Oil Companies' Properties in Mexico"* (N.Y., Standard Oil Co. [N.J.], 1940), *The Atlantic Monthly*, July, 1938, and speeches and articles in the daily press, 1938–42. For a hostile view of the companies' propaganda activities, see Josephus Daniels, *Shirt-Sleeve Diplomat* (Chapel Hill, N.C., University of North Carolina Press, 1947), Chap. XXII.

23. Address by Roscoe B. Gaither before the Mining and Metallurgical Society of America, April 16, 1940 (N.Y., Mining and Metallurgical Society of America, 1940). See also letters by George S. Montgomery, Jr., in New York *Times*, July 2, August 20, 1939, in which it was asserted that "Good Neighborliness which depends for its existence upon meek submission to seizures of our properties is not only unhealthy but cannot long endure."

24. November 11, 1938. This editorial, entitled "The Policy of the Good Neighbor Cannot Be Reconciled with a Managed Economy," employed language more vehement than customary for *La Prensa*.

25. *La Prensa* (Buenos Aires), November 11, 1938. This guarded statement appeared in stronger terms in the United States, where the New York *Herald Tribune*, November 11, reported that Ortíz had asserted that dumping of wheat in South America would constitute a "violation of the Good Neighbor policy."

26. *La Prensa* (Buenos Aires), November 11, 1938, reported, however, that when Theis arrived in Rio de Janeiro, he was met at the airport by the agricultural attaché of the United States Embassy.

27. *Ibid.*, November 13, 1938. Foreign Minister Oswaldo Aranha said in Rio de Janeiro that the wheat deal was not one that concerned the governments of either Argentina or the United States; it was simply a matter of getting bread for the Brazilian people as cheaply as possible. *Ibid.*, November 12, 1938.

XII. Factors External to Policy (*pages 298–308*)

1. Some of the elements of the attitudes of Latin Americans are considered in *What the South Americans Think of Us*, by Carleton Beals, Bryce Oliver, Herschel Brickell and Samuel Guy Inman (N.Y., McBride, 1945).

2. The Assistant Secretary of State (Francis White) to American Diplomatic Officers in Latin American Countries, October 10, 1930. DS, 710.G/4A.

3. It was undoubtedly the Nicaraguan experience that gave rise to the comment that military intervention created news and antagonism: "When military intervention is found necessary, no effort or expense should be spared to make it promptly overwhelming and decisive." Despatch 2323, the Minister in Colombia (Jefferson Caffery) to the Secretary of State, Bogotá, March 11, 1931. DS, 710.G/18.

4. Despatch 676, from Caracas, January 7, 1932. DS, 710.G/57; and Despatch 138, from Montevideo, January 6, 1931. DS, 710.G/8.

5. "The motion picture also plays its part [in campaigns against the United States], and I am sometimes prone to wonder whether the so-called censorship considers the implied immorality in many pictures or bears in mind the prestige of the United States." Despatch 386, from the Minister in Uruguay (Josiah Butler Wright) to the Secretary of State, Montevideo, December 30, 1932. DS, 710.G/123.

6. "Without suppressing or distorting legitimate news, much benefit would ensue if the volume of despatches on murders, divorces, etc., were decreased by the Press Associations, and news of scientific, cultural, and other developments substituted." Despatch 138, from Montevideo, January 6, 1931. DS, 710.G/8. Also Despatch 758, from the Ambassador in Cuba (Harry F. Guggenheim) to the Secretary of State, Havana, June 29, 1931. DS, 710.G/33. However, the general tone of Brazilian comments on reports of gangsters and kidnappers "and related phenomena of con-

temporary American civilization is almost invariably kindly." Despatch 4179, from Rio de Janeiro, July 31, 1933. DS, 710.G/197.

7. E.g., Despatch 676, from Caracas, January 7, 1932. DS, 710.G/57.

8. Despatch 2359 from Bogotá, March 18, 1931. DS, 821.51/891.

9. See, for example, the series of studies entitled *United States Business Performance Abroad*, begun in 1953 by the National Planning Association, Washington, D.C.

10. Despatch 22 from Bogotá, March 3, 1939. DS, 711.21/931.

11. Despatch 444, from San José, May 29, 1931. DS, 710.G/32.

12. Despatch 4179, from Rio de Janeiro, July 31, 1933. DS, 710.G/197.

13. "Probably the greatest single factor toward a better conception of the policy of the United States has been the determination of the present administration to withdraw the Marines from Nicaragua and to remould its policy in Haiti and the Dominican Republic." Despatch 386, from Montevideo, December 30, 1932. DS, 710.G/123.

14. Press conference 786, November 25, 1941. FDRL, Press Conferences, XVIII, 317–19. The article, critical of the President of Chile, Pedro Aguirre Cerda, appeared in the November 17, 1941, issue of *Time;* the fact that the article came out a few days before the Chilean President's death undoubtedly intensified the official reaction in the United States. The offensive statement was: "While the Popular Front swayed, bushy-mustached President Aguirre felt more & more like a man who does not govern but merely presides. He spent more & more time with the red wine he cultivates. Fortnight ago he was reported ill."

15. President Alfonso López of Colombia wrote to President Roosevelt in 1936 about a favorable atmosphere for strengthening continental unity because Roosevelt's policy was a healthy rectification of previous policies. Further: "The same interests that strive to maintain their economic privileges in the United States in opposition to your own government, and which you have pointed to as being prejudicial to the well being of the United States, formerly exercised a perturbatory influence on our relationships with the homeland of George Washington." Letter, February 18, 1936. DS, 710 Peace/16. An editorial in *Uruguay* (Montevideo), June 7, 1936, stated: "The defeat of plutocratic dominance in domestic politics in the United States has been accompanied by its defeat in foreign policy. The United States is becoming less and less each day that detestable oligarchy of the trusts and the bankers."

16. Letter to Roosevelt, April 11, 1934. This letter was in response to one from Roosevelt (March 22, 1934), probably inspired by Ambassador Daniels, praising "the progress your country has made and is making along the lines of social reform leading to social justice and the education and welfare of the Mexican people." Both letters in FDRL, PPF 1354. Similar sentiments appear in a letter from Mexican Foreign Minister Puig Casauranc to Ambassador Daniels. Shortly after meeting Roosevelt, Puig wrote that he had been impressed by Roosevelt's sincerity, unselfishness and intelligence. "While . . . he may not admit it perhaps, he gives one the impression of being a social revolutionary in the highest and noblest sense of the term. I am so certain that this impression of absolute

respect and perfect confidence which he inspired in me will last always that I did not hesitate to write him so." Letter, October 24, 1933. FDRL, PSF, Box 12 (Mexico).

17. "Roosevelt between Two Fires in Cuba," *El Universal Gráfico* (Mexico City), September 27, 1933. Dávila singled out United States policy in Mexico: "What other power, given the same circumstances and aggravations, would have withdrawn its forces, after Vera Cruz and Columbus?" (The last reference was to Pancho Villa's murderous raid in 1917.) Compare Augustín Edwards, owner of *El Mercurio* (Santiago, Chile), who declared: "I find myself among those who do not believe in North American imperialism." Interview quoted in *El Comercio* (Lima), March 9, 1935. He asked whether we could be sure that the Panama Canal, "one of the most decisive factors in the progress of the nations of the Pacific," could have been opened by less forceful measures than were taken at the time.

18. For a European comment on this point see David Mitrany, *American Interpretations: Four Political Essays* (London, Contact, 1946), pp. 68–70.

19. *El Mercurio* (Santiago, Chile), February 9, 1936. This position was echoed elsewhere; see, e.g., the statement by ex-President of Costa Rica, Julio Acosta, in *La Prensa Libre* (San José), February 18, 1936. *El Diario* (Montevideo), April 14, 1936, noted that the lack of understanding between Latin America and the United States had largely disappeared thanks to the Good Neighbor policy and hoped that a new international organization in the Americas would have no ties with Geneva—"this decadent Geneva, center of more or less hidden interests and of implacable struggles, and responsible for present difficulties that America should shun while it tries to offer to the world a new formula of effective collaboration."

20. *Anales del Senado* (Colombia), No. 34, September 2, 1937, pp. 407–8.

21. Quoted in Despatch 674, from Stockholm, January 11, 1937. DS, 710. Peace/1270. *The Times* (London), August 22, 1936, admitted that "contemplation of the affairs of Europe cannot but intensify the desire of all the participants [in the Buenos Aires Conference] to safeguard the peace of their own continent in every way practicable."

22. Letter, December 19, 1936. FDRL, PPF 1212.

23. Memorandum from Laurence Duggan to the Under Secretary of State, Edward R. Stettinius, Jr., October 19, 1943. DS, 710.11/10–1943.

24. See *History of the Office of the Coordinator of Inter-American Affairs*, Historical Reports on War Administration (Washington, U.S. Government Printing Office, 1947), pp. 91–105.

25. Memorandum, March 17, 1939. DS, 710/118.

26. Despatch from Otto Langmann, German Minister to Uruguay, to the German Foreign Ministry, Montevideo, April 21, 1938. *Documents on German Foreign Policy, 1918–1945*, Series D, V, 830. See in this same volume similar reports from other Latin American countries, especially that of April 8, 1938, from Mexico, accurately predicting that the good relations between Mexico and the United States resulting from the Good

Neighbor policy would "sustain the present test with regard to the petroleum conflict" (p. 829).

27. On this last point see José Vasconcelos, *Hoy* (Mexico City), January 14, 1939, who, in hailing the stand of Argentina at the Lima Conference, spoke of the necessity for the separate evolution of the two races of the New World; for the Monroe Doctrine the Lima Conference was "another fiasco," but "for the freedom of commerce and the cultural freedom of Spanish nations, it was a triumph, and also a rescue of their honor." In contrast, an editorial in *La Mañana* (Montevideo), December 7, 1936, went so far in praise of Roosevelt's speech at the Buenos Aires Conference as to say that "now the voice of Ariel comes from the North," and, when General Franco was reported as saying in Madrid that "a bastard culture" had come to separate America from Spain, *El Tiempo* (Bogotá), October 20, 1939, rebuked him, saying: "The separation of America from Spain is something more than a cultural phenomenon; it is the inevitable consequence of the coming of age of new races which have come to realize their historic destinies without the tutelage of an ethnic relationship occasioned solely by one of the strange chances of history."

28. See e.g., *Vanguardia* (Buenos Aires), November 4, 1936, which praised the "dignity and maturity" shown by the people of the United States in the presidential election; and *El Universal* (Mexico City), November 8, 1946, which commented that the gaining by the Republican party of a congressional majority in the 1946 elections "was a new proof of the effectiveness of the democratic institutions" of the United States. "For peoples politically backward, which is the condition of most of those in Spanish America, this election is a valuable lesson in democracy."

29. Above, p. 228.

30. "Human Dignity," Editorial, *El Comercio* (Quito), November 25, 1943. The editorial compared unfavorably the position of the Ecuadoran soldier.

31. Speech during the 1920 presidential campaign, quoted in Frank B. Freidel, *Franklin D. Roosevelt* (Boston, Little Brown, 1952), II, 81.

32. Editorial, January 26, 1927.

33. Compare, for example, the great concern exhibited in the private correspondence of Theodore Roosevelt and some of his friends about racial issues in foreign affairs. Howard K. Beale, *Theodore Roosevelt and the Rise of America as a World Power* (Baltimore, Johns Hopkins Press, 1956). Roosevelt wrote to Henry White: "It is to the interest of civilization that the English speaking race should be dominant in South Africa, exactly as it is . . . that the United States . . . should be dominant in the Western Hemisphere" (pp. 32–33). Omissions as given by Beale.

XIII. The Evocation of Reciprocity (pages 309–14)

1. Quoted in *Hoy* (Mexico City), October 11, 1941, p. 8.

2. Rafael Rodríguez Altunaga, in *Finanzas* (Havana), September 30, 1939.

3. Despatch 355, from Rio de Janeiro, February 25, 1938. FR, 1938, V, 392–93.

4. William L. Langer and S. Everett Gleason, *The Challenge to Isolation* (N.Y., Harper, 1952), p. 208.

5. Letter to an official in the Department of Commerce, October 31, 1942. DS, 710.11/2906. Welles went on to say that the official publication of "specific gains" made by the United States through the policy "might tend to confirm the views of some of our enemies to the effect that the Good Neighbor policy is a cloak for imperialistic or self-seeking aims on the part of the United States."

XIV. *Latin America Appraises the Good Neighbor* (*pages 315–26*)

1. December, 1943, pp. 21–25.

2. *Hoy* (Mexico City), January 29, 1944, in an editorial entitled "Those Who Betray Mr. Roosevelt," charged that Mumford had written the article and that the Senator had merely signed it.

3. Senator Joseph F. Guffey (Dem.) of Pennsylvania, was reported to have declared that his colleague from Nebraska was a "catspaw in a bit of journalistic ghost-writing"; and to have said that the "editors of *Reader's Digest* were abusing his trust and employing his personal prestige to foist on America and the world a mass of misinformation." He suggested that the editors of the magazine should apologize to Senator Butler for having made him "appear an international fool," and apologies should also go to the Senate and to the governments and people of every friendly American nation." Quoted in New York *Times*, December 8, 1943. On behalf of the *Reader's Digest*, editor De Witt Wallace denied that the magazine had made a "catspaw" of Senator Butler; "all figures used in the article" were the Senator's own, the editor was reported to have said, and the article contained "nothing 'to offend Latin America.'" *Ibid.*

4. On this point, Sr. Claudio Urrutia stated that the value of United States contributions to Venezuela in the form of fish stocking amounted to trout eggs to the value of $125, and the payment of freight amounting to $96 on two lots of live fish sent to Venezuela. In return, he, as an official of the Venezuelan Ministry of Agriculture, had taken some fish from Venezuela to the United States; the fish were used in an antimalarial campaign in the southern part of the United States after being delivered to the New York Aquarium. Sr. Urrutia said he had paid for the freight on these fish himself as a way of repaying the United States and helping fight malaria in that friendly country. Letter in *El Universal* (Caracas), December 17, 1943.

5. "Expenditures and Commitments by the United States Government in or for Latin America," Report by Hon. Hugh Butler, November 26, 1943, and the "Reply to Such Report Made by Hon. Kenneth McKellar," December 18, 1943. Senate Document 132, 78th Congress, 1st Session.

6. The form was good Tennessee florid: "I doubt if Ananias, Baron Munchausen, or Jules Verne, singly or combined, ever conceived or

ever uttered such monumental and inaccurate guesses in all their lives as
have been included in this marvelous so-called report." From Senator
McKellar's speech in the Senate, December 18, 1943. *Ibid.*, p. 98. Mc-
Kellar asserted that Butler and his companions "were bent upon stirring
up trouble and strife between the independent states of America," and
he inquired "how much this marvelous airplane trip over the highest
mountains in South America cost, and who paid for it?"

7. As appendices to McKellar's speech there were printed comments
on the Butler report by the Department of State and other agencies. *Ibid.*,
pp. 116–70.

8. "They Are Still Deep, Dark Secrets," *Reader's Digest*, February,
1944, pp. 107–11.

9. Despatch 5335, from Havana, December 6, 1943. DS, 710.11/3069.

10. *El Universal* (Caracas), November 29, 1934. However, the editorial in this paper proceeded to say that the Senator's intention in presenting evidence of waste was "misleading and tendentious" because he
tried thereby to show that Venezuelans had taken advantage of North
American generosity to engage in "orgies of spending"—an interpretation
that the paper rejected. See also *Hoy* (Mexico City), January 29, 1944,
which took occasion to say that there were certain United States government officials in Mexico who had betrayed their trust by engaging in
private business transactions with Mexican citizens. Such individuals,
in the opinion of *Hoy*, should be removed from governmental service,
since their actions were contrary to the "generous policy" of President
Roosevelt.

11. *Hoy* agreed with Senator Butler on another point by saying that
Latin Americans could not be convinced of the "democratic sincerity"
of the United States when they saw propaganda favorable to the President of the Dominican Republic issued by the Office of the Coordinator
of Inter-American Affairs and read reports of the official reception in
Washington of the President of Nicaragua.

12. Whether or not this statement was a veiled attack on the government of Ecuador, it was at least expressed in nonpartisan terms. In
Mexico, on the other hand, *El Sinarquista*, December 9, 1943, used the
Butler article as a text for an attack on the Mexican government, and
raised the question whether the United States was really a Good Neighbor when it exercised no influence in Mexico against a regime that the
paper considered repressive. In this connection, it may be noted that
Ahora (Caracas), November 25, 1943, observed that the appearance of
the article by Senator Butler demonstrated that in the United States
everyone was permitted to have his say, no matter how "senseless and
dangerous" his words might be. The range of opinion that has been
quoted above from Mexican papers may be said to demonstrate the
large measure of freedom of the press enjoyed in that country.

13. Butler's declarations demonstrated to "Próspero" in *Ultimas
Noticias* (Quito), November 26, 1943, "the ferocity of domestic political
strife in the United States." The writer noted that Butler was a Republican and deplored the bad impression of the United States that would be

given by Butler's charges, despite Roosevelt's considerable success in dissipating Latin America's suspicions of North America. See also *Hoy* (Mexico City), December 4, 1943; and Austregesilo de Athayde in *Diario da Noite* (Rio de Janeiro), December 17, 1943. An editorial in *El País* (Havana), January 4, 1944, stated flatly that the Butler attack was that of "a political opponent attempting to lessen the prestige of his adversary [Roosevelt], who by being elected a fourth time would again defeat Butler's party."

14. B. Sanín Cano, in *El Tiempo* (Bogotá), November 29, 1943. In Honduras, the travelers' stay was no longer than twenty-four hours, giving rise to the comment in *La Epoca* (Tegucigalpa), December 9, 1943, that the Senator had committed an offensive action in assuming "to make judgments about the internal politics of Latin American countries by virtue of the fact of having passed over like a meteor."

15. See, for example, *Ultimas Noticias* (Quito), November 24, 1943. *Excelsior* (Mexico City), February 1, 1944, carried a story stating that a group of administration senators in the Mexican Congress ("bloque del PRM") had declared that it would not take notice of Senator Butler's references to Mexico, nor bother to refute them "because it considered the Senator's attitude as being of no 'importance.' "

16. *Hoy* (Havana), November 28, 1943, stated that "only a partisan of the Axis would be capable of maintaining that our production was not usefully serving the cause of democracy."

17. *Correio da Manha* (Rio de Janeiro), December 11, 1943.

18. *Ultimas Noticias* (Quito), November 24, 1943. The Ecuadoran papers gave considerable space to defense of their country because it was named several times in the article.

19. *La Tribuna* (San José), December 1, 1943. Such a suggestion by Butler amounted to "dishonoring the fine international policy of Roosevelt, Wallace, and Welles." See also *La Esfera* (Caracas), December 1, 1943.

20. *Correio da Manha* (Rio de Janeiro), December 16, 1943.

21. *El Día* (Quito), November 26, 1943.

22. *El Universal* (Caracas), November 29, 1943.

23. See also *Ultimas Noticias* (Quito), November 24, 1943. This paper countered Butler's charges by figuring that if Ecuador should demand rent of the United States for the use of the Galápagos Islands at the rate of ten cents a square meter per year, the annual figure would be about $5,000,000, apart from the fact that United States armed forces would consume "without any charge whatever, the wild cattle that are abundant in the Islands."

24. *Ahora* (Caracas), December 1, 1943.

25. *La Prensa* (Mexico City), November 29, 1943. *Novedades* (Mexico City), November 28, 1943, stated that Senator Butler need have no fears about Mexico; dollars or no dollars, Mexico would remain a good friend out of a sense of fraternity that had no price.

26. *Congressional Record*, House of Representatives, December 8, 1943, p. 10466.

27. Buenos Aires, December 11, 1943. Even *La Prensa* (Buenos Aires), December 11, 1943, which had no Axis sympathies, commented that this remark had given rise to justified indignation in Latin America, for the policies of the governments had not been established in return for dollars.

28. *El Mercurio* (Santiago, Chile), December 15, 1943. *Noticias* (Arequipa), December 16, 1943, said that Butler, with a typical North American attitude, had quoted amounts in dollars as being excessive loans and grants to Latin America. Even though Hull had shown Butler's figures to be incorrect, said the paper, "it is nevertheless disgusting to attempt to establish a relationship between money on the one hand and sentiments and principles on the other."

29. *El Tiempo* (Bogotá), November 29, 1943. The editorial referred to the policy as "this humane and civilized manner of understanding the relationships between the peoples of the American continent." See also *El Diario* (Montevideo), November 30, 1943.

30. This editorial characterized Senator Butler as "a member of a genus that was disappearing in the United States—the 'rough riders' of money, who hoped for the backing of each dollar by a bayonet."

31. "Próspero" in *Ultimas Noticias* (Quito), November 26, 1943. The *Star & Herald* (Panama), January 23, 1944, charged Senator Butler with making an attack "on the Good Neighbor, a policy that his fellow-partisans of the past never had the foresight to devise, foster and develop."

32. *Hoy* (Mexico City), January 29, 1944. *Hoy* stated that this declaration was made at a political banquet in December, 1934; no reference to such a statement, however, was found in Roosevelt's papers or in United States newspapers at the time. *Hoy* gave tribute to Roosevelt for having carried out the Good Neighbor policy "with a personal sincerity that it would be despicable to doubt."

33. "The Latin American countries have seen in the Roosevelt policy of the Good Neighbor, honorably applied, the only certain route toward true friendship and fraternal cooperation in the Continent." *El Popular* (Mexico City), November 29, 1943.

34. This editorial noted that both Herbert Hoover and Henry L. Stimson had claimed for the Republican party the paternity of the Good Neighbor policy, and expressed faith that the policy was firmly embedded in popular sentiment in the United States, a country where public opinion was of great importance. Similar views were aired by *Correio da Manha* (Rio de Janeiro), December 13, 1943.

35. *Hoy* (Mexico City), January 29, 1944.

36. Text in Department of State *Bulletin*, December 18, 1943, pp. 430–31.

37. Text in *ibid.*, December 25, 1943, pp. 443–48.

38. Memorandum by the Office of the Special Consultant, Public Attitudes on Foreign Policy, January 7, 1944. DS, 710.11/3281.

39. Letter from Nelson A. Rockefeller to Secretary of State Cordell Hull, December 20, 1943. DS, 710.11/3184.

XV. The Good Neighbors (pages 327–61)

1. For studies giving greater attention to the institutional structure, see, among others, M. Margaret Ball, *The Problem of Inter-American Organization* (Stanford, Calif., Stanford University Press, 1944), and John P. Humphrey, *The Inter-American System* (Toronto, Macmillan, 1942).

2. "El sistema interamericano," *Revista de Educación* (Santiago, Chile), April–May, 1938, p. 6.

3. Roosevelt said: "Since the 4th of March 1933 Dollar Diplomacy is no longer recognized by the United States government." Quoted in Memorandum from Stephen T. Early to the Secretary of State, September 4, 1935, referring to a statement by the President to newsmen, made on that day. FDRL, OF 20, Box 3.

4. Letter to Roosevelt, December 30, 1942. FDRL, OF 535 (Venezuela).

5. See above, p. 265.

6. As one straw in the wind, it was in 1942 that the Pan American Agricultural School at Zamorano, Honduras, was founded by Samuel Zemurray, president of the United Fruit Company, "as a practical symbol of the company's appreciation for the collaboration of the Spanish American people." Stacy May and Galo Plaza, *The United Fruit Company in Latin America*, Seventh Case Study on United States Business Performance Abroad (Washington, National Planning Association, 1958), p. 192.

7. Quoted on p. 270.   8. See above, p. 273.

9. See above, p. 314.

10. The phrase is used in Eduardo Yrarrázaval Concha, *El Hemisferio postergado* (Santiago, Chile, Zig-Zag, 1954), p. 27.

11. For the views of a former Mexican diplomat on the matter of style, see Isidro Fabela, *Buena y Mala Vecindad* (Mexico City, América Nueva, 1958).

12. See above, p. 305.

13. Convention for the Maintenance, Preservation and Reestablishment of Peace, article II.

14. A projected study by the author will examine the policy of the United States in the Chaco, Leticia, and Marañón disputes.

15. It may be noted that the opinion that "the standard proclaimed and observed by the United States of America to the effect that its international policy must be founded on that of the 'Good Neighbor' is a general criterion of right and a source of guidance in the relations between States," was approved by the Rio de Janeiro Conference of 1942, which declared that "the principle that international conduct must be inspired by the policy of the Good Neighbor is a norm of international law of the American Continent." "Resolution XXII" in *Report on the Third Meeting of the Ministers of Foreign Affairs of the American Re-*

publics, January 15–28, 1942 (Washington, Pan American Union, 1942).

16. "The Continuing Struggle for Liberalism," speech, June 30, 1938, in Franklin D. Roosevelt, *Public Papers and Addresses,* 1938 vol. (N.Y., Macmillan, 1941), p. 412.

17. Sumner Welles, *Where Are We Heading?* (N.Y., Harper, 1946), p. 183.

18. One of the younger officers in the Division of American Republics at the time has made the comment that in the three years 1938–40 only one divisional meeting had been held, and then the occasion was to present a gift to a colleague who was the proud father of a baby girl.

19. The New York *Times,* for example, did not carry accounts of the negotiations, and only sketchy information was provided in the *Oil and Gas Journal.* An article entitled "New Venezuela Oil Law Raises Taxes Sharply" (February 18, 1943), summarized the new law and stated that "also interested in the negotiations was Max Thornburg, as a representative of the U.S. State Department" (p. 30). Later, this trade journal reported that the Department of State thought that "a real problem" was involved in the desire of the Venezuelan government to secure a greater return from its oil economy, and the Department "suggested to the companies that it would be wise to reopen negotiations with Venezuelan officials in a cooperative spirit." "Impact of Venezuelan Oil Law May Blanket Western Hemisphere," *Ibid.,* March 18, 1943, pp. 24–25.

20. "The Good Neighbor policy had created an inter-American system—a regional system of sovereign states, sovereign in all that affected their purely internal affairs, but prepared to mold their external relations in such shape as would best advance the common welfare of their peoples." Sumner Welles, *Where Are We Heading?* p. 184. See also Chapter V in Welles's *The Time for Decision* (N.Y., Harper, 1944), where emphasis is given to changes in recognition policy after he left office. Hull's *Memoirs* (N.Y., Macmillan, 1948), which contains some interesting sidelights, gives little attention to problems of protection of nationals, and Duggan's posthumous *The Americas* (N.Y., Holt, 1949) remarks that only a few members of the foreign service, "threw themselves enthusiastically into the development of the Good Neighbor policy" (p. 75), but his book gives scant space to an explanation of the policy itself.

21. It should be noted that, for a host of lesser cases of protection of business interests, the Department of State continued its routine methods of giving support. See, for example, exchanges with Brazil over claims of the Foreign Bondholders Protective Council in 1939. FR, 1939, V, 357ff. See also FR, 1938, V, 549–50, where the Department noted that the government of Ecuador had made known to the press its belief that the Department had "acted 'officiously' and . . . intervened in the domestic affairs of Ecuador," because it had asked that the South American Development Company in Ecuador be given a reasonable period of time to consider a decree requiring it to pay pensions to Ecuadoran employees. The Department protested that it was its policy not to intervene, and

that its action in this case was in "complete harmony and conformity with the Good Neighbor policy."

22. March 24, 1938, p. 19.

23. Similarly, see the correspondence on Colombia's resumption of foreign debt payments, in which the Department undertook to "do everything that it appropriately can" to secure acceptance of the so-called "Laylin formula" by the Foreign Bondholders Protective Council. Putting pressure on the Council was by no means a customary action by the Department, and Duggan recorded that he "took pains to make it clear to the Ambassador that this was a most unusual step for the Department to take." FR, 1939, V, 513.

24. Press conference 452-A, held with the Associated Church Press, April 20, 1938. FDRL, Press Conferences, XI, 330.

25. January 7, 1941. FDRL, PSF Box 22. Mr. Paley, of the Columbia Broadcasting System, stated in a letter to the author, September 13, 1960, that the memorandum "was the result of a trip . . . throughout South America during the latter part of 1940 for the purpose of organizing a Pan American network. . . . President Roosevelt was most interested in my objective, particularly because at that time the Germans had made great progress in getting an unusual degree of cooperation from Latin American broadcasters."

26. Letter from Welles to Roosevelt, March 17, 1941. *Ibid.*

27. January 7, 1941. FDRL, PSF Box 22.

28. These negotiations have been described in detail in William L. Langer and S. Everett Gleason, *The Undeclared War* (N.Y., Harper, 1953), pp. 147ff, and 610ff; the above quotation, citing an informal memorandum of the Division of American Republics, December 17, 1940, is at p. 150.

29. Quoted in *ibid.*, p. 614. Langer and Gleason state: "No evidence has turned up to support the charge that American representatives were privy to the action taken to replace Arias by a new chief executive, Ricardo Adolfo de la Guardia" (p. 614).

30. Letter, September 27, 1940. FDRL, OF 87 (Pan American Affairs) Box 2.

31. On this delicate question of insisting on reciprocity, but avoiding *quid pro quo* negotiations, see correspondence with Cuba in FR, 1938, V, 472ff, especially p. 480; and FR, 1939, V, 530ff. Many facets of this question shine forth in the latter volume, since all parties concerned apparently regarded the willingness of the United States to make loans and other financial arrangements at the Panama Conference as an appropriate opportunity to review many long-standing claims and other politico-economic issues.

32. On the high degree of inter-American unity reached after 1938, see Whitaker, *The Western Hemisphere Idea*, pp. 144ff.

33. John M. Cabot, speech before the joint meeting of the Export Managers Club of New York and the Export Advertising Association, March 17, 1953. Department of State, Press release 139, March 16, 1953.

34. Quoted in New York *Times*, February 20, 1955.

35. Sir Ivone Kirkpatrick, "As a Diplomat Sees the Art of Diplomacy," New York *Times*, March 22, 1959.

36. See above, p. 278.

37. Department of State *Bulletin*, January 2, 1943, p. 6.

38. Sir Arthur Salter seems to have shared Welles's broader view when he inquired whether good neighborliness were expansible, so that the United States might also become "a good citizen." *Security: Can We Retrieve It?* (N.Y., Reynal and Hitchcock, 1939), p. 46.

39. Press conference 614-A, January 12, 1940. FDRL, Press Conferences, XV, 75–78. Compare Welles's warning: "United States capital must no longer be invested in other American republics in such a way as to create an empire within another sovereign state. . . . The only practicable plan is for capital from this country always to be associated with capital obtained in the country where it is invested. That kind of partnership will eliminate the political and economic evils resulting from foreign control of the national resources or public utilities of a country, and will enable the peoples of countries where industries are being developed or natural resources exploited to derive their full and just share of the benefits." *The Time for Decision*, pp. 240–41.

40. For an official expression of this judgment, see Nelson A. Rockefeller, "The Fruits of the Good Neighbor Policy," New York *Times*, May 14, 1944. Rockefeller was then Coordinator of Inter-American Affairs.

41. E. H. Carr, *The Twenty Years' Crisis, 1919–1939* (London, Macmillan, 1940), p. 300.

Index